Experimenting with Democracy

The chronic instability in the Balkan states of South-East Europe has prevented the end of the Cold War becoming an era of genuine peace in Europe. Against a background of competing nationalisms, economic decline and the resilience of authoritarianism, it is easy to forget that experiments with democracy have taken place since 1990 with relative success. Now, for the first time, the region is genuinely engaging with open politics; the outcome will determine whether the Balkans can cease being a byword for instability, and an area whose shock-waves have disturbed the peace of Europe on many occasions.

This book explores the obstacles impeding the consolidation of democracy, and even preventing a state like Serbia from going very far down the democratic road. Social scientists with expert knowledge of each of the Balkan states, and their political and economic systems, examine why progress in building free institutions has been slow compared to that of Central Europe, the Iberian peninsula and Latin America.

Using a theoretical framework to explore Balkan experiments with regime change, the volume considers the relationship between political culture and democracy-building, and the problematic of nationalism. Economic forces and the effect of Western organizations show the influence of internal and external pressures. *Experimenting with Democracy* is a coherent and timely analysis of transitions and regime change since the collapse of communist systems in 1989; it will be an important resource for students of political science and European studies as well as those interested in democratization in general.

The Editors: Geoffrey Pridham is Professor of European Politics and Director of the Centre for Mediterranean Studies at the University of Bristol. He has written extensively on democratization; his publications include *Stabilising Fragile Democracies: Comparing New Party Systems in Southern and Eastern Europe,* and he was co-editor of *Democratisation in Eastern Europe* and *Securing Democracy: Political Parties and Democratic Consolidation in Southern Europe,* all published by Routledge. **Tom Gallagher** holds the Chair of European Peace and Conflict Studies at Bradford University; his books include *Romania after Ceausescu: The Politics of Intolerance.*

Routledge Studies of Societies in Transition

Experimenting with Democracy
Regime Change in the Balkans

Edited by Geoffrey Pridham and Tom Gallagher

London and New York

In Association with the Centre for Mediterranean Studies, University of Bristol

First published 2000
by Routledge
11 Fetter Lane, London EC4P 4EE

Simultaneously published in the USA and Canada
by Routledge
29 West 35th Street, New York, NY 10001

Routledge is an imprint of the Taylor & Francis Group

© 2000 Geoffrey Pridham and Tom Gallagher for selection and
editorial matter

Typeset in Baskerville by Exe Valley Dataset Ltd, Exeter
Printed and bound in Great Britain by MPG Books Ltd, Bodmin

British Library Cataloguing in Publication Data
A catalogue record for this book is available
from the British Library

Library of Congress Cataloguing in Publication Data
Experimenting with Democracy: regime change in the Balkans /
    edited by Geoffrey Pridham and Tom Gallagher.
        p.   cm. — (Routledge studies of societies in transition ; 13)
    Includes bibliographical references and index.
    ISBN 0–415–18726–5 (hc. : alk. paper)
    1. Balkan Peninsula—Politics and government—1989–
    2. Post-communism—Balkan Peninsula.   3. Democracy—
    Balkan Peninsula.
    I. Pridham, Geoffrey, 1942–   . II. Gallagher, Tom, 1954–   .
    III. Series.
    DR48.6.D46   1999
    949.6055´9   dc21   99-31059
                                                              CIP

ISBN 0–415–18726–5

Contents

Contributors

Will Bartlett is Reader in Social Economics at the School for Policy Studies and Deputy Director of the Centre for Mediterranean Studies, University of Bristol. His research activity covers the problems of economic and social transformation in the Balkans, co-operatives and small firms in Southern Europe, and welfare state reforms. He has published a number of articles on economic developments in the Yugoslav successor states. He is Editor of *Economic Analysis: Journal of Enterprise and Participation*.

Stefano Bianchini is Director of the Centre for Studies on East-Central and Balkan Europe of the University of Bologna, where he teaches the history and politics of Eastern Europe. He is author of *La Questione Yugoslava* (Castermann, 1996), and *Sarajevo: Le Radici dell'Odio* (Edizioni Associate, 1993). Recently, he has co-edited with George Schöpflin *State Building: Dilemmas on the Eve of the 21st Century* (Longo, 1998). His main research interests are focused on state and nationalism in the Balkans, political culture and politics in post-communist transition countries, and Balkan geo-politics.

Aurelian Craiutu is author of *Elogiul Libertatii* [In Praise of Liberty] (Iasi, 1998), and translator into Romanian of Edmund Husserl, *Cartesian Mediations* (Humanitas, 1994). He will reissue a new edition of F. Guizot, *History of the Origin of Representative Government* with Liberty Fund. He is preparing a Ph.D. thesis at Princeton University.

P. Nikiforos Diamandouros is the Ombudsman of Greece. He is also Professor of Comparative Politics at the Department of Political Science, University of Athens, and Co-Chair of the Sub-Committee on Southern Europe of the Social Science Research Council (New York). In 1995–98 he served as Director and Chairman of the Greek National Centre for Social Research (EKKE). He is co-editor (with Richard Gunther and Hans-Jurgen Puhle) of *The Politics of Democratic Consolidation: Southern Europe in Comparative Perspective* (Johns Hopkins University Press, 1995), and author, most recently, of 'The political system in post-authoritarian Greece, 1974–96: outline and interpretation', in P. Ignazi and C. Ysmal, eds, *The Organisation of Political Parties in Southern Europe* (Praeger, 1998) and of 'Politics and judiciary in the Greek transition to democracy', in J. McAdams, ed., *Transitional Justice and the Rule of Law in New Democracies* (University of Notre Dame Press, 1997).

Kyril Drezov is Lecturer in the Politics of South-East Europe at Keele University and a leading researcher at the Keele South-East Europe Unit. He studied international relations at the University of Economics in Sofia, and did research at the Bulgarian Academy of Sciences before taking up doctoral studies at Oxford. He has published on problems of transition, modernization and nationalism in Bulgaria and Macedonia and on the Russian factor in Bulgarian politics. His main research interests are post-communist politics, Slav nationalisms and Panslavism, modernization and nationalism in the Balkans, with particular emphasis on Bulgaria and Macedonia. He is also a regular contributor on Balkan, Bulgarian and Macedonian affairs for the BBC World Service, Oxford Analytica and Eastern Europe.

Tom Gallagher holds the Chair of European Peace and Conflict in the Department of Peace Studies, Bradford University. He is author of *Romania after Ceausescu: The Politics of Intolerance* (Edinburgh University Press, 1995), a Romanian translation having been published by Editura All, Bucharest, in 1999. His major research is the politics of identity in Western and Eastern Europe and its impact on democratization processes. He is currently researching a book *Europe's Turbulent South-East: Radical Nationalism and Strategies for Containment*, which is due to be published by Gordon & Breach in 2002.

Stephen Larrabee is a senior staff member at RAND in Washington DC. He has taught at Columbia University, Cornell University, New York University, the Paul Nitze School of Advanced International Studies, Georgetown University and the University of Southern California. In 1978–81 he served on the US National Security Council staff in the White House as a specialist on Soviet-East European affairs and East–West political–military relations. He is co-editor (with David Gompert) of *America and Europe: A Partnership for a New Era* (Cambridge University Press, 1997), author of *East European Security after the Cold War* (RAND, 1994), editor of *The Volatile Powder Keg: Balkan Security after the Cold War* (American University Press, 1994), co-editor (with Robert Blackwill) of *Conventional Arms Control and East–West Security* (Duke University Press, 1989) and editor of *The Two German States and European Security* (St Martins Press, 1989).

James Pettifer is Visiting Professor in the Institute of Balkan Studies, University of Thessaloniki, and Research Fellow of the European Research Institute, University of Bath. He writes on the southern Balkans for a number of newspapers and periodicals, principally *The*

Times. His most recent books are *The Turkish Labyrinth* (Viking, 1997) and *Blue Guide to Bulgaria* (A. & C. Black, 1998).

Geoffrey Pridham is Professor of European Politics and Director of the Centre for Mediterranean Studies at Bristol University. He has authored numerous works on democratization in both Southern and Central & Eastern Europe, including (editor) *Transitions to Democracy: Comparative Perspectives from Southern Europe, Latin America and Eastern Europe* (Dartmouth, 1995) and (co-editor) *Stabilising Fragile Democracies: Comparing New Party Systems in Southern and Eastern Europe* (Routledge, 1996).

Valentin Stan is Lecturer in International Relations and International Contemporary History at the Faculty of History, University of Bucharest. He is a board member of the Centre for Euro-Atlantic Studies of the University of Bucharest and editorial board member of the bi-annual foreign affairs journal *Euro-Atlantic Studies*. He has authored several studies on international security issues and Euro-Atlantic integration. His most recent book is *Romania and its Failure to Integrate with the West* (Bucharest University Publishing House, 1999). He is preparing a Ph.D. thesis on the concept of subsidiarity and minorities issues in the new European security architecture.

Bogdan Szajkowski is Professor of Pan-European Politics and Director of the Centre for European Studies at the University of Exeter. He has written extensively on questions of transition of the former communist countries to democracy. His most recent books include *Encyclopaedia of Conflicts, Disputes and Flashpoints in Eastern Europe, Russia and the Successor States* (Longman, 1994) and *Political Parties of Eastern Europe, Russia and the Successor States* (Catermill, 1997). He is co-editor of *Muslim Communities in the New Europe* (Ithaca, 1996). He is currently completing a monograph on the politics and society of contemporary Macedonia and also writing a book *Which Europe and What Kind of Europe?* His current research concentrates on the political, economic and religious conflicts, politicized ethnicity, and the development of political parties and party systems.

Ivan Vejvoda has taught political science and European studies at the Sussex European Institute, University of Sussex, at Macalester College, Minnesota, and most recently at the Government Department of Smith College, Massachusetts. He has edited the works of La Boetie, Robespierre and Saint-Just. He is co-editor of *Yugoslavia and After: A Study in Fragmentation, Despair and Rebirth* (Longman, 1996) and of *Democratisation in Central and Eastern Europe* (Cassell Academic Publishers, 1999). He was one of the founders of the Democratic Forum in Belgrade (1989) and the Belgrade Circle–Association of Independent Intellectuals (1992). He is currently Executive Director of the Fund for An Open Society–Yugoslavia.

Preface

This book follows an international conference held at Bristol University in May 1997. It was organized by the Centre for Mediterranean Studies and received financial support from the British Academy. There were participants from a variety of European countries as well as the USA and UK. The papers were subsequently revised in two stages for finalization in this book form.

This conference and project followed a series of similar events on regime change in Europe held under the Democratization Research Programme of the Centre for Mediterranean Studies. It also formed part of the Centre's new Balkan Studies Research Programme, the twin emphases of which have so far been regime change and economic transformation.

In the case of regime change, it was felt a suitable moment to review the state of progress in a region commonly regarded as providing difficult examples of democratization. The war in Bosnia ended in late 1995, and changes of power in Romania and Bulgaria gave some encouragement to the prospects of democratization there. More than nine years after the end of communist rule, it has nevertheless become quite clear that in the Balkans the transition to democracy has overall proved more qualified and problematic than has usually been the case in the countries of East-Central Europe.

At the same time, one cannot generalize too absolutely about the Balkans. Strong common inheritances there certainly are and these have left deep marks on the course of regime change there; but cross-national variation is also apparent by now, whether comparing different successor states to the former Yugoslavia or these with other countries in the Balkans. Altogether, the transitions in Central and Eastern Europe as well as in the states from the former Soviet Union have been very diverse with the prospect of variable regime change outcomes in the offing. General categories based firmly on different regions here have become less convincing, and national particularities have begun to emerge more strongly.

The editors decided to combine comparative analyses of relevant themes with case studies of most of the Balkan countries. Slovenia was omitted as being not typically Balkan but rather Central European by both historical background and geographical location. Bosnia was not included for quite a different reason, because it has only survived in outline form since 1995 thanks to massive intervention of the West and has little control over half the territory's population. We have also included some discussion on theories of democratization to complete the survey.

Finally, it should be noted that this book was completed before the recent war on Kosovo. The immediate outcome of that crisis is known, but at the moment of writing its wider consequences for democratization in the region cannot be accurately assessed. In the light of this, we as the editors decided not to make changes in the text. This makes some chapters, especially that by Vejvoda on the Federal Republic of Yugoslavia, seem dated where references are made to Kosovo. We hope the reader will understand.

Overall, a mixed picture emerges with some countries providing guarded optimism and others suggesting a more gloomy scenario. In further cases, it is not yet clear whether liberal democracy will be the eventual outcome of regime change. Almost a decade since the collapse of communist systems, the evidence of consolidation of new democracies in the Balkans is not yet compelling.

Geoffrey Pridham   Tom Gallagher
University of Bristol   University of Bradford

1 Democratization in the Balkan countries

From theory to practice

Geoffrey Pridham

Introduction: focusing on the Balkans

Studying the recent process of regime change in the Balkan countries confronts one with some special and rather fundamental problems. Not least, there is the burden of complex historical legacies which seems to weigh so heavily with efforts in these countries to make a success of their new democratic regimes. This perspective lies behind the common view among transitologists, but also Western policy-makers, that the Balkans present a far more dubious prospect for political stability than East-Central Europe. In particular, the demands of state-building, national identity and ethnicity are much more to the fore in the former; and they have to a significant degree distracted from the priorities of democracy-building and economic reform.

Managing a triple transformation is undoubtedly a very daunting task within the relatively short period allowed so far in the 1990s, so that pessimism about regime change outcomes, while understandable, is nonetheless over-hasty. It goes without saying, too, that war in parts of the former Yugoslavia resulted in democratization being effectively shelved, for this experience until 1995 tended rather to reinforce authoritarian practices if not institutions, while flouting human rights and highlighting the breakdown of pluralist tolerance. Given these difficulties, this chapter explores whether the approach of democratization theory can be of any help in understanding regime change in the Balkans.

Predominant theoretical approaches have as a whole tended to caution against determinism in judging the process and outlook of democratization. The study of democratization has shifted its priorities over time, moving from attention to democratic prequisites for democracy on to actor-based concerns with the transition moment. This might at first suggest that one should be relatively less pessimistic about the Balkan countries with their difficult historical inheritances. However, the subsequent broadening of concerns that came with work on democratic consolidation has had undoubted consequences for theory-building. To some extent, this has led to reconsidering approaches that had been abandoned – notably, structural approaches emphasizing socio-economic conditions – if only because they seem, after all, to have some relevance to the longer-term process involved in consolidation. Transition is almost by contrast a usually brief process – invariably around a few years – except perhaps with those new democracies that fail to move easily into consolidation. In retrospect, therefore, it looks almost artificial to adopt actor-based approaches in too exclusive a manner when their relevance is particularly linked to such a short, albeit crucial, period.

The collapse of communist regimes in Central and Eastern Europe and the Soviet Union has generally reactivated a strong interest in the problems of democratic transition, not least because of the abundance and rich variety of examples. In doing so, it has led to many assumptions held in earlier work on regime change being challenged. Thus, the focus of transition theory on elite actors has not matched up to the experience of multiple and simultaneous transformation, even though it still has a partial relevance in many of these cases. Above all, work in this area should embrace the democratization process as a whole and not just the transition or the consolidation stage, if only because of the interlacing of different levels of change. The regime change literature has long recognized that transition and consolidation may well overlap to some extent and even proceed in parallel.[1] It may furthermore be said that work on transition or consolidation has tended to be rather ahistorical as well as acontextual, suggesting the need for relating the dynamics and prospects for regime change to earlier developments. Some transitologists have implied this need in seeing a link between the nature of authoritarian collapse and transition as well as between the nature of transition and the prospects for consolidation.[2]

Given the deficiencies of democratization theory, but also a growing recognition of its need to expand its concerns, it is inevitable that its scope and relevance for the Balkan countries might be questioned. Their historical experience and current problems seem to be in many ways a world apart from that of Southern Europe and Latin America, on which much theorizing has been based. Above all, the impressive Spanish model of transition through elite transaction and consensus, which influenced actor-based approaches, is so untypical of what has been happening in the Balkans.

In this chapter, therefore, we look at the background of democratization theory and efforts to adapt it to the demands of change in Central and Eastern Europe, before asking whether and, perhaps, in what ways it may serve some purpose in understanding the dynamics of transformation in the Balkan countries. Discussion then turns to whether they present unique problems if not new lessons for democratization theory. And this raises the final question of whether they represent a special 'model' of regime change or, alternatively, whether national diversity in the region argues against this.

Democratization theory and its evolution

Four groups of theories will be discussed in turn: the functionalist; the transnational; the genetic; and the interactive. These emphasize or concentrate respectively on socio-economic structural conditions, international influences and trends, political elite strategy and decisions, and lastly the dynamic relationship between the political and the socio-economic. The first and third are commonly regarded as the prominent schools of thinking in transition theory, while the other two are convenient labels to describe two different forms of approach.

Functionalist theories

These have focused on the requisite economic, social and cultural preconditions for democracy, and have drawn lessons from modernization theory with its twin focal points of economic development and social mobilization. Their guiding observation was that some societies were not as ready for democracy as others, leading to the view that the chances of democracy depended crucially on the level of socio-economic development. Thus, modernization was seen as producing value change which favoured democratization. From this developed a political-cultural version of functionalist theory. According to this, some political cultures are conducive to the establishment of democracy, while others are not, for certain mass orientations must be present before embarking on democracy.[3]

Functionalist theories have as a whole emphasized the overriding importance of prerequisites. Typical of this is Dahl's study of polyarchy, which highlights complex sets of factors that impinge on democratic development, including historical sequences, levels of socio-economic development, concentrations of power, socio-economic inequalities, subcultural cleavage patterns, political beliefs and foreign domination.[4] These theories of democratization have generally been criticized for being deterministic, for espousing a linear view of political development and for paying too much attention to material factors. One major reaction was a new approach to this problem emphasizing the crucial role played by political choice. Others have continued to find validity in the link between economic development and democracy.[5]

Such a link has to some degree been rehabilitated in work on democratization in the past few years, owing to the global shift to democracy in the 1990s. There are many more empirical cases and, it is claimed, the correlation between economic development and democracy has strengthened compared with the late 1950s, when Lipset wrote his original article.[6] It hardly needs saying too that in the case of Central and Eastern Europe the combined transformation at both economic and political levels has obviously highlighted this link and forced transitologists to take more note of what Rustow called 'the deeper layer' of socio-economic conditions[7] and to consider interactions with political democratization. While all this happened, the original claims of the modernization theories have been scaled down from causality (economic development as a cause for the emergence of democracy) to environment (economic development as providing a milieu favourable to democracy).[8] This modification connects with the view that economic development may not be a necessary prerequisite for democratic transition, but it correlates well with the sustainability of democracy, hence with the consolidation process.

Transnational theories

These have a broad-sweep or semi-historical approach in common with functionalist theory, and have developed from the latter towards a more complex array of factors both internal and external. For instance, structural explanations based on socio-economic conditions have come to be seen as strengthened through diffusion tendencies.[9] These theories have the virtue of drawing attention in an imprecise way to the importance of international factors and their influence on domestic change.

For instance, Samuel Huntington sought to explain the transition to democratic regimes in terms of a variety of factors – economic, social, cultural and external – and developed the thesis of 'waves' of democratization.[10] He defines a 'wave' as 'a group of transitions from non-democratic to democratic regimes that occur within a specified period of time and that significantly outnumber transitions in the opposite direction during that period of time'.[11] A 'snowball' effect occurs as a function of transnational influences or interactions and of geographical proximity. Particularly important in the recent wave has been the expansion of global communications, thanks to which the image of a 'worldwide democratic revolution' has 'become a reality in the minds of political and intellectual leaders in most countries of the world'.[12] References to the collapse of communist regimes in Central and Eastern Europe as a 'media revolution' – because of the effects of transmitting news about the one case on another – is convincing, although obviously not to the exclusion of other factors.

But this approach lacks a viable framework for estimating cause and effect. What are the exact conditions that allow diffusion to be successful? On the one hand, the emphasis in the globalization literature on decline in state authority, the consequent increase in political opportunities for international organizations and the expansion in transnational forces[13] does raise important issues about *how* these might impact on domestic change. On the other hand, it is certainly erroneous to interpret democratization as primarily the outcome of common patterns involving greater interdependence – what Held calls 'growing global interconnectedness' – between states.

Genetic theories

Such theories differ fairly radically from the functionalist and, to some extent also, the transnational theories, both in their specific focus on the process of systemic change and emphasis on political choice and actions of elites as well as in their belief in the intrinsic uncertainty of transition. It is the way transition pans out that determines regime outcomes. Structural preconditions, if treated, tend to be regarded primarily as background factors. The main contribution of genetic thinking to the democratization literature is that it has usefully centred attention on the dynamics of the process, although – not always admitted – its concern has been essentially the transition to, rather than the consolidation of, liberal democracy.

Various approaches have been developed, including those of pactism, political crafting, path-dependent analysis and contingency. 'Pactism' makes a number of assumptions, the most prominent of which is that it is individual action by leaders of groups who make strategic calculations and engage in pragmatic choice. Work on 'elite settlements' and 'transition by transaction' is very much in the spirit of this concept. Closely related, too, is the concept of 'political crafting', which draws attention to the style and means whereby elite settlements are carried out, and understandably it places an onus on the quality of leadership. It is essentially an optimistic notion, for 'greater investment in crafting (so as consciously to steer clear of repeated authoritarian involutions) can open novel possibilities for democracy in contexts previously deemed unfavourable'.[14] 'Path dependency' refers to an approach that starts by rejecting the idea of common causality in democratic transitions and opts for accepting the different paths to democracy; while the closely related concept of 'contingency' lends a more definite angle to the way transition develops. Contingent factors embrace speed, timing and sequence.[15]

Genetic theories have become increasingly criticized on several grounds – for being too elitist, over-voluntaristic and for disconnecting political action from socio-economic factors. In other words, there is a marked tendency to assume too much freedom on the part of transition actors, notwithstanding the fluidity and uncertainty of that process. There is a need to counter this by placing the study of transition within a framework of structural-historical constraints.[16]

Interactive theories

These relate to genetic theory but set it in a broader and more dynamic framework. Furthermore, they have a potential for exploring the democratization process as a whole and not simply the transition stage. In fact, interactive thinking has been present in some form or other in regime theory from the beginning; but it did not develop much until multiple transformation in the 1990s required much greater consideration of this approach.

According to Rustow, 'any genetic theory of democracy would do well to assume a two-way flow of causality, or some form of circular interaction, between politics on the one hand and economic and social conditions on the other; wherever social or economic background conditions enter the theory, it must seek to specify the mechanisms, presumably in part political, by which these penetrate to the democratic foreground'.[17] A link with political crafting is made: 'given uncertainty, how do structural and conjunctural factors recombine in the transition; to what extent are they recombined by actors; and how influential do structural factors remain?'.[18] The very realization that the overall democratization process is not merely uncertain but also rather complex and multi-dimensional encourages a broader and more open-minded approach to regime change theory. Kirchheimer's theory of 'confining conditions and revolutionary break-throughs' was in fact the first serious attempt to develop an interactive approach to the problem of regime change.[19] In his 1965 article, he explained 'confining conditions' as 'the particular social and intellectual conditions present at the births of these regimes' and sought to answer the question: to what extent do circumstances attendant at the emergence of a new regime determine its subsequent actions? What matters 'is the inter-relation between socio-economic conditioning and the discretionary element left to the decision of the regime'.[20]

It is the changes in Central and Eastern Europe that have urged fresh thinking because of the compelling need to work out the relationship between economic and political transformation in terms of relative priority but also mutual interdependence. This has led to a persistent debate about 'simultaneity', 'sequencing' and even 'asynchrony'.[21] Claus Offe recognizes the unprecedented overload in confronting the triple transformation (the problem of stateness as well as politics and economics). He nevertheless argues that political and economic change may in fact enhance each other in the form of a virtuous circle, which however may be threatened by the third form of change (territorial integrity and ethnicity). Crucial nonetheless is the question of the temporal structure of these different processes of change and possibilities for buying time and creating trust and patience.[22]

Of the various theoretical approaches, it is the interactive that offers the best scope for accommodating the growing diversity and complexity of factors in regime change and, above all, for responding to the need to embrace multiple transformations. Furthermore, interactive approaches have a dynamic potential that is particularly attractive as it allows us to bring into play such determinants as the historical and how legacies from the past impact on the present as well as the interplay between top-down dictates and bottom-up pressures.

Reviewing democratization studies in the age of the revolutions in Central and Eastern Europe

It is evident from the foregoing survey of regime change theory that future work on democratization needs to devote more attention to certain broad concerns. To summarize, it needs to:

1 take into account a historical dimension as not merely passive background;
2 embrace the democratization process as a whole from pre-transition liberalization under authoritarian regimes through transition and then consolidation out to regime outcome;
3 accommodate different levels of this process while focusing on its dynamic qualities;
4 embrace the multiple transformation (whether dual or triple) that is perhaps the greatest particular challenge.

It is certainly possible to suggest specific ways in which democratization studies should develop. An aspect that is much underplayed in comparative work on democratization is the societal. This is a major omission given the importance of looking at both top-down and bottom-up pressures in authoritarian collapse as well as in transition. Popular mobilization has been neglected in the democratization literature, with its focus rather on elites and the implicit if not explicit assumption that popular action could be dangerous to the fragile exercise of constructing elite agreements to keep the transition on course.[23] Nevertheless, civil society has emerged as significant in the transitions in Central and Eastern Europe, drawing attention to an obvious, and in retrospect surprising, area of neglect in democratization theory.[24]

One root problem in developing regime change theory has been its origin in one area study or another, notably Latin America and Southern Europe. The focus on the role of elites in transition is certainly influenced by the experience of the latter, and especially of the 'Spanish model'. This example of an evolutionary non-violent transition much impressed contemporaries as well as, subsequently, transition elites in some countries in Central and Eastern Europe, and developed into a paradigm. But its focus on path dependency and elite behaviour did not take sufficient account of wider or contextual considerations. Transitions to democracy in Latin America have not only been more diverse – and numerous – than in Southern Europe, but they have tended to encompass problems of social inequality and economic development. While there has been some shift to emphasizing the autonomy of political factors, concern with economic failure has traditionally prevailed in generalizations about transitions there, thus explaining why democratic instability has been to the fore.[25]

Such area-boundness has been criticized since regime change theory is seen as having little or no bearing, for instance, on the recent series of transitions in Africa, a continent where such change was not expected to happen for a variety of reasons, cultural, economic and historical. These include problems of state legitimacy linked to ethnicity and inheritances from the colonial period.[26] As a result, Africanists feel they are lacking a 'ready-made explanatory framework or set of defining conditions that can simply be tested in the African context' with respect to democratization.[27] In East Asia, conventional models of transitions have tended to be 'imported' from the West, although in fact there are convincing arguments for drawing lessons from East Asia such as with regard to cultural, socio-logical, institutional and also international explanations of the move towards democracy.[28] Similar comments may be made with respect to Central and Eastern Europe, and especially the Balkan countries.

The transitions in Central and Eastern Europe have differed from earlier ones especially in Europe in different ways. Sarah Terry, for example, lists five differences: the dual-track nature of the transitions, with the simultaneous construction of pluralist democracy and a market economy, an effort which is historically unprecedented; the fact that most earlier transitions took place in countries with a lower level of socio-economic and industrial development, making it easier for a change in development strategy, which was inhibited in Central and Eastern Europe by public attachment to the 'nanny state'; that previous transitions had not involved the same degree of ethnic complexity; the role played by civil society, or rather in Central and Eastern Europe the obstacles to its emergence; and the influence of the international environment.[29]

Matters relating to culture raise a nest of linked and often contentious issues that make the regime change in Central and Eastern Europe especially complex. These include problems of nationalism and state and society, but also point to historical inheritances and influences. The question of nationalism in parts of East-Central Europe, and especially the Balkans, forces us to confront its importance in relation to democratization. It represents one potentially basic threat to the new democracies there, as acknowledged in Nodia's view that 'unless resentment against the democratic model somehow recruits the deepest feelings of national identity, there will not be any open rebellion against it'.[30] The relationship between state and society involves the nature of conflict between the two, and how much the former is rooted in the latter or not. The role of the party-state as a means for the dominance of society in the communist regimes furthermore underlines the importance in democratization theory, and to some degree also in empirical work, of the need to think through more carefully the implications and consequences of prior-regime type. This is one dimension where the difference between authoritarian regimes in Southern Europe and Latin America and communist ones in Central and Eastern Europe needs highlighting.

Probably the main difficulty facing the application of standing democratization theory to Central and Eastern Europe, and above all the Balkans, is that several of its main assumptions or 'givens' have been called into question. As Offe has put it succinctly, 'the core problem of the political and economic modernisation of the former socialist societies resides in their lack of any non-contingent "givens" which would be suitable fixed parameters . . . precisely because the system is at such a deadlock, everything becomes contingent and nothing can self-evidently remain as it is'.[31] Studies of democratization in the former communist states have continued to call into question the relevance of paradigms in the transitions literature, 'just as some economists have challenged the applicability of models drawn from non-Communist societies to the dilemmas of economic reform in post-Communist states'.[32] A frequent, indeed obvious, stricture of regime change theory has been that it has essentially been posited on countries having a capitalist framework and that claims like 'no market – no democracy' are simply non-applicable.[33] Offe goes so far as arguing that 'designer capitalism' runs the risk of 'a post-socialist repetition of the structural problem or "rationalist fallacy" of state socialism'. He also sees genetic theories as having little application because of the gloomy scenario after communism of 'perfect destructuration comparable to the situation when "the earth was deserted and empty" – everything is possible and nothing can be excluded'.[34]

This suggestion of elite impotence, aside from the 'decisive role . . . played by individual charismatic personalities', seems too negative. Rather more pointed is the criticism that rational choice thinking behind genetic theories is weakened by its failure to predict mass upheavals, for what they explain is the rarity of these, i.e. they interpret why people don't take risks, not why they actually do so.[35] Others have found the focus on elites as useful in helping to understand internal tensions within outgoing communist regimes and the early phase of transition.[36] But it clearly has limited use in approaching the complex dynamics of the democratization process as a whole in Central and Eastern Europe.

The Balkan countries and democratization theory

It is evident then that regime change theory has some severe limitations for assessing regime change in the countries of the Balkans. While it offers various relevant angles in exploring this process, it is however quite obvious that the experience with regime change in these countries in the 1990s suggests new avenues in developing theory on democratization. Thus, we begin to address the question of a possible 'Balkan model'. We turn to both these lines of enquiry.

A brief reference back to the four groups of theories highlights where they may be relevant. Given criticism of traditional functionalist approaches concerning the chances of democracy occurring, it has to be recognized that democratization may commence in countries that lack the kind of developmental or cultural prerequisites previously regarded as vital. However, these developmental or cultural aspects – including the extent to which they remain traditional or backward – usually become very pertinent for democracy succeeding and rooting itself. In the Balkan countries, therefore, complex historical legacies do not as such prevent a change of regime, but they may well inhibit its fulfilment and may also, depending on the specific problem, help to divert this process from a democratic outcome. In particular, one would expect such legacies to surface in the dual or triple transformation and to account for the magnitude of issues facing their new democracies.

Regime change may for instance take place because the non-democratic regime collapses through internal divisions, external pressures or simply its failure to cope with mounting policy problems. In other words, political variables may be uppermost and these can be strengthened by inter-national events, notably Moscow's tolerant line towards change in Central and Eastern Europe but also the example set by the first transitions in East-Central Europe. Thus, the Balkans were far from immune to the 'snowball' effects of a democratization 'wave' starting elsewhere to the north. These domino-style transnational influences were also evident within the Balkans, where the dramatic collapse of Ceauşescu's regime in Romania prompted the early erosion of the totalitarian system in Albania, which then sought to discourage growing mass discontent through cautious reform. When this failed, the shift to democratization occurred, although alternation in power in favour of the opposition did not prevent totalitarian legacies and their impact on the functioning of Albania's shaky new democracy.[37]

While political factors of a more immediate than long-term nature can be decisive in explaining the onset of transition, it does not follow that such factors will secure a successful transition once it has started. Political choice has indeed been evident in the Balkans, but of a distinctly more conflictual than consensual kind. There was little effort at elite settlements or pacts more commonly found elsewhere, save initially in Bulgaria in the early 1990s. There cross-party negotiations moderated the first stage of the transition, but increasingly politics became more contentious and problems of overcoming the past – especially visible in the largely unreconstructed composition of the former ruling party, now the Socialists – persisted and held back the reform process.[38] The role of mass pressures at different points in the transitions of the Balkan countries, not to mention the incidence of violence in cases like Romania, demonstrated that the elitist assumptions of genetic theory carried limited conviction. In any case, the actions of various leaders in some countries illustrated not so much political crafting for democracy's sake as the utilization of historical legacies for nationalist designs, notably on the part of former communists seeking a new political message. Thus, state-building, ethnicity and other aspects of the third form of transformation threatened to derail the process of democratization if not disrupt that of economic reform. The war in parts of the former Yugoslavia illustrated how this negative dynamics could be carried to an extreme length.

While some Balkan countries demonstrated that political choice could have disastrous consequences during regime change, interactive approaches serve better than genetic ones in measuring how structural and political variables relate. Thus, historical legacies – whether in the form of ethnic cleavages, totalitarian inheritances, weak civil society or simply political patterns – may be defined as 'confining conditions' that act as a constraint on political choice once democratization begins. At the same time, as Kirchheimer notes, the power of these conditions may alter once that process is in train due to the discretionary element that remains for political elites and the possibilities for mass mobilization created by the democratic game. Clearly, both may play an important part in how cross-effects between multiple transformations occur. In broad terms, an interactive approach allows us to focus on factors such as the cultural that might otherwise be too difficult to incorporate in analysis of regime change. This approach may also encompass dimensions of regime change highlighted by the Balkans but generally neglected in theoretical concerns. These are also dimensions that should for general reasons be included or more developed in comparative and theoretical studies of democratization. Three in particular are worth mentioning.

First, the Balkan countries usually remind us how much complex historical legacies may enter transition politics and help determine the prospects for democratic consolidation. Historical determinants of regime change require spelling out in a way that avoids bland assertions about 'the rebirth of history' or 'the weight of the past'. This may be done by regarding historical patterns – such as the existence or absence of democratic or authoritarian traditions – as a powerful though not predictive force. Historical patterns may be modified or strengthened by more recent historical experience; and it is here that four decades of communist rule should be compared with previous methods of government and tendencies in political culture. Issues of change and continuity have featured in some empirical literature on case studies of regime change. But this is of largely descriptive interest. It is more useful to focus on questions like historical memory, how this is transmitted and what effects it has on elite choice and public response once transition commences. Problems of national identity too are relevant for these tend to convey historical experiences, and it is a reasonable assumption that self-images linked to national identity may influence early trends in political culture in new democracies. But, of course, national identity may also be divisive in societies with ethnic cleavages, thus reinforcing the argument that issues of national identity need to be resolved in a way that is positive for implanting democratic and pluralist values. Finally, it is important to recognize that historical legacies may be multi-form – social and economic as well as political – and that they may not always deter the emergence of democratic politics.

As to authoritarian legacies, mentalities and practices are more important than institutional forms, for the latter may be dismantled in a relatively short time. This leads us to consider how such legacies are handled during transition itself, where, clearly, an onus is placed on the right political choice by new democratic leaders. This is often a matter of drawing a fine balance between different and sometimes conflicting considerations, such as truth, revenge, retribution, justice and reconciliation when it comes to dealing with human rights abuses under dictatorial government. This issue brings together the past (the hard edge of authoritarianism) with the present (democratic transition and possible demands for responding to revelations of abuses) and the future (the question of national unity and the prospects for democratic consolidation). Similarly, political learning is an important concern in any democratic transition, particularly – although not exclusively – if a previous pre-authoritarian democratic experiment has failed. Thus, the most telling form of this derives from a country's own political past, although it may also come – admittedly, less painfully – from lessons abroad, most likely on institutional matters. Nancy Bermeo has rightly relativized the degree of learning required in early democratization for it does not occur uniformly nor does it necessarily have to involve a deep normative commitment to democracy at this stage. What is important is that there develops a 'criticial mass' of learners in key groups and that political learning is cumulative as this will feed into the eventual consolidation process.[39]

Second, the relationship between the three types of transformation (of political regime, economic system and that linked to nation-building) may to a significant extent be explored with reference to the state, regime and society. This is particularly pertinent for the Balkans because of cross-national patterns of a pronounced statist tradition, patrimonial rule and the late emergence of independent states as well as weak civil societies and a potential for inter-ethnic strife. The question of the state/regime relationship is important to clarify with respect to democratization. This is not merely because it reflects on the extent of change involved, but rather as it highlights complexities in the process. Confusion may arise because, under non-democratic regimes, these two different entities tend to merge to a greater or lesser degree, most of all in the totalitarian version and to a varying extent under authoritarian models. Hence, regime and state may become virtually indistinguishable; whereas in liberal democracies the regime becomes demarcated from the state just as government (or rather, successive governments) becomes distinguished from the regime.

In general, it is expected that under democratic rule the state is less intrusive or at least less all-encompassing in its attempt to penetrate society. A border is drawn between the public and private spheres, and this applies notably to the retraction of the state from socio-economic life. This aspect is especially pronounced in Central and Eastern Europe with marketization replacing state-run economies. This is sometimes known as the 'orthodox paradox', whereby the state is expected to organize its own withdrawal from the economy. In the Balkan countries, implementing this 'paradox' has been especially difficult with a pattern of strong state centralism combining with weak civil society. Destatization has been a gigantic and multi-dimensional task involving liberalization, privatization, a radical reduction in state expenditure and the state's retreat from the allocation of credits – to name the main requirements.[40] Beyond that, it is a matter of defining and establishing legal and financial institutions; and there are implications here for the general process of bringing into being the rule of law.

It is clear, then, that regime change can have major effects on the role of the state. But there is another aspect to this problem which reflects on authoritarian inheritances. The blurring of the distinction under non-democratic rule invariably affects popular perceptions, so that it is quite common for public mistrust towards the state to persist after democracy has been introduced. However, it is likely that positive demonstrations by the new democratic regime of clear differences from authoritarian rule will gradually have a positive effect on the standing of the state. The diffusion of authority in the state structure is likely to help produce this political sea-change. On the other hand, if the third transformation is on the agenda, then the relationship between state and society may become highly com-plicated as nation-building involves creating a new state, defining the citizenry and shaping national identity as well as regulating relations with neighbouring and other countries. In practice, though, nation-building can often result in an over-emphasis on state power, an exclusive notion of citizenry, an overblown sense of national identity and hostile relations towards abroad. If national minorities are present, the temptation to abuse human rights may well arise. For all these reasons, the impact on democra-tization can be lethal. We need, therefore, to distinguish between those countries which face state-building challenges (notably those from the former Yugoslavia) and those where the state existed but was weakened or deformed by communist rule.

Thirdly, some Balkan countries offer lessons concerning the question of hybrid regimes and transition trajectories. Normally, regime legitimacy is a fairly linear process once the constitutional settlement is firm and institutional design is relatively clear. The way is open, so to speak, for a new democracy's institutionalization. But this is another matter in the case of hybrid regimes or cases where the constitutional settlement is unclear or contested, for such a situation is likely to inhibit institutionalization and legitimation. In the 1990s, the global wave of democratization has in fact produced some diversity of post-authoritarian regimes, with many of them differing significantly if not profoundly from democracies in advanced industrial countries. In certain cases, they are considered as not fully democratic.[41] Such regimes are usually categorized as hybrid as they meet only minimum standards for democracy and operate in some way contrary to democratic practice. They are sometimes labelled *democraduras* ('hard democracies') which retain some authoritarian elements, as in a degree of political power for the military or in being 'delegative' as opposed to representative democracies leading to weak or non-existent accountability. A post-communist version of hybrid regimes may occur with a retention of power by former regime elites who – predominantly unreconstructed – exercise that power in a way not readily conducive to easy democratization despite meeting formal requirements. It follows that there is likely to be a weak legitimacy of democratic rules, although much may depend on the degree of social backwardness and traditional political culture, hence the acceptability of such hybrid outcomes of regime change.

There are, indeed, several examples of this pattern in the Balkans. This is one important point of differentiation from the transitions in East-Central Europe, with the possible exception of Slovakia under Mečiar's rule, although some new nations deriving from the former Soviet Union offer further examples of hybrid regimes.[42] Croatia is, for instance, a convincing case of a *democradura*. In the words of one recent study, 'post-Communist Croatia has exhibited important aspects of both incipient democratization and residual authoritarianism'.[43] That is, the one-party communist regime has been abandoned, there have been competitive elections and economic transformation has commenced, but the Tudjman government has continued to exhibit an executive-centred and anti-pluralist approach such as in curbing the activities of opposition parties and democratic expression in the media. Since these authoritarian tendencies depend to a considerable degree on the ageing figure of Tudjman, the post-communist regime in Croatia is seen as moving towards a crossroads against a background of growing opposition pressure.[44] Undoubtedly, Tudjman's credit for achieving statehood and the war situation in the former Yugoslavia impeded the democratization process there. Similarly, in Serbia, presidential rule by Milošević has been domineering and highly manipulative in an authoritarian way. Accordingly, while the institutions for a democratic transition have been in place since 1990, these dictatorial practices together with an inability of the opposition to articulate any message other than an ethnic nationalist alternative have limited their potential effectiveness.[45] Problems of ethnicity only illustrate the failure to achieve political inclusiveness that is crucial for democratic consolidation. Thus, in cases like Serbia and to some degree Croatia the necessary contextual conditions that favour constitutional legitimacy have been lacking.

The existence of such hybrid regimes and, in other cases, the retention of power by former regime elements have affected the nature of transition trajectories in the Balkan countries. Whereas regime change in East-Central Europe broadly followed a procedural pattern familiar to transitologists, in the Balkans it has often followed a hesitant and sometimes ambiguous path. This usually satisfied formal requirements of democracy, but often cast doubt on the qualitative direction of regime change. The weakness of opposition, reflecting the lack of pre-authoritarian democratic traditions and limited civil society, was one factor here, as was the preference of ex-regime elites (e.g. in Romania) or even new democratic elites (e.g. in Albania) for authoritarian practices. But, from the mid-1990s, various influences have changed the situation: the end of the war in the former Yugoslavia which lifted pressures for national solidarity on security grounds; growing international demands for economic reform; and a late flowering of democratic mobilization at home.[46] The outcome has been a second democratic transition in some of these countries, offering less mixed prospects than the first round of transitions in 1989–91, especially after alternation in power as in Romania, Bulgaria and Albania during 1996–7. Such alternation is usually of symbolic importance in transitions, showing how rival political elites accept their own loss of office as part of the new democratic game. In the Balkan cases, such alternation has had distinctly systemic implications.

A Balkan model of regime change – or national diversity?

These particular features of regime change in the Balkans suggest that the area concept may be applicable in understanding the process there of democratization. This concept argues there is a common environment that has shaped the evolution of political systems, economic development and social change, and has produced uniform political patterns; and that this environment consists of historical similarities as well as geographical location. However, our examination above, while suggesting strong similarities among the Balkan countries, also points to significant differences between them as regime change has progressed. This cautions against asserting there is a clear-cut Balkan model. Moreover, one should guard against any cultural bias that may be present in any argument about Balkan exceptionalism. For there is also a convincing case to be made for late development in these countries.

The Balkans are commonly seen as a special set of cases in the study of regime change, representing chronic political instability and a lack of socio-economic modernization as well as much poorer prospects for democratiz-ation and for acceptance into the European Union (EU) compared with the countries of East-Central Europe. This is partly due to influential long-term patterns or 'confining conditions' insofar as they continue to carry weight during regime change itself. They include various effects of long Ottoman rule over centuries in these countries, belated national independence, the frequent absence of democratic traditions, a tendency for political conflict and violence, and territorial disputes with neighbouring states. Overcoming such a past has been exacerbated by the experience of four decades of communist rule, which have resulted more often than not in a strengthening of traditional patterns through authoritarian practices.[47]

The consequences for regime change in the 1990s have been predictably the lack of widespread liberal values, weak and sometimes non-existent elements of civil society and a propensity for oligarchical and loosely accountable methods of government. In particular, the weakness of the rule of law tradition suggests that eventual democratic consolidation will be a difficult task. Moreover, the economic context of regime change presents further problems here, for the general absence of a commercially based middle class committed to the rule of law and political pluralism means implanting democracy in shallow cultural soil. The deterioration of living standards on a scale not seen in Europe since the Great Depression places a major additional burden on what must be seen as still fragile new regimes.

How far can one therefore speak of a Balkan model of regime change, producing ambiguous if not insecure democratization, and distinctive from other regions of Europe if not elsewhere in the world? The answer must lie in how far the aforementioned historical patterns have actually become significant 'confining conditions' which continue to inhibit seriously the establishment of new democracies and uniformly so across the region. In other words, how much is the image of the Balkans replicated in current reality?

As several chapters in this book show, these 'confining conditions' are considerable and very present in these societies, although with some cross-national variation. Diamandouros and Larrabee identify, for instance, five salient features which characterize these new democratic regimes in the Balkans, including patrimonialist, sultanistic and (post-)totalitarian inheritances in state/society relations, non-liberal concepts of democracy, ethnic concepts of the nation and the expected use of public office for private gain. The ability of nationalism to shape political culture is furthermore highlighted by Gallagher, while Bianchini notes the continuing struggle between contending political cultures, the liberal and the nationalist. Difficulties in nurturing pluralist ideas are evident too in areas like the media because of the legacy of doctrinaire communism and older traditions of political partisanship, as shown too by Gallagher. Altogether, therefore, the 'confining conditions' in these countries are powerful and have had an undoubted imprint on the course of democratization there. But, given the relatively brief time-span involved of less than a decade, that is hardly surprising. Historical legacies and forces of this nature are not likely to disappear soon, if disappear they can. Nationalism, at least, has usually an enormous potential for mobilizing identities and political emotions, not to mention for being exploited by ruthless politicians, and is therefore a force of some staying power. The best that can be hoped for in the short term (i.e. during transition) is for its effects to be progressively neutralized by counter-influences; and these must include democratic practices and judicious leadership by new democratic elites.

Referring again to regime change theory, it is evident that historical legacies of the magnitude witnessed in the Balkans need not and did not prevent democratic transition occurring, but they are likely to complicate the course of democratization if not inhibit the prospects for regime consolidation. It is also clear that there is, despite the power of these 'confining conditions', much scope for political action that may, with some degree of luck, help shift the dynamics of regime change in a positive rather than destructive direction. International influences too are a notably important factor in the region, and these may well serve to help or hinder developments. Externally driven change has possibly ensured that countries like Romania and Bulgaria have not followed the authoritarian path of Serbia. Pro-active Western efforts to sustain fragile democracies have been a strong by-product of the Dayton peace process.

Given, therefore, a degree of openness in the situation of regime change in the Balkans, it is relevant at this stage to consider cross-national variation in the incidence of different 'confining conditions'. We turn now, briefly, to the individual countries as a final test of how far there may or may not be a Balkan model of regime change.

Some significant differences soon become apparent. There is a marked variation in the styles of transition, say between revolution in Romania and evolution in neighbouring Bulgaria, with intermittent chaos in Albania; but also so far in regime change outcomes especially between republics of the former Yugoslavia. Slovenia has quietly established a reasonably functioning democracy but also one with signs of a healthy civil society, thus pointing to some optimism with respect to consolidation. As strictly non-Balkan by background, location and culture, Slovenia may be seen as the exception that proves the Balkan rule. However, the transitions in Central and Eastern Europe as a whole have become increasingly diverse with the prospect of quite variable regime change outcomes in the offing. And this makes for caution in generalizing about either East-Central Europe or the Balkans in too strict a manner. Indeed, in the latter case so far, these outcomes have produced one likely candidate for democratic consolidation (Slovenia), two hybrid regimes (Croatia and Serbia), three still somewhat fragile democracies (Romania, Bulgaria and Macedonia) and one seemingly dubious case of democratization (Albania).

Croatia and Serbia have – as previously noted – created formal democracies with authoritarian tendencies; while Macedonia has notwithstanding a divisive historical past and threatening circumstances (including an initial dispute about its international status) survived as a new democratic system. Undoubtedly, the war situation in the former Yugoslavia during 1991–5 dramatizes the main difference in the region so far as the actual process towards democratization is concerned. In the belligerent states, this process was effectively stalled while elsewhere it continued, albeit sometimes in a chequered fashion. This war furthermore reminds us that problems of ethnicity have indeed varied between these countries. In some parts of ex-Yugoslavia, anti-minority nationalism has not been prevalent, such as in Slovenia and Macedonia – in the latter instance owing much to Gligorov's leadership skills as President. In Bulgaria and Romania, minority issues have become inflamed at times but then the minorities in question – Turks in the former, Hungarians in the latter – have also been represented in coalition governments at other times. It is in Serbia, Croatia and especially Bosnia-Hercegovina that ethnic relations led to tragic violence. In addition, states from the former Yugoslavia have been involved in nation-building, while other Balkan countries have not.

Various countries in the Balkans have also of late shown a capacity for a renewed start at democratization, notably in Romania and also Bulgaria. The changes of power there in respectively 1996 and 1997 hold out better prospects for the future of their regime changes; and, indeed, this development was emphasized in the official opinions of the European Commission on their applications for accession to the EU. And in Serbia and Croatia new signs of democratic pressures emerged once the Bosnian war situation and its requirements for national solidarity passed and lifted constraints on internal dissent. The chances for their regimes to persist as somewhat authoritarian now look less promising. All this suggests, although cautiously, that progress towards democratization may be improving, even if it is still too soon to call a final judgement on the likely outcome.

For different reasons, therefore, it is difficult to claim there is a strict Balkan model of democratization. Our study of regime change in this region warns us that culturalist notions of democratization's chances or the lack of them on grounds of historical burdens and overwhelming problems – not to mention conventional images about 'the Balkans' – are dangerously monolithic. They do little to advance serious research, let alone encourage new thinking deriving from cross-national comparisons. Indeed, they recall the early writing on regime change – long since contested – about preconditions for democratization. Common legacies and common patterns there certainly are; and, to some extent, one may say there is some evidence of common tendencies insofar as these legacies and patterns affect regime change itself. Thus, in terms of background, there are good reasons to consider these countries as a Balkan area study. But the different forms of national diversity, and also differences in regime outcomes, argue against any uniform process of democratization across the region. Hence, it is in the final analysis difficult to argue there is a 'Balkan model' of regime change. This becomes even clearer when we turn to looking at the prospects for democracy in the region.

Conclusion: prospects for democracy and its consolidation

It is clear that if the historical past is any guide to regime change in the Balkans, then there is ample cause for pessimism. There are, especially in certain countries in the region, enough major problems with long legacies to overload any fragile new democracy, thus increasing the pressures against successful regime change. However, while the past and its influence may be described as black, the present is unsettled or grey just as the future cannot be referred to in any form of colour since the process is sufficiently open to further change and therefore unpredictable. The very dynamics of democratization can make a significant difference and help to relativize the actual impact of such legacies. Much depends on the strength, unity and energy but also moderation of pro-democracy forces and their ability to constrain other forces, which are either reluctant about democracy or seek to promote alternative models of government. When viewing the democratization process as a whole in the Balkan countries, it is only possible to draw tentative conclusions; and this is of course a further reason for arguing against a Balkan model.

Any assessment of progress in regime change is therefore likely to produce a mixed picture in most national cases, with both positive and negative signs. For example, Romania has showed signs of hope, deriving in part from the 1996 change in power but also evident in media pluralism and some evidence of participatory politics. At the same time, the slow pace of economic reform, the persistence of mentalities from the former communist regime and a still quite undeveloped civic culture present a more sombre picture. But it is also important to observe movement in regime change and not merely focus analysis on snapshots at a particular, even recent, moment. For this reason, we have in this volume sought to combine cross-national comparative studies on relevant themes with case studies of the main examples of regime change in the countries of the Balkans. Moreover, and first of all, the democratizations in the Balkans are approached from the standpoint of regime change theory. There are thus three sets of chapter contributions: theoretical, comparative and national case study. What do they reveal about the prospects for democracy in this region?

For Diamandouros and Larrabee (Chapter 2) the chances for democratic consolidation there are unsettled and open. Much depends on how elite and collective actors manage to eliminate obstacles in moving their countries beyond electoral regimes to liberal democracies. This is particularly true of Albania and states from the former Yugoslavia; while in Bulgaria and Romania it is a matter of crystallizing and institutionalizing democratic practices as a means towards consolidation. But in all cases these actors have to operate against different structural constraints relating to the state, the nation and society. Bianchini (Chapter 3) emphasizes the imprint of traditional patterns as well as conflicting forms of political culture. While the outcome here is uncertain, nevertheless interaction with Western Europe is likely to be a vital influence in encouraging democracy-building in the Balkans. Tom Gallagher (Chapter 4) also sees links with Europe as providing a challenge to the absolutist view of nationalism. But they must be set against factors that may continue to promote the latter, and these include severe economic and social hardship. His other chapter (Chapter 5) identifies a range of problems which have inhibited the development of the print and electronic media from becoming a significant support for the emergence of liberal democracy. Legacies from the former regime through state restrictions combine with strong partisanship but also erosive economic pressures to prevent independent tendencies in the media from stabilizing.

Difficulties of economic transformation are examined by Bartlett (Chapter 6), who notes that privatization has been largely manipulated by the political elites and sees democratization being constrained by the absence of sustained economic growth from which a middle class could develop. A flourishing small business sector has been unable so far to become a driving force behind growth. While cross-national variation in economic transformation is evident, in general the vicious circle commonly found in the Balkans is only likely to be broken through privatization enabling radical restructuring, small business having a more dynamic effect and patterns of internalization through inward investment. The role of external forces, highlighted in several other chapters, are explored by Stan (Chapter 7). Western aid will continue to be quite crucial in assisting the magnitude of change, and there is an extraordinary readiness of govern-ments in the Balkans to seek support from outside. However, in the end this role of the West remains one of strong influence, and a significant one, although it is internal developments that may prove decisive in deter-mining the final outcome of regime change. Differences between the countries are apparent, with the degree of their links with the EU being the single most important factor.

Cross-national variation with regard to the prospects for democracy in the region emerges again when looking at the various country studies in this volume. In Romania's case (Craiutu, Chapter 8), the early 1990s saw change leading to a quasi-pluralist regime marked by chronic dis-equilibrium and ideological confusion, with polarization between those who were reluctant about democracy or looked to less tarnished elements of the communist past and those who wanted a clear if not radical break with that past. The 1996 elections provided a new chance for democratization to proceed, although the lack of elite consensus remains an obstacle to eventual consolidation and the question of state/society relations will still condition how this occurs. Bulgaria (Drezov, Chapter 9) also evidences some problem of elite disunity (save on the constitution and EU membership). While alternation in power in 1997 raised hopes about the prospects for democracy there, nevertheless severe difficulties with economic performance and the tendency for party-political colonization of the state and resulting corruption continue to cause doubts about the course of democratization in that country.

Croatia and Serbia (Vejvoda, Chapter 10) are virtually in a category of their own because of the war situation during the first half of the 1990s and the overwhelming impact of the communist legacy. In Serbia in particular, the ideology of the former regime has been transmuted into strong nationalism alongside which old practices have to some extent continued within the framework of formal democracy. As a result, a *sui generis* form of regime has emerged combining traditional features with new elements, although the latter have failed to crystallize let alone institutionalize in a way suggestive of possible democratization.

The remaining two cases of Albania and Macedonia present somewhat differing prospects. Albania (Pettifer, Chapter 11) has suffered from a particularly difficult historical background as well as from being the poorest of the Balkan countries, and embarked on regime change slightly later than elsewhere. But habits and mentalities from the communist period have persisted albeit in democratic forms, while the collapse of law and order has called into question the prospect of success with democratization. There is undoubtedly a large democratic deficit in Albania with a long way to go before regime change can be secured. Turning to Macedonia (Szajkowski, Chapter 12), this country has turned out to be the failure that did not happen. Macedonia demonstrates many severe problems relating to legacies – no democratic tradition, deep inter-ethnic tensions, problems of economic development and threats from regional insecurity – that should have halted the move to democracy. But up till now this process has not collapsed and this is a tribute to the way in which transition itself – in particular, elite choices – may help to counter the effects of problems from the past. Thus, Macedonia contrasts with some other countries in the Balkan region where historical legacies have been exploited for political ambitions.

Altogether, the evidence so far of democratic consolidation in the countries of the Balkans is not compelling. This does not mean that at some levels it has not started, as the more hopeful signs identified in this chapter suggest. Democratic consolidation is a multi-level process and it does not follow that advances at one level are automatically paralleled by advances at another. Moreover, some consolidation may commence before transition is complete. It is tempting to see the Balkan countries as somewhere in this stage, but as we have discovered there is significant cross-national diversity so that generalization is not very possible. The other main conclusion must be that these countries, or some of them, cannot be – as yet – relegated to any hopeless category of democratization cases. Our study shows that, even against a background of weighty historical legacies, the dynamics of regime change may alter perspectives and produce interactions that may hold out the possibility of departures from previous patterns of political behaviour.

Notes

1 E.g. R. Gunther, N. Diamandouros and H-J. Puhle, *The Politics of Democratic Consolidation*, Baltimore: Johns Hopkins University Press, 1995, p. 3.

2 Ibid., pp. 399–402. Also see J. Linz and A. Stepan, *Problems of Democratic Transition and*

Consolidation: Southern Europe, South America and Post-Communist Europe, Baltimore: Johns Hopkins University Press, 1996, chapter 4.

3 G. Almond and S. Verba, *The Civic Culture: Political Attitudes and Democracy in Five Nations*, Princeton: Princeton University Press, 1963.

4 See Robert Dahl, *Polyarchy: Participation and Opposition*, New Haven: Yale University Press, 1971.

5 For example, see K. Bollen, 'Political democracy and the timing of development', *American Sociological Review*, vol. 44, 1979, pp. 572–87; E. Muller, 'Democracy, economic development and income inequality', *American Sociological Review*, vol. 53, 1988, pp. 50–68; L. Diamond, 'Economic development and democracy reconsidered', *American Behavioral Scientist*, March/June 1992, pp. 450–99. See also S. Lipset, 'The social requisites of democracy revisited', *American Sociological Review*, February 1994, pp. 1–22.

6 See S. Lipset, S. Kyoung-Ryung and J. Torres, 'A comparative analysis of the social requisites of democracy', *International Social Science Journal*, vol. 45, 1993, pp. 155–75. Cf. also D. Rueschemeyer, E. Stephens and J. Stephens, *Capitalist Development and Democracy*, Chicago: University of Chicago Press, 1992.

7 D. Rustow, 'Transitions to democracy: toward a dynamic model', *Comparative Politics*, April 1970, p. 343.

8 See discussion of this point in H. P. Schmitz, 'Why structural and agency-based approaches fail to explain – a constructivist perspective on democratisation', ECPR paper, March 1997, pp. 5–8.

9 E.g. see J. Londregan and K. Poole, 'Does high income promote democracy?', *World Politics*, 1, 1996, pp. 1–30, for the argument that the democratizing effect of growing incomes is significantly increased by external influences.

10 S. Huntington, *The Third Wave: Democratisation in the Late Twentieth Century*, Norman: University of Oklahoma Press, 1991.

11 Ibid., p. 15.

12 Ibid., pp. 101–2.

13 D. Held, *Democracy and the Global Order*, Cambridge: Polity Press, 1995, pp. 89–90.

14 Ibid., pp. 8–9 and 22.

15 P. Schmitter, 'The consolidation of political democracies', in G. Pridham, ed., *Transitions to Democracy: Comparative Perspectives from Southern Europe, Latin America and Eastern Europe*, Aldershot: Dartmouth, 1995, pp. 560–63.

16 T. Karl and P. Schmitter, 'Modes of transition in Latin America, Southern and Eastern Europe', *International Social Science Journal*, Vol. 43, 1991, p. 271.

17 Rustow, 'Transitions to democracy', p. 344.

18 G. Di Palma, *To Craft Democracies: An Essay on Democratic Transitions*, Berkeley: University of California Press, 1990, p. 6.

19 O. Kirchheimer, 'Confining conditions and revolutionary breakthroughs', *American Political Science Review*, 59, December 1965, pp. 964–74.

20 Ibid., pp. 964, 965.

21 See A. Przeworski, *Democracy and the Market: Political and Economic Reforms in Eastern Europe and Latin America*, Cambridge: Cambridge University Press, 1991; Rueschemeyer, Stephens and Stephens, *Capitalist Development and Democracy*; and B. Crawford, ed., *Markets, States and Democracy: The Political Economy of Post-Communist Transformation*, Boulder: Westview Press (1995).

22 See Claus Offe, *Varieties of Transition: The East European and East German Experience*, Cambridge: Polity Press, 1996, chapter 3.

23 See N. Bermeo, 'Myths of moderation: confrontation and conflict during democratic transitions', *Comparative Politics*, April 1997, pp. 305–22.

24 See G. Ekiert, 'Democratisation processes in East Central Europe: a theoretical reconsideration', *British Journal of Political Science*, 1991, 21, pp. 298–300.

25 See discussion of transition theory and Latin America in S. Mainwaring, 'Transitions to

democracy and democratic consolidation', in S. Mainwaring, G. O'Donnell and J. S. Valenzuela, *Issues in Democratic Consolidation*, Notre Dame: University of Notre Dame Press, 1992, pp. 326–9; and K. Remmer, 'New theoretical perspectives on democratization', *Comparative Politics*, October 1995, p. 114.

26 C. Clapham, 'Democratisation in Africa: obstacles and prospects', ECPR paper, April 1993.

27 R. Joseph, 'Democratisation in Africa after 1989: comparative and theoretical perspectives', *Comparative Politics*, April 1997, p. 364.

28 This line of argument is developed by J. Ruland, 'Theoretische, methodische und thematische Schwerpunkte des Systemwechselforschung zu Asien', in W. Merkel, ed., *Systemwechsel 1: Theorien, Ansatze und Konzeptionen*, Opladen: Leske & Budrich, 1994, pp. 271–99.

29 S. Terry, 'Thinking about post-Communist transitions: how different are they?', *Slavic Review*, Summer 1993, pp. 333–7.

30 Nodia, 'How different are postcommunist transitions?', *Journal of Democracy*, October 1996, p. 28.

31 Offe, *Varieties of Transition*, p. 41.

32 B. Parrott, 'Perspectives on postcommunist democratisation', in K. Dawisha and B. Parrott, eds., *The Consolidation of Democracy in East-Central Europe*, Cambridge: Cambridge University Press, 1997, p. 2.

33 See review of theories on transition and their bearing on Eastern Europe in D. McSweeney and C. Tempest, 'The political science of democratic transition in Eastern Europe', *Political Studies*, September 1993, pp. 408–19.

34 Offe, *Varieties of Transition*, pp. 137–8.

35 See T. Kuran, 'Now out of never: the element of surprise in the East European revolution of 1989', in N. Bermeo, ed., *Liberalization and Democratisation: Change in the Soviet Union and Eastern Europe*, Baltimore: Johns Hopkins University Press, 1992, p. 14.

36 E.g. P. Lewis, 'Patterns of democratisation and perspectives on regime change in Eastern Europe', paper for conference on Regime Change and the Transition to Democratic Politics, Sofia, September 1995.

37 A. Agh, *The Politics of Central Europe*, London: Sage, 1998, p. 185.

38 Ibid., pp. 180–2.

39 N. Bermeo, 'Democracy and the lessons of dictatorship', *Comparative Politics*, April 1992, p. 275.

40 J. Elster, C. Offe and U. Preuss, *Institutional Design in Post-Communist Societies: Rebuilding the Ship at Sea*, Cambridge: Cambridge University Press, 1998, chapter 5 on building capitalism in Eastern Europe.

41 D. Collier and S. Levitsky, 'Democracy with adjectives: conceptual innovation in comparative research', *World Politics*, April 1997, p. 430.

42 Notably Belarus, where there has been a democratic inversion under Lukashenska. In the case of Slovakia, the outcome of the 1998 election with Meciar's defeat has to be consolidated through effective performance and the new government's own stability.

43 L. Cohen, 'Embattled democracy: postcommunist Croatia in transition', in K. Dawisha and B. Parrott, eds, *Politics, Power and the Struggle for Democracy in South-East Europe*, Cambridge: Cambridge University Press, 1997, p. 69.

44 Ibid., pp. 111–13.

45 N. Miller, 'A failed transition: the case of Serbia', in Dawisha and Parrott, *Politics, Power and the Struggle for Democracy in South-East Europe*, p. 179.

46 Agh, *The Politics of Central Europe*, p. 186.

47 T. Gallagher, 'Democratisation in the Balkans: challenges and prospects', *Democratization*, Autumn 1995, pp. 337ff.

2 Democratization in South-Eastern Europe

Theoretical considerations and evolving trends

P. Nikiforos Diamandouros and F. Stephen Larrabee

Introduction

If the study of democracy has an ancient pedigree, the study of democratization, conceived as a process of regime change, is much more recent. Systematic analyses of how democracies come about, how and under what circumstances they consolidate, and how they expire are a phenomenon of the last three decades. Prior to that, social science inquiry remained very much the hostage of Cold War preoccupations, which placed greater emphasis on contrasting democracy with totalitarianism than on peering inside democratic political systems and trying to understand the dynamics of their development or failure.[1]

The collapse, in April 1974, of the longest non-democratic regime in Europe, Portugal's 48-year-old Estado Novo, set off a powerful international dynamic in support of democratic regimes, which in the course of the ensuing quarter century has profoundly transformed the balance between democracies and non-democracies around the world. Aptly labelled the 'third wave of democratization', this unfolding dynamic initially swept through Southern Europe, subsequently engulfed Central and Latin America, reached out to East Asia, and culminated in the concatenation of momentous events unleashed by the fall of the Berlin Wall and intimately linked to the collapse of the Soviet Union and the end of the Cold War.

Closely following this rapidly accumulating experience, social scientists sought to develop conceptual tools capable of understanding the properties of unfolding developments and of providing credible theoretical generalizations concerning the emerging brave new world of different types of democracies. The result was a new and burgeoning subfield of comparative politics, whose own intellectual horizons have been steadily expanding, in response to the evolving logic of the overarching democratization process. In its initial phase, the study of democratization focused on the immediate problem at hand – the demise of non-democratic regimes and the transition to democratic politics. Subsequently, as some societies successfully negotiated their transitions and produced institutionalized democratic regimes, the focus of attention of both scholars and, increasingly, policy-makers shifted to the requisites of democratic sustainability and, more specifically, democratic consolidation. More recently yet, as the study of consolidation began to yield its first systematic insights and to generate its first critics, analysis has tended to shift towards considering the properties of consolidated democratic regimes and especially their quality. The still greatly under-theorized notion of the 'quality of democracy' seems at present to constitute the natural next frontier for students of democratization.[2]

Within this broader universe of concerns, the study of democratization in Eastern Europe holds a special place. This is so because, along with the successor states of the Soviet Union, these states represent a new pheno- menon for analysts of democratization which is qualitatively different from earlier empirical cases. Their chief distinguishing characteristic lies in the fact that these countries' transitions to democracy have been occurring at the same time as they move from a centrally planned economy to some variant of the market mechanism. An additional distinctive feature, differen- tiating the democratization experience in the overwhelming majority of these societies from that of most other parts of the world, especially Southern Europe and Latin America, is their imperative need to confront serious challenges to the legitimacy of the state. These challenges issue from profound social, political and cultural divisions linked to ethnic and national minorities, established within the boundaries of these states and potentially, if not actually, contesting their territorial integrity. As Robert Dahl originally pointed out and Juan Linz and Alfred Stepan have more recently forcefully demonstrated, the democratic process presupposes the existence of an undisputed territorial unit:

> we cannot solve the problem of the proper scope and domains of democratic units from within democratic theory. Like the majority principle, the democratic process presupposes the unit. The criteria of the democratic process presuppose the rightfulness of the unit itself. If the unit itself is not [perceived as] proper or rightful – if its scope or domain is not justified – then it cannot be made rightful simply by democratic procedures.[3]

The virtual incapacity of these societies to disentangle these three different challenges and to confront each of them in a more or less isolated manner, seriatim, greatly increases the problems and risks associated with their quest for democracy, significantly complicates the prospects for its successful completion, and makes them very distinctive as an object of analysis. In practice, the systematic study of this cohort has proceeded in an uneven manner. By far the greatest attention has, so far, been paid to the democratization process in the countries of East-Central Europe (Poland, Hungary, the Czech Republic and Slovakia), the Baltic region and Russia.

The rest of the former Soviet Union and, especially, South-Eastern Europe (Albania, Bulgaria, Romania, and the states issuing from the dissolution of former Yugoslavia), which constitutes the central concern of this chapter, have received much less attention.[4]

This chapter has three intertwined goals: to place the evolution of South-East European democracies to date within the theoretical context of the study of democratization; to draw insights from the experience of South-Eastern Europe which are useful for the comparative study of democratization; and to evaluate critically perceptions concerning the region which inhibit a more balanced assessment of their democratic experiments and of the prospects for their successful completion. We shall endeavour to address these broader concerns while attempting to answer two specific questions. First, what are the distinctive characteristics of the South-Eastern European democratization process and what are the observable differences from other similar experiences, whether in East-Central Europe, Southern Europe, or elsewhere? Second, what explains these differences? But first, a short theoretical digression.

Theoretical considerations

Two analytical approaches compete for primacy in the systematic study of democratization – those privileging culture and those emphasizing politics. The former tends to focus on longer-term developments and trends and to underscore the significance of historical continuities, which often constrain human action. By contrast, the latter privileges choice and hence the capacity of human agency decisively to influence the course of events surrounding individual and collective social actors and the conditions affecting their existence. It has gained increasing prominence in social and political analysis during the last two decades, as the reaction against Marxist interpretations maximizing the importance of 'objective' factors in history and commensurately minimizing 'subjective' ones gathered momentum. On the whole, and taking into account the inevitable degree of conceptual distortion implicit in such exercises in reductionism, approaches emphasizing culture are often implicitly, if not explicitly, equated with determinism, while those privileging politics are charged with being excessively voluntaristic.

Our inclination in this instance is to argue in support of an eclectic approach favouring the complementarity rather than the mutual exclusivity of these two modes of analysis. We support this option because we believe that the analytical requirements of different components in the overall democratization process vary, and that one or the other of these analytical approaches may be more appropriate in understanding the nature and dynamics of a particular element of that process. Thus, transitions, which are by definition periods of pronounced indeterminacy and uncertainty, are the grounds *par excellence* where the freedom of human action can be greatly expanded. In this instance, politics can be decisive in producing policy options, developing new rules for their implementation, crafting new institutions, and, above all, fashioning the rules of the democratic game and generating the requisite support for their adoption and implementation. It is the crafting of the rules of the democratic game that, after all, defines a transition. In these moments, the constraints of the social environment are significantly attenuated, the weight of the past becomes less decisive, and social reality tends to be more malleable, allowing us to think of transitions as the classical loci for 'crafting'.[5]

Conversely, the legacies of the past, which can, and invariably do, have an admittedly variable impact on a transition, constitute parameters constraining the freedom of human action and limiting choice. As such, they can leave their imprint on transition and consolidation processes but also on the type of democracy crafted through human agency during these two critical subcomponents of the overall democratization process. In assessing the significance of these factors for democratization, an analytical approach more sensitive to choice-constraining rather than choice-maximizing conditions seems to be more appropriate. Finally, consolidation, conceived as a process, whose salient characteristics are the gelling and crystallization of often newly invented or, at least, newly agreed upon practices, their gradual (though occasionally rapid) institutionalization, and the application and implementation of the rules of the democratic game fashioned during the transition, produces an environment for choice that is clearly more constraining than that of the transition but less confining than the legacies of the past just referred to. The task facing the student of democratization, therefore, is to identify the appropriate mixture of these two approaches that will render intelligible the dynamics of a particular moment of the democratization process(es). In Kirchheimer's terminology, the task entails identifying the confining conditions for human action, which have to be overcome for breakthroughs, conceived as environments facilitating, if not maximizing, the room for choice to occur.[6]

Democratization, conceptualized as a process, entails a combination of background factors and subprocesses affecting and, more often than not, cumulatively determining its evolution. The particular path or trajectory that democratization will take in a given country will ultimately depend on the specific manner in which each of these factors will combine with the others, as well as on the intensity which each of these assumes in a particular case. Outcomes are certain to vary. Some societies produce successful transitions and consolidations, which lead to varying types of democratic regimes of varying quality. In others – to date a much larger number – transitions become stalled, fail to institutionalize the democratic rules of the game, and produce fragile and precarious democracies. In still others, the democratic experiment proves unable to survive, their democracies break down, and give way to some form of authoritarian involution, exit from which may (or may not) occur in the future, setting in motion yet another democratization cycle. This is not to imply that consolidated democracies are free of the dangers of breakdown. Deconsolidation is clearly a theoretical possibility, which can be followed by either re-equilibration or by breakdown. But empirical evidence suggests that in consolidated democratic regimes breakdown occurs much more infrequently than in non-consolidated ones.[7]

The relation of transition to consolidation deserves a short comment. Temporally, transition precedes consolidation and, as such, greatly influences it. This, however, does not necessarily imply that they relate to one another in a sequential way. More often than not, the two processes overlap and the origins of the consolidation can be traced to some point in the transition itself. More frequently, their end points will vary, too, with the end of consolidation following that of transition. It is, however, possible for the two processes to reach completion at the same time. The Chilean democratization may be a case in point. According to many observers, the expiration of limitations, which the constitution devised by General Augusto Pinochet imposes upon the authority of the country's democratic government, is quite likely to lead to the completion of the Chilean transition and consolidation at the same time. In their recent work on transition and consolidation, Juan Linz and Alfred Stepan have argued that the same phenomenon is true of Portugal, where, in their estimation, both processes came to an end in 1982, following the constitutional revision that removed the *de jure* limitations on the authority of parliament created by the existence of the Council of the Revolution, dominated by the military. In the cases which concern us here, South-East European countries find themselves in various points of their transition processes in the late 1990s. In none has democratic consolidation been achieved. Only one among them, Slovenia, can be said to be in the very early stages of consolidation.[8]

In our view, the most important factors affecting democratization are socio-economic development, the legacy of the predecessor non-democratic regime, the mode of its expiration, prior democratic experiences or learning that can be made use of during the transition, leadership, and the nature of the transition itself. To these, we would add the longer-term heritage of state–society relations. This term is designed to capture two important dimensions: first, the historical legacy of the state in a given society, the mode of its operation, and the degree of its legality; and second, the level of development in civil society, the degree of its organization, and the patterns of its interaction with the state. For reasons we shall explain shortly, we believe that this parameter has special importance for South-Eastern Europe, where the mode of political domination associated with Ottoman rule has left its lasting imprint on both states and societies in the region. Given its theoretical importance for our argument, we shall begin our analysis of the political factors affecting democratization with this parameter.

The long-term heritage of state–society relations

An important difference distinguishing South-Eastern from East-Central European societies stems from the fact that until the second decade of the twentieth century each of these regions formed part of large imperial states, the Habsburg and the Ottoman empires, whose principles of political, social and economic organization were, in an ideal type sense, distinctly different. As part of the Habsburg empire, the societies which comprise East-Central Europe today were politically organized under a variant of Western absolutism, which, since the time of Maria Theresa and especially Joseph II in the eighteenth century, had systematically sought to pursue reformist policies designed to render the imperial state administration more enlightened and rational. An additional feature of absolutism, pertinent to our concerns, was that, its name notwithstanding, it was a system in which the exercise of political power, and thus the relation between rulers and subjects, was mediated by powerful intermediate bodies, such as the aristocracy. The significance of these *corps intermediaires*, to which Montesquieu devoted considerable attention in his *Spirit of the Laws*, lay precisely in the fact that they contributed to the greater organizational density and, hence, capacity of society, and in an embryonic form served as the foundation for the subsequent emergence of more articulate and relatively strong civil societies.[9]

The relative rationality of the state and the mediated exercise of power in these territories had profound positive implications for the structuring of state–society relations in the newly independent nation-states of Czechoslovakia, Hungary and Poland, which emerged from the ruins of the Habsburg empire in the aftermath of the First World War. Of these countries, Czechoslovakia stands out as the one which best managed to capitalize upon these legacies of the absolutist past to build a successful democratic system in the inter-war period, and to generate an important amount of democratic learning for both its elites and masses. Taken together, democratic learning (that is, the accumulated experience with democratic rules of the game, to be more fully discussed below) as well as the traditions of state rationality and the mediated exercise of power constituted an impressive amount of cultural and political capital that could subsequently be tapped and made available to imaginative leaderships, when the proper circumstances materialized. But even in Poland and Hungary, which succumbed much more to the temper of the inter-war period and experienced breakdowns of their fledgling democracies, the legacies associated with the state and the mediated exercise of power were not completely lost. They were to prove immensely valuable subsequently to the leaderships of these states.

The significance of these legacies cannot be overemphasized. A recent work by Shain and Linz emphasizes the crucial significance which the presence or absence of a legal rational state tradition in non- or

pre-democratic settings has for a successful negotiation of democratic transitions. Put otherwise, the legality of the non- or pre-democratic state,
which in and of itself tends to generate a certain amount of self-legiti-
mation, can also serve as a potent source of cultural and political capital
and of political learning, which under the proper circumstances can greatly
facilitate a democratic transition.[10]

From the perspective of the long-term factors favouring the generation
and accumulation of cultural and political capital that could be profitably
tapped by democratizing actors, the legacies of the Ottoman empire were
significantly less favourable. In sharp contrast to the practices associated
with absolutism, the exercise of power in the Ottoman state closely
conformed to the logics of two types of rule described in varying degree of
detail by Max Weber: patrimonialism and sultanism, an extreme variant of
the former. The distinctive features of patrimonialism are the highly
personalized exercise of power; the lack of a clear distinction separating the
state from the ruler's household and the official from the private; the
discretionary, unrestrained, and unmediated exercise of power; the personal
subservience of officials to the ruler; the use of tradition as its major
principle of legitimation; and, more generally, the tendency to regard the
state as a source of provisioning for the ruler. What distinguishes sultanism
from mere patrimonialism is the former's tendency to break with tradition,
thereby freeing the ruler from the types of restraint, often significant, that
tradition can place upon his/her freedom in exercising power.[11]

Throughout its long history, the Ottoman empire was a classical example
of a patrimonial state. The authority of the Sultan, the manner in which he
related to the state, to his officials and to his subjects, closely conforms to
Weber's analysis. In the final centuries of its long history, especially from
the mid-eighteenth century on, when the empire entered a period of sharp
deterioration as centrifugal forces began to tear its ruling institutions apart,
and when the power of tradition to serve as a restraint upon the ruler
greatly declined, it becomes increasingly possible to assert that the exercise
of power conformed to the principles of sultanism rather than to
patrimonialism.

Two points need to be stressed with respect to the legacy of patrimonialism. First, the gradual disintegration of the imperial institutions in
the nineteenth century, the rise of nationalism in its territories, and the
gradual emergence of aspirations among subject peoples for the creation of
separate nation-states coincided with the period of the sultanistic rather
than the more benign and, at times, enlightened (e.g. Suleiman the
Magnificent) patrimonial phase of the empire's history. In turn, this
development helped impart sultanistic logics concerning governance and
administration in collective as well as elite attitudes towards the state and
its relations with civil society. Second, the combination of sultanistic practices with the gradual disintegration of the central imperial institutions and
the incapacity of the imperial state to exercise effective control over much

of its provinces and periphery resulted in the replication of such practices and logics at all levels of governance. These ranged from the powerful regional pashas to the more lowly local ayans, all of whom exercised power within the level of their jurisdictions in a manner that closely replicated the model practices at the imperial centre based on the complete elimination of the line separating the private from the official and resulting in the appropriation of the state for personal use.[12]

The type of state–society relations fostered by such a state legacy is likely to be characterized by weak organizational capacity of social actors and, consequently, by low levels of interest articulation in civil society. Herein lies a crucial difference between the absolutist and the sultanistic models of political organization. The unmediated exercise of power, the absence of the *corps intermediaires*, which Montesquieu identified as critical structures contributing to the imposition of effective restraints on the power of absolutist rulers, and the potent tradition of personal subservience of office-holders and private subjects to the ruler effectively combine in undermining civil society's capacity to define itself proactively (rather than reactively) *vis-à-vis* (and even in opposition to) the state and to articulate a forward-looking, self-empowering sense of collective identity. This is what is generally referred to as the notion of the 'weakness' of civil society and this deserves further examination.

In the various bodies of literature dealing with the 'weakness of civil society', whether in the context of democratization or in terms of its relations with the state, weakness is usually conceptualized and treated as a function of low capacity for self-organization and for the articulation of interests and demands. While such an approach is clearly accurate in its depiction of the social realities it wishes to analyse, its emphasis on incapacity (or low capacity) for organization effectively prevents the analyst from grasping an important social dimension of weakness, which is the enormous tenacity of such societies and their capacity to resist. The Yale political scientist James C. Scott has systematically focused on what he has called the 'weapons of the weak' and on the power dynamics involved in 'domination and resistance'. Scott's work pointedly focuses our attention in the direction of the 'strengths of the weak' and on the logics and cultures peculiar to them. Without challenging the accuracy of analyses focusing on the weakness of civil society, these insights enhance our understanding of the inner working of such societies, by bringing out qualities and logics inadequately captured by the more dominant conceptualization.[13]

In the context of the concerns informing this analysis, Scott's insights help us capture a number of important characteristics of the legacies fostered and shaped by the dominant pattern of state–society relations, under which the elites and masses of South-East European societies articulated their fledgling aspirations for nationhood and statehood. The highly personal and unmediated exercise of power by the ruler combined with the personal subservience of office-holders and private individuals alike to foster social realities characterized above all by the weak capacity of formal structures (offices, institutions) to 'protect' their incumbents from arbitrary action from above. The result was the emergence of a powerful culture of levelling egalitarianism in the region, built around the solidarity of the weak and directly linked to the collectivist ethos (discussed in the next section on socio-economic modernization), which has had a lasting, variable and ambiguous influence upon the political organization of these societies. In certain ways, it can be said to have facilitated the rise of communist regimes in the region and enhanced their capacity to stay in power without experiencing the type of eruptions encountered in East-Central Europe (East Germany in 1953, Hungary in 1956, Poland in 1956 and again from the 1970s on, and Czechoslovakia in 1968).

On the other hand, its lingering presence has greatly complicated the pace and scope of democratization in these countries and has adversely affected the quality of their fledgling democracies. For whereas the egalitarian component of this legacy can be said to contribute positively to the construction of a democratic regime, the absence of a liberal-pluralist component – which the levelling element of its egalitarianism *inter alia* implies – imparts a potentially populist dimension to the democratic process. It also inhibits the emergence and proliferation of social actors capable of contributing to the deepening and thickening of democracy and of favourably affecting its quality. Above all, however, the levelling effect of egalitarianism and the sultanistic logic of the state which underpins it have contributed to the generation of a profoundly ambiguous perception of political power and of its most powerful institutional manifestation – the state. Simultaneously combining the logic of appropriation of public office for private ends with the logic of resistance to authority, such a perception effectively undermines the capacity of the state, greatly weakens its legitimacy, and results in large but ultimately weak states, often likened to colossi with clay feet.[14]

A further legacy of the Ottoman past which has a bearing on the democratization process in contemporary South-Eastern Europe derives from the relatively peaceful coexistence that, on the whole, characterized the state of interreligious relations among subject peoples under Ottoman rule. During the early centuries of the Ottoman empire, tradition, the central legitimating principle of patrimonial rule, served as an effective underpinning of formal and informal arrangements, ensuring the peaceful coexistence of the various ethnic and religious groups constituting the subject populations and reducing conflict to tolerable levels. Such an assessment is all the more persuasive when seen in the context of the religious intolerance (e.g. wars of religion, expulsion of the Jews from Spain) that was wreaking havoc in Western European societies at the time. In the more recent past, when tradition became greatly eroded as a principle of legitimation and the Ottoman state acquired increasingly sultanistic characteristics, the institution of the millets (administrative structures containing subjects of the same religion and, thus, separating one religious group from another), served as insulating mechanisms, which ensured the continuation of peaceful coexistence among peoples of different religions. And, since religion was by far the single most powerful factor in determining individual and collective identity under this arrangement, inter-ethnic conflict was also commensurately contained. In the case of South-Eastern Europe, the existence of what has been referred to as an '[Eastern] Orthodox Commonwealth' served to provide the empire's Orthodox populations with an additional sense of separateness from other subject peoples and, through the powerful institution of the Orthodox Church, to reinforce a sense of commonality among them which discouraged conflict.[15]

It was only when, in the course of the nineteenth century, the rise of nationalist aspirations among subject peoples progressively eroded the primacy of religious identity, and as a result existing ethnic and religious cleavages gradually began to be recast in the exclusivist logic of the nation, that the powerful solidaristic bonds of traditional arrangements enhancing peaceful coexistence became increasingly attenuated and the 'problem of the Balkans', with all the pejorative associations attached to such a conceptualization, was born. In sharp contrast, therefore, to conceptualizations of the region's contemporary politics as being steeped in cultural legacies of 'ancient hatreds' and 'centuries-long enmities', the intractable problems bedevilling the democratization process in South-Eastern Europe are the products of relatively recent developments and form part and parcel of its belated and protracted transition to modernity during the twentieth century. And they are intimately related to the rise of nationalism in the region, and to its greatly complicating impact on the relations among the successor states of the Ottoman empire. Nationalism in South-Eastern Europe is often accurately referred to as virulent, aggressive, intolerant or overweening. Its power derives from two sharply contrasting factors, which, paradoxically, are intimately interrelated and mutually reinforcing: the fragility of its social foundations and its strength as a principle of legitimation for relatively new states hampered almost throughout their short existence by weak legitimacy.

Nationalism in South-Eastern Europe is fragile not because it is relatively young. The cause for its fragility lies, rather, in the fact that, in the face of multi-ethnic and multi-religious social settings, which constitute the dominant reality in the region, the logic underpinning it and decisively influencing the state-building strategies linked to it has been ethnic. As a rule, this has meant that the ethnicity of the dominant national group within a given state has served as the organizing as well as exclusive principle informing its nationalism. The non-recognition of other ethnic groups, which such an arrangement implies, narrowed the social foundations upon which the nationalist ideology rested, severely eroded the legitimacy of the state identified with it, and often gave rise to strategies of coping with the problem that adhered to one of three alternative logics: of assimilation, expulsion or liquidation. None of these was reassuring for that part of the new state's populations left out of the dominant con-ceptualization of the nation.

The existence of large excluded minorities within their boundaries greatly contributed to the weakness of the new states by raising implicit, if not explicit, concerns and fears regarding their territorial integrity. Fearing that the recognition of the existence of minorities within their territories would open the backdoor to irredentist claims on the part of their neigh-bours and weakened by the estrangement and covert (if not overt) hostility which non-recognition and frequent repression engendered, the successor states of the Ottoman empire became ever more entangled in a mortal embrace with their own ethnic nationalisms, in a vain and desperate search for legitimation, however narrowly based and therefore fragile. The international challenge posed by the rise of an avowedly anti-nationalist ideology, communism, at the very moment when these states attained independence, and strove to carve out a place for themselves in the modern world, exacerbated the problems facing them, reinforced the tendency to search for security in aggressive and intolerant nationalism, and cut short their early experiments with democracy. The resulting deficit in prior democratic learning was to become painfully obvious during the difficult search for new and more promising democratic formulas in the years following the collapse of communism in the region.[16]

A final dimension of the pre-communist legacies in South-Eastern Europe on which we should like to focus concerns the strong antipathy towards political division characteristic of these societies. The fear of division, which modern politics implies, is a pre-political phenomenon in no way peculiar to a particular set of societies. It constitutes, rather, a feature typical of pre-modern settings and of their usual correlate, exten-sive peasant populations. Indeed, the collectivist solidarities generated in peasant societies strongly militate against the notion of division, which is regarded as a sinister force threatening the pristine unity of the peasant world. In quite a different setting, the same antipathy towards division was a salient feature of the mercantile Venetian republic, in which concern with the adverse by-products of division was a central preoccupation of the ruling elite. In either case, the result was the perpetuation of conditions militating against the emergence of pluralist structures in society, contri-buting to the survival of zero-sum conceptualizations of power relations, and inhibiting the gradual accumulation of learning geared more to the acceptance of interest, compromise and positive-sum logics as constitutive aspects of an alternative, modern type of politics.

As already noted, the overwhelmingly peasant nature of South-East European societies fostered the emergence of powerful collectivist attitudes and practices, including the distrust of political divisions. Such perceptions of reality were further reinforced by another feature of the region, to which we have already alluded: the administrative organization of the subject peoples of the Ottoman state into separate, corporate entities based on religion. Within these pre-modern settings, religion, the single most important force defining, reproducing and reinforcing individual and collective identities, combined with administrative separation as well as minority and subject status to produce a strong emphasis on in-group solidarity. Under these circumstances, division was seen as a mortal threat to the integrity and, indeed, the survival of these communities. As we shall endeavour to establish in our discussion of the communist phase in the region's protracted and delayed transition to modernity, the communist regimes which prevailed in these societies after the end of the Second World War built upon this pre-existing heritage of aversion towards division. The intense ideological preoccupation of these regimes with notions of monopoly and unity in the organization of politics, economy, society and the state effectively exacerbated this heritage.

As we conclude the discussion on what we call the long-term factors having a bearing on democratization, we should like to repeat an earlier word of caution. These factors should not be regarded as ostensibly constituting, in and of themselves, insuperable obstacles to democratiz-ation. That would imply a deterministic understanding of legacies of the past, which we strongly reject. Rather, we see them as parameters, which human agency, whether in the form of individual leaders, elites or collective actors, will have to confront and cope with in the course of the transition to democracy, seeking to minimize their restraining impact and commensurately to maximize its own freedom to craft new arrangements conducive to successful democratic outcomes. Moreover, not all of these factors need to become activated or to exhibit the same levels of salience during the transition. Some of them may lie quiescent or be sufficiently neutralized through imaginative political choices and leadership action designed to limit their impact. Others may become more salient during consolidation. In the final analysis, their ultimate importance lies in the manner in which they are dealt with during the transition. This will influence the type of outcome to emerge from the overall democratization process – be that a stalled transition, a problematic consolidation, the quality of democracy to be arrived at, or, *in extremis*, some form of non-democratic involution.[17]

Socio-economic modernization and democratization

The literature on democratization generally acknowledges the existence of a strong positive, albeit not a causal, link between socio-economic development and democratic consolidation. The democratization experiences of Southern Europe and other regions provide ample evidence confirming this linkage. Transitions to democracy and consolidation processes that unfolded within relatively undeveloped socio-economic settings were much more problematic and protracted than those which unfolded within relatively modern and more affluent societies. To a significant extent Italy and Spain bear out this observation. In Italy, the transition to democracy took place in the aftermath of the Second World War at a time when extensive socio-economic structures retained characteristics more typical of the nineteenth century than of the twentieth. The protracted nature of its transition was directly linked to this situation. In Spain, conversely, democratization in 1970s and 1980s occurred in socio-economic settings that had undergone profound modernization in the preceding two decades and had, in many ways, transformed Spain into a modern society. As a result, transition and consolidation were achieved more easily in a much shorter time-span. Closer to the Italy of the 1940s but more pertinent to our concerns, the democratization experience in Latin America has, as Terry Karl has repeatedly pointed out, been severely complicated by lasting problems associated with, among others, great socio-economic inequalities linked to late development.[18]

Viewed from this perspective, the societies of South-Eastern Europe embarked upon their own uncertain journey into the uncharted waters of democratic politics with a significant disadvantage stemming from their late socio-economic development. Two major factors account for this. First, the incorporation of the region in the Ottoman empire in the course of the fifteenth century effectively meant that, with the exception of Slovenia, which came under Habsburg domination in the fourteenth and fifteenth centuries, and partly of Croatia, which formed part of the Hungarian monarchy (until the 1520s) or the Habsburg Empire (after 1718), South-Eastern Europe did not partake of the momentous changes that in the course of the ensuing centuries shaped the modern world. More specifically, most of the region did not directly experience the Renaissance, the Reformation and the Counter-Reformation, the Scientific Revolution, the Enlightenment, or the Industrial Revolution. Thus, when, beginning in the late nineteenth and early twentieth centuries, South-Eastern Europe societies began their belated encounter with modernity, they constituted what Alexander Gerschenkron, in an influential essay, labels 'late late developers' – that is, societies characterized above all by the predominance of the agrarian sector, in which powerful anti-industrial and anti-modern landowning classes ruled over landless masses, by the extreme weakness of the urban sector, the virtual absence of a bourgeoisie, pervasive illiteracy, rampant poverty, pre-modern cultures, and, more generally, profound underdevelopment. Directly issuing from this state of affairs was a powerful cultural tradition rooted in the collectivist ethos arising from the agrarian solidaristic arrangements prevalent in the region and fostering, among others, strong anti-urban and anti-modern mentalities in South-Eastern European societies. With significant variations across countries and despite perceptible erosion brought about by gradual modernization, it has retained its salience until the present.[19]

The four decades of communist rule in the years after the Second World War only partially rectified this situation. The rural–urban balance shifted in favour of the latter, as the logic of centrally planned economies generated a form of economic development that transformed the region. The pathologies of totalitarianism, however, and above all the virtual lack of pluralist structures in economy, society and politics that such a regime type implies, left their deep imprint on South-East European societies and ill-prepared them for the enormously complex challenges of democratization they were suddenly called upon to confront once the communist systems established in the late 1940s abruptly collapsed in the late 1980s and early 1990s.

In addition, and with the sole exception of Slovenia, the economies of the communist countries of South-Eastern Europe remained poor and underdeveloped in comparison to those in Southern Europe and East-Central Europe. Albania had the lowest per capita income in Eastern Europe. Romania's per capita income was only slightly better. To be sure, Yugoslavia was better off because of its ties to the West and its more open economy. But within Yugoslavia strong regional differences existed. Slovenia and Croatia enjoyed relatively high standards of living, while the southern regions, especially Kosovo, Macedonia and Montenegro, were quite underdeveloped. (The standard of living in Kosovo, however, was higher than that in Albania proper.)

This legacy of economic underdevelopment severely complicated the economic and political challenges facing the new elites in South-Eastern Europe during the transition process. As a result, the overall process of socio-economic transformation in this region was both slower and more problematic than in East-Central Europe. Indeed, low levels of socio-economic development combined with the mismanagement of the economy by the communist and post-communist elites to produce in South-Eastern Europe shock effects and severe social discontent during the initial transition to the market economy. These developments differentiate South-Eastern from East-Central Europe, where relatively higher levels of socio-economic development produced more of a cushion to buffet the initial disruptions and deprivations caused by the introduction of market mechanisms. All in all, then, 'late late' socio-economic development constituted for South-Eastern Europe a heavy and adverse legacy that severely burdened and complicated its democratic transitions and, more generally, its democratization to date.

The character of the predecessor non-democratic regime

The character of the predecessor non-democratic regime is one of the most important factors influencing the prospects for successful democratization. Though originally confined to authoritarian regimes, the analytical scope of studies on democratic transitions was greatly expanded after the collapse of communism to take into account the new empirical universe produced by the attempt of post-communist regimes simultaneously to develop democratic political systems and to introduce some variant of a market economy. While the general consensus among scholars has been that this 'dual transition' greatly complicates the transitions to democracy, an equally important finding concerns the much greater transition problems facing post-communist societies compared to post-authoritarian ones. Put otherwise, specific properties of totalitarian regimes, not found or found at much lower levels of frequency or intensity in their authoritarian counterparts, are much more inimical to successful democratization.

As Linz and Stepan emphasize in their recent work, *Problems of Democratic Transition and Consolidation*, post-totalitarian regimes, defined as regimes that have experienced some degree of evolution away from the totalitarian ideal type, can be broken down into three subtypes. The first, early post-totalitarian, exhibits the least amount of evolution away from the ideal type of totalitarian regime, identified in particular with the period of high Stalinism. Usually, this takes the form of an abandonment of the use of terror as a systematic policy instrument, the adoption of collective leadership styles, and the abandonment of personality cult practices, which constitute an important feature of the totalitarian type. The second subtype, frozen post-totalitarian, refers to regimes whose evolution away from totalitarianism become arrested and a deliberate attempt is made to freeze their evolution away from the totalitarian ideal type. Czechoslovakia after the end of the Dubcek liberalization in 1968 is the classic example of such a subtype. Finally, mature post-totalitarian regimes are characterized by significant movement away from the totalitarian ideal type, which brings them closest to the point of transiting to another regime type, be that authoritarian or even democratic. In the analysis provided by Linz and Stepan, Hungary fits most closely to this last subtype, whereas Poland is regarded as already having crossed the threshold to authoritarianism before the 1989 convulsions. In short, at the time their transitions were initiated, the former Habsburg territories now constituting the states of East-Central Europe examined by Linz and Stepan occupied positions farthest removed from the totalitarian end of the post-totalitarian range in which they were inscribed. Poland had already crossed the boundary to the authoritarian type, Hungary was closest to the democratic, Czechoslovakia was situated in the middle of the range, and none were at its extreme end closest to the totalitarian ideal type.[20]

In sharp contrast to this state of affairs, the former Ottoman territories now constituting the countries of South-Eastern Europe were, for the most, situated at the end of the range closest to the totalitarian regime type or even within that type. Thus, Bulgaria fell squarely within the early post-totalitarian subtype. On the basis of current evidence, the Albanian case would appear to fall within the totalitarian type. Until the end of Enver Hoxha's rule in 1985, Albania strongly resembled the Soviet Union during the height of Stalinism. Terror was still utilized as a policy instrument, the cult of personality remained the rule, the economic system was totally centralized, and society appeared to be under the state's absolute control. Ceauşescu's Romania straddled two different regime types, totalitarian and sultanistic, reflecting its highly repressive character and extraordinarily personalized exercise of power. The only part of South-Eastern Europe that, at the moment communism collapsed in 1989, could be said to have moved closer to the mature post-totalitarian end of the range was former Yugoslavia, a country whose dramatic collapse and disintegration has enormously complicated the prospects for democracy in the successor states. Significantly, the successor state that has made the greatest progress in its democratization is Slovenia, a country with a Habsburg rather than an Ottoman pre-communist legacy.

What explains this qualitative difference between the north and south of Eastern Europe? We believe that the legacies of the pre-communist period with respect to the three areas on which we have already concentrated – that is, the configuration of the state, its relations with society, and the weakness of civil society itself – go a long way in providing a convincing explanation for the extent to which post-totalitarian regimes in South-East Europe proved unable to move significantly beyond the totalitarian end of the range defining their subtype.

These same legacies were significant in at least two additional ways. In the first place, they served as a firm and, in many ways, fertile ground upon which the communist regimes of the post-Second World War period were erected. The patrimonial and sultanistic heritage of the state as well as its domination of civil society could be, and were, taken over by the new regimes and used in ways that served their purposes. (This was particularly true in Romania under Ceauşescu.) At the same time, the weakness of civil society facilitated rather than obstructed the advent of communist regimes in the region.

Second, and most importantly, the political and organizational imperatives of the communist regimes greatly expanded and magnified the scope of these pre-communist legacies. To be sure, this was not a linear process of appropriation and adaptation. Rather, it was a complex and often contradictory process of inventive and selective borrowing. Its net result, however, was a major exacerbation of those structural problems of South-East European societies and states that were to prove most intractable and dysfunctional during democratization. The concerted drive for the penetration, conquest and domination of civil society by the state, typical of all totalitarian regimes, and the resulting levelling of that society, is the most obvious example of the manner in which the communist regimes served further to enfeeble what was already a very weak social setting. The conquest of the state by the party and its use for the benefit of a small part of the population (or, in Ceauşescu's case, for the benefit of one family and its acolytes) was rendered easier by the prior existence of a patrimonial and sultanistic legacy in the region. The pre-modern aversion to division facilitated acceptance of the communist quest for monopoly of power and the elimination of pluralism in state or society. The cumulative result of all this was the patent inability of these societies to generate the requisite social and political forces that might slowly inject their post-totalitarian regimes with an evolutionary dynamic capable of moving them towards a transition to another regime type, whether authoritarian, as was the case with Poland in the 1980s, or democratic, as appeared to be the trend in Hungary during the same period. And it was with these types of regimes, and with the political, social and cultural capital associated with the logics informing them, that South-East European societies had to confront the challenges of democratization once they commenced in late 1989.[21]

Prior democratic learning

Prior democratic learning refers to accumulated experience in a given society with democratic practices. These can range from a minimum of familiarity with elections and electoral practices to habituation with an increasingly demanding set of rules geared to ensuring the application of the rule of law, the guarantee of civil and political rights, and all the other attributes of consolidated democracies. In this sense, prior democratic learning can entail both negative and positive dimensions respectively rooted in the successes or failures of previous democratic experiments. Such learning can be thought of as contributing to the accumulation of a 'democratic capital', the presence or absence of which can significantly affect the critical period of the democratic transition and commensurately affect the chances for successful consolidation. In turn, democratic capital should be understood in two distinct senses. The first involves diffuse learning that derives from a 'negative legitimation' of democracy, seen as a regime preferable to other alternatives and allowing it to become 'the only game in town'. At a more concrete level, democratic capital refers to specific memories and learning arising from the loyal, semi-loyal or dis-loyal attitudes or behaviour of critical institutions such as the monarchy, the armed forces, or political parties in prior democratic experiments. The greater the accumulation of such capital, the better the chances for a smooth transition and for eventual consolidation.[22]

In this respect, the countries of South-Eastern Europe embarked upon their transitions with very weak prior democratic learning derived from failed democratic experiments in the inter-war period, which never met the basic requirements of a democratic regime and resembled rather what a number of recent analysts have referred to as electoral regimes. Prior democratic learning was further eroded by the longevity of the communist regimes that dominated the area for more than four decades and by their adherence until the very end to practices and norms associated with totalitarian and, in time, post-totalitarian regimes. Under the circumstances, the democratic capital available to the South-Eastern European countries at the outset of their most recent democratization experiment was very small. Thus, at the moment of the communist regimes' expiration, negative legitimation of democracy was perhaps the only capital available to the elites attempting to steer their countries through the unpredictable currents of open politics. As we shall see in the section concerning the nature of the transition, even that legitimation of democracy was partial and in many ways conditional.[23]

The mode of expiration

The mode of the predecessor non-democratic regime's expiration can strongly influence the path of democratic transitions and can have important, long-term implications, whether positive or adverse, for consolidation. The critical issue here is the circumstances under which the transfer of power from the old to the new regime is effected. Violent transfers are more likely to produce turbulent and protracted transitions and to increase uncertainties concerning the new regime's capacity to consolidate. Conversely, peaceful transfers tend to serve as facilitating factors for a successful consolidation.[24]

The character of the predecessor non-democratic regime can affect the mode of its expiration to the extent that its own internal organization renders possible or precludes the emergence, within the regime, of distinct constellations of actors that can be labelled as hardliners and moderates. Put otherwise, the presence or absence in a non-democratic regime of a sufficient amount of non-responsible political pluralism, which makes possible the coalescence of actors espousing different policy options with respect to the regime's evolution, can have a decisive impact on the latter's capacity to effect a peaceful extrication from power. The closer a regime is to the totalitarian type, the fewer the chances of a peaceful exit, given the emphasis of such regimes on monolithic control of state and society and their unrelenting opposition to any form of pluralist arrangement in society or the state. Such a situation effectively precludes a peaceful expiration and opens the way for violent regime overthrow, which as a rule tends to give the momentary advantage to more radical and better organized forces and to disadvantage the more moderate and usually less organized ones.

Romania provides a case in point. As noted earlier, the Ceauşescu regime combined elements of the totalitarian and sultanistic models. Power was essentially personal, rather than institutional. Ceauşescu consciously sought to weaken the communist party and to accumulate power in his own hands and those of a few close family members. Dissent, even within the party, was practically non-existent. Consequently, when his regime collapsed, there were no political institutions or groups that could effectively organize authority. The result was that the transition in Romania was marked by considerable violence and political chaos, which only gradually subsided after the insurgents, with the aid of the army, defeated the supporters of the Ceauşescu regime, led by the Securitate (secret police).

The weak organizational density of civil society and the frailty of political institutions severely complicated the transition process. Because of the sultanistic nature of the Ceauşescu regime, the opposition remained weak and disorganized. This allowed representatives of the *ancien régime*, led by Ion Iliescu, a reform communist and one of the original leaders of the National Salvation Front, the political formation he hastily helped assemble, to win an overwhelming victory in the May 1990 elections and to retain key positions of power in the state apparatus, especially the media. As a result, it was not until the end of 1996 that the democratic forces, reorganized and led by Emil Constantinescu, were able to gain power.

Bulgaria, by contrast, had by 1989 entered the phase of early post-totalitarianism. While power was highly centralized in the hands of the communist party, led by Todor Zhivkov, there was a higher degree of political pluralism in Bulgaria than in Romania. By 1988, a small but vocal dissident movement had begun openly to challenge party policy. Within the Bulgarian Communist Party, distinct factions advocating greater reform had emerged. This limited but greater degree of political pluralism facilitated a peaceful transition, which was initiated by Zhivkov's ouster in what amounted to a 'palace coup' in November 1989. From the outset, the transition was controlled and dominated by the communist party, which won the 1990 'founding' elections, after having renamed itself the Bulgarian Socialist Party (BSP).

At first glance, Albania would seem to call into question the idea that the closer the regime type is to the totalitarian model, the fewer the chances of a peaceful exit. Of all the regimes in South-Eastern Europe, Albania came closest to the totalitarian model, especially during the rule of Enver Hoxha, the country's first communist leader. But the Albanian system underwent some evolution after Hoxha's death in 1985. Under growing popular pressure, Hoxha's successor, Ramiz Alia, introduced a series of limited reforms, including legalization of opposition parties and the convocation of democratic elections. As in Bulgaria, the former communists were able to capitalize on the weakness of civil society and of the opposition to win the founding elections in March 1991, only to be defeated by the democratic opposition, led by Sali Berisha, in elections held a year later. Berisha became Albania's first democratically elected President. However, once in office he showed increasing contempt for the democratic rules of the game and was eventually forced to resign, once widespread financial scandals touching large segments of the population unleashed violence protests that swept the country in the spring of 1997. The elections which followed brought the Albanian Socialist Party back to power and its leader, Fatos Nano, to the premiership. The country's bitter division between a pro-

Berisha north and a pro-Nano south and the government's virtual incapacity to impose law and order throughout the state greatly complicated the democratization process. In September 1998 a series of violent incidents orchestrated by pro-Berisha forces with an eye to gaining power by force shook the country and led to Nano's resignation. He was replaced by Pandeli Majko, a 30-year-old leader of the ruling Albanian Socialist Party, who pledged to steer Albania back to some semblance of order.[25]

The violence that led to both Berisha's and Nano's resignations underscores the difficulties Albania faces in its transition to democracy. At the same time, the Albanian experience would seem to confirm the general hypothesis about the relationship between the character of the predecessor non-democratic regime and the nature of the transition. In the Albanian case, the lack of economic, political and social pluralism under communist rule increased the prospects for a non-peaceful extrication. The outbreak of violence, which came in the later phase of the transition, severely complicated the democratization process in that country.

The democratization experience of countries in East-Central and Southern Europe provides further confirmation concerning the strong link between the character of the predecessor non-democratic regime and the mode of expiration. The greater organization density of civil society in Hungary and Poland during the later phases of communist rule, and the significant degree of social, economic and political pluralism that this implied, greatly facilitated the peaceful unfolding of the transitions in these countries and commensurately increased the prospects for successful consolidation. Finally, Spain stands as the most impressive example confirming this generalization. The extensive social and economic pluralism that was a salient feature of the late Franco regime combined with a high degree of non-responsible political pluralism to create the preconditions that acted as a major factor facilitating the smoothness of the Spanish transition and decisively contributing to democratic consolidation.

Two additional features of predecessor non-democratic regimes that can directly affect the mode of expiration deserve mention: the civilianized or military character of the ruling elite(s) and the hierarchical or non-hierarchical organization of the military elite in control of the non-democratic regime. Experience has shown that the probability for less turbulent expiration and for a successful democratization is higher if the predecessor non-democratic regime is more civilianized than military. The highly protracted nature of the democratic transition in Brazil, where the military had profoundly penetrated the regime, stands out as an example to be avoided. Conversely, the highly civilianized nature of the late Franco regime in Spain undoubtedly served as a facilitating factor for both a peaceful expiration cum self-transformation and a smooth transition. Finally, as Felipe Aguero, among others, has argued with respect to Southern Europe and Latin America, the organization of the military-as-institution along lines disrupting its natural hierarchy can severely complicate the predecessor non-democratic regime's mode of expiration and, in turn, adversely affect the chances for a smooth and successful democratic transition.[26] In this respect, the firm control over the military traditionally exercised by communist regimes and the resulting absence of non-hierarchically organized military institutions effectively translated into modes of expiration that facilitated the democratic transitions in East-Central and South-Eastern Europe.

Romania stands as the main exception to this generalization. In that country, the role of the military was crucial in the transition. Initially the army supported the government but later it switched sides and joined the insurgents. Indeed, without the army's help, the insurrection would probably not have succeeded. In the transition period leading up to the June 1990 elections, the army also played a critical role in helping preserve order. In some areas, in fact, it ruled directly. The army's unique role in the Romanian transition was related, in part, to the sultanistic nature of the Ceauşescu regime and to the highly personal exercise of power that this entailed. The main pillar of Ceauşescu's rule was the security forces or Securitate, which he built up as his own personal elite paramilitary police force. The Securitate was composed of well-equipped, well-paid professionals, who were personally loyal to Ceauşescu. The army, on the other hand, was poorly equipped, poorly paid, and composed of conscripts. Moreover, it was often required to perform non-military duties such as running power plants, building bridges, and taking in the harvest. These side duties were a source of irritation within the officer corps and accentuated rivalry with the Securitate, whose privileged position was deeply resented by most top military officers.[27] Hence, when the unrest broke out in December 1989, the Securitate fought viciously to defend the *ancien régime*. The military, on the other hand, equivocated and eventually switched sides, joining the insurgents. Moreover, during the period immediately following Ceauşescu's execution, the army was the only force capable of restoring and preserving order. Without its support, the National Salvation Council – the self-appointed, interim government that held power during the transition period leading up to the May 1990 elections – might not have survived.[28]

Romania, however, was the exception not the rule. In Albania, the army remained largely neutral during the transition and did not try to rescue the communist regime. In Bulgaria, the military did not intervene directly, although General Dobri Dhzurov, Bulgarian Defense Minister for twenty-eight years, is widely thought to have played a key role behind the scenes in engineering Todor Zhivkov's resignation as party leader in November 1989.[29]

The passive role played by the military in the East-Central and South-East European transitions (Romania excepted) is, in large part, explained by the fact that under the predecessor communist regimes the military had been subordinated to strict party control, had always maintained its hierarchical structure intact, and had developed little tradition of acting independently. All this reduced its temptation to involve itself actively in the transition process and made it easier for the military-as-institution to transfer its loyalty to new civilian elites. Moreover, in contrast to Latin America, in East-Central and South-Eastern Europe the military had, for the most part, not been associated with mass repressions against the civilian populations during the time of non-democratic rule. The most egregious acts of repression were carried out not by the army but by the security organs. This was true even in Poland, where the Zomo, the special riot police, not the army, were the main instruments of repression during the imposition of martial law in 1981. Hence, one of the first acts taken by the transition governments in almost all East European countries, including those in South-Eastern Europe, was to disband or reorganize the security organs.

Because of the military's lesser degree of complicity in acts of repression, the new civilian authorities found it less necessary to punish or purge the military. This, together with the strong tradition of civilian, that is, party, control in the predecessor communist regimes, made it easier for the military to transfer their allegiance to the new forces which assumed power after the collapse of communism in the region. At the same time, it spared the new democratizing regimes in South-Eastern Europe the type of problems associated with the deep involvement of the military in many Latin American predecessor authoritarian regimes, which greatly complicated the democratic transitions in these countries.[30]

Leadership

The comparative study of democratization strongly suggests that leadership can serve as an important factor facilitating successful transitions and consolidations. To be sure, leadership does not manifest itself in the manner of a *deus ex machina*, somehow external to the socio-political context in which it operates. Rather, the leaders' importance lies in their capacity to take advantage of the opportunities provided by the structural parameters of the unfolding democratization process. 'Capacity', in this context, effectively translates into a sense of vision, judgement and tactical acumen (or what Machiavelli long ago called *virtu*), which can help determine the proper timing for action that can significantly, if not decisively, affect the course of events.

Without a doubt, Greece, Portugal and Spain benefited enormously in the 1970s and 1980s from the presence of leaders endowed with such qualities at the helm of their respective governments. Salient illustrative examples of such leadership include King Juan Carlos's choice of Adolfo Suarez as the man to whom he entrusted the responsibility for the Spanish transition and, especially, his dramatic defence of the new democratic regime against the military coup of 1981; Mario Soares's determined defence of the democratic rules of the game during the radical phase of the Portuguese Revolution; and Constantine Karamanlis's measured strategy for prosecuting and trying the protagonists of the Greek military regime – a strategy which resulted in the incarceration of the principal figures for life.[31] Strong leadership played a significant role in all the East-Central European transitions. Vaclav Havel's towering moral presence greatly benefited the Czechoslovak transition. *Mutatis mutandis*, so did Lech Walesa's and Jozsef Antall's steady leadership in Poland and Hungary respectively.

The countries of South-Eastern Europe were less fortunate in that regard. The leaders who rose to power during the transitions, that is, at the very moment, when the opportunity for crafting is greatest and the room for human agency is maximized, were for the most part the products of the predecessor totalitarian or early post-totalitarian regimes and, in many ways, the carriers of mentalities and attitudes fostered by them. As such, they proved to be ill-equipped to confront the challenges associated with the search for, and institution of, pluralist practices in the political, economic and social spheres of their new democratic regimes.

The main exception to this generalization was Bulgaria's president, Zheliu Zhelev, who had been a dissident during the Zhivkov regime. A philosopher by training, Zhelev had more in common with Czechoslovakia's Vaclav Havel than with the rest of the transitional leaders in South-Eastern Europe, most of whom were neo-communists or former communists turned nationalists like Croatia's Franjo Tudjman and Serbia's Slobodan Milošević. As President, Zhelev was a strong supporter of reform and acted as an important democratic counterweight to the neo-communist leaders, who controlled the Bulgarian government during most of the transition period.

Slovenia's President Milan Kučan can also be regarded as a partial exception. Although part of the *ancien régime* in Slovenia, Kučan was a reformer and had been in the forefront of Slovenia's fight for independence in the period preceding Yugoslavia's collapse. Thus, he enjoyed great respect and prestige among broad segments of the Slovene population. He was also seen by many Slovenes as a factor of stability during a period of rapid change and uncertainty. Both factors greatly helped him to win the founding presidential elections in 1990 and facilitated his re-election in 1997.

By contrast, Franjo Tudjman in Croatia and Slobodan Milošević in Serbia, both former communist officials, sought to exploit deeply felt nationalist sentiments to further their political ambitions and consolidate their personal power. Under Tudjman, Croatia has evolved into a strong nationalistic, semi-authoritarian state, not unlike some of the authoritarian regimes that existed in Eastern Europe during the inter-war period. While relatively free elections have been held, Tudjman has circumscribed freedom of expression, closing down several independent newspapers and radio stations, and has generally ruled in a highly autocratic manner. This has severely hindered Croatia's transition as well as its attempts to forge closer ties with Europe.

Serbia, too, has moved in an authoritarian direction since the collapse of Yugoslavia. As in Croatia, Milošević has used nationalism – in this case Serb nationalism – to enhance and consolidate his power. At the same time, and in a style strongly reminiscent of the region's sultanistic legacies, he has maintained strong control over the agents of repression, especially the police and army, as well as over the media and the economy, which is largely controlled by profiteers with close contacts to Milošević and his family.

The failure of democratic leadership in South-Eastern Europe, observable during the early transition period, has its roots in the debility of political institutions and the weak organizational density of civil society in the countries of the region. Slovenia has been the notable exception. Its better performance is largely linked to its different legacies, to experiences rooted in absolutist Habsburg rule, to cultural affinities with East-Central Europe, and to the absence of the type of patrimonial and sultanistic traditions that characterize the rest of South-Eastern Europe.

The nature of the transition

Four major clusters of distinctive characteristics distinguish the South-East European transitions from their counterparts in the post-authoritarian settings of Southern Europe, Latin America and East Asia and in the post-totalitarian situations in East-Central Europe. Two derive their specificities from the totalitarian or early post-totalitarian nature of the predecessor regimes and set them apart from their frozen (Czechoslovakia) or mature (Hungary) post-totalitarian (or even authoritarian [Poland]) East-Central European counterparts. The third springs from the region's imperial past and its belated encounter with nationalism. The last relates to the influence of international factors on regime change.

The dual nature of the transition

The first, critical implication flowing from the totalitarian or early post-totalitarian nature of the predecessor regimes was that the South-East European transitions necessarily entailed the need to negotiate a dual shift away from political and economic systems lacking even the limited degree of pluralism encountered in their East-Central European counterparts. This situation greatly complicated the course of the South-East European transitions and burdened them with major challenges from which countries in Southern Europe, Latin America and East Asia, exiting from authoritarian settings endowed with variable degrees of economic, social and non-responsible political pluralism, had been largely spared.

The simultaneity of the dual transition was a further factor burdening the democratic transitions of post-communist regimes, including those in South-Eastern Europe. Put otherwise, these regimes could hardly afford to opt for the type of policies geared to decoupling political from economic changes that their post-authoritarian relatives could and did adopt with much success and considerable benefit for their nascent democracies. The existence in these latter countries, whether in Southern Europe, Latin America or East Asia, of significant economic pluralism linked to some variant of the market mechanism made it possible for the elites in charge of the transition to postpone economic reform and restructuring until after the political requisites of democracy had been sufficiently met. The inability of post-communist regimes, as a whole, to decouple the political from the economic transition effectively meant that their transitions became burdened with significantly more complex tasks and challenges that were further complicated by the weak organizational capacity of their societies. These complications were greatly magnified and rendered all the more formidable in the case of South-East European countries, where the combination of Ottoman patrimonialism and sultanism had combined with totalitarianism or early post-totalitarianism to produce societies marked, above all, by great organizational debility and a great dearth of democratic capital.[32]

The two-step nature of the transition

The second set of distinctive characteristics distinguishing South-Eastern Europe from its northern neighbours in East-Central Europe concerns the political dimension of the transitions and stems from the totalitarian or early post-totalitarian as opposed to the mature post-totalitarian nature of its regimes. In this instance, the absence of pluralism and, hence, the pronounced organizational weakness of civil society implicit in these regime types translated into the lack of any significant opposition to the outgoing regime capable of taking the lead or, at the very least, of playing a central role in the transition to democracy. It is this very absence of credible alternative democratic actors capable of organizing power or of channeling political participation in areas conducive to a democratic outcome, which imparted in the South-East European transitions their distinctive two-step logic that profoundly influenced the course of their democratization trajectories and left its distinct imprint on them. In the initial phase, the transitions were dominated by the hurriedly reorganized forces of the outgoing regime. Taking advantage of the weak organizational capacity of the democratic opposition, the reformist elements of the predecessor regime moved swiftly to occupy, control and dominate the central institutions of the emerging regime. Effectively, this meant that the transitions in South-Eastern Europe were, in their initial phase, dominated by erstwhile adherents of the predecessor regime striving to minimize or prevent change from completely eliminating their power positions. A direct by-product of this situation was that the substantive transfer of power in the region was delayed for a considerable amount of time and was not achieved until a second wave of elections in the mid-1990s brought to power democratic opposition forces that had meanwhile managed to increase their organizational capacity and to emerge as credible alternatives.[33]

This delay in the advent of democratic forces to power, however, had a crucial implication, which constitutes a second critical by-product of this delayed pattern of transition: it facilitated the colonization of many of the new structures, both political but also economic, associated with the emerging regime by forces loyal to the old regime and resulted in their entrenchment in positions of power, which they could, henceforth, use as bastions from which to fight their rearguard battles against their democratic opponents. The net effect of all this was greatly to complicate the nature of the democratic transition in the region, to add to the uncertainties of the democratization process, and to raise further questions concerning its outcomes.

By way of contrast, it is worth pointing to the qualitative differences distinguishing the situation just described from the transition experiences of East-Central Europe. In that region, much more articulate and better organized democratic oppositions were able quickly to replace the forces of the old regime and to take charge of the democratization process. This development afforded the new democratic elites critical time in which, taking advantage of the disorganization and delegitimation of old regime forces and of their incapacity to act as an effective opposition, to introduce structural changes designed to ensure the success of the transition and to pave the wave for eventual consolidation of the new democratic regimes.[34]

The integrity of the state

The problem of stateness, as Linz and Stepan have called it, has already been alluded to in the introduction to this chapter. Shorn to its essentials, it refers to the fact that the integrity of a territorial state is, as Dahl has argued, a condition prior and external to democracy. In the case of post-imperial states, such as the ones found in former Habsburg or Ottoman territories, challenges to the territorial integrity of the successor states ultimately came from three main sources: (a) new boundaries that were artificial in the sense that they cut through long-established population settlements and, in the process, created minorities within the new states; (b) the construction of national identities along lines based on the exclusive logic of ethnicity rather than on the more secular and inclusive principle of citizenship and the elevation of the most populous ethnic and often religious group into the position of political, social, economic and cultural dominance; and (c) the inevitable emergence, within the new states, of disgruntled minorities, experiencing marginalization or exclusion, refusing, whether overtly or covertly, to accept the legitimacy of the new state, exhibiting semi-loyal or disloyal attitudes and, quite often, behaviour towards that state, and harbouring latent or open secessionist aspirations. A partial, but nevertheless important, interpretation accounting for the rise of authoritarian, quasi-fascist, or fascist regimes in the post-imperial states during the inter-war period is that they constituted, *inter alia*, a policy option taken by the dominant ethnic groups within each successor state in an attempt to stem the challenges to their rule and to the integrity of the state emanating from oppositions directly linked to, and supported by, semi-loyal or disloyal ethnic minorities.[35]

The advent of communism put a temporary lid on these pressures, which the convulsions of the Second World War and the realities of Nazi or Fascist rule had exacerbated to an explosive degree. The new communist regimes made full use of the international and, therefore, anti-national character of Marxism-Leninism and, much more importantly, of its monistic logic in effectively repressing conflict based on ethnic cleavages or, at the very least, marginalizing it politically and keeping it, for the most part, below the surface of national politics.[36]

It is tempting to argue, as many do, that the end of communism brought about the resurfacing of these cleavages and that this development has severely complicated the course of the democratic transitions in South-Eastern Europe. Such an argument, however, is too simplistic and mechanistic, because it fails to take into account the critical role of human agency and of institutional arrangements in lending renewed salience and dynamic to these cleavages and, in the process, elevating them to prominence. Put otherwise, it is political factors and not some type of primordiality that best explains the degree to which ethnic cleavages have emerged as a prominent aspect of South-East European transitions and as an important factor complicating the democratization process in the region.

In this context, former Yugoslavia provides the most poignant example. Its disintegration was not particularly the result of 'primordial ethnic hatreds' – although their exploitation clearly played a role. Rather, the country's collapse had its roots in the institutional weaknesses of the Titoist system itself and in the political choices made by leaders, elites and collective actors as the crisis unfolded. The decentralization and devolution of power that had begun before Tito's death but gathered momentum after his demise in 1980 accentuated regional and ethnic grievances that had been papered over during his lifetime. As long as he was alive, the potential problems linked to regional and ethnic cleavages were held in check. But once the strong force of his leadership and authority was removed, his successors, seeking to establish their ascendancy over their competitors and to ensure their own future, chose to exploit these cleavages. Within a short period of time, economic, political and ethnic tensions that had long been held in check beneath the surface acquired a pernicious momentum and erupted with full force. The Serbs, who felt that Tito's reforms had come at their expense, favoured a re-establishment of stronger central control in order to ensure their own dominance over the other republics. The Croats and the Slovenes, ever fearful of Serb hegemony, saw the weakening of the federation as an opportunity to expand their autonomy and to realize long-standing national agendas. At the same time, a number of leaders in the member republics, especially Milošević and Tudjman, sought to use nationalism as a means to enhance their own political power. The result was a general conflagration and a proliferation of atrocities that gave renewed rise to culturally determinist arguments concerning the region's tradition of hatreds and failed to accord due attention to political choices made at the local, regional, national and international levels which contributed to the crisis and Yugoslavia's eventual collapse.[37]

An instructive illustrative example, which confirms this point *a contrario*, is the manner in which Romania handled the long-festering problem of its relations with the large Hungarian minority that became part of the Romanian state following the demise of the Habsburg empire in 1918. The overwhelming desire of the Romanian leadership to increase the country's prospects for membership in the North Atlantic Treaty Organization (NATO) and the European Union (EU) led it to resolve its differences with Hungary (September 1996) and Ukraine (June 1997). In the Romanian case, in other words, the alleged and much abused salience of primordial sentiments was successfully attenuated by the desire to attain broader political goals. Bulgaria provides another positive example. Under the communist regime, the Turkish minority in that country faced severe restrictions on its political rights and freedom of expression – a fact that led to the forced emigration of nearly 300,000 ethnic Turks in 1989. However, the new democratic elite in Bulgaria restored the rights and property of many of these emigrants. As a result, nearly half of the 300,000 Bulgarian Turks have returned and the Turkish minority issue has significantly receded as a domestic political problem and as a disruptive factor in Bulgaria's democratization and its relations with Turkey.

At the other end of this spectrum is the blatant manipulation of ethnic cleavages for shameless political gain by Slobodan Milošević and the Serbian leadership in former Yugoslavia. To be sure, this case constitutes the extreme example illustrating the extent to which the legitimacy of the territorial state is a prior condition for the viability of democratic regimes. Still, the fact remains that, albeit at lower levels of intensity, conflicts based on the political manipulation of ethnic cleavages continue to plague transition politics in South-Eastern Europe and to complicate severely the prospects for democratic consolidation in the region.

To conclude, most of the states in South-Eastern Europe are the products of the disintegration of former empires. Almost all had large minorities on their territories. What has determined whether these minorities became threats to the integrity of the state, however, has been the policies pursued by the new leaderships in the various successor states undergoing democratic transitions. Those governments, such as Serbia and Croatia, that have chosen to pursue 'exclusionary' policies based on zero-sum conceptualizations of politics have faced significant unrest among their minorities. Those, like Bulgaria, that have opted for more inclusionary policies subscribing to positive-sum logics have faced fewer expressions of discontent. In short, the threats to the integrity of the state have come primarily from failures in leadership and political choices rather than from unchanging primordial sentiments lying beyond the capacity of human agency to contain or neutralize.

The international factor

The decisive role which international factors played in the East-Central and South-East European transitions to democracy constitutes the fourth area where the region's experience departed from the transition patterns observed in other parts of the world. In Latin America, Southern Europe and South-East Asia, direct international involvement in the transitions played a marginal to negligible role in the unfolding of the democratization dynamic, which tended to follow the logic of domestic developments. Portugal is the lone exception to that generalization. Even in this case, however, the influence of the international actors was felt after the onset of the transition and once the radicalization dynamic that set in in the course of late 1974 had mobilized international actors in support of more moderate, democratic forces in the Portuguese political scene.[38]

In East-Central as well as South-Eastern Europe, by contrast, the international factor – specifically the policies of the Soviet hegemon – played a critical role in triggering the transition process. Three specific developments served as milestones in this context. First, there were attempts by the Soviet leader, Mikhail Gorbachev, who, beginning in the late 1980s, deliberately sought to promote a liberalization of the East-Central and South-East European regimes in line with the unfolding of *perestroika* in the Soviet Union. The goal of such a strategy was to foster the emergence of more durable and viable regimes in these countries. Gorbachev's many public statements stressing that members of the Soviet bloc were free to pursue their own road to the fuller development of socialism had a profound effect on the political evolution of Eastern Europe and directly contributed to the collapse of the communist regimes in the states of the region. Second, the open abandonment of the Brezhnev doctrine of limited sovereignty came in early October 1989, when the Soviet Union refused to intervene militarily to support the collapsing Honecker regime in the German Democratic Republic. More than any other event, this development effectively signalled the death of the old regimes and triggered the transition dynamic in Eastern Europe. Finally, the failure of the Soviet hardliners' *putsch* on 19 August 1991 eliminated the last possibility of a Soviet policy reversal that could play into the hands of the hardliners in the countries of the former Soviet bloc and could enhance their capacity adversely to affect democratization in the region. Freed from that danger, the transition processes in East-Central and South-Eastern Europe accelerated and gained new momentum.

The international factor played a greater role in both the East-Central and the South-East European transitions in yet another important way. Following the collapse of the Soviet bloc and the end of the Cold War, the EU and NATO emerged as international actors, membership in which would bestow not only respectability but also legitimacy and security to the two regions' fledgling democratic regimes. To be sure, the new democratic regimes in Southern Europe had also sought to reap similar benefits, when they applied for membership in the European Community and, in the case of Spain, eventually NATO. What distinguishes the two cases, however, is that in the case of East-Central and South-Eastern Europe the terms for entry were much more concretely spelled out than they had been in the case of the Southern European countries. The European Council meetings in Copenhagen (June 1993) and Essen (December 1994) as well as the Treaty of Amsterdam (June 1997) itself specifically stated the rules governing the pre-accession process for candidate countries. The net outcome of this has been that international factors have, to date, played a particularly prominent role in promoting the democratic transition process in East-Central and South-Eastern Europe.

Evolving trends, uncertain prospects

The cumulative impact of the background factors so far examined and of the two-step nature of the South-East European transitions has resulted in a delayed pattern of democratization, whose salient feature is uncertainty with respect to evolutionary trends and, especially, the prospects for con-solidation. Succinctly put, the cumulative impact of patrimonialism, sultanism, totalitarianism and post-totalitarianism has been a cultural, social, economic and political environment that has considerably slowed down the democratization process and complicated the prospects for consolidation.

To be sure, the region's democratic experiments are still young. The delayed pattern of their unfolding effectively means that, in substantive terms, open democratic politics has existed for considerably less than a decade. Within that short span of time, notable change has occurred and progress has been achieved in a number of areas. Elections have been held, rules of the democratic game have been and are being crafted, violence has largely been contained and is declining, alternation in office has taken place, overt challenges to democratically elected governments have, again with the exception of Albania, been rare. At a deeper level, however, the structure of democratic politics in the region remains riddled with severe problems that are likely to plague South-East European democracies for a long time and effectively to serve as confining conditions for successful consolidation. Put otherwise, it is these structural characteristics of the South-East European democratic systems which pose the greatest challenges to human agency and to its capacity to use politics to 'craft' solutions to these problems. We shall conclude our analysis with a few remarks concerning these issues.

The evolution of South-East European democracies, to date, suggests a fairly clear conceptual range defined by Slovenia at one end and Albania at the other. The former has made the greatest progress in its democratization and stands the best chance of consolidating its democracy in the foreseeable future. Socio-economically, Slovenia is the most developed country in South-Eastern Europe, with good prospects to join both the EU and NATO in the medium term. The construction of a moderate party system, based on consensus politics, has also helped it avoid the sharp polarizations characteristic of transitions elsewhere in the region.

Albania's transition has been most problematic. Corruption and violence have been widespread, hindering the emergence of a stable democratic order. Strong regional and ethnic cleavages involving the northern-based, mostly Muslim Ghegs and the southern-based, mostly Christian Tosks have contributed to political polarization. In addition, decades of isolation under the communist regime have bred a strong sense of nationalism and xenophobia that provides fertile soil for political manipulation and extremism. As a result, further disruptions and breakdowns of democracy cannot be excluded.

Closest to Albania stand a number of states issuing from the break-up of Yugoslavia. As noted earlier, Croatia and Serbia share many similarities with authoritarian regimes in inter-war Eastern Europe. In both cases, the media, the army, the police, and much of the economy are tightly controlled and their leaders show scant regard for the rules of the democratic game. Both rely heavily on a form of exclusionary nationalism as a mobilizing and unifying force. The Former Yugoslav Republic of Macedonia has made considerable progress toward democratization since 1991. But its transition has been hindered by serious conflicts between the Slav majority and the Albanian minority as well as by the new state's weak sense of national identity. President Kiro Gligorov, a reform communist who served in the top echelons of power in former Yugoslavia, has provided an important element of continuity and stability during the transition period. Montenegro has until recently been little more than a Serb client. However, the victory of Milo Djukanović, a reformer and opponent of Yugoslav President Slobodan Milošević, in the October 1997 presidential elections, coupled with the success of forces loyal to him in the legislative elections of May 1998, suggests that Montenegro may slowly begin to emancipate itself from Serbia's grip and make progress in its attempts to democratize. Bosnia is a special case, since it is not really an integral state. Despite the Dayton Accord, there is little contact between the three ethnic communities (Bosnians, Serbs and Croats) and the Muslim-Croat federation has ceased to function. It is, thus, difficult to speak of a democratization process as such in this case.[39]

Bulgaria and Romania are situated near the centre of the range. Bulgaria seemed off to a good start with the victory of the democratic opposition (United Democratic Forces – UDF) in the October 1991 elections. Severe problems in both its economy and politics which became especially acute in the mid-1990s have significantly hindered the unfolding of its democratic transition. However, since the return to power of the democratic opposition forces in 1997, Bulgaria has made considerable progress in carrying out its democratic transition. Reflecting the pathologies of its hybrid nature as a post-totalitarian and sultanistic regime, Romania made a highly problematic start. However, since late 1996, when elections brought the democratic opposition to power, it has exhibited a renewed commitment to economic and political reform, allowing for a less pessimistic assessment concerning future prospects.

Five salient features seem to characterize the democratic regimes that South-East European societies have, with varying degrees of success, been constructing over the past decade. Their common underlying characteristic is twofold. In the first place, they all, in many ways, represent attempts to reconstruct state–society relations through a reconciliation and adaptation of the imperatives and logic of the new democratic game with the multiple and contradictory legacies of patrimonialism, sultanism, totalitarianism and post-totalitarianism. At a higher level of abstraction, they graphically express an agonizing ambivalence arising from these societies' latest encounter with modernity and from the inexorable pressure for multiple breaks with the past that this implies. In actual practice, this ambivalence is reflected in the emergence of two competing and, to a certain extent, mutually exclusive cultures within the new democracies. The social strata adhering to the first of these cultures consist of potential winners in the emerging democratic political system and market economy and, with varying degrees of commitment, strongly identify with the cause of reform and structural change. The second culture rallies together social forces directly threatened by the prospects of a more pluralist economic and political landscape and seeking, as a result, to contain change within areas that do not completely undermine their sources of power. Taken together, these constitutive features, which while by no means unique to South-Eastern Europe are nevertheless particularly salient there, directly affect both the nature of the transition unfolding in each of the countries in the region and lend an added degree of indeterminacy to the overall democratization process.

The first of these features stems from the pronounced ambivalence which the region's societies feel towards the abandonment of a legacy of collectivist solidarities rooted in the distant past but greatly strengthened by the more recent encounter with communism. This ambivalence takes the form of a widespread rejection of communism as an organizing principle for state–society relations coupled with a pronounced diffidence towards the market mechanism and a strong preference for socio-economic and political arrangements according the state a major social role in the area of job security, full employment, and protection from the perils of competition implicit in open political or economic systems. Such 'statist' attitudes are in accord with the traditional perception of the state as the senior and guiding partner in its relationship with society and reflect the latter's weak organizational capacity and late development features.

The second constitutive feature issues directly from the first. The tenacity of the statist tradition, strongly reinforced by the success of forces linked to the old regime in colonizing the new regime's institutions during the initial phase of the two-step transition, has spawned, in reaction, a dogmatic pro-market, neo-liberal temper prone to ahistorical conceptualizations of the market mechanism according the state a minimal role, if any. The result has been the construction of political and economic systems exhibiting a high propensity for polarization, in which the dogmatic opposition to the statist tradition fosters the emergence of and, ultimately, dependence on illicit and outright illegal practices, sharp social dislocations, and enormous and new-found inequalities that are deeply offensive to the collectivist and egalitarian ethos still widespread in these societies. Again, these phenomena can be encountered in East-Central Europe as well. But they have been accentuated in South-Eastern Europe by the war in Yugoslavia, which has put a premium on and rewarded profiteering and illegal activity. The net effect has been to place additional burdens on the democratization process and to render more difficult the tasks associated with the negotiation of the dual transition in the region.

The third constitutive feature of the new democratic regimes in South-Eastern Europe springs from the widespread inclination of elite and collective actors alike to conceptualize democracy in ways that decisively privilege its egalitarian as opposed to its liberal principles. To be sure, this is not a characteristic peculiar to this region. Rather, it constitutes a property common to democracies in late developing societies and has recently begun to receive scholarly attention. In the case of South-Eastern Europe, this conceptualization of democracy is rooted, among others, in the levelling egalitarianism that was such a salient characteristic of Ottoman patrimonialism and especially sultanism, and was subsequently reproduced and greatly amplified by the region's totalitarian and post-totalitarian regimes.

Implicit in such a conceptualization of democracy is an overemphasis on the principle of majority rule as the single most important feature of the new regimes. The monistic logic underpinning such an approach to democracy, however, inevitably tends to discount and to underprivilege the significance of the liberal component of democracy and of the pluralist associations implicit in it. A reflection of the traditional weakness of civil society in the region, such a conceptualization of democracy has translated into lopsided political systems showing low tolerance for institutionalizing oppositions, for respecting and enforcing the rights of political, ethnic or religious minorities, and, more generally, scant willingness to comply with the imperatives of the rule of law. A further negative by-product of this structural imbalance between the egalitarian-democratic and the liberal-pluralist logics of democracy is the South-East European regimes' reduced capacity to provide for effective mechanisms of checks and balances and, more generally, of accountability capable of reining in powerful actors, whose illicit or illegal activities in both the private and public sectors adversely affect the democratization process and undermine these regimes' legitimacy.

The fourth constitutive feature of South-East European regimes stems from a combination of the problems relating to the integrity of the territorial state discussed earlier and the low salience accorded the liberal-pluralist dimension of democracy in the countries of the region. The specific form that it takes is the use of ethnicity as the foundation upon which to build the dominant conceptualization of the nation – and hence the nation-state – in the region. Given the presence of significant minorities in these countries, such a conceptualization, which inevitably accords lower status to minority populations, seriously undermines the egalitarian dimension of democracy and poses direct challenges to the enforcement of the rule of law.

To date, the alternative policy option which bases the conceptualization of the nation on citizenship rather than ethnicity has failed to gain favour in the region. Yet this option has been utilized by countries such as Spain, which used it successfully in order to cope with the severe problems facing that multi-ethnic society's transition to democracy, and, earlier on, by France. There can be little doubt that the prospects for successful democratization are significantly enhanced by the degree to which multi-ethnic societies manage to eschew the dangers of polarization inherent in adopting the exclusivist logic of ethnicity as the organizing principle of their politics, and resort instead to the alternative of conceptualizing the nation in terms of multiple, overlapping, and not mutually exclusive identities. The destructive nature of the wars that accompanied the emergence of new states built upon an ethnic definition of the nation in the northern and central parts of former Yugoslavia and the lingering concerns that similar developments may yet occur in the southern parts of that former country are ample reminders of the dangers to democratization inherent in the conceptualizations of the nation that prevail in the region so far.

Finally, the fifth constitutive feature of South-East European regimes is the tendency to reproduce in new settings the traditional patrimonial and, especially, sultanistic heritage of appropriation and use of public office for private gain. Once again, this is not a characteristic unique to the regimes in this region. Many of the late developing societies in which the distinction between the private and the public spheres is not clearly drawn exhibit similar traits. The intensity of the phenomenon, however, seems to constitute a feature peculiar to the South-East European democracies and to be linked to the lingering legacies of sultanism, totalitarianism and post-totalitarianism as well as to the two-step nature of their democratic transitions. More specifically, the capacity of significant elements of the old regimes to take charge of the initial phase of the transitions in their countries and pre-emptively to colonize the state has greatly amplified this practice and has helped adapt it to the requisites of a more pluralist democratic environment. The result has been the emergence of a nexus of interests linking together private and public sectors in extensive activities of an often illicit and illegal nature that are ultimately detrimental to the legitimation of the new regimes. The war in former Yugoslavia has reinforced this trend by creating and rewarding a stratum of profiteers and entrepreneurs, who have become wealthy by exploiting their connections to the old elites for their own personal profit.

It is against these structural constraints or confining conditions that social and political actors committed to democratization have to struggle in their attempts to secure the viability and institutionalization of democracy in South-Eastern Europe. Benefiting from its Habsburg and attendant absolutist heritage, Slovenia is certainly ahead of the pack and is well on its way to achieving consolidation. Bulgaria and Romania come next and are striving to establish the rule of law, secure the success of their transitions, and pave the wave for eventual consolidation. Albania and most of the states issuing from former Yugoslavia fall short of the minimum criteria for democratic regimes and would appear more logically to fit into the category of electoral regimes conceptualized by Terry Karl, in order to refer to political systems providing for electoral competitions but unable to ensure the conditions of their fairness and of the rule of law.

The future of democracy in the South-Eastern Europe, then, ultimately depends on the capacity of the elite and collective actors in the region to achieve two sets of distinct goals. In the case of Albania and the successor states of former Yugoslavia, the challenge lies in their capacity to eliminate the conditions preventing them from moving beyond the category of electoral regimes to that of democracies. In the case of Bulgaria and Romania, on the other hand, the goal remains how to secure the crystallization of democratic practices and to bring about the conditions for their institutionalization that can substantively enhance the chances for consolidation. Success in this direction will help move forward the third wave of democratization that in the course of the 1990s appears to have been stalled and will demonstrate the capacity of the leaders, political elites and domestic and international actors through which human agency manifests itself to craft solutions imaginatively recombining past legacies and present options and successfully to overcome confining conditions. As such it will constitute a victory for politics and culture and a successful negotiation of these countries' latest encounter with modernity. Failure, on the other hand, will confront these countries with the unenviable prospect of remaining confined to the large universe of non-consolidated democracies or electoral regimes, with all the dangers for potential deconsolidation and breakdown that this entails. It will symbolize a defeat for politics and will bring to mind Winston Churchill's pejorative aphorism about the 'Balkans [being] a region that produces more history than it can consume'. At the moment, however, the jury on this matter is still out.

Notes

1 The search for a better understanding of the origins and nature of non-democratic regimes remained from the early 1940s to the mid-1960s fixated on totalitarian political systems, whether communist or fascist. Classic examples of this preoccupation are Carl J. Friedrich and Zbigniew K. Brzezinski, *Totalitarian Dictatorship and Autocracy*, New York: Praeger, 1962, and Franz Neumann, *Behemoth: The Structure and Practice of National Socialism, 1933–1944*, Oxford: Oxford University Press, 1942. The 1960s witnessed a move away from this preoccupation which, *grosso modo*, took two distinct forms: the renewal of interest in the comparative study of democracy and the attempt to move beyond the dichotomous conceptualization of political systems implicit in the distinction between democratic and totalitarian. Typical early examples from the first category are Sigmund Neumann, *The Democratic and the Authoritarian State*, Glencoe IL: Free Press, 1957, and Barrington Moore, Jr, *The Social Origins of Dictatorship and Democracy: Lord and Peasant in the Making of the Modern World*, Boston: Beacon Press, 1966. The move beyond totalitarianism in the study of non-democratic regimes is best exemplified by Juan J. Linz, 'An authoritarian regime: Spain', in Erik Allardt and Yrjo Littunen, eds, *Cleavages, Ideologies and Party Systems*, Helsinki: Transactions of the Westermarck Society, 1964, pp. 291–341, and his subsequent, more expanded 'Totalitarian and authoritarian regimes', in Fred I. Greenstein and Nelson W. Polsby, eds, *The Handbook of Political Science*, Reading MA: Addison-Wesley, 1975, vol. 3, pp. 175–411.

2 On the 'third wave' of democratization, see Samuel P. Huntington, *The Third Wave: Democratization in the Late Twentieth Century*, Norman: University of Oklahoma Press, 1991. For studies concerning the transition to democracy, see Guillermo O'Donnell, Philippe C. Schmitter and Laurence Whitehead, eds, *Transitions from Authoritarian Rule: Prospects for Democracy*, Baltimore MD: Johns Hopkins University Press, 1986, as well as the more recent work by Stephen Haggard and Robert R. Kaufman, *The Political Economy of Democratic Transitions*, Princeton: Princeton University Press, 1995. The literature on democratic consolidation is by now huge. For a general comparative statement, see Juan J. Linz and Alfred Stepan, *Problems of Democratic Transition and Consolidation: Southern Europe, South America, and Post-Communist Europe*, Baltimore MD: Johns Hopkins University Press, 1996. For studies with a more regional focus, see, among others, Richard Gunther, P. Nikiforos Diamandouros and Hans-Jurgen Puhle, eds, *The Politics of Democratic Consolidation: Southern Europe in Comparative Perspective*, Baltimore MD: Johns Hopkins University Press, 1995; Scott Mainwaring, Guillermo O'Donnell and J. Samuel Valenzuela, eds, *Issues in Democratic Consolidation: The New South American Democracies in Comparative Perspective*, Notre Dame IN: University of Notre Dame Press, 1992, John Higley and Richard Gunther, eds, *Elites and Democratic*

Consolidation in Latin America and Southern Europe, Cambridge: Cambridge University Press, 1992; and Larry Diamond, Marc F. Plattner, Yun-han Chu and Hung-mao Tien, eds, *Consolidating the Third Wave Democracies*, Baltimore MD: Johns Hopkins University Press, 1997.

3 For the quotation, see Robert A. Dahl, *Democracy and its Critics*, New Haven: Yale University Press, 1989, p. 207. On the challenges of democratization in Eastern Europe, see, among others, Geoffrey Pridham and Paul G. Lewis, eds, *Stabilising Fragile Democracies: Comparing New Party Systems in Southern and Eastern Europe*, London: Routledge, 1996; Adam Przeworski, *Democracy and the Market: Political and Economic Reforms in Eastern Europe and Latin America*, Cambridge: Cambridge University Press, 1991; Vladimir Tismaneanu, *Reinventing Politics: Eastern Europe from Stalin to Havel*, New York: Free Press, 1992; and Attila Agh, *The Politics of Central Europe*, London: Sage, 1998, which also deals with South-Eastern Europe.

4 This is not the place to examine the complex reasons underlying this development. Suffice it to say that they reflect the coincidence of, *inter alia*, (a) real international and regional concerns and political priorities in the United States, the European Union, and Germany, (b) the troubled, protracted, and uncertain democratization experiences in the region, but also (c) the persistence of powerful stereotypes concerning the cultures and societies of South-Eastern Europe, very often pejoratively referred to as the Balkans, and their perceived incapacity to free themselves from their ostensible 'ancient' enmities, hatreds and conflicts. Important exceptions to this generalization notwithstanding, the combined result of this trend has been the relegation of the study of South-Eastern Europe to a sphere of relative oblivion, which effectively undermines the generation of fresh knowledge concerning the region and dampens intellectual curiosity regarding the prospects for democracy in the region.
   Two studies which look at the international and security dimensions of the problem are F. Stephen Larrabee, ed., *The Volatile Powder Keg: Balkan Security After the Cold War*, Washington DC: American University Press, 1994, and Susan L. Woodward, *Balkan Tragedy: Chaos and Dissolution After the Cold War*, Washington DC: Brookings Institution, 1995. A recent noteworthy study focusing on the region is Karen Dawisha and Bruce Parrott, eds, *Politics, Power, and the Struggle for Democracy in South-East Europe*, Cambridge: Cambridge University Press, 1997. See also P. Nikiforos Diamandouros, 'Prospects for democracy in the Balkans: comparative and theoretical perspectives', in Larrabee, ed., *The Volatile Powder Keg*, pp. 3–26.

5 A forceful analysis of the importance of politics in the crafting of new democratic regimes is Giuseppe Di Palma, *To Craft Democracies: An Essay on Democratic Transitions*, Berkeley: University of California Press, 1990.

6 For the concept of confining conditions, see Otto Kirchheimer, 'Confining conditions and revolutionary breakthroughs', *American Political Science Review*, 59, December 1965, pp. 964–74.

7 We consider a democratic regime to be consolidated when all politically significant groups regard its key political institutions as the only legitimate framework for political contestation and adhere to democratic rules of the game. For a fuller discussion of this issue, see Gunther, Diamandouros and Puhle, eds, *The Politics of Democratic Consolidation*, pp. 5–9. For the definition of a democratic regime, see, among others, Juan J. Linz, 'Totalitarian and authoritarian regimes', pp. 182–3.

8 For a general discussion of the democratization cycle, see, among others, Linz and Stepan, *Problems of Democratic Transition and Consolidation*, pp. 3–15 and Richard Gunther, Hans-Jurgen Puhle and P. Nikiforos Diamandouros, 'Introduction', in Gunther, Diamandouros and Puhle, eds, *The Politics of Democratic Consolidation*, pp. 1–32. On the breakdown of democracies, see Juan J. Linz, *Crisis, Breakdown, & Reequilibration*, Baltimore, MD: Johns Hopkins University Press, 1978.

9 On Montesquieu's discussion concerning the significance of *corps intermediaires*, see

Baron de Montesquieu, *The Spirit of the Laws*, New York: Hafner, 1962, pp. 66–70 and 120–5. On absolutism, see Perry Anderson, *Lineages of the Absolutist State*, London: New Left Books, 1974, as well as the pertinent sections in Immanuel Wallerstein, *The Modern World-System II. Mercantilism and the Consolidation of the European World-Economy, 1600–1750*, New York: Academic Press, 1980, and in Michael Mann, *The Sources of Social Power, Vol. 1*, Cambridge: Cambridge University Press, 1986.

10 On the significance of a legal rational tradition for democratic regimes, see Yossi Shain and Juan J. Linz, *Between States: Interim Governments and Democratic Transitions*, Cambridge: Cambridge University Press, 1995, pp. 10–14.

11 For Weber's discussion of patrimonialism, see Max Weber, *Economy and Society*, ed. Guenther Roth and Claus Wittich, Berkeley: University of California Press, 1978, pp. 227–41 and 1006–70. For the reference to sultanism as a subtype of patrimonialism, see ibid., pp. 231–2. Finally, for a recent, theoretical work on sultanism, see H. E. Chehabi and Juan J. Linz, *Sultanistic Regimes*, Baltimore MD: Johns Hopkins University Press, 1998, and esp. pp. 3–48.

12 On the Ottoman empire, see, among others, Halil Inalcik, *The Ottoman Empire: The Classical Age, 1300–1600*, New York: Praeger, 1973; Halil Inalcik and Donald Quataert, eds, *An Economic and Social History of the Ottoman Empire, 1300–1914*, Cambridge: Cambridge University Press, 1994; Huri Islamoglu-Inan, ed., *The Ottoman Empire and the World Economy*, Cambridge: Cambridge University Press, 1987; and the old but still useful works by H. A. R. Gibb and Harold Bowen, *Islamic Society and the West*, London: Oxford University Press, 1950, and Leften Stavrianos, *The Balkans Since 1453*, New York: Holt, Rinehart, Wilson, 1958.

13 See James C. Scott, *Weapons of the Weak: Everyday Forms of Peasant Resistance*, New Haven: Yale University Press, 1985; *Domination and the Arts of Resistance: Hidden Transcripts*, New Haven: Yale University Press, 1990; and *The Moral Economy of the Peasant. Rebellion and Subsistence in South-East Asia*, New Haven: Yale University Press, 1976.

14 For a discussion of levelling egalitarianism as it pertains to the case of Greece, see P. Nikiforos Diamandouros, *Cultural Dualism and Political Change in Postauthoritarian Greece*, Madrid: Instituto Juan March, 1994, Working Paper 50, pp. 13–15.

15 On the nation of the Orthodox Commonwealth, see Paschalis M. Kitromilides, '"Imagined communities" and the origins of the national question in the Balkans', in Martin Blinkhorn and Thanos Veremis, eds, *Modern Greece: Nationalism and Nationality*, Athens: Sage-ELIAMEP, 1990, pp. 23–66.

16 The belated emergence of nationalism in South-Eastern Europe and the problems associated with its grounding on ethnicity rather than citizenship has increasingly attracted scholarly attention. For relevant studies, see, among others, Rogers Brubaker, *Nationalism Reframed: Nationhood and the National Question in the New Europe*, Cambridge: Cambridge University Press, 1996; Liah Greenfeld, *Nationalism: Five Roads to Modernity*, Cambridge MA: Harvard University Press, 1992; John Breuilly, *Nationalism and the State*, 2nd edn, Chicago: University of Chicago Press, 1993; and Ernest Gellner, *Nations and Nationalism*, Ithaca NY: Cornell University Press, 1983. For an earlier but still valuable study, see Peter F. Sugar and Ivo J. Lederer, eds, *Nationalism in Eastern Europe*, Seattle: University of Washington Press, 1969, and, for the historical dimension of the issue, Eric Hobsbawm, *Nations and Nationalism Since 1780*, Cambridge: Cambridge University Press, 1990.

The inclination to think of South-Eastern Europe as a region where primordiality prevails and where 'ancient hatreds' persist unaffected by the passage of time is graphically reflected in the decision of the Carnegie Endowment for International Peace to reissue in 1993, at the time of the conflagration in the former Yugoslavia, its report on the Balkan Wars of 1912–13 with the telling title *The Other Balkan Wars: A 1913 Carnegie Endowment Inquiry in Retrospect with a New Introduction and Reflections on the Present Conflict by George F. Kennan*, Washington DC: Carnegie Endowment for

International Peace, 1993. This stereotypical view of the region is cogently criticized by Maria Todorova in *Imagining the Balkans*, Oxford: Oxford University Press, 1997. See also her 'The Ottoman legacy in the Balkans', in L. Carl Brown, ed., *Imperial Legacy: The Ottoman Imprint in the Balkans and the Middle East*, New York: Columbia University Press, 1995, pp. 45–77, and Elizabeth Prodromou, 'Paradigms, power and identity: rediscovering Orthodoxy and regionalizing Europe', *European Journal of Political Research*, 30, Sept. 1996, pp. 125–54.

17 The aversion to division and to factionalism typical of pre-modern settings was also a salient feature informing the debates of the American Constitutional Convention in 1787 and some of the more seminal of the Federalist papers. On this point, see Robert A. Dahl, ed., *Political Oppositions in Western Democracies*, New Haven: Yale University Press, 1966, p. xvii.

18 On the link between socio-economic development and democracy, see Seymour Martin Lipset, 'Some social requisites of democracy', *American Political Science Review*, March, 1959, pp. 69–105, and 'The social requisites of democracy revisited', *American Sociological Review*, February, 1994, pp. 1–22; and Dietrich Rueschemeyer, Evelyn Huber Stephens and John D. Stephens, *Capitalist Development and Democracy*, Oxford: Polity Press, 1992. For Terry Karl's views, see Terry Lynn Karl, 'Dilemmas of democratization in Latin America', *Comparative Politics*, 23, 1, 1990, pp. 1–21.

19 For Gerschenkron's concept of 'late' and 'late late developers', see Alexander Gerschenkron, *Economic Backwardness in Historical Perspective*, Cambridge: Harvard University Press, 1962. See also Ivan Berend and Gyorgy Ranki, *The European Periphery and Industrialization 1780–1914*, Cambridge: Cambridge University Press, 1982; Daniel Chirot, ed., *The Origins of Backwardness in Eastern Europe*, Berkeley: University of California Press, 1989; and John R. Lampe and Marvin R. Jackson, *Balkan Economic History, 1555–1950: From Imperial Borderlands to Developing Nations*, Bloomington IN: Indiana University Press, 1982.

20 For the discussion concerning the significance of predecessor regimes for democratic transitions and consolidation as well as for the typology of political regimes, see Linz and Stepan, *Problems of Democratic Transition and Consolidation*, pp. 55–66.

21 For background on developments in South-Eastern Europe during the communist period, see in particular: James F. Brown, *Nationalism, Democracy and Security in the Balkans*, Aldershot: Dartmouth, 1992; Jonathan Eyel, ed., *The Warsaw Pact and the Balkans*, New York: St. Martin's Press, 1989; Larrabee, ed., *The Volatile Powder Keg*; Paul Lendvai, *Eagles in the Cobwebs: Nationalism and Communism in the Balkans*, New York: Doubleday, 1969; Daniel Nelson, *Balkan Embroglio: Politics and Security in Southeastern Europe*, Boulder CO: Westview Press, 1991; and Paul S. Shoup and George W. Hoffman, eds, *Problems of Balkan Security*, Washington DC: Wilson Center Press, 1990.

22 For a discussion of 'negative legitimation' as it pertains to democratization in Southern Europe, see Leonardo Morlino and Jose Ramon Montero, 'Legitimacy and democracy in Southern Europe', in Gunther, Diamandouros and Puhle, eds, *The Politics of Democratic Consolidation*, pp. 234–5.

23 For a discussion of electoral regimes, see Terry Lynn Karl, 'Imposing consent? Electoralism vs. democratization in El Salvador', in Paul Drake and Eduardo Silva, eds, *Elections and Democratization in Latin America, 1980–85*, San Diego: Center for Iberian and Latin American Studies, 1986, pp. 9–36. See also Guillermo O'Donnell, 'Horizontal accountability and new polyarchies', unpublished paper, September 1997; and L. Diamond 'Is the third wave over?', *Journal of Democracy*, July 1996, pp. 21–2.

24 For useful analyses of the mode of expiration, see Robert Fishman, 'Rethinking state and regime: Southern Europe's transition to democracy', *Comparative Politics*, 42, April 1990, pp. 422–40, and Linz and Stepan, *Problems of Democratic Transition and Consolidation*, pp. 55–65. For a useful discussion of conditions facilitating democratization and, especially, consolidation, see J. Samuel Valenzuela, 'Democratic consolidation

in post-transitional settings: notion, process, and facilitating conditions', in Mainwaring, O'Donnell and Valenzuela, eds, *Issues in Democratic Consolidation*, pp. 57–104.

25 For a detailed discussion, see Elez Biberaj, *Albania in Transition*, Boulder CO: Westview Press, 1998, pp. 81–114. Also Nicholas Pano, 'The process of democratization in Albania', in Dawisha and Parrot, eds, *Politics, Power and the Struggle for Democracy in South-East Europe*, pp. 298–314.

26 Felipe Aguero, 'Democratic consolidation and the military in Southern Europe and South America', in Gunther, Diamandouros and Puhle, eds, *The Politics of Democratic Consolidation*, pp. 124–65.

27 The military appears to have been plotting for some time to remove Ceauşescu. A *putsch* was apparently planned for the summer of 1984, when Ceauşescu was due to make an official visit to the Federal Republic of Germany. However, it never materialized, because key units of the army, meant to be used in the *putsch*, were sent to do agricultural work. The plot that removed Ceauşescu in December 1989 appears, at least in part, to have been based on the plans drawn up in 1984. Both Ion Iliescu, who subsequently became head of the National Salvation Front, and General Nicolae Militaru, who became Minister of National Defense after Ceauşescu's ouster, were involved in that initial plot. For information on this point, see Michael Shafir, 'New revelations of the military's role in Ceauşescu's ouster', *Report on Eastern Europe*, 11 May 1990, pp. 24–27.

28 During this transition period, there was a close symbiosis between the military and the ruling National Salvation Council. Two military officers were members of the Council. Military officers also occupied important positions in the National Salvation Front (NSF) government after the founding elections of May 1990.

29 On the role of the army in the Albanian transition, see Adem Copani and Constantine P. Danopoulos, 'The role of the military in the democratization of Marxist-Leninist regimes: Albania as a case study', *Mediterranean Quarterly*, 6, 2, Spring 1995, pp. 117–34.

30 On the role of the military in Latin American democratizations, see Felipe Aguero, 'Democratic consolidation and the military in Southern Europe and Latin America', in Gunther, Diamandouros and Puhle, eds, *The Politics of Democratic Consolidation*, pp. 124–65. For earlier but valuable studies, which focus on Chile and Argentina, see respectively Marcelo Cavarozzi, 'Political cycles in Argentina since 1955', and Manuel Antonio Garreton, 'The political evolution of the Chilean military regime and problems in the transition to democracy', in Guillermo O'Donnell, Philippe C. Schmitter and Laurence Whitehead, eds, *Transitions from Authoritarian Rule: Latin America*, Baltimore: Johns Hopkins University Press, 1986, pp. 19–40 and 92–122.

31 The importance of leadership in democratization is discussed in, among others, Gianfranco Pasquino, 'Political leadership in Southern Europe: research problems', *West European Politics*, 13, October 1990, pp. 118–30, and in Juan Linz, 'Innovative leadership in the new transition to democracy and a new democracy: the case of Spain', in Gabriel Sheffer, ed., *Innovative Leadership in International Politics*, Albany: State University of New York Press, 1993, pp. 141–86.

32 The problems associated with the dual (or, according to some, triple) nature of the transition in post-communist regimes has been the object of extensive attention in the literature on democratization. On this, see, among others, Adam Przeworski *et al.*, *Sustainable Democracy*, Cambridge: Cambridge University Press, 1995; Linz and Stepan, *Problems of Democratic Transition and Consolidation*, pp. 435–53; and Claus Offe, 'Capitalism by democratic design? Democratic theory facing the triple transition in East Central Europe', *Social Research*, 58, Winter 1991, pp. 865–92.

33 On the two-step nature of the transition to democracy as a distinguishing feature of democratization in South-Eastern Europe, see F. Stephen Larrabee, 'Uncertain democracies: regime change and transitions', unpublished ms., 1991, and P. Nikiforos Diamandouros, 'Prospects for democracy in the Balkans', in Larrabee, ed., *The Volatile Powder Keg*, p. 18.

34 For the most recent comparative assessments of democratization in East-Central Europe, see Karen Dawisha and Bruce Parrott, eds, *The Consolidation of Democracy in East-Central Europe*, Cambridge: Cambridge University Press, 1997, and the pertinent sections in Linz and Stepan, *Problems of Democratic Transition and Consolidation*.

35 For the discussion of the significance of stateness as a factor affecting democratization in Linz and Stepan, see their *Problems of Democratic Transition and Consolidation*, pp. 16–38.

36 For a systematic and superb treatment of the politics of post-imperial states in East-Central Europe since the inter-war period, see Joseph Rothschild, *East Central Europe Between the World Wars*, Seattle: University of Washington Press, 1977, and *Return to Diversity: A Political History of East Central Europe Since World War II*, New York: Oxford University Press, 1989.

37 For a good analysis of the reasons accounting for Yugoslavia's collapse, see Woodward, *Balkan Tragedy*; Mihailo Crnobrnja, *The Yugoslav Drama*, London: McGill-Queens University Press, 1994; John R. Lampe, *Yugoslavia as History*, New York: Cambridge University Press, 1996; and Laura Silver and Allen Little, *Yugoslavia: Death of a Nation*, New York: TV Books, 1996.

38 The significance of international factors in triggering the democratic transitions in East-Central and South-Eastern Europe is widely acknowledged. For a discussion of the theoretical literature, see Geoffrey Pridham, 'International influences and democratic transition: problems of theory and practice in linkage politics', in Pridham, ed., *Encouraging Democracy: The International Context of Regime Transition in Southern Europe*, Leicester: Leicester University Press, 1991, pp. 1–29. See also Laurence Whitehead, 'International aspects of democratization', in O'Donnell, Schmitter and Whitehead, eds, *Transitions from Authoritarian Rule*, pp. 3–46. For East-Central and South-Eastern Europe, see Alex Pravda, ed., *The End of the Outer Empire: Soviet-East European Relations in Transition, 1985–90*, London: Royal Institute of International Affairs-Sage, 1992. Finally, for South-Eastern Europe, see the contributions by F. Stephen Larrabee, Loukas Tsoukalis, James B. Steinberg and Uwe Nerlich in Larrabee, ed., *The Volatile Powder Keg*, pp. 201–18, 219–31, 233–74 and 275–92 respectively.

39 Indeed, Steven Burg has explicitly referred to Bosnia-Hercegovina as 'a case of failed transition'. See Steven L. Burg, 'Bosnia-Herzegovina: a case of failed transition', in Darwisha and Parrott, eds, *Politics, Power and the Struggle for Democracy in South-East Europe*, pp. 122–45.

3 Political culture and democratization in the Balkans

Stefano Bianchini

Competing cultures and the changes in the Balkans

A controversial discussion on political culture in Eastern Europe emerged after the communist collapse among a narrow circle of scholars, although it clearly had broad implications for the democratization process in the region. Although attention focused on the Soviet Union/Russia and to a certain extent on Central and Baltic Europe, more than on the Balkans, this discussion nevertheless offers relevant lessons for countries in this region.

This debate was controversial not least because of criticism which arose particularly towards Sovietology, which had failed to predict the demise of communism. The reasons for this failure were traced back to mainstream political culture: more specifically, the behavioural or subjectivist civic culture model was charged with being powerless in explaining the growth of democratic values and the civic activism in the Soviet Union after 1987. Similarly, most analysts and scholars, policy-makers and international public opinion were caught by surprise when the Yugoslav secession war erupted and affected the whole post-communist transition in the Balkans to differing degrees. They underestimated the impact of political cultures or followed the dominant civic culture model; and, as a result, they were ill-equipped to recognize the relay race between two dominant political cultures, namely the set of political beliefs, knowledge and rules referred to as Marxism and the set referred to as nationalism.[1]

A recent, challenging study by Nicolai Petro on Russian democratization and political culture strongly criticized two flaws of mainstream political culture: 'first, the notion that political culture is a given, rather than a multifaceted and evolving identity; and second, the view that political culture is at best a haphazard collection of beliefs whose concrete expression can be measured only by the quantitative analysis of attitudes and behaviors'.[2] In other words, according to Petro, the behaviouralism of Almond and Verba is in the Soviet context inadequate for understanding the changes which occurred in communist society. Moreover, it is well known that the decrease of state-sponsored terror under Khrushchev encouraged most American scholars, and particularly the Harvard school, to emphasize the apparent popularity of Soviet institutions with the aim of identifying trends towards gradual reform of the system 'from within', rather than understanding the reasons of this popularity.[3] Accordingly, the political passiveness of the population towards the political system was misunderstood, because it was considered a retreat from politics rather than a defence mechanism. Hence, Sovietologists believed that the lack of claims (or inclinations) of the population in favour of democratic rules revealed the strengthening of Soviet communism. These considerations led analysts to stress how much communist political culture was able to permeate the society and become deeply rooted.[4] Their emphasis on the dominant (and/or official) political culture under communism followed mainstream political culture approaches in presuming that only one version of political culture could exist at a time.[5] As a result, competing political cultures within a single state were not considered and increasing differences in political attitudes or beliefs interacting in communist societies were underestimated.

However, the symbolist or interpretativist approach, advocated by scholars such as Robert Tucker, Lowell Dittmer and Howard Wiarda, allowed a more expansive definition of culture than the behaviouralist.[6] Studies on political culture received a great impetus from anthropology, and political symbols and political myths were considered crucial topics in understanding changes which occurred in a set of values. For instance, Geoffrey Hosking and George Schöpflin effectively pointed out the role of symbols and myths in the emergence of modern nationalisms in post-communist Eastern Europe.[7] In addition, this interpretativist approach is helpful when investigating the alternative values which emerged so quickly after communist collapse. Petro's category of *underground society* (or the parallel polis, in Vaclav Benda's terminology[8]) is particularly effective when explaining the simultaneous influence of different symbols, myths, values, political beliefs and knowledge which grew under communism and still characterize post-communist transitions, affecting the further democratic transformation of these societies.[9]

In the Balkan context, the underground society played a decisive role in preparing the way for post-communist developments, certainly much more than political emigration. The actors who took the lead in initiating change came from communist ranks or emerged from the anti-communist opposition *within* their countries. Admittedly, in the Yugoslav case, emigration lobbies played a significant role in events leading to the collapse of the Federal State. Serbian and Croatian *émigrés* influenced international public opinion and policy-makers in the United States, the Vatican, Germany, Great Britain and France, just as Albanian *émigrés* supported economically the suppressed population in Kosovo and contributed to arming extremist groups. However, in the Balkans a generation of actors who represented alternative political cultures *within* their own countries was nurtured despite communism. New expectations and beliefs arose with communist modernization, particularly in the newly promoted social strata. These generations are amongst the actors who are at the forefront of democratization in the area.

However, in departing from Petro's argument, the Balkan countries revealed distinctive forms of political behaviour, rules and beliefs which cannot, however, be accommodated by the dichotomy 'communist political culture–alternative political culture'. In fact, the underground society nurtured a plurality of ideas and expectations, which generated different political cultures. When communism collapsed, at least two of them – the nationalist and the reformist – competed in their impact on the process of democratization. Apparently, they seemed to converge initially because both opposed communism. Actually, they were in serious potential conflict. The future of democratization in South-Eastern Europe will mainly depend on the possible outcomes of this conflict.

Social change and modernity under communism

This emergence of different political cultures occurred in spite of the lack of autonomous institutions which made these countries unable to develop civil society.[10] In fact, despite strong communist control over public life, such societies with social and economic structures radically transformed by communism were increasingly in search of new forms of political representation and this helps to explain why alternative values emerged so quickly after the communist collapse.

Countries like Yugoslavia, Romania and Bulgaria in particular achieved impressive industrial growth with high industrial employment between the 1950s and 1970s.[11] Economic changes produced radical social changes as well. In Bulgaria, the urban population rose from 27.5 per cent in 1950 to 54.7 per cent in 1971; in Romania from 24.7 per cent in 1950 to 41.1 per cent in 1971; and in Yugoslavia from 21.7 in 1953 to 38.6 in 1971 (and 46.5 per cent in 1981). Even Albania followed these patterns, at least initially: influenced by the Soviet experience, migration flows towards the main cities were encouraged. Nevertheless, later, when de-Stalinization threatened Hoxha's personal dictatorship and the Chinese experience was emphasized, migration flows from the countryside were contained in order to exploit natural resources to the utmost and to keep strict control over the population in the towns and villages. Accordingly, the Albanian population living in rural areas diminished only from 78.7 per cent in 1945 to 66 per cent in 1991. Simultaneously, a great educational effort was started all over the Balkans, with illiteracy becoming drastically reduced from the 1950s. An increasing number of people had the opportunity to enter higher education. New academies of science were created, notably in Albania. This process was even more evident in the Yugoslav context, where the decision to open up the country, despite some restrictions, encouraged contacts with the rest of the world, tourism and freedom of movement, making society more sensitive and permeable to international culture, at least among the more conscious strata.

Initially, communist values determined social change in the Balkans, although eventually transformation encouraged differences so that former rural societies were characterized twenty years later by social complexity. Marxism was intended as an 'objective science', creating society without classes and conflicts, applying egalitarian values and emancipation as universal rights; and socialist realism as the art mirroring the logic of the 'perfect' society. In addition, modernity was identified with industrial growth and the rationality of large enterprises both in the centrally planned and self-managed economies. This identification was strengthened during the first phase of development, when heavy production, limited consumerism and autarchy appeared to be the main characteristics. However, the approach did not essentially change in the following decades, although attempts aimed at differentiating industrial production, encouraging consumerism and/or turning the countries to Western and Third World economies for trade and credit were made, albeit mostly by Yugoslavia after 1965, but also by Romania in the early 1960s and, more timidly, by Bulgaria at the beginning of the 1960s and 1970s.

Furthermore, communist ideology shares with modernity the idea that development is characterized by linearity and coherence. It was not by chance that communism sought to inculcate in the population the belief that the evolution of human societies leads inevitably to the overcoming of capitalism, to the stage of socialism and, eventually, to communism through an endless effort of 'further improvements'. As a result, the words 'reform', 'radical transformation', 'turning-point' were rarely used in communist terminology before the collapse appeared to be a concrete possibility. Finally, both in the Soviet-style command economy and in self-managed society the role of the administration was rapidly strengthened in the form of centralism and/or bureaucracy, following the French pattern which was popular all over Eastern Europe from the nineteenth century.

However, communism applied centralism extensively to all aspects of society, and not only in state administration. As a result, market relationships did not exist at all or (in the Yugoslav case) they had limited opportunities to work. On the contrary, the state became the owner/entrepreneur of the means of production, the distributor of goods and the sole institution able to guarantee social services and assistance to the population. In these fields the Yugoslav exception was only partial. On the one hand, self-management, particularly in the 1970s and later, ensured a high degree of autonomy to the economic sphere. On the other hand, the decentralization of the federal system created a 'multiple' state, by restricting the role of federal institutions and strengthening the role of republics, autonomous regions and municipalities, which proved able to affect economic and social activities as a whole.[12]

The emerging of alternatives to communism

Crucially, the way that modernity was rooted in the Balkans was mediated during communist rule by its perception of modern values and its ideological commitments and the state-building experience. Economically, these factors provoked an inflexibility which inhibited innovation and the spread of technology. Modernization was contained in a 'do it yourself' approach, with a too-long containment of consumerism, a too-strong state control over population mobility (especially in the Albanian and Romanian cases), and a too-rapid urbanization.

Culturally, socio-economic changes occurred while ideological inflexibility and the emphasis of the dictatorship of the proletariat intertwined with inflexibility towards 'otherness', identified with the 'capitalist enemy'. This helped to root in the population a rigid cultural mentality and the fear of contamination as well as the belief that ideological homogeneity is a prerequisite for defending a specific set of values. We may mention the emphasis on: (a) ideological purity by Enver Hoxha in Albania; (b) the 'indigenization' of Marxism promoted by Nicolae Ceauşescu in Romania; (c) Soviet orthodoxy and criticism towards Titoism in Bulgaria; and (d) and the ideology of self-management in Yugoslavia, in contrast with 'Soviet dogmatism' and 'anarcho-liberalism' (namely the theories of Djilas).

The needs of cohesion and homogeneity were particularly widespread in the countryside and in the suburbs, where social and cultural integration processes had yet to start. But this did not mean that society as a whole had such a restricted perception of reality. Social differentiation generated under communist rule revealed a growing differentiation with respect to political knowledge and expectations in people. Social classes concentrated in city centres showed a more open-minded and dynamic attitude towards 'otherness' which proved somewhat resistant to the appeals in favour of ideological cohesion or national homogeneity.

Despite peculiarities in each communist country, similar developments fermented in different periods in the main Yugoslav cities and to a lesser extent in Sofia, Tirana and Bucharest. This strengthened an intelligentsia 'in some respect highly developed, both in terms of class consciousness and a shared cultural experience',[13] as well as sport, literary and cultural organizations which enjoyed a relative autonomy. In other words, despite repeated repressive waves, a new intellectual elite emerged which was sensitive towards the evolution of society, anxious to interpret its trends and attentive to Western considerations. This phenomenon was significant in Yugoslavia during the 1960s and 1970s, particularly in Ljubljana, Belgrade and to a lesser extent in Zagreb and Sarajevo.

If the study of political culture has to be recast as the study of systems of political communication, as recently,[14] then it may be said that the recent phase of modernization multiplied the systems of political communication, affecting the predominant role of communist values, in spite of the fact that they were broadcast mainly by the media or spread throughout the schools, the unions and the political organizations strictly controlled by communist rule.

Crucially, dissent encouraged the development of an underground society, despite its limited membership. Dissent, in fact, was characterized by a broad variety of ideas. In the Yugoslav case[15] – the most permeable to Western ideas, at least in the Balkan context – it included personalities who radically differed from each other, as for instance Milovan Djilas and the Serbian liberals expelled from the party in 1972, Croatian and Slovenian nationalists who led the unrest between the 1960s and the 1970s, the movements of students and ecologists, the intellectual group of 'Praxis' and the university professors of Belgrade and Zagreb. Similar trends of dissent emerged in other Balkan countries despite the rigidity of their dictatorships.

The set of tools for political communication differed as well. In Yugoslavia, it included even the publication of 'alternative' journals (later suppressed by the party), heterodox articles in the official press and university lectures. Furthermore, and particularly in the other Balkan countries, it relied on 'samizdat' activity, illegal meetings – sometimes promoted by communist personalities criticizing mainstream party orthodoxy – and other kinds of civic resistance, as for instance in the arena of private life or the rejection of communist political ceremony. These trends were nurtured by the development of international contacts, receptiveness towards Western ideas, the growth of social complexity, and finally – particularly in the Bulgarian, Albanian and Romanian cases – by the experience of Soviet perestroika. In this situation, the role played by intellectuals proved crucial in influencing people, although this had changed over time. Whereas intellectuals of the humanities had traditionally dominated, a new group of technicians, managers and directors of enterprises emerged under communism and sought to dominate in society. This meant the traditional intellectuals had to become either the 'clergy of the nation' (as happened with members of the Serbian Academy and Slovenian intellectuals of the journal *Nova Revija*) or exponents of the most challenging Western ideas concerned with secular, multicultural and feminist ideas in their countries.[16]

The last aspect is to be considered in many respects a novelty, however generated by the communist emphasis on the category of emancipation (of the peoples, the working class, the women and humanity as a whole). Recent studies made by Katherine Verdery and Deema Kaneff have pointed out how modernization that was capital-poor has been crucial in Romania and Bulgaria in order to encourage a labour policy able to include everyone regardless of sex.[17] In Yugoslavia and Albania during the 1950s and 1960s the situation was similar and this explains why gender equality was supported. On the one hand, the needs of an industrialization programme based on quantity rather than quality facilitated generous maternal leave, child-care and free access to abortion. On the other hand, emancipation as an instrument aimed at guaranteeing equality between genders was regarded as consistent with the modern ideological commitment of which communism is part.

Actually, this approach, and particularly access to abortion, were restricted in Romania after 1966, but in general women's participation in the labour force increased relatively their authority within family units in the whole of the Balkans. In addition, to some extent, communism reorganized household tasks. This had different consequences in society, particularly in Yugoslavia after the 1970s, when the impact of liberalization was more incisive. In this case, feminist theory penetrated more easily from Western societies and feminist groups were created in the main cities. Although limited in number and politically controlled, they made a relevant contribution to the process of formation of an underground society under communism.[18]

Paradoxically, industrialization and modernization under communism generated in Balkan societies growing differences of economic and social interests as well as helping to articulate underground society. Both represented a radical change in comparison with the predominantly peasant and rural culture of the 1940s. By contrast, neither the underground society nor the pluralism of interests were mirrored by political institutions under the hegemony of the communist party, and these proved inadequate to manage change. In this situation, political reform involving democratization was hindered by ideological commitments, while contrasting interests were mediated within the framework of the Central Committee. When this mediation became impossible, because the contrasts required other instruments and institutions to express themselves and find solutions, the communist party exploded and the system collapsed.[19]

Modernity and democratization: Balkan perspectives

The disintegration of heterogeneous communist values

The increasingly heterogeneous set of values, beliefs, focal points of identification and loyalties nurtured by communism disintegrated when its political system collapsed. Underground political cultures emerged and polarized into two tendencies: the nationalist and the reformist. Meanwhile, new parties were created and new rules had to be established. This process suffered from the impact of different features, particularly insecurity, institutional instability and the lack of sources of power legitimation. Operating in a vacuum so far as rules for the functioning of state and political systems were concerned, the process of social implantation of a legal multi-party system had to confront the controversial questions of identities and solidarity as well as organizations until then politically discriminated against, like the religious.

Religious appeals to identity and solidarity values interacted with political parties and the recasting of political cultures. Wishing to play again a predominant role, official religious institutions sought to re-establish strong links with state and territory. Contributing significantly to re-legitimate power in historical and metaphysical terms, they emphasized the holy and transcendental dimension of the nation.[20] This approach was particuarly marked in the case of Orthodox Christianity. Nonetheless, similar attitudes emerged in the Catholic Churches of Croatia and Slovenia, which persuaded the Vatican to dismember the common bishops' conference for the purpose of strengthening their identification with their republics as reference points.[21] Identity and solidarity values were identified to a lesser extent with Islam, albeit leading Bosnian Muslim theologians, priests (imam) and activists increasingly supported fundamentalism. Ethnic cleansing and ethnic persecutions during the war encouraged radicalism within the Muslim community. However, decades of secularization, the lack of a strong confrontation between Islam and communism under Tito and the habit of multicultural cohabitation softened the impact of Islam on political beliefs.[22] Its role was even more marginal in other Balkan countries, such as Albania and Bulgaria, where clashes between cultural groups had a less relevant impact.

However, identity and solidarity values were politically encouraged in ways other than religious. The *zadruga* tradition in Yugoslavia and Bulgaria, *fis* in Albania, and *sat* in Romania – all expressive of the rural patriarchal community – were utilized by communist collectivism to solidify support for the regime through group loyalty and pride.[23] In the end, the *zadruga* tradition was effective for rooting group loyalty and pride; but later, nationalism exploited it for mass mobilization, for example against Romanies, Turks or Hungarians in Romania and Bulgaria. National pride was emphasized in order to oppose the country's 'sell-out' to the West, as through privatization. This was the case with Slovenia where rightist and nationalist parties claimed independence and later opposed the association with the EU.[24] In Albania, Sali Berisha appealed to kinship and *fis* loyalties within his party and in the country in order to secure his leadership. Any criticism of the President of the Republic was banned in line with the prerogatives of the 'headman' established in the Kanun and supported by principles such those of *besë* (loyalty) and *pabesë* (disloyalty). In Yugoslavia, despite its higher level of industrialization, its permeability to Western ideas and the aims of the communist leadership, self-management intertwined with the *zadruga* culture. Lacking democracy, the mix of new ideas and old traditions produced a peculiar set of values, which hindered further evolution of the country when the economic crisis erupted.

Identity and solidarity embodied in the *zadruga* culture remained reference values for the implantation of parties when communism collapsed. In particular, nationalist political viewpoints took advantage of this, seeking to take root in society and instigate mass mobilization. Emphasizing group homogeneity as a prerequisite for political consent, nationalism forced groups and individuals to take sides and, in order to preserve homogeneity, it did not hesitate to blackmail morally and even sanction as traitors of the nation those whose criticized the state or nationalist parties.

As a reaction to this, reformist political culture strengthened claims for radical democratization based on civil society, multiculturalism and citizenship, with the support of the most sensitive and educated strata of society. By competing with each other in their beliefs and values, these alternative political cultures promoted public politicization when a vacuum of rules emerged at the beginning of the 1990s. Accordingly, high politicization in the Balkans is a matter of fact and the post-communist clash of political cultures (nationalist versus reformist) demonstrates how the democratization process depends on the outcome of this clash.

The post-communist exclusiveness of groups versus democratization

The end of communism did not imply the end of discrimination. Rather, a new set of discriminations has emerged from nationalist political culture. During communism, ideology justified discrimination: the members of a community were divided between good and bad party members, or between party members and others. After communism, nationalists recast discrimination along cultural lines. Members of the community are requested to share the same cultural values in order to have access to all the rights usually granted to legal citizens. Homogeneity has been imposed as a value over complex and differentiated societies, by encouraging myths and symbols able to strengthen the sense of belonging to a group, to select the sources of identification and judge the loyalty of individuals. Once the communist myths of the wartime Resistance, Tito and '*bratstvo i jedinstvo*' (brotherhood and unity) were eroded, the Yugoslav secession war has allowed the destruction of previous symbols of power legitimation and the praise of new ones, like the images of the 'Sacrificed Nation'. Mixing the sacred and the profane, and using religion as a mark of identity, nationalism established new sources of legitimation, while perpetuating discrimination and increasing conflict.[25]

Hence, the display of national symbols has hindered post-communist democratization. For example, there is the great monument built in Shumen, a mixed area with large minorities of Turks and Romanies, with the aim of celebrating 1,300 years of the Bulgarian state. It is the symbol of a nation-state continuity, which cannot be shared by all the citizens of the country. As a result, it has become a source of disloyalties or suspicions of disloyalty. Similarly, the celebration of the days of Vasil Levki, a hero of Bulgarian independence who was hanged by Turks, does not encourage a shared love of freedom and Bulgarian laws by both Turkish and Slavic speaking populations. In sum, nationalist political culture strengthens political myths as a category of thought and a tool for action. Drawing inspiration from Herder's and Von Schlözer's philosophy of history at the end of eighteenth century, it emphasizes both epic deeds (which are considered the 'soul' of the nation) and a new form of distorted history in order to claim an ethnic and statehood continuity since the Middle Ages. Nor has the later contribution of Sorel's theories, and of rightist and Nazi racism, been absent.[26]

The fear of the 'otherness' encourages nationalist political culture to turn attention to demography. 'Strength lies in numbers': this commitment is clearly related to the rural tradition of defence against enemies, which also furthers patriarchal values that persisted under communism. Basically, the communist party took over the role played by the *zadruga* headman, drawing inspiration from the Soviet Family and Wedding Act which declared in 1922 that 'the family must be replaced by the party'. According to Julie Mostov and Katherine Verdery, the paternalist approach aimed at finding a strong framework of security for the members of the community.[27] They could obtain from the Father-Party acceptable life conditions, such as the welfare state, justice, social promotion, co-optation to leading roles and a solid ideological reference system. Moreover, the image of the country leaders – Ceauşescu, Hoxha, Zivkov and Tito – was generally identified with the 'wise, old headman', although the impact of this image was different in each country and, indeed, Ceauşescu and Hoxha particularly appealed to it in order to strengthen their power by removing or liquidating their opponents. In this way, a sort of consensus on the basis of customary laws and collective values adapted to the new conditions took place, and a sort of *zadruga*-socialism was created.

When communism collapsed, the cultural pattern of *zadruga* adopted by communism was re-interpreted within the set of ethnic values, because it was helpful for dealing with insecurity and ethnic imbalances.[28] In particular, the predominance of patriarchal values was evident in two approaches: on the one hand, by strengthening the personification of power management, as in the cases of Berisha in Albania, Milošević in Serbia and Tudjman in Croatia, who all sought to build an image of themselves as the 'wise, old headman', and the last even promoting himself as the 'Father of the Country'; on the other hand, by supporting policies aimed at forcing women out of the labour force and returning them to their 'original' reproductive task.

In the post-communist transitions, the nationalist approach to society has been characterized by a consistent cultural pattern whereby the role of *zadruga*-socialism is recast as *zadruga*-nationalism. It would be misleading, however, to consider this as simply an outcome of an 'ancestral' or archaic reaction against communist modernization and/or globalization. Truly populist solutions urged by policy-makers (like Tudjman, Milošević or Iliescu) appealed to solidarity and identity values preserved by the rural socio-political system. To this end, the past has been reinterpreted with the aim of rejecting communist ideological homogeneity. And, in this context, nationalism became the most consistent political culture alternative to communism.

Nonetheless, the border between continuity and rupture along the communist–nationalist line is quite unclear. Communist 'indigenization' anticipated nationalism, when it emphasized rural and popular traditions (with Ceauşescu and Zivkov and Hoxha), although it never opposed the urban and industrialist goals of communism. Furthermore, communism preserved those rural values which were compatible with modernity, such as egalitarianism. Indigenization was often considered by local bureaucracies an effective tool for strengthening their power by appealing to the solidarity of the nation, which made it possible for them to join nationalist ranks later, when the system collapsed. In the end, socialism and *zadruga* nationalism nurtured their political cultures in connection with modernity despite their different sets of values.

As a result, the approach to democratization has faced significant limitations, in spite of the fact that all Balkan countries have developed multi-party systems. At best, pluralism is perceived as a value only within an ethnic group, the broadest being the titular nation and the others the legally 'included' or recognized minorities: Croatia, Serbia and Kosovo are good examples of this. As a result, a hierarchy of groups is established, while cross-group political communication is regarded as a factor of destabilization of groups and national feelings (the charge of 'national traitor' traces its origin to this political belief).[29]

In this context, formal political equality is affected by a dominant ethnic group and the fact that observance or assertion of rights depends on whether individuals are members of socially or constitutionally 'included' ethnic groups. Otherwise, those excluded cannot even partake of fundamental civic rights (passive electorate, equality before the law, equal fiscal system). Systematically, the admission to political life, administration, education and military commands is based on these exclusionary assumptions and individual rights are in this way neglected or marginalized.

Democratization and differences as a political value

Despite several past waves of ethnic cleansing since the 1870s and their often being legitimated by international diplomacy, differences have persisted and still mark society in the countries of the Balkans. These differences are interconnected, and act at different levels. The sense of belonging to a group, particularly in South-Eastern Europe, lies both in a set of ethnic codes (related to affinities of language, religion, culture and moral codes) and in a set of supranational features (related once again to religion, but also to a common origin and material culture).

By way of clarification, it is a shared belief that Serbs, Croats and Bosnians are united by language and divided by religion (and partially by alphabet) in the wider Yugoslav cultural framework. However, not all Serbs are Orthodox, not all Croats are Catholic or Bosnians Muslims. In addition to non-believers, there are culturally important groups of Catholic Serbs in the Dubrovnik area, as well as Protestant Croats in Slavonia (likewise a part of the Slovenians). At the same time, all are Slavs. While Romanians are of Latin origin, the majority of the population is Orthodox, like the Slav Bulgarians, the Turk Gagaouzes and the Tosk Albanians. In addition, pre-existing ethno-cultural and religious differences have intertwined with social and economic differentiation, which has derived all over the Balkans from communist and capitalist modernization after the Second World War. In fact, despite their peculiarities and the different international context, a simultaneous radical change took place in Greece and Turkey in terms of industrial development, urbanization and mass education. As a result, when communism collapsed, Greece and Turkey were again included in their regional framework as crucial actors.

In sum, differences have been increased in the Balkans in the last decades. These differences have permeated both the groups and the individuals, but not on the basis of a typical patriarchal and dualistic antagonism ('us' versus 'them') as suggested by nationalist political culture. On the contrary, they persist within groups and in individuals. These considerations are the source of a specific reformist political culture based on multicultural values and beliefs, federal perspectives and secularization, which trace their origins back to the Yugoslav ideals and in Balkan federation or co-operation perspectives, which prospered in the mid-nineteenth century.[30] Sectors of underground society nurtured liberal and democratic claims, while dissident intellectuals and personalities expelled from communist political power circles because of their liberalism or democratic attitudes had opportunities to establish illegal but fruitful contacts with the Western democratic world. Meanwhile, the social changes provoked by communism and new challenging ideas from the West made possible the emergence of a constellation of several albeit small and scattered organizations promoting multiculturality and the protection of women's rights.

Shared by circles with a support more limited than that of nationalists (except for women's groups, which still represent the most structured and consistent organizations), reformist political culture emphasizes a direct link between the political system and the social/ethno-cultural pluralism of the Balkans.[31] Nonetheless, reformist political culture suffers from several flaws. Its secularization has difficulty in identifying effective myths and symbols able to attract support from less educated people. Without significant financial and media backing, channels of reformist subculture have often shown a lack of ability in organization and mediation. Movements and parties often divide, but when they are able to find agreement, their chances of playing an influential political role increase immediately, as the victories of Constantinescu and the Zajedno alliance in Romania and Serbia have respectively shown. Broadly speaking, the contribution of the whole liberal set of values is crucial in order to encourage democratization and peace in the region.

In this context, aside from groups of dissidents and – particularly in the late communist period – the emergence of actors for protecting the environment and multiculturality, the civil service and conscientious objection, the role played by the theory and practice of women concerning gender differences has had a special impact. Thanks to social and cultural influences after the 1960s, feminist theories penetrated from Western societies easily. Although limited in number and politically controlled, feminist groups influenced society by reconfiguring the male role in urban environments. Although they were more active in Yugoslavia,[32] they gradually became rooted also in the capitals of Bulgaria and Romania, while in Albania a similar process started when isolation came to an end in 1990.

Concerning the notion of emancipation, feminism criticized the enlightened assumption that equal rights can be guaranteed through a process of imitation of the male gender. On the contrary, by stressing that human beings are physically different and interact in different social, economic and cultural environments, they emphasized that equal rights can be guaranteed only through the recognition of differences. This approach had a crucial impact on political culture, because it challenges the traditional idea of the state or, rather, the beliefs and expectations that people have in politics. The 'modern state' and 'nationalism' are then severely criticized as patriarchal structures based on the prevalence of *one* political subject. At the same time, many family obligations have been eroded as a consequence of economic and health improvements (including a drastic fall in child death rates and an increasing use of different contraceptives). As a result, feminist groups are increasingly acting as a distinctive political actor and vehemently reject the dual antagonism ('us' versus 'them') in social relations. Rather, their emphasis focuses – following a postmodern approach[33] – on differences *within* groups *and* individuals. Culturally, the political impact of this attitude is relevant, because it presents a set of radically new rules of political participation, new values and beliefs in open confrontation with those supported by nationalism.

In this context, new values are having an interactive influence on democratization processes offering a recasting of relations *within* the group through the 'secularization' of ethnicity, which therefore hinders attempts to make it homogeneous. Altogether, they involve a new balance between collective and individual rights, permitting legal citizenship to offer a better solution than ethnicity while defining state membership.[34] In the Balkan countries, this is a revolutionary political culture, since individual rights have so far been regularly neglected. In terms of democratization, the autonomy of the citizen is an essential prerequisite in order to dismantle the state's monopoly, and to encourage the plurality of political subjects and an emergent civil society.[35]

Accordingly, the autonomy of the citizen and individual rights have been increasingly claimed in Bulgaria, Romania or Albania.[36] Similar approaches emerged in the former Yugoslavia, when the Prime Minister Ante Marković emphasized the idea of *gradjanska drzava* (civic state) in contrast with *nacionalna drzava* (nation-state) supported by Tudjman and Milošević. Although politically defeated, Markovic's approach is still the main reference point for several groups of intellectuals and young educated people who are aware that citizenship requires restricting or containing predominant collective (ethnic) rights.[37]

Significantly enough, these political beliefs attracted women's organizations, which opposed nationalism in Yugoslavia by promoting the most effective actions against the war in the whole area. Only movements such as 'Women in Black' had the courage to demonstrate solidarity in Belgrade with women of Kosovo in early 1998, while feminist groups protected deserters in Croatia.[38] In Bulgaria, women lead the most relevant centres for intercultural activities. With their activities and ideas, women have been able to attract support from educated younger generations. In other words, feminist movements are converging with educated younger generations who are increasingly in conflict with the older rural generations educated under communism. Their values and approaches to work and politics differ significantly thanks to the impact of new technologies and new dynamic relations with Western societies which encourage the initiative of individuals, their claims for individual rights and the observance of differences from the values of older generations.

However, it is still questionable whether reformist political culture is able to take the lead in promoting democratization or whether nationalism maintains a predominant or influential role given economic difficulties may emerge any time and support it. In this case, a possible outcome is the evolution of societies towards cultural autism with a neo-authoritarian collective control over individuals while preserving multi-party systems. In other words, the failure of democratization is possible once again in the Balkans. Much depends on whether political culture based on differences and liberal options is doomed to submerge itself or, even worse, to be expelled. The lack of a receptive environment may encourage new migration flows towards the West, which can provoke an impoverishment of intellectual energies in the Balkans. As a result, democratization in the Balkans strictly depends on both domestic developments and foreign pressures, and whether the latter supports what we can define an 'anti-nationalist political culture' or, better, a political culture aimed at establishing a *liberal* management of differences.

Conclusions: whither democracy? An interpretativist approach

In conclusion, after the breakdown of communism, alternative political cultures emerged from the underground society and became polarized and divided. Nationalist political culture is still seeking to promote itself as the 'natural' heir of communism not only because both share the same attitude towards politics, but also because both are attracted by modernity and an antagonistic approach to 'otherness', although expressed by different symbols and myths. By contrast, reformist political culture is still working as an alternative (to nationalism, instead of communism), but it runs the risk of being rejected and of returning to the underground.

The nationalist approach relies on an effective set of symbols and myths, while its political beliefs and values are either shared by a plurality of parties (as in Romania or Serbia), or are a monopoly of one party and one leader (as in Croatia or Bosnia). Generally, it enjoys a good implantation in society and a great ability to use and control the media, even when not included in the government (as in the case of Slovenia, Romania and Macedonia). In other words, nationalist subcultures – through the action of nationalist parties – accept political polarization when the priority of ethno-cultural values of a community are not disputed *within* the community itself. Here, democratization provides a constraint albeit within ethno-cultural limitations. Nationalist political culture has been promoted by the implantation of Western autarchic and anti-liberal ideas, which are incompatible with the *existing* multicultural and religious web of the Balkans. As a result, it nurtures instability, which is – in the form of a vicious circle – the main source of its strength. In order for it to be successfully implemented, neo-authoritarian outlets, ethnic cleansing and wars are unavoidable. In this context, the democracy-building process is a perspective for the future, not an issue for today.

The reformist approach is quite different. It is based on the ideal of a broad pluralism, which is expressed by scattered and widespread subcultures shared by many groups and movements whose memberships are often unstable. Albeit divided and often competing in terms of political organizations, its political culture suggests a worldwide idea of freedom based on the observance of differences and human and citizens' rights. Values and political beliefs reveal a post-modern approach to democratization, which takes priority over ethno-cultural community concerns. Reformist political culture, while rejecting community autism, is a result of the existing multicultural and religious web of the Balkans. It intertwines with the most advanced Western ideas and it is shared mainly by highly educated people who have the technological knowledge for developing their countries. Reformists consider that democracy-building processes are not an issue for tomorrow, but an immediate need in order to create stability and economic growth. Culturally, democratization is intended as a political process able to guarantee the widest free flow of ideas and an equal representation of the existing differentiated cultural web in the Balkans. In this respect, a specific contribution comes from the most recent theories on gender identities, which challenge patriarchal values and the idea of homogeneity of the individual and the community.

The situation regarding these competing Balkan political cultures and their evident European characteristics confirms how groundless is Huntington's theory of a clash of civilizations in Europe. His map dividing the Protestant–Catholic world from the Muslim–Orthodox is powerless in explaining democracy for instance in Greece, recent electoral/political changes in Romania and Bulgaria, or the similarities of aggressive nationalisms from Slovenia to Cyprus.[39] Albeit based on attractive literary images, Huntington fails to focus on different fundamental political beliefs and focal points of loyalties, which are affecting European societies, while offering a patriarchal and homogeneous image of each country, which is in fact consistent with the nationalist political culture approach. By contrast, modern Balkan nationalism is not a genuine spontaneous feeling. Rather, it is a tool for the organization of support conducted through the media by policy-makers, but is not supported by significant groups in society which prefer to emigrate.

From this perspective, the Balkan problems of democratization are often misrepresented in the West. Analysts and policy-makers prefer to turn their attention to outer forms of nationalist myths and symbols, concluding that clashes of civilization generate nationalist conflicts. In fact, it is exactly the contrary: nationalist conflicts occur between those who share a common set of values and a common political culture. Furthermore, the idea of a clash of civilizations legitimates a deterministic idea of history which stems from religions and/or philosophies of history predicting that certain people have missions of civilization, or a 'natural' right to dominate. This obviously presents a substantial problem for reintegrating the Balkans into the European framework with serious repercussions for democratization in the region.

In other words, categories of interpretation appealing exclusively to a 'certain' history and a 'certain' European culture, when applied to the Balkans, run the risk of misleading so far as the complexity of the region is concerned, and of underestimating the Western and modern origin of Balkan nationalism as well as the impact of post-modern liberal and feminist political culture on democratization. In this sense the Balkans and whole of Europe do need the 'end of history'. This is not because the conflicts or the events related to human actions can come to an end (this can happen only in the event of human beings disappearing), but because the deterministic idea of history – seeking to explain how the nation-state is the final result of an unavoidable evolution – is increasingly threatened by the crisis of the nation-state.

The current fragility of this socio-symbolic structure is a matter of fact: threatened by both disintegrative and integrative phenomena, its crisis tragically emerged in the Balkans through the Yugoslav and Albanian collapses, the risk of Bulgarian collapse and the still not avoided Romanian collapse. In a sense, overthrown by a deep crisis of adjustment, the Balkans are anticipating in a dramatic way a decline of socio-symbolic structures, which is perceived in Western countries too.

Moreover, Balkan political cultures are perfectly able to interact with Western European political cultures, so that the future of Balkan democratization will mainly depend on these interactions. If Western policy-makers and analysts are aware of it and act consistently, Balkan democratization will be encouraged decisively. In fact, any attempts at treating the democracy-building process in the Balkans as an issue which is separate from Europe, which is 'simply' affected by 'war legacies' and 'traditional' violence, is illusory. This approach can only increase misunderstanding and affect peace and stability all over the Continent. In a sense, Mangu Dibango's sentence on Africa can be applied effectively to the relations between Western and Balkan societies: 'Most peoples of Western thinking want to maintain Africa as a museum. I mean, they want Africa to continue to play tom-toms because Africa is tom-tom; that's it. They don't think we can play electronics. I think it is most important that people understand that the electronic Africa does exist.'[40]

Notes

1 However, a restricted number of analysts emphasized these changes. See for example Viktor E. Meier, *Neuer Nationalismus in Südosturopa*, Opladen: C. W. Leske Verlag, 1968, or Carl Gustav Ströhm, *Ohne Tito kann Jugoslawien überleben?*, Wien-Köln: Verlag Stiria Graz, 1977. On the nexus of communism and nationalism before communist collapse see also Stefano Bianchini, *Nazionalismo croato e autogestione*, Milan: La Pietra, 1983, and 'Il nemico è il nazionalismo economico', *Rinascita*, 4, 1982, p. 22.

2 V. Nicolai N. Petro, *The Rebirth of Russian Democracy: An Interpretation of Political Culture*, Cambridge, MA: Harvard University Press, 1995, pp. 3–8.

3 See the classical studies of Gabriel Almond, 'Comparative political systems', *Journal of Politics*, 18, 1956, pp. 391–408; Gabriel Almond and Sidney Verba, *The Civic Culture: Political Attitudes and Democracy in Five Nations*, Princeton: Princeton University Press, 1963; Lucian W. Pye, 'Culture and political science: problems in the evaluation of the concept of political culture', *Social Science Quarterly*, 53, 2, 1972, along with Alex Inkeles and Raymon A. Bauer, *The Soviet Citizen: Daily Life in Totalitarian Society*, Cambridge, MA, Harvard University Press, 1961, and Roger Kanet, *The Behavioral Revolution and Communist Studies*, New York: Free Press, 1971.

4 Cf. Archie Brown, ed., *Political Culture and Political Change in Communist States*, New York: Holmes & Meier Publishers, 1977, pp. 7–8; Grzegorz Ekiert, 'Democratic processes in East Central Europe: a theoretical reconsideration', *British Journal of Political Science*, 3, 1991, pp. 285–313, and Giuseppe di Palma, 'Legitimation from the top to civil society: politico-cultural change in Eastern Europe', in Nancy Bermeo, ed., *Liberalization and Democratization*, Baltimore: Johns Hopkins University Press, 1992.

5 V. Lucian W. Pye and Sidney Verba, *Political Culture and Political Development*, Princeton: Princeton University Press, 1965; Gabriel Almond and Sidney Verba, *The Civic Culture Revisited*, Boston: Little Brown and Co., 1980; Frederick C. Barghoorn and Thomas F. Remington, *Politics in the USSR*, Boston: Little, Brown and Co., 1986.

6 Cf. Robert C. Tucker, 'Culture, political culture and communist society', *Political Science Quarterly*, 2, 1973; Lowell Dittmer, 'Political culture and political symbolism: toward a theoretical synthesis', *World Politics*, 29, 4, 1977; Howard J. Wiarda, 'Political culture and national development', *The Fletcher Forum*, 2, 1989.

7 Geoffrey Hosking and George Schöpflin, eds, *Myths and Nationhood*, London: Hurst, 1997.

8 Vaclav Benda *et al.*, 'Parallel polis, or an independent society in Central and Eastern Europe: an inquiry', *Social Research*, 1–2, 1988, pp. 211–46.

9 Petro, *The Rebirth of Russian Democracy*, p. 21.

10 Geoffrey Hosking *et al.*, *The Road to Post-Communism*, London: Pinter, 1992, and Mary Kaldor and Ivan Vejvoda, 'Building democracy in Central and Eastern Europe', in *International Affairs*, 1, Jan. 1997, pp. 76–82.

11 John Lampe and Marvin Jackson, *Balkan Economic History*, Bloomington: Indiana University Press, 1982. Wlodzimierz Brus, *Storia economica dell'Europa Orientale 1950–1980*, Rome: Editori Riuniti, 1983; Daniel Chirot, *The Origins of Backwardness in Eastern Europe*, Berkeley: University of California Press, 1989.

12 Cf. Marijan Korosic, *Jugoslavenska kriza*, Zagreb: Naprijed, 1989; Vladimir Goati, *Politicka anatomija Jugoslovesnkog drustva*, Zagreb: Naprijed, 1989; Zagorka Golubovic, *Kriza identiteta jugoslovenskog drustva*, Beograd: Filip Visnjic, 1988; Branko Horvat, *Jugoslovesko drustvo u krizi*, Zagreb: Globus, 1985. Recent studies are those of John R. Lampe, *Yugoslavia as History*, Cambridge: Cambridge University Press, 1996; Sabrina P. Ramet, *Balkan Babel*, Boulder, CO: Westview Press, 1996.

13 Trond Gilberg, *Nationalism and Communism in Romania*, Boulder CO: Westview Press, 1990, p. 138.

14 Cf. Michael Brint, *A Genealogy of Political Culture*, Boulder, CO: Westview Press, 1991; Lowell Dittmer, 'Comparative communist political culture', *Studies in Comparative Communism*, Spring–Summer 1983, pp. 11ff. and Dittmer, 'Political culture and political symbolism', p. 557.

15 Stefano Bianchini, *La diversità socialista in Jugoslavia*, Trieste: Est, 1984.

16 See Nebojsa Popov, ed., *Srpska strana rata*, Beograd: Republika, 1996, and the group of intellectuals of the journal *Republika*, or Zarana Papic, *Sociologija feminizma*, Beograd: Istrazivacko-izdavacki centar SSO Srbije, 1989.

17 Katherine Verdery, 'From parent state to family patriarchs: gender and nation in contemporary Eastern Europe', *East European Politics and Societies*, 2, Spring 1994, pp. 225–55, and Deema Kaneff, 'State building and local resistence: a Bulgarian case', in Stefano Bianchini and George Schöpflin, eds., *State Building in the Balkans: Dilemmas On the Eve of the 21ˢᵗ Century*, Ravenna: Longo, 1998.

18 See Smiljana Novosel, *Zene – politicka manjina*, Zagreb: Narodne Novine, 1990; Slavenka Drakulic, *Smrtni grijesi feminizma*, Zagreb: Znanje, 1989; Zarana Papic and Lidya Sklevicky, *Antropologija zene*, Beograd: BIGZ, 1983.

19 François Fejtö, *La Fin des démocraties populaires*, Paris: Editions du Seuil, 1992.

20 Srdjan Vrcan, *La guerra in ex Jugoslavia: una guerra di religione contemporanea o una guerra con le religioni impegnatissime o una guerra di fede?*, Split: Manuscript, 1993; Vrban Todorov, 'Etniceski i religiozni problemi na Balkanite. Mjastoto na B'lgarija', *Politiceski Izsledvanija*, 4, 1995, pp. 341–53; Mient Ian Faber, ed., *The Balkans: A Religious Backyard of Europe*, Ravenna: Longo Editore, 1996, p. 240.

21 Cf. P. Stanko Duje Mijic, *Hrvatska do pakla i natrag*, Zagreb: Samostan Sv. Duha, 1993, and Bodgan Djurovic, ed., *Religija, rat i mir*, Nis: Junir, 1994.

22 David Steele, 'Religion as a fount of ethnic hostility or an agent of reconciliation?', in Dusan Janjic, ed., *Religion and War*, Beograd: European Movement in Serbia, 1994, p. 180.

23 These traditions were successfully described by leading anthropologists and economists such as Jozo Tomasevich, Joel and Barbara Halpern, Henry H. Stahl or Joseph Obrebski. See in particular the more recent work of Barbara K. Halpern, 'An anthropologist in the village', in John B. Allock and Antonia Young, eds., *Black Lambs and Grey Falcons: Women Travellers in the Balkans*, Bradford: Bradford University Press, 1991, pp. 145–61.

24 See, for example, Andrej Aplenc, *Prodaja Slovenije*, Ljubljana: Mladinska Knjiga, 1997; Janez Jansa, *Premiki*, Ljubljana: Mladinska Knjiga, 1992.

25 Srdjan Vrcan, *The War in Ex-Yugoslavia and Religion*, Split: Manuscript, 1993, and Ivan

Cvitkovic, 'On the role of religions in a war', in Janjic, ed., *Religion and War*, pp. 197–209.

26 On political myths and ideology see George Schöpflin, 'The functions of myths and a taxonomy of myth', in Hosking and Schöpflin, *Myths and Nationhood*, pp. 19–35; Alida Rizova, 'Politiceskite mitove i utopii', *Politiceski Izsledvanija*, 3, 1995, pp. 301–12, and the classics Benedict Anderson, *Imagined Communities*, London: Verso, 1991; Eric Hobsbawm and Terence Range, eds., *The Invention of Tradition*, Cambridge: Cambridge University Press, 1983; John Armstrong, *Nations before Nationalism*, Chapel Hill NC: University of North Carolina Press, 1982.

27 See Julie Mostov, 'Democracy and the politics of national identity', *Studies in East European Thought*, 46, 1994, pp. 9–31; Katherine Verdery, *National Ideology under Socialism*, Berkeley: California University Press, 1995, and again Julie Mostov, '"Our women"/"their women": symbolic boundaries, territorial markers and violence in the Balkans', *Peace and Change*, 4, 1995, pp. 515–29.

28 These factors are also connected with the lack of a democratic habit deeply analysed in the context of the political parties in Bulgaria by Zeljo Georgiev. See Zeljo Georgjev, 'Demokraticnijat "etos" v postkomunisticeska B'lgarija', *Politiceski Izsledvanija*, 4, 1996, pp. 371–87.

29 Dusan Janjic, ed., *Ethnic Conflict Management: The Case of Yugoslavia*, Ravenna: Longo Editore, 1997; Stefano Bianchini and Dusan Janjic, *Ethnicity in Postcommunism*, Belgrade: Institute of Social Science, 1996; Michael Freeman, Dusan Janjic and Dragan Pantic, eds., *Nationalism and Minorities*, Centre for Human Rights, University of Essex, 1995; Silvo Devetak, *Manjine, ljudska prava, demokratija*, Sarajevo: Oslobodjenje, 1989.

30 Cf. Dobrica Vulovic, ed., *Balkan krajem 80–ih godina*, Beograd: CMU, 1987, and Angelo Tamborra, *L'Europa Centro-Orientale nei secoli XIX e XX*, Milan: Vallardi editoriale, 1971.

31 Anna Krasteva, ed., *Obstnosti i identicnosti*, Sofija: Petekston, 1998; Bozidar Jaksic, ed., *Frontiers: The Challenge of Interculturality*, Beograd: Forum za etnicke odnose, 1997; Anna Krasteva, Nina Dimitrova, Nonka Bogomilova and Ivan Kacarski, *Universalno i nacionalno v B'lgarskata kultura*, Sofija: IMIR, 1996; Antonina Zeljazkova, *Relations of Compatibility and Incompatibility between Christians and Muslims in Bulgaria*, Sofija: IMIR, 1995.

32 See *Talking About Women and Men*, special issue of *Transition*, January 1998 and the numbers 1, 2, 18, 27, 30, 36 of *War Report*; Rada Ivekovic, *Le Pouvoir nationalist et les femmes*, Europe and the Balkans Int. Network/Occ. Papers, Longo, 1996; *La balcanizzazione della ragione*, Rome: Manifestolibri, 1995; Marina Padovese and Salvo Vaccaro, *Donne contro la guerra*, Palermo: La Zisa, 1996; Ru'ica Rosandic and Vesna Pesic, eds, *Warfare, Patriotism, Patriarchy*, Belgrade: Center for Antiwar Action, 1994.

33 See the document of Italian feminists 'È accaduto non per caso', *Sottosopra*, January 1996; see in addition A. Huyssens, 'Mapping the post-modern', *New German Critique*, 33, 1984, pp. 5–52.

34 See Joseph Marko, 'Equality and difference: political and legal aspects of ethnic group relations', in Franz Matscher, ed., *Minority Protection in Europe*, Kohl: N. P. Engel Verlag, 1997.

35 See Julie Mostov, 'Endangered citizenship', in Michael Kraus and Ronald D. Liebowitz, eds, *Russia and Eastern Europe after Communism*, Boulder, CO: Westview Press, 1995, pp. 35–50, and Zoran Pokrovac, ed., *Gradjansko Drustvo i Drzava*, Zagreb: Naprijed, 1991.

36 See Antonii Todorov, 'Trudnostite pred Grazdanskoto obstestvo: kritika na prehoda k'm demokracija', *Politiceski Izsledvanija*, 3, 1995, pp. 227–31.

37 See Esad Zgodic, *Gradjanska Bosna*, Tuzla: Ritam, 1996; *Federacija Bosna i Hercegovina. Drzava i civilno drustvo*, Zagreb: Erasmus; Svjedocanstva, 1995; Vojin Dimitrijevic, ed., *Suppressed Civil Society*, Belgrade: Manuscript, 1996.

38 See Bozidar Jaksic, ed., *Ka jeziku mira*, Beograd: Forum za Etnicke Odnose, 1996; *Deserters from the War in Former Yugoslavia*, Belgrade: Zene u Crnom, 1994.

39 Samuel P. Huntington, 'A clash of civilizations?', *Foreign Affairs*, 3, 1993, p. 30.

40 Mangu Dibangu, *Melody Maker*, 1984 reported in the Seattle Art Museum, Art of Africa, Seattle.

4 Nationalism and Democracy in South-East Europe

Tom Gallagher

Introduction

The Balkan states of South-East Europe entered the phase of post-communism with the collapse of Soviet power after 1989. But the shift to liberal democracy was much weaker there than in Central Europe, as was the influence of communist reformers genuinely committed to going down the pluralist road. Instead, an improvised transition from above was attempted by unreformed elements of the communist elite, which largely abandoned the Marxist ideology but tried to retain a monopoly of power. The nomenklatura (the self-selecting communist elite used to control state and society) saw the best chance of prolonging their political ascendancy in new political conditions if competitive politics could be shaped along ethnic lines. Most of the countries of South-East Europe were fertile ground for the politics of ethnicity owing to the traditional ability of nationalism to shape the political culture irrespective of the social system that happened to be in place. The mobilizing capacity of nationalism was already apparent in countries whose communist rulers had occasionaly sought legitimacy by appealing to patriotic symbols, scapegoating minorities, or reviving dormant quarrels with neighbouring states, as in Romania.

Thus, the start of the 1990s witnessed a rapid ideological conversion to nationalism by ex-communists intent on retaining political power under new rules which required the legitimacy of opposition and competitive elections. The espousal of ethnic politics was seen as offering a 'clean identity' and removing the stigma of being attached to the old, bankrupt regime.[1] The most successful appeals to nationalism occurred in states where civic values were weak and associational growth limited (Romania) or where there were tangible nationalist grievances that could be manipulated by resourceful ethnic entrepreneurs (Serbia). In such contexts, rulers were able to sabotage the transition to democracy at an early stage or else enable the power of a small group of authoritarian-minded individuals to be perpetuated through a façade democracy. Thus it became possible for unreformed ex-communists to defy the winds of democratic change by relying on a new form of collectivism, that of nationalism, which, like communism, was capable of downgrading or delaying the onset of individual freedoms.

The second claim made here is that nationalism only had limited applicability for the ruling ex-communist left. It was a strategy that enabled them to re-group rather than pioneer a new form of long-term political control. Ex-communists were usually unauthentic nationalists who, if necessary, were ready to jettison their nationalist programmes if these got in the way of conserving power. Moreover, it became harder to conceal from ordinary citizens that nationalism had been used as a screen to permit the misallocation of public resources and wholesale corruption by post-communist elites. Where the regime tolerated public opposition and per-mitted elections in which the results were not decided in advance (usually under pressure from abroad), electorates disillusioned by the ex-communist left's misuse of power have deserted it in growing numbers.

Thirdly, the politics of ethnicity is unlikely to perish with the decline of the ex-nomenklatura left. Parties of the nationalist right comparable to Le Pen's Front National in France exist which are sometimes capable of promoting solidarity for atomized individuals and declining social groups facing bleak prospects. More worrying is the possibility that reformers, unable to honour electoral promises, will appeal to nationalism in order to prolong their credibility. The strength of collective values and the weakness of individual and civic ones are not just shortcomings which the ex-communist left or extreme right are prepared to exploit for their power-conserving ends; they are outcomes which arise from the region's difficulties in adapting to important aspects of modernization.

The final claim made here is that purposeful efforts by multilateral international organizations to assist democracy in the region and promote economic reform and co-operation between states may, in no small way, help to determine whether the balance of power can shift decisively away from authoritarian nationalists, of whatever political hue. External inter-vention needs to be carried out in a sensitive and disinterested way to prevent it being exploited by local nationalist forces. If what initially were bogus democratic transitions carried out from above by nomenklatura forces blossom into genuine democratization efforts thanks, in no small part, to external assistance from the Western democracies, it will be another example of foreign powers shaping developments in the Balkans, but one of the most constructive ones seen over a long historical period.

The legacy of authoritarianism

South-Eastern Europe's mainly negative experience of communism and a much longer record of misrule by foreign or local rulers have not prepared the region for competitive politics within an orderly legal framework. Lengthy periods of foreign rule, a briefer period of self-government in which a majority nation usually dominated an ethnically mixed polity, followed by first Soviet-sponsored and then native communist rule, have left damaging legacies that now impair attempts to operate democratic political systems, or else have sabotaged democratization efforts as in Serbia.

Different empires, civilizations and social systems have collided in the Balkan peninsula over a long historical period.[2] The resulting instability and the eruption of conflicts which have led to wider conflagrations, have given the Balkan region a reputation which today is one of the most negative paradigms in international relations.[3] But it would be wrong to view South-Eastern Europe as a region of perennial conflict and oppression of groups whose identity may be regarded as suspect by rulers. Under the Ottoman empire, religious toleration was permitted by a despotic political system. However, in the nineteenth century, Western-style nationalism imposed itself upon the multicultural traditions of the Ottoman world. Intellectuals and political agitators dreamt of freeing and uniting subject peoples from the Sultan's rule. But the Balkans was an ethnographic mosaic and the complex distribution of languages, religions and proto-nationalities meant that political and ethnic boundaries could not be easily made to coincide.

Self-governing states emerged in Greece (1830), Serbia (1815), Romania (1859) and Bulgaria (1878). Where the acquisition of freedom occurred by violent means, constitutional politics was frequently interrupted by armed revolts. Romania was the only Balkan country to achieve its independence largely through diplomacy, and it may be no coincidence that in the first half-century of self-rule constitutional government there was never interrupted by coups or the assassination of government leaders.

The creation of new states or the enlargement of existing ones after 1918 made national self-determination the new organizing concept for a region shorn of multinational empires. Liberal constitutions were drawn up and competitive elections held, but liberty was defined as essentially meaning collective freedom from foreign domination rather than liberty of the individual. Nationalist elites usually ruled in the name of an ethnic majority or sought to impose cultural uniformity on the rest of the population. Emphasis was placed on defending the 'national homeland' (usually seen as reaching to the furthest limits of the territory inhabited by the ethnic majority) rather than on safeguarding individual freedoms or advancing material prosperity. When nationalism was elevated almost to the status of a state religion, it not only led to friction with unreconciled minorities but to inter-state conflicts over territory. In the end, nationalism was unable to provide fractious elites with the coherence to undertake the task of state-building. Weak states found it hard to integrate new territories even where inhabited by the majority nationality. In Yugoslavia and Romania cultural and economic divisions on internal regional lines were arguably more responsible for the collapse of democracy than the activities of non-Slavic or non-Romanian minorities.[4]

The communist era strengthened aspects of Balkan political culture inimical to democracy-building. Ruthless violence was used to demolish much of the old social system, a course followed owing to the weakness of communist parties across much of the region. Force was periodically used to settle political disputes within ruling elites and always employed to deal with dissent from below. Civil society was flattened as the totalitarian party sought to abolish any boundaries between state and society. Given the strength of the sanctions employed to discourage free worship of religion or civic associations, it is not surprising that many citizens fell back on ethnic identity to provide a collective sense to their lives.

Ruthless social engineering policies, designed to create a new 'communist man' by directing peasants from the over-populated countryside into urban heavy industry, also left disturbing legacies for the post-communist era. Much of this industry was unviable and even before 1989 nationalism was being rehabilitated by the state in order to reach out to the new working class. Internationalism on Soviet terms had made it difficult for communist rule to acquire legitimacy. Soviet-led internationalism was never strong enough to overcome the national and sub-national differences between Balkan states and peoples. Starting with Tito's Yugoslavia in 1948, most Balkan states were to reject Soviet tutelage and nationalism was revived in order to preserve their authority. Industrialization was depicted as the culmination of the struggle for independence. More ominously, relations with communist neighbouring states suffered in this new climate of national communism. The idea of the state as the preserve of the majority ethnic group revived in Romania and Bulgaria and was accompanied by the ill-treatment of minorities, especially where co-ethnics had a neighbouring state to which they were able to look. Even Tito, lauded for his success in defusing internecine South Slav quarrels during his 36–year rule in Yugoslavia, was prepared to 'accommodate many nationalist demands because he believed that nationalism and communist authoritarianism were compatible'.[5] According to Aleksa Djilas (son of the celebrated Yugoslav dissident Miloslav Djilas), 'he was much more afraid of liberal reforms than of nationalism, since reform directly challenged the communist monopoly of power and his personal rule'.[6]

Communism and nationalism

Communism as a doctrine was much more suited to ethnic homogenization than to promoting ethnic pluralism. The first theoreticians of communism may have dismissed nationalism as a bourgeois tool to distract the masses, but affinities between communism and nationalism allowed national values to be rehabilitated by Balkan communists. Both are systems of ideas built around an impersonal force – the nation or the working class – which becomes the sole focus of loyalty in society. Solidarity between rulers and society is sought by identifying 'national' or 'class' enemies that threaten the very survival of the state. There is a stress on unity behind individuals able to uphold the collective will in societies based on nationalist or communist principles. The emphasis on uniformity of thinking and action can leave little room for autonomous institutions allowing the individual to lead a social life independent of the state.[7]

The failure of the communist industrial model in the agrarian societies of the Balkans increased the likelihood that elites would seek to preserve their authority by appealing explicitly to nationalist values. They had far less inclination to vacate the political stage than their counterparts in Central Europe after the Soviet Union made it clear in the late 1980s that it would not use force to uphold communist rule in any of its satellites. The mistakes and abuses of power carried out by Balkan communists were usually of a worse order than anywhere else in the Soviet bloc. Opposition to their rule was much weaker owing to the scale of coercion directed against potential or actual dissidents. Western pressure for internal reform was weak in comparison to that exercised on Poland or the Czech Republic. Indeed Balkan communist leaders as different as Yugoslavia's Marshal Tito and Romania's Nicolae Ceauşescu had received important diplomatic and financial support from the West because their nationalist regimes were seen as weak links in the chain of Soviet power in Eastern Europe.[8] So there were not a few apparatchiks in South-Eastern Europe who assumed that the use of nationalism, which had enabled them to defy Soviet power, might conceivably enable them to survive the complete collapse of the Soviet edifice.

Yugoslavia in the 1980s provides the path-breaking example of communists who were ready to appeal to the masses through nationalism in order to safeguard their power in a time of disturbing regional transition. At different times, Tito had sought to foster all-Yugoslav solidarity by adopting a hostile stance to neighbours like Albania and Bulgaria who were thought to have designs on Yugoslav territory owing to the presence of national communities – the Albanian Kosovars and the Slavic Macedonians – that previously had been identified with Greater Albanian and Greater Bulgarian state-building projects.[9] A new twist was then given to this strategy of appealing to solidarity by identifying a national threat *when the threat was seen to come from within*, from disloyal minorities like the Albanians or treacherous fellow South Slavs like the Croats.

The innovator in this respect was Slobodan Milošević, who after 1987 was the leader of the communist party in Serbia, the largest of the six republics and two provinces making up federal Yugoslavia.[10] He exploited simmering discontent among public officials and intellectuals unhappy that Serbia had lost its traditional pre-eminence in Tito's federal system. It will long be debated whether he exploited accumulating grievances about Serbia's subordinate position or whether he was responsible for licensing and spreading nationalist feelings previously only at a low level.[11] But in 1989–90 he enjoyed enormous popularity among Serbs when he successfully abolished the autonomy of the provinces of Voivodina and Kosovo and brought them under direct Serbian control. This move was seen as a step to end Serbia's 'second-class status' within Yugoslavia. Peasants and small-town residents were mobilized in 'spontaneous' demonstrations to drive from office local bureaucrats in these provinces loyal to Tito's decentralist precepts. People's power was being manipulated to forestall genuine democratic change and channel discontent along nationalist lines. Thus Milošević anticipated post-communist nationalists elsewhere in the region who in the 1990s would also pursue top-down populist campaigns for their own power-conserving ends. An orthodox communist with no nationalist programme of his own, he was prepared to borrow the 'narratives of suffering' of Serb intellectuals who had been complaining ineffectually that the Serbs had been punished for their 'large numbers' when in fact they deserved to be seen as the state-building people of Yugoslavia on account of being the first of the South Slav peoples to acquire territorial independence.[12]

Elsewhere in Yugoslavia, Milošević's assertion of Serbian national demands was seen as a power-grab designed to reconstitute the federation around its most numerous ethnic grouping. The Slovenian communist party, followed reluctantly by its counterparts in Croatia and eventually Macedonia, formulated national demands of its own based on resistance to absorption in a 'Greater Serbia'. In the face of this threat, the Slovenian and Croatian communists abandoned the Yugoslav communist party in January 1990, eighteen months before the state ceased to exist. (In the end only Montenegro opted not to break away, choosing to remain with Serbia in a Yugoslav federation after a referendum in 1992.)

The seeds of disintegration had already been sown in Tito's time. The 1974 constitution had devolved power away from the centre to the republican leaderships. The aim was to preserve a communist multi-ethnic state after Tito (who died in 1980) by allowing each of the constituent elements in the federation to exercise power. Instead, the unwieldy post-Tito framework left a vacuum at the centre and encouraged rivalry between regional communist parties which had rival interests based, in large part, on the differing economic conditions and needs of the republics. By the late 1980s, Yugoslavia appeared to be evolving from a decentralized republic to a loose association of states.[13] Serbia's attempt to fill the power vacuum on its terms hastened the process of dissolution, especially when force was seen as a legitimate goal.

Elections were held in each of the Yugoslav republics in 1990. These were supervised by the local communist party and the aim was to acquire popular legitimacy for the objective of the republican leaderships whether it be Serb centralism, confederalism or secession. Democratization was not the chief priority of the post-communist national elites. Whatever chances there were of Yugoslavia embarking upon a Spanish-style transition depended on federal elections taking place.[14] Federal elections were urged in 1990 by the reformist federal Premier Ante Marković and might have resulted in a transnational coalition of forces committed to a looser but democratic federation. Significantly, hardliners in Serbia and reform communists in Slovenia and Croatia were at one in agreeing that under no circumstances should federal elections be held.[15]

The emergence of nomenklatura nationalism

In Romania and Bulgaria, communists regrouped under the banner of nationalism, but the stakes were not as high as in former Yugoslavia and the tactics employed were not as reckless. There was no perceived threat to the national territory which could justify draconian steps against untrustworthy minorities. Turkey and Hungary, though concerned about their large minorities in Bulgaria and Romania, never pursued an irredentist strategy to recover territory which had previously been under their rule. Besides, in their mature stages, the Romanian and Bulgarian regimes had already exploited nationalism for crude political advantage. The negative images of their systems, which were despotic even by communist standards, arose partly through the nationalist excesses associated with personal dictators, Nicolae Ceauşescu in Romania and Bulgaria's Todor Zhivkov, who invested a great deal of energy in seeking to assimilate or expel their problematic minorities. So post-communists seeking a new identity could not embrace nationalism with impunity as it had already been taken out of the communist refrigerator and employed as a weapon by now discredited party bosses. They had to move with circumspection. Nevertheless, in the scramble for power involving hardline and reform communists, nationalism was not a weapon that could easily be discarded. It remained a key form of mobilization in societies with collapsing institutions and was the only collective appeal which the masses had responded to with any degree of enthusiasm during the communist era. Ion Iliescu, who became Romania's leader in 1990 after years of disgrace in which he had disassociated himself from Ceauşescu's national communism, may have concluded that the requirements of political survival compelled him to make an accommodation with nationalism. Surveying the Balkans in the early 1990s, one Belgrade sociologist made the following perhaps apposite comment:

> the leaders who refuse to be swept away from the competitive political scene have no other choice but to revert to nationalism. Extremism is forced upon leaders by the competitive forces and those who are not ready to accept nationalistic ways will be ruthlessly displaced by those who are.[16]

In Albania, national communism may have been pursued longer and with more irrational energy than anywhere else under the xenophobe Enver Hoxha (in power from 1944 to 1985). But when his successors engaged in a cosmetic form of liberalization in the early 1990s, they were unable to appeal to popular nationalism in a bid to perpetuate their rule: there were no highly visible or problematic minorities other than a small Greek one; no serious threat to the territorial integrity of the state could be observed; and the Albanians in Kosovo were too remote after two generations of rigid isolation to offer a rallying cry when their persecution from Belgrade got underway. The rapid collapse of the post-communist regime of Ramiz Alia may, in no small measure, have been due to its failure to manufacture nationalist diversions that could have lessened popular indignation about appalling living standards.

What will henceforth be described as nomenklatura nationalism enjoyed the longest lease of life wherever leaderships were able to convince large numbers of citizens that there was a perceived threat to national survival from within and without and that physically defending the 'homeland' should take precedence over all other state responsibilities.[17] The threat to national survival was most easily communicated to the wider populace in Serbian parts of the former Yugoslavia. Milošević generated mass emotions about the province of Kosovo, overwhelmingly Albanian in population but seen as the historic cradle of the Serb nation. His rise to the top coincided with a campaign by the state media in which Albanians were de-humanized and branded as 'terrorists', 'secessionists', 'rapists' or 'tourists' who had no right to be occupying Serbian land and whose position in Kosovo was a transitory one.[18] The scale of the perceived threat was used as an excuse to suspend political rights existing elsewhere in the federation, and after Serbia took full control of Kosovo in early 1990 the Albanian population was subjected to systematic discrimination.[19] When other republics, notably Croatia and Bosnia, broke away from a Serb-dominated Yugoslavia in 1991–2 they became the targets of Serb aggression. Milošević warned that the break-up of Yugoslavia (which he more than anyone else had engineered) was turning the Serbs of Croatia and Bosnia, into minorities likely to face persecution. He offered to place them under his protection and he financed and armed groups in both territories ready to oblige him by asking for the intervention of the pro-Serb central state.

In Romania and Bulgaria government leaders condemned demands for 'affirmative action' programmes from minorities arguing that they would fuel unacceptable aspirations for autonomy and undermine the security of the state.[20] Chauvinists close to the government demanded martial law and even firmer measures against 'the enemy within'. But, unlike ex-Yugoslavia, extremists – though politically useful to post-communist rulers – were not able to translate their maximalist demands into action.

To differing degrees, Iliescu and his much weaker Bulgarian counter-parts felt that the stabilization of their regimes was dependent on Western diplomatic and financial assistance, so they could not indulge the crude ambitions of their chauvinist allies. In Romania, not without success, Iliescu adroitly manoeuvred between his ethnocentric domestic allies and inter-national agencies before alienating the former during the final years of his presidency.[21] But during the years marking the eclipse and violent break-up of Yugoslavia (1990–3), Milošević first ignored and then brazenly defied international opinion. An incongruous group of countries and power centres, from Germany, Austria and the Vatican to Turkey and Iran, were seen as plotting the utter destruction of Serbdom.[22] The outside world was seen as fundamentally hostile to Serb interests. In May 1992 when the United Nations (UN) voted to impose trade sanctions on Serbia, it was seen by the state media as confirmation of a global conspiracy, and it contributed to the siege mentality gripping a large part of the population.

A sense of isolation and threat desensitized apolitical citizens and provided a convenient screen for an acquisitive and corrupt governing style to be established. Milošević and his influential wife Mirjana Markovic acquired tight control over the state economy by issuing licences and contracts to favoured supporters. Elsewhere in South-East Europe privatization was carried out on a discretionary basis. Capitalists with a background in the nomenklatura were the chief beneficiaries of an ill-planned lurch towards the semblance of a market economy, or a pseudo-privatization. Often the new economic oligarchy enjoyed a privileged relationship with the regime which enabled 'nomenklatura capitalists' to evade taxes and profit from the black economy, with the complicity of very senior officials. Huge fortunes were made through exploiting powerful connections, by speculative practices (obtaining unsecured loans from state banks for instance), by seizing private property in war conditions, or by smuggling arms, drugs or people. In Romania, the redistribution of state wealth was carried out more judiciously than in Serbia or even Bulgaria, but in ethnically divided Transylvania privatization went ahead according to ethnic criteria. Ex-members of the nomenklatura distributed prime assets among themselves, arguing that Hungarians must be excluded on the grounds that their true allegiances were to a neighbouring state.[23] Nationalism was therefore manipulated in order to 'reinforce longstanding patterns of corruption and clientelism in the region'.[24]

Perhaps an even greater threat to ethnic peace was the elevation into senior positions of groups ready to take nationalism much further in order to obtain sectional advantages or else because they were 'true believers'. In Serbia organized criminals have patronized nationalist associations and causes in order to find a respectable cover for their activities. In Serbia, Croatia and Bosnia bands of youths made a living through violence, or threats of violence, enjoying the protection of politicians.[25] Unreconstructed elements of the state intelligence service in a number of countries have promoted ethnic strife at the local level to justify their continued existence or else at the behest of influential patrons.[26] *Émigrés* with a romantic view of their former homeland have bankrolled militant nationalist causes and, in the case of Croatia, have become a powerful lobby inducing the Tudjman government to emulate many of the hardline policies of its Serbian counterpart.

The manipulation of democracy

Nomenklatura nationalists deemed it expedient to obtain a popular mandate for their rule. In Romania, Serbia and Bulgaria there was no delay in the holding of elections. Early excursions to the polls took place before opposition forces could properly organize themselves. In each of these countries, the ruling left relied on much the same electoral power-bases: voters in small towns and villages, the new working class, old people and mothers who feared that tenuous family security would be jeopardized by the introduction of the market economy.[27] They had grown used to being centrally directed by the state and often found the sudden eruption of noisy, competing parties difficult to accept. Left-wing populists knew how to appeal to their sensibilities, offering social protection and a defence of national values to bewildered citizens fearing the disruption of routines established in communist times. Balkan ex-communists talked the language of democracy for foreign consumption, but at best they were committed (as in Romania) to an enlightened brand of autocracy with some democratic mechanisms and at worst (as in Serbia) to a predatory gangster state where the rule of law scarcely applied and where the ruling family was usually unrestrained by any constitutional checks and balances.

As late as 1989, Milošević described himself as 'a communist by conviction': when asked about the prospects for a multi-party system, he said that he preferred 'a system without parties'.[28] In Romania, the National Salvation Front (NSF) initially called for democratic mechanisms within the ruling party which would, in Iliescu's words, become 'a platform of national unity'.[29] But when such an approach proved untenable, it quickly moved to hold early elections in which it sought to preserve its monopoly of power by denying any competitive advantage to the opposition.

A fragmented opposition was composed of personality-based parties with diffuse programmes unaware of which classes or social groups constituted their electoral base. In desperation, they sometimes latched on to nationalism in a usually forlorn effort to outdo the ruling party in patriotic zeal.[30] Unable to campaign in rural areas because of intimidation or a lack of resources, the opposition found its progress impeded in many of the cities. Thanks to the social engineering policies of the communist era, ex-peasants formed a numerically significant grouping in the huge housing estates which ringed Balkan cities. Heavy industry drives from the 1950s onwards had created a social formation whose members can be described as 'worker-peasants' or neo-urbanites. Often poorly educated and trapped between a rural world they couldn't return to and an urban world in which their future prospects were bleak, they were a ready-made constituency for nationalists rather than the liberal opposition. The Serbian civic activist Vesna Pesić has written that 'liberalism offered only uncertainty and little in the way of identity. It identified itself with an unfamiliar civic culture which would take a long time to gather strength after having been pulverised under communism.'[31] Nationalists, who offered disorientated or alienated workers a social category within which they could locate themselves, obviously were in a much stronger position.[32]

Perhaps the hardest thing for reluctant or bogus democrats, like Iliescu and Milošević, to swallow was not the presence of liberal critics but the fact that the ruling party could no longer monopolize expressions of nationalism. Separate nationalist parties emerged which regarded foreign models of politics and economic change with suspicion and refused to abide by international norms in handling national minorities, often calling for mass repression or expulsions. There is plenty of evidence that elements in the Romanian and Serb elites initially promoted extremist parties to weaken the opposition and make the ruling party look good abroad in comparison to such dangerous forces. But whatever degree of collusion may have existed between them, nationalist parties were soon able to carve out an existence independent of nomenklatura forces. They acquired support in areas where the nationalist majority was in danger of being outnumbered by the minority or where workers facing economic threats could be persuaded that assertive minorities were somehow behind them. A party like Vojislav Šešelj's Serbian Radical Party (SRS) was able to benefit enormously from the popular indignation stemming from economic sanctions against Serbia and the huge influx of refugees when the wars of the Yugoslav succession started to turn against Belgrade. The Serbian and Romanian ex-communists won convincing pluralities in elections held in December 1989 and May 1990 respectively.[33] But in subsequent polls, Milošević's Socialist Party of Serbia (SPS) and Iliescu's National Salvation Front/Party of Social Democracy lost their overall majorities thanks not least to the strength of the nationalist blocs. In Bulgaria, the Socialists won an overall parliamentary majority in the two-round elections of 10 and 17 June 1990, but they were not strong enough to hold the line against the urban anti-communist opposition.[34] The Bulgarian left was divided over strategy and there was no one able to play the nationalist card with the skill or ruthlessness seen in other Balkan states. It suffered a major defeat in August 1990 when Zheliu Zhelev, a veteran dissident and enemy of ultra-nationalism, was elected President.

Constitutions were rapidly promulgated in 1990–1 which gave elevated positions to the majority nation and (except in Bulgaria) bestowed strong executive powers on the President.[35] The holders of these posts in Serbia and Romania were men without ideology, skilled at fashioning a consti-tuency of support from the vast party–state bureaucracy and who focused most of their energies on retaining power. Milošević relied more heavily on nationalism than Iliescu once it became clear to him that he had no chance of being leader of a multi-ethnic Yugoslavia. Instead, his aim (at least from 1989 to 1993) was to unite the Serb-populated areas in other republics outside Serbia in a state joined with his own known as the Federal Republic of Yugoslavia. Serb revolts in Croatia and Bosnia, which led to the expulsion and killing of non-Serbs in large numbers, were prepared under Milošević's supervision well in advance of formal declarations of independence in Croatia and Bosnia according to Borislav Jović, a former President of Yugoslavia and long-standing ally of Milošević.[36]

External factors strengthen nomenklatura nationalism

Western disarray in responding to the Yugoslav crisis, and the tendency of most major international players to regard the crisis as a humanitarian one rather than a political emergency that required outside intervention, emboldened Milošević in his defiance of world opinion. A policy of containment in the Balkans, preventing its nationalist tensions contaminating the rest of Europe and upsetting an uneasy Cold War power balance, hardened into a solid reflex. Milošević may well have known, through the extensive contacts he enjoyed with US diplomats and financiers, that Western policy-makers did not have high expectations of the Balkans; for there was indeed a long track-record of recognizing ambitious and unscrupulous authoritarian leaders as truly representative of their peoples. It is certainly true that, up to 1996, less energy and resources have been committed by Western governments and transnational bodies to nurturing democracy in South-East Europe than to Central or Southern Europe. The sense of fatalism about the potentialities of local Balkan elites and their populations to aspire to good government and reasonable forms of conduct has been high in the West for a century or more. Milošević, an English speaker who had resided in the USA before 1985, must have known the reputation of the Balkans in the metropolitan West: he may have assumed that a nationalist power-grab would have been viewed as a typical local occurrence rather than a violation of post-1945 European values, among influential statemen who may not really have regarded the Balkans as part of Europe.[37]

But though Milošević may have shrewdly anticipated the broad Western reaction to his power-grab, it is not at all clear that he knew how destructive were the forces of nationalism that he was playing with. It has been argued that the Serb leader did not expect his aggression in Bosnia to spiral into a three-year war unsurpassed for fifty years in its brutality at least in Europe.[38] The renowned Belgrade journalist Milos Vasić has written that 'the Pandora's Box of ethnic war went out of control and ... he himself [Milošević] was surprised ... that the war of ethnic extermination gained such a momentum as to make it a self-supporting suicidal machine'.[39]

Despite the grave setbacks his nationalist strategy encountered, Milosevic's brand of ethnic politics was sufficiently attractive to be emulated to varying degrees in countries which had been the victims of Serbian war aims or saw themselves as threatened by them. President Franjo Tudjman of Croatia emulated Milošević's expansionism, being even more obsessed with the idea of acquiring as much territory from the remains of Yugoslavia as possible, however flimsy Croatian claims were. The two state leaderships, which were at war in 1991–2, could nevertheless agree on the desirability of partitioning Bosnia-Hercegovina between them, if not the exact demarcation lines. Tudjman insisted that Croatia was an integral part of 'enlightened' Central Europe but his party's, 'symbiotic relationship with the Croatian state makes it more like the old communist party state than a 'normal' western-style political party'.[40]

Tudjman managed, unlike Milošević, to keep violent chauvinists within the ruling party fold where they shared the spoils of dubious privatization measures with ex-communists. The influence of militants from western Hercegovina (part of Bosnia rather than Croatia) in national politics helps to explain why state-led chauvinism has been pursued more ruthlessly in Croatia than in Serbia. Even the beleagured Muslim-led state in Bosnia has seen the rise of a majoritarian party, the Party of Democratic Action (SDA), which combines an increasingly ethnic appeal with a desire to monopolize important positions in politics, the economy and the military. It has become the vehicle for a confessional nationalism as a Muslim state nationalism begins to takes its place with the others in former Yugoslavia.[41]

Finally, the last years of President Sali Berisha's increasingly arbitrary rule in Albania (1991–7) also saw a gradual increase in bellicose nationalism in a bid to divert attention from domestic troubles.[42] Each of these countries (excepting Bosnia) had adopted a presidential system, the head of state rejecting the constraints of a civic state based on a clear separation of powers. It is hardly surprising that Milošević, Tudjman and Berisha have used similar language when claiming that they were ideally suited to interpret the national will and complete the process of nation-building, if necessary by enlarging the territory of their existing states.

Not until the 1995 NATO intervention in Bosnia were there concerted international efforts to persuade Balkan leaders to renounce their most flagrant authoritarian practices. It is unfortunate that Greece, the only Balkan state which has had a long-standing engagement with democratic institutions, declined to act as a champion of democracy in the area. Instead, in 1990, when Milošević was in dispute with the reformist Yugoslav Premier, Marković, Greece took the side of the former, which, according to one Greek critic of his country's Balkan policy, 'obstructed Serbia's democratization and sacrificed the interests of the Serbian people'.[43] Under different governments, Greece identified with the pan-Serb goals of Milošević's regime and indeed was Serbia's most consistent diplomatic ally up to 1995.[44] The cultural threat to Greece's sense of identity posed by the tiny Republic of Macedonia resulted in Athens imposing an economic blockade of its northern neighbour from 1993 to 1995. Domestic parties (with the exception of the far left), which had no economic incentives or record of competence to offer the Greek electorate, instead tried to outdo each other in their uncompromising approach to Greece's land-based neighbours with each of whom it was locked in some kind of dispute. That the only full EU and NATO member in the Balkans was prepared to act in such a high-handed way did not contribute to a cooling of ethnic passions in the region, nor does it suggest that the acquisition of democratic government can insulate a Balkan state and its society from the furies of nationalism.

Resistance to the ethnic appeal

Despite these tendencies, there are other Balkan states where, instead of victimizing minorities, the ruling elite has left them alone or even conciliated them. In Bulgaria during early 1990, the still-ruling Bulgarian Communist Party (BCP) sought to dampen down inter-ethnic tensions. This was a time when mass anti-Turkish rallies in the provinces were mobilizing larger numbers than the pro-democracy ones which had occurred a short time before. One analyst reckons that the progressive wing of the BCP assisted the non-nationalist opposition, seeing this strategy as the best way of absorbing the anti-Turkish vote into its own ranks.[45] Uncertainty about whether or not to use the ethnic card weakened the ruling party and resulted in nomenklatura nationalism failing to achieve its undoubted potential in the transition period. All the major players in politics also adopted a reasonable stance towards the new state of Macedonia. Bulgaria became the first state to recognize Macedonia, but it was reluctant to concede that there was a separate Macedonian nation, owing to the close affinity between the two Slavic peoples and to the widespread Bulgarian perception that they were unjustly robbed of Macedonia by the machinations of the great powers when Bulgaria was formed in 1878.[46]

There are also several new states which emerged from the collapsing Yugoslav and Soviet federations where anti-minority nationalism was not pursued – Macedonia is clearly in the Balkans, Moldavia as part of Romania from 1918 to 1940 was a Balkan entity, while the Ukraine is not. In each of them, parties descended from the ex-ruling communist parties have retained control in usually free and open elections. Inter-ethnic co-operation has been promoted for a number of reasons. The need for these fragile new states, each of which obtained independence in unexpected circumstances, to win international legitimacy by adhering to recognized norms of conduct in their treatment of minorities is one obvious factor. The reluctance to antagonize a powerful neighbour whose co-ethnics make up a large portion of the minority population is certainly a factor which weighed upon the minds of the post-independence Moldavan and Ukrainian leaderships, which needed to secure the loyalty of Russian minorities whose fate is closely followed in Moscow. Finally, in Macedonia, the popularity and leadership skills of Kiro Gligorov, a former communist committed to Tito's pragmatic ethnic policies, helped to keep in check tensions between the Slav majority and the growing Albanian minority. Until 1998 Gligorov's Social Democratic Union ruled in conjunction with moderate Albanian parties. But radical Albanian parties, growing in popularity, demand constituent nation status and a degree of autonomy. In response, the state authorities insist on individual equal rights rather than group rights for non-Slavic minorities. However, Albanian discontent is mounting in the late 1990s because of accumulating evidence that lower-ranking state officials discriminate against them and even deny them proper access to basic individual rights.[47]

The danger is that if the external threat to Macedonia recedes (from the larger and hitherto unfriendly states of Serbia and Greece) the incentive for the ex-communist elite to conciliate its minorities may, in turn, recede, increasing the chances of acute internal instability. A history of rivalry or conflict between dominant and subordinate ethnic groups in the Balkans (and further afield) means that few states are ready to accept minority demands with equanimity. States and boundaries have proven transient for the last century or more so that yesterday's minorities have sometimes become today's majorities and vice versa. The tendency of nation-building efforts following the collapse of dynastic empires to be in turn subverted by invasion, war and revolution has made the national majority wary about conceding territorial autonomy or the status of constituent nation to large or concentrated minorities.

Minority demands

The demands of national minorities vary in scale and intensity. The goal of secession, so that a minority can join up with a neighbouring state controlled by its co-ethnics, has openly been seen in the former Yugoslavia, whereas it was a fairly common aspiration in earlier waves of Balkan state-building. The ambition of 'all Serbs in one state' animated militants in Bosnia and Croatia in 1991–2 and was later emulated by Croats from the Hercegovina region of Bosnia. The only other minority with an explicitly separatist agenda is the Albanians of Kosovo, who are actually a majority in the province annexed by Serbia in 1990. Their leaders argue that since other Slavs could not tolerate Serbian rule, why should they, as Albanians, be attached to Serbia: when Yugoslavia was destroyed so was the Albanian ability to remain, claims Ibrahim Rugova, the leader of a parallel Albanian state in Kosovo.[48] But until 1998 the Kosovar Albanians pursued a strategy of non-violent civil disobedience, perhaps aware that there is no well-organized kin state ready to come to their assistance. Albania is too feeble to offer protection to its co-ethnics.

All Balkan minorities with a national consciousness seek institutions or laws which will give official recognition and protection of their identity.[49] Language is seen as the kernel of identity and demands for the public use of a minority language in the courts and the local administration – as well as the right to be educated in it up to university level, and to enjoy access to radio and TV broadcasts in it – are usually the most common ones in the minority platform. The achievement of many of these rights by minorities in Western Europe after 1945 gives Balkan minorities a benchmark upon which to base their claims. Encouragement has also been provided by attempts by the Council of Europe to codify minority rights and draw up a minimum standard binding on its members.[50] Membership of this body is seen as an important gateway which will prepare ex-communist states for possible membership of NATO or the EU. A supportive international environment has encouraged most Balkan minorities to use pragmatic rather than militant tactics to obtain cultural and economic rights rather than pursue the high-risk strategy of secession or territorial autonomy. But fear of the ruthlessness of nomenklatura nationalism as it was seeking to burnish its patriotic credentials and erase the stain of communism may have also been a restraining factor for discontented minorities.

Nationalism becomes a liability

Gradually, ex-communists like Milošević and Iliescu found the nationalism which they had licensed was of declining effectiveness and even posed a threat to their long-term survival. To his chagrin, Milošević lost control of the Bosnian Serb leadership which had already used exceptional brutality by driving out non-Serbs from large areas of Bosnia so as to create an ethnically pure territory. In May 1993, when his rebellious protégés rejected the UN-sponsored Owen–Vance agreement which would have given them control of 49 per cent of Bosnia, Milošević told the self-styled Bosnian Serb Assembly that 'I don't know what you want. You have to understand that I cannot help you anymore.'[51] By now international sanctions were beginning to cripple the Serbian economy and Milošević felt the need to distance himself from political and military officials who would shortly be facing international war crimes charges. In August 1994, after his pleas for the acceptance of a new peace plan were rejected, he severed ties with the Bosnian Serb leadership, closing the border to all traffic save humanitarian aid.[52]

Milošević was an inauthentic practitioner who used nationalism as an instrument to fulfil his wider ambitions. Not without success, he underwent a metamorphosis after 1993 from 'Butcher of the Balkans' to 'the man who was the indispensable key to regional peace'. The volte-face was a cruel blow to the 'true believers' of the Greater Serbia project. The party, military and state media were purged of elements who could not adapt quickly enough to the new position. But the internal upheavals were limited because it is clear that the bulk of his officials also had an instrumental view of nationalism. There were no powerful indigenous bodies such as a state church, peasant movements, or sporting and cultural organizations which had promoted nationalist values as ends in themselves, and would refuse to brook any scaling down of national demands. So, in his opportunistic approach to nationalism, Milošević was representative of the power-elite as a whole.

Even on the war front, deals were made by supposedly deadly enemies, involving the sale of weapons or material goods, which suggested that not a few of the protagonists in a war of 'ancient ethnic hatreds' were primarily motivated by greed and plunder. A British journalist who covered the Yugoslav wars has written that 'Serbia has conducted the war in Croatia and Bosnia with such cynicism that it is hardly surprising that for many "defending Serbdom" was indistinguishable from making money'.[53]

But Milošević had a credibility problem in trying to explain to his own people why he was abandoning Serb minorities in Croatia and Bosnia who were after all the pretext for his rush into war in 1990–1. By 1993 the sanctions with which the West had retaliated had cut industrial output by two-thirds, and in a country of ten million people had left only one million in formal jobs. Such a record of failure was bound to invite a backlash perhaps even in a country whose traditions of social protest were as weak as Serbia's.

In Romania, not a few citizens were also able to see that nationalist rhetoric had been a convenient screen behind which a new class of state-backed capitalists could become fabulously wealthy, while living standards plummeted and the unreformed economy sunk deeper into recession. But at least Iliescu had avoided territorial adventures (such as trying to regain Moldova which had been part of Romania before 1940) or active persecution of the Hungarian minority. He walked a tight-rope seeking to satisfy the West that Romania was shedding its communist past and embracing pluralism and the free market, while giving radical nationalists influence via the media, local government and the privatized economy. Chauvinists who had shored up a pro-Iliescu minority government in parliament finally deserted him in 1996 when he made what were seen as unacceptable concessions to the West, above all a bilateral treaty ending the long-running quarrel with Hungary.[54] The loss of nationalist backing was a prelude to his defeat in the presidential election of November 1996. By now, evidence from across the region suggests that appeals to ethnic prejudices were proving less effective as vote-winners. All the ex-nomenklatura regimes of the Balkans had records of economic incompetence or worse and voters were starting to scrutinize their records and intentions far more sceptically than before. There was growing accept-ance of competing parties and programmes and growing awareness that prospects for a peaceful existence and economic recovery were not advanced by constant references to race and nation.

The decline of Balkan left nationalism

Ruling left-wing parties faced unprecedented popular opposition in Serbia, Romania and Bulgaria in 1996–7. The challenge took different forms and specific local circumstances shaped its character and outcome. But the broad regional context in which nomenklatura rule was being challenged should not be ignored. First, the forces of militant Serb nationalism and their erstwhile patrons in Belgrade suffered resounding military and political defeats which were formalized by the Dayton Peace Accord of November 1995. The belated but firm actions by the international community in ex-Yugoslavia, culminating in NATO's direct intervention, could not be ignored by other left nationalist rulers in the area. Indeed they may have restrained rulers with an anti-minority agenda from carrying through some of their plans.

Second, a number of decisions were taken by the Western powers which suggest, perhaps for the first time, a willingness on the part of the Atlantic democracies to incorporate the Balkan states in post-Cold War security plans for Europe. NATO launched a Partnership for Peace programme in 1994 which Balkan states were able to join in 1995, and it invited former Warsaw Pact members to apply to join NATO as full members. Moreover, the USA actively promoted the South-East Europe Co-operation Initiative in 1996–7 in order to improve multilateral links between Balkan states. There was now an awareness on the part of the architects of the Dayton Accord that the success of the initiative depended in part on efforts to delegitimate conflictual nationalism in the Balkans as a whole. So not only were there greater costs to be incurred by leaders who exploited the politics of ethnicity; but there were some grounds for hoping that a rejection of strident nationalism might bring positive rewards for Balkan states which had known only isolation and economic decline since the end of the Cold War.

The Romanian elections of 1996 were the first indication that the balance of power was starting to swing away from ruling ex-communists due to their policy failures and the changing geo-political environment across the region. Largely conspicuous by its absence was the manipulation of nationalism, which in the previous two elections (1990 and 1992) had been 'an enormous diversion destined . . . to indefinitely delay the democratization of Romanian society and the alternation of power'.[55] A peaceful campaign, a high turnout and the election to the presidency of a leading liberal committed to pacifying inter-ethnic conflict suggested that Romanian political culture might be outgrowing the Balkan stereotype dominated by images of nationalism, partisanship and collectivist values.[56] Meanwhile in Bulgaria, the reckless economic policies of the BSP, re-elected with an absolute majority in 1994, produced huge demonstrations, forcing the party to abandon office in January 1997 and agree to early elections. These were won the following April by the centre-right UDF, which abandoned the pro-Russian orientation of its predecessor and showed itself far more willing to mend fences with the Muslim minority.

Overshadowing these regime changes were the unprecedented mass protests in Serbia against Milošević's rule which lasted through the winter of 1996–7. Centre-right opposition parties overcame their divisions and were prepared to make overtures to the Albanians in Kosovo which hitherto would have been viewed as political suicide, given the widely held Serbian view that Serb control of the province was non-negotiable. Faced with demonstrations of up to 500,000 people which latterly included many from the middle and even working classes who had hitherto remained on the sidelines, Milošević made unprecedented concessions to his opponents. The opposition Zajedno alliance was allowed to gain control of town halls in the main cities which it had won in the 1996 local elections and Milošević temporarily relaxed his grip on the state media. But the opposition failed to capitalize on its advantage and Milosevic soon recovered the initiative. Instead of pushing for an interim all-party administration pending free and fair parliamentary elections, rival opposition personalities quarrelled about how to divide up power which was not yet in their grasp. Miodrag Perišić summed up their failure succinctly: 'we had public opinion on our side, and the international community, and the media, but we made the same old silly mistake. We fragmented.'[57] A disillusioned electorate swung to the ultra-nationalist SRS in the September 1997 parliamentary elections. It took one-third of the seats on a platform of social demagoguery which appealed to apolitical voters 'fed up with years of economic deprivation, corruption . . . and isolation by a hostile West'.[58] The SRS leader, Šešelj, actually won the run-off presidential election held on 5 October 1997, but the election was declared invalid owing to the fact that less than half the electorate turned out. Reformist chances had been dashed by the huge exodus of young people from Serbia (perhaps as many as 200,000) during the war years. Already by 1992, one-third of voters consisted of pensioners, many of whom were suspicious of the democratic opposition.[59]

Where the liberal opposition offers no viable alternative to a corrupt regime and where a seemingly hostile West appears ready to confine Serbia to limbo for years to come, it is no surprise that an electorate desensitized by war and sanctions opts in large numbers for a quasi-fascist ready once more to make Serbia a force to be reckoned with in the Balkans. Interestingly, the hardline option was rejected in October 1997 in presidential elections held in the smaller republic of Montenegro which, with Serbia, makes up rump Yugoslavia. There the ruling party was split between pro-Milošević loyalists and modernizers keen to mend fences with the West; the modernizers' candidate, Milo Djukanović, won a narrow victory. Montenegro, with its access to the sea and limited responsibility for the war, enjoys better prospects of normalizing ties with the West than its landlocked and overpopulated partner. Its minorities are also prepared to vote in elections, unlike the Albanians in Kosovo who, by boycotting the polls, give Serb hardliners an in-built advantage. For these reasons, Montenegran voters were better able to envisage a brighter future for their territory than their Serb counterparts, which explains why a nationalism anchored in the past enjoys less appeal. When the defeated candidate contested the validity of the result at the behest of Milošević and started to stir up inter-ethnic tension, the West intervened to assert that the election (supervised by the Organization for Security and Co-operation in Europe, OSCE) had been fair and that any attempt to overturn the results would prove very costly for the Belgrade regime.[60] Such external backing for local moderates had been conspicuous by its absence in ex-Yugoslavia during the early 1990s.[61] As a new ingredient it can play a role in reviving stalled transitions, but only where the democratic opposition gives evidence of a capacity to supplant authoritarian nationalism.

Nationalism outlives the Left: the case of Romania

It should not be assumed that the decline of parties with roots in the communist era will mark the eclipse of nationalism in the Balkans. As long as falling living and health standards characterize the Balkan states, there will be a receptive audience for chauvinists who seek scapegoats in this time of troubles and who emphasize ethnic purity, indigenous values and the subjugation of minorities. Evidence from Serbia and Romania in the late 1990s suggests that chauvinist parties promoting classic right-wing nationalist themes will be able to survive the decline of nomenklatura parties which originally nurtured them.

An even bigger worry is that reformist parties unable to offer economic relief to demoralized voters will seek to soften the blow by appealing themselves to a sense of ethnic solidarity. This need not be an entirely negative phenomenon. In the past small states in Northern and Western Europe have invoked a sense of patriotism in order to obtain popular backing for reforms requiring austerity, patience and endurance. Judy Batt has written that 'nationalism has the potential to breathe life into new democracies by mobilising dispirited and apathetic electorates, but at the same time relieving the pressure of popular material demands which the economy cannot satisfy'.[62] But for such an appeal to work, the public administration must enjoy a reputation for efficiency and honesty and pro-reform party interests must be prepared to shelve their normal political ambitions.

In Bulgaria during 1997, the quiet way in which the new UDF government has gone about dealing with a disastrous economic situation suggests that it might be capable of such self-limiting behaviour. By contrast, in Romania, the first year in office of the centre-right government showed how difficult it was for even a liberal and well-meaning figure like Premier Victor Ciorbea to carry out institutional reforms and deal with immediate crises. The inexperience of ministers, the poor calibre of many top civil servants, and the inefficient two-chamber parliament meant that progress in re-starting a stalled political and economic reform process was slow. To make matters worse, factionalism within and between parties led to weeks of governmental paralysis in 1997. Thus, it was confirmed that the polarized pluralism and disdain for compromise emerged as salient features of Romanian political culture.

Within elites characterized by a high degree of infighting, rejection of 'the other' can easily extend to unassimilated minorities or to a neighbouring state which has been a historic rival. At the outset, the Ciorbea government pledged to address minority concerns and normalize relations with Hungary. But it soon became clear that the divided reformers would be unable to combine austerity policies and a pragmatic approach to the Hungarian minority and the Hungarian state without paying a high political price. Not only have sections of the mainstream press been ready to flirt with chauvinism amidst a battle for a shrinking pool of readers, but elements in the linchpin of the coalition, the National Peasant and Christian Democratic Party (PNTCD), have done the same in order to advance their careers. Thus, only slow progress has been made by government moderates who wish to soften the state's rigid approach to ethnic diversity.

The convention that the state must govern in the name of the ethnic majority has influential adherents beyond the leftist and openly chauvinist parties in South-East Europe. The desirability of reconciliation with problematic minorities is still not cherished as an end in itself which can subdue debilitating quarrels and strengthen the cohesion of state and society as they are confronted by the immense challenge of breaking free from communist structures and mentalities. Instead, it is viewed as an inconvenient extra tariff required to board the European train and win the favour of multilateral organizations like NATO and the EU.

A fractious political elite in Romania sees European integration as necessary for national recovery (and perhaps even survival), but there are deep reservations about renouncing the nationalist complexes which the founders of the European integration project challenged in the 1940s and 1950s. Since 1995 whenever prospects for integration with European institutions have faltered, so has Romanian enthusiasm for a post-nationalist agenda. It is no coincidence that Romania seemed to discard its anti-Hungarian complex in the first half of 1997 when it looked like having a real chance of being invited to join NATO at the July Madrid summit. There were cordial top-level bilateral meetings, declarations of a strategic partnership between Romania and Hungary, and laws were drawn up in Bucharest to give the Hungarians some of the cultural and linguistic rights they had long been demanding. But when NATO gently rebuffed Romania and the European Commission declined to recommend that she be one of the countries invited to open negotiation for EU membership, a mood of introspection allowed nationalist frustrations to return.[63] Gesture politics based on manipulating nationalist symbols took over: a nationalist mayor snatched the Hungarian flag from a newly opened Hungarian consulate in his city; then a young ambitious PNTCD Senator, seeking a popular following, blocked a law facilitating Hungarian-language education in state schools, unless the subjects of history and geography were taught at all times in Romanian. Across the region, there is a long tradition of such trivial incidents poisoning inter-ethnic relations and endlessly delaying reconciliation prospects.

However, given the popularity of the desire to 'return to Europe' and the advance of global communications which challenge the absolutist world-view of nationalism, chauvinists may well find it far harder to make capital out of the politics of ethnicity than in times past. Perhaps in a country like Romania, mainstream politicians as well as their supporters will acquire dual identities based on pro-Europeanism and nationalism, whichever element being in the ascendant depending on the degree of national security or insecurity felt at a given moment.

The future

In South-East Europe the resilience of intransigent nationalism has derived from historic experiences which left weak states in possession of contested territories and unable to evolve the institutions and laws capable of eliciting consent from the populations under their jurisdiction. Long periods of foreign occupations, wars, revolutions and local efforts to repulse unwelcome external interference and form states around indigenous values have shaped the history of the Balkan states down to the 1990s. In the post-communist years, nationalism has shaped, to differing degrees, the way Balkan states have recast their political and economic systems. But it is no longer an absolute 'given'. Bulgaria and Albania have experienced periods of prolonged instability but nationalism has not been the chief driving force behind upheavals which have had more to do with popular alienation at chronic misgovernment. In what was Yugoslavia, there is a sense of heightened nationalism in many of the new states which have emerged from Tito's broken federation. But even here qualifications need to be made. Contrary to expectation, Macedonia, once the most ethnically mixed part of Yugoslavia after Bosnia, has avoided chronic ethnic strife, and so far some efforts have been made to reflect the multicultural nature of the state in its governing arrangements. The other states of the federation have privileged nationalism, but so do new states in Central Europe like Slovakia and Latvia.

Nationalism will probably have plenty of staying power unless states begin to overcome their chronic economic difficulties. Majorities are less inclined to make room for minorities and more willing to listen to nationalist demagogues when economic prospects are bleak. The shift from a state-led to a market economy has led to millions of social casualties and has allowed new groups to prosper owing to their political connections and ability to bend or break the law. Even in Serbia, where no privatizations have taken place, the rise of a new 'red oligarchy' enables national populists to exploit the resultant social resentment. If parts of South-East Europe follow a Latin American developmental path with an entrenched oligarchy ruling a socially polarized and demoralized society, then nationalism will act as 'a seemingly natural bond uniting otherwise atomised members of a decayed society into meaningful groups'.[64] The state-versus-society cleavage is a chronic one in the Balkans, and unless it is narrowed native democracy will find it hard to put down sturdy roots. Nationalism is often the only thing that can fill the vacuum in states where civic associations are weak and the main political institutions lack prestige due to chronic malfunctioning.

But the social classes and cultural formations which nurtured ethnic appeals before are lacking or have diminishing strength. The numerically dominant peasantry has vanished and the poorly integrated working class, though capable of being 'a dangerous class' for some years ahead, is unlikely to be able to offer secure backing for chauvinists. Intellectuals, a key element in promoting radical nationalism before 1945, are more receptive to international liberal values. It was mediocre intellectuals, promoted by the communist state for their ideological services, who turned to nationalism in the early 1990s when it became clear that they lacked the professional skills to do well in meritocratic democracies.[65] Now that the challenges of globalization and European integration require university graduates with qualities and skills matching those to be found in the West, then it is perhaps the time when the East European nationalist intellectual with his inferiority complexes will start to retreat into history. The decline of religion as a variable that can be exploited by nationalists may well also reduce the capacity of nationalism to grow. In most Balkan countries where the Orthodox Church is the dominant faith, religion has lost much of its popular influence as a result of the damagingly close links the former often had with the communist authorities.

The only new social formation with a vested interest in promoting nationalism appears to be organized crime. Gangsters and entrepreneurs dealing in illegal commodities have a vested interest in ensuring that international conventions and laws do not impede their activities. Therefore it is natural for them to back chauvinist politicians who insist that only nationalist norms should shape state policy. In parts of ex-Yugoslavia there is already a close connection between local mafias and ultra-nationalists. War has prevented the growth of economies which supply the needs of the domestic market, employ large numbers of citizens in productive rather than speculative activities, and earn revenue from legitimate trading abroad. If the subterranean economy thrives elsewhere in the Balkans and criminal influence extends to the heart of the state, then it will not be surprising if an unapologetic chauvinism becomes an accessory of rogue capitalism.

The degree to which the European integration process extends to South-East Europe will probably have the most crucial bearing on the fortunes of nationalism. The desire to belong to a common European economic and security system enjoys an appeal in many Eastern lands only previously matched by extremist ideologies in the 1930s; this is especially so among intellectuals and the young. But if the European project falters or its benefits are confined to a select group of Central European states, with the Balkans relegated to an outer-Europe, then the resulting disillusionment could give a powerful impetus to radical nationalism.

There are at last some encouraging signs that Western policy-makers are no longer responding to Balkan instability with the policy of 'containment' which in the past allowed authoritarian rulers to be supported as guarantors of fitful stability. At the end of 1997, US President Bill Clinton's success in persuading his defeated presidential rival, former Congress leader Bob Dole, to support US troops staying in Bosnia beyond the original withdrawal date of 1998, suggests that radical nationalism in the Balkans is now seen as a threat to Western security as a whole rather than to the well-being of a few states on the margins of the continent. The decision of EU governments in the same month to overrule the Commission in Brussels and include Romania and Bulgaria in the enlargement process, though at a slower pace than their Central European neighbours, suggests that the risks of banishing these countries behind a new European partition might be seen as too great. Of course, the West will almost certainly make it clear that the pace at which integration takes place for Balkan states depends on how willing they are to pursue a post-nationalist strategy of guaranteeing minority rights, improving ties with neighbours, and pursuing regional co-operation.

NATO states, led by the USA, have imposed what in some quarters is seen as a protectorate over Bosnia, in order to turn a truce between warring factions into a lasting peace and begin the reconstruction of that shattered country. If followed through, the engagement is likely to be far longer than the one undertaken by Western forces to oversee the reconstruction of West Germany and its return to the community of free nations. In the spring of 1999 NATO launched an air war against the Milošević regime following the Serbian leader's failure to concede self-rule within Yugoslavia to the Kosovar Albanians and the launch of an intensified campaign of repression against them. A two-month air offensive forced Milošević to the negotiating table and in June 1999 a NATO-led international force took charge of the administration of Kosovo. NATO leaders have pledged to make the reconstruction of Kosovo part of a wider programme of integrating the Balkan region with west European economic and security structures. But the forces of conflictual nationalism may have been emboldened in countries profoundly shaken by the war, Serbia obviously but also Macedonia, and great sensitivity will be required by outside powers to keep these from overwhelming a tenuous peace process.

The tendency to view liberty as meaning primarily freedom from foreign control still has plenty of adherents in the region. It is unlikely that the Balkans will see the emergence of a powerful cosmopolitan movement promoting European values and downgrading nationalist ones. After all, no EU state (possibly with the exception of Italy) has yet seen such a phenomenon. Feelings of collective insecurity are bound to provide fertile ground for national populists even if, at last, democracy begins to sink firmer native roots in the region. Greece is an obvious example of how a myriad of social and economic frustrations have enabled nationalism to flourish in a fully democratic context. But if, with the assistance of multilateral organizations like the EU and NATO, economic and social reconstruction generates hope in the future, borders cease to be contested or act as insuperable barriers to regional co-operation, the mix of resentments and fears on which local nationalisms thrive might then begin to retreat.

Transnational co-operation in Western Europe after 1950 relegated the politics of ethnic antagonism that in the previous eighty years had caused more destruction in what today is known as 'the Golden Triangle', on account of its economic prosperity, than anything seen in the Balkans this century. Hopefully, if the initiative starts to swing slowly away from the devotees of national specificity towards liberal and civic forces at ease with multiple identities, it will become clear that South-Eastern Europe is not fundamentally different from the rest of the continent in terms of its political aspirations and democratic capabilities. But the extent of the region's problems suggest that quite a long time may have to elapse before it can be assumed that the age of nationalism has run its course. In Western Europe, state nationalism has only made way for the forces of globalization, interdependence and regional integration because economic contentment and a belief in collective security have eroded territorial identities. In parts of South-East Europe, the young and urban-based citizens clearly desire to be part of a broadly liberal international system based on interdependence and cultural pluralism. But the initiative will probably lie with devotees of collective nationalist values until the security and prosperity taken for granted by perhaps most West Europeans become recognizable features of life in the Balkans. As long as material prospects remain so uncertain, the politics of the region will probably revolve around non-negotiable values and absolutes to a greater extent than anywhere else in Europe.

Notes

1 Claus Offe, *Varieties of Transition: The East European and East German Experience*, London: Polity Press, 1996, p. 62.
2 See Charles and Barbara Jelavich, *The Balkans*, Englewood Cliffs: Prentice-Hall, 1965, chapter 1.
3 See Maria Todorova, 'The Balkans: from discovery to invention', *Slavic Review*, 53, 2, 1994.
4 A monograph which explores the failure of the inter-war South-European state to establish its authority is Irina Livezeanu, *Cultural Politics in Greater Romania*, Ithaca: Cornell University Press, 1995.
5 Aleksa Djilas, 'Fear thy neighbour: the break-up of Yugoslavia', in Charles Kupchan, ed.,

Nationalism and Nationalities in the New Europe, Ithaca: Cornell University Press, 1995, p. 91.

6 Ibid.

7 Zagorka Golubovic, 'Nationalism and democracy: the Yugoslav case', *Journal of Area Studies*, 3, 1993, p. 72.

8 See Mark Percival, 'Britain's political "Romance" with Romania in the 1970s', *Contemporary European History*, 4, 1, 1994, pp. 67–87.

9 R. R. King, *Minorities Under Communism*, Cambridge: Harvard University Press, 1971.

10 A succinct account of how Milosevic spent a decade manipulating nationalism is provided by Stan Markotich, 'A consummate politician and a pathological liar', *Transition*, 2, 18, 6 September 1996, pp. 18–21.

11 The former position is taken by V. P. Gagnon Jr, 'Serbia's road to war', in Larry Diamond and Marc Plattner, eds, *Nationalism, Ethnic Conflict and Democracy*, Baltimore and London: Johns Hopkins University Press, 1994, p. 118; the latter by Jovan Teokarevic's 'Neither war nor peace: Serbia and Montenegro in the first half of the 1990s', in D. A. Dyker and I. Vejvoda, eds, *Yugoslavia and After: A Study in Fragmentation, Despair and Rebirth*, London: Longman, 1996, pp. 180–1.

12 For the 'narratives of sufferings' phrase see Ivan Vejvoda, 'Yugoslavia 1945–91 – from decentralization without democracy to dissolution', in Dyker and Vejvoda, *Yugoslavia and After*, p. 20.

13 Teokarevic, 'Neither war', p. 181.

14 The importance of having all-state elections prior to regional ones in multi-ethnic states is emphasized in Juan Linz and Alfred Stepan, *Problems of Democratic Transition and Consolidation: Southern Europe, South America, and Post-Communist Europe*, Baltimore and London: Johns Hopkins University Press, pp. 99, 366–7.

15 Bogdan Denitch, *Ethnic Nationalism: The Tragic Death of Yugoslavia*, Minneapolis and London: Minnesota University Press, 1994), pp. 67–8.

16 Ljubomir Madzar, 'The roots of nationalism', *Balkan Forum*, 2, 1, 1994, p. 23.

17 The term 'nomenklatura nationalism' has previously been used by D. A. Dyker. See his article, 'Nomenklatura nationalism: the key to the new East European politics', *Australian Journal of History and Politics*, 41, 1995. The term 'chauvino-communist' is preferred by George Schöpflin. See his chapter, 'Nationalism and ethnicity in Europe, East and West', in Kupchan, ed., *Nationalism and Nationalities*, pp. 37–65. Meanwhile, 'apparat nationalism' is used by an international team who investigated recent conflicts in the Balkans. See *Unfinished Peace: report of the International Commission on the Balkans*, New York: Aspen Institute/Carnegie Endowment For International Peace, 1996, p. 149.

18 Tony Barber, *Independent*, London, 9 May 1993.

19 One of the best documented sources for internal conditions in Kosovo is the International Helsinki Federation for Human Rights, *From Autonomy to Colonization: Human Rights in Kosovo 1989–93*, New York: IHFHR, 1994.

20 Janusz Bugajski, 'The fate of minorities in Eastern Europe', in Diamond and Plattner, eds, *Nationalism*, p. 104.

21 His tactics are explained in Tom Gallagher, 'A feeble embrace: Romania's engagement with democracy, 1989–94', *Journal of Communist Studies and Transition Politics*, 12, 1996, pp. 145–72.

22 G. Parks, 'Cause or consequence: religion and the Balkan Wars', *Warreport*, April 1996, p. 20.

23 Tom Gallagher, *Romania After Ceauşescu: The Politics of Intolerance*, Edinburgh: Edinburgh University Press, 1995, p. 158.

24 Jacques Rupnik, 'Finishing the revolution', *Warreport*, March 1997, p. 17.

25 Mary Kaldor, 'Cosmopolitanism versus nationalism: the new divide', in Richard Caplan and John Feffer, eds, *Europe's New Nationalism: States and Minorities in Conflict*, Oxford: Oxford University Press, 1996, p. 52.

26 Hardline elements of Ceauşescu's repressive apparatus are widely thought to have been implicated in inter-ethnic strife which convulsed the city of Tirgu Mures in Romania during March 1990. See Gallagher, *Romania*, chapter 3.

27 Vesna Pesic, 'The cruel face of nationalism', in Diamond and Plattner, eds, *Nationalism*, pp. 134–5.

28 *Le Monde*, 12 July 1989, quoted in *Unfinished Peace*, pp. 25–6. Five years later, his influential wife observed that 'parliamentary democracy . . . suits the English but really does not look good on the Serbs': Laura Silber, *Financial Times*, 29 December 1994.

29 M. Calinescu and V. Tismaneanu, 'The 1989 Revolution and Romania's future', *Problems of Communism*, 1991, p. 52, n. 38.

30 Ivan Vejvoda, 'Opposition parties and movements', *Warreport*, June–July 1994, p. 4. For a Romanian example, see Gallagher, *Romania*, pp. 159–60.

31 Pesić, quoted in Gagnon Jr, 'Serbia's road to war', p. 118.

32 For an example of how this was done in the Transylvanian city of Cluj in 1992, see Tom Gallagher, 'Ultra-nationalists take charge in Transylvania's capital', *RFE-RL Research Report*, 1, 27 March 1992, p. 25.

33 In Serbia, in two-round elections held on 9 and 26 December 1990 the SPS won 77.6 per cent of the parliamentary seats with 45.8 per cent of the votes and Milosevic was elected President with 63.5 per cent of the votes cast. B92, Open Serbia, Belgrade, 19 December 1997, http://www.b92eng.opennet.org

   In Romania, the ruling FSN won 66.3 per cent of the votes on 20 May 1990 and Ion Iliescu was elected President with just over 85 per cent of the votes cast. Bogdan Szajkowski, ed., *Political Parties of Eastern Europe, Russia and the Successor States*, London: Longman, 1994, p. 346.

34 The BSP and its allies won 52.75 per cent of parliamentary seats. See Szajkowski, *Political Parties*, p. 104.

35 Vojin Dimitrijevic, 'Ethnonationalism and the constitutions: the apotheosis of the nation-state', *Journal of Area Studies*, 3, 1993, pp. 50–7.

36 Julian Borger, 'Wartime ally denounces Milosevic', *Guardian*, 31 January 1997. In September 1991 Ante Markovic, the last Premier of Yugoslavia, showed his cabinet the transcript of a wire-tap of a conversation between Milošević and the Bosnian Serb leader Radovan Karadžić which clearly suggests that Milošević had been orchestrating the first stages of fighting in 1991. See Tim Judah, *The Serbs: History, Myth and the Destruction of Yugoslavia*, New Haven and London: Yale University Press, 1997, p. 191.

37 The way a negative appraisal of the region and its peoples influenced the policy of a major West European state towards the Yugoslav crisis is examined in Jane O. Sharp, *Honest Broker or Perfidious Albion: British Policy in Former Yugoslavia*, London: IPPR, 1997.

38 Judah, *The Serbs*, p. 192.

39 Milos Vasić, 'The Yugoslav army and the post-Yugoslav armies', in Dyker and Vejvoda, eds, *Yugoslavia and After*, p. 132.

40 Anthony Robinson and Guy Dinmore, *Financial Times*, 28 May 1997.

41 Allusions are made to this in Xavier Bougarel, 'Bosnia and Hercegovina – state and communitarianism', in Dyker and Vejvoda, eds, *Yugoslavia and After*, pp. 108–13. Izetbegovic declared in 1997 that the SDA contains some extremists but is basically a bastion of 'tolerant Islam'. See RFE/RL NewsLine, South Eastern Europe, 29 December 1997. The Internet address is, http://www.rferl.org/newsline

42 See Miranda Vickers and James Pettifer, *Albania: From Anarchy to a Balkan Identity*, London: Hurst, 1997, p. 162.

43 Leonidas Hatziprodromidis, 'Forward to the past', *Warreport*, February 1995, p. 36.

44 *Uneasy Peace*, p. 132. Milošević, after meeting the Greek Premier, Andreas Papandreou, in 1994, said 'there is hardly a sphere in which our views differ'. Serbian radio, Belgrade, 19 December 1994, quoted by BBC Survey of World Broadcasts, Eastern Europe, 21 December 1994.

45 See Kyril Drezov's chapter in this volume. The BCP renamed itself the Bulgarian Socialist Party (BSP) in April 1990.

46 Andrei Georgiev and Emil Tzenkov, 'The troubled Balkans', in Hugh Miall, ed., *Redefining Europe: New Patterns of Conflict and Co-operation*, London: Pinter, 1995, p. 54.

47 Kerin Hope, 'Minorities: image shattered by clashes', *Financial Times*, 17 December 1997.

48 *Unfinished Peace*, p. 115.

49 For the programmes of various minorities, see Hugh Poulton, *The Balkans: Minorities and States in Conflict*, London: Minority Rights Publications, 1991.

50 See Jennifer Jackson Preece, 'National minority rights vs. state sovereignty in Europe: changing norms in international relations?', *Nations and Nationalism*, 3, 3, 1997.

51 Ian Traynor and Yigal Chazan, *Guardian*, 7 May 1993.

52 Stan Markotić, *Transition*, 2, 18, 6 September 1996, p. 19.

53 Judah, *The Serbs*, p. 242.

54 I discuss the the the new Romanian situation in 'Danube detente: Romania's relations with Hungary after 1996', *Balkanologie*, 3, 1998.

55 Andrei Cornea, *22*, Bucharest, 3–9 July 1997.

56 Tom Gallagher, 'To be or not to be Balkan: Romania's quest for self-definition', *Daedalus*, 126, 3, Summer 1997, pp. 73–4.

57 Andrew Gumbel, 'Revolution fails as Serbia's winter storm blows over', *Independent*, 29 July 1997.

58 Guy Dinmore, *Financial Times*, 25 September 1997.

59 Gagnon Jr, 'Serbia's road to war', pp. 128–9.

60 Information on the Montenegran poll and its aftermath was obtained from the excellent newservice provided by Belgrade's Radio B92 whose website is entitled Open Serbia: http://b92eng.opennet.org/

61 Vesna Pesić, one of the most active leaders of the Serbian opposition, claimed in 1993 that what she saw as the West's capitulation to Serbian demands to split up Bosnia had contributed to the collapse of democratic hopes in Serbia itself: 'everything we said in favour of human rights and against "ethnic cleansing" looks ridiculous. The West has recognized the use of force to change borders, betraying their own values. Lord Owen is the real war criminal in all this. After he endorsed genocide in Bosnia against Muslims, you may as well forget democracy inside Serbia.' This last reference to the UN negotiator David Owen concerned his willingness to treat Bosnian Serb leaders as respectable negotiating partners and promote a partition plan which had little in it for people of mixed ethnicity and those committed to a multicultural Bosnia.
   Pesić was supported by Milovan Djilas, the veteran dissident. After Owen had praised Milosevic as a peacemaker, the 83–year-old Djilas said: 'we are in the era of Chamberlain and Daladier, of believing that if you signed a treaty you avoided trouble, never mind that a whole nation has been sold out' (a reference to the Bosnian Muslims). See Marcus Tanner, 'Serbia subtly stifles democracy', *Independent*, 24 June 1993.

62 Judy Batt, *East Central Europe: From Reform to Transformation*, London: Frances Pinter, 1991, p. 8.

63 One sign of returning introspection was the number of Romanian publications which chose this time to abandon the websites which they had opened on the Internet in the previous year.

64 Victor Zaslavsky, 'Nationalism and democratic transitions in post-communist societies', *Daedalus*, 121, 2, Spring 1992, p. 107.

65 A good example are the intellectuals who founded the Vatra Românescâ Union in Romania as a means to prevent Hungarians recovering positions that they had enjoyed before the communist regime entered its chauvinist phase.

5   The media and the search for democracy in the Balkans

Tom Gallagher

Introduction

The role of the print and broadcasting media did not occupy a key place in the transitions literature when democratization processes were largely confined to Southern Europe and Latin America. The media were not a strategic resource absolutely vital for the power-conserving plans of dictators or single parties. Limited diversity in the media permitted differing viewpoints and sources of news to exist in all but the most punitive of right-wing dictatorships. Allowing a substantial widening of press freedom was often one of the most painless gestures that moderates in one-party regimes could make in order to assert their liberal credentials. But it was different in South-East Europe where manipulation and control of information were seen as vital requirements by the ex-communists who, in all the states of the region, tried to shape the post-communist order around their own limited agenda for change. The degree to which they succeeded depended on how successful they were in controlling information in altered political conditions. Therefore, it is appropriate to view media freedom as a key variable that determines the degree to which Balkan states are able to break out of the shadowlands of post-communism, where restrictions on genuine pluralism abound, towards genuine multi-party democracy where the media increasingly enjoys the freedoms taken for granted now in Southern Europe.

The state-led transitions from communism witnessed in most of the Balkan states after 1989 made the media a key issue in post-communist politics. How mass communications were to be regulated, the degree to which state broadcasting should reflect views outside the ruling party, the extent of the new freedoms to be enjoyed by private newspapers, and the degree to which the state was prepared to lift its monopoly over the electronic media were just some of the issues which envenomed politics as power struggles erupted between former top communist officials and newly legalized parties on the centre and right of politics.

Unlike Central Europe, transitions to democracy involving pacts between communist reformers and new movements deriving their strength from the vitality of civil society were conspicuous by their absence. In South-East Europe, civic, religious and intellectual bodies, which had acquired some autonomy from the communist state in Poland and Hungary, never had a chance to flourish owing to the severity of communist rule. Old-guard figures wishing to retain as much political control as competitive politics would permit, and determined to pursue a limited agenda of change, usually outnumbered pragmatic communists prepared to throw their weight behind a process of genuine democratization.

Censorship and control of information had enabled communists with a totalitarian outlook to retain their ascendancy in South-East Europe (or else recover it in Yugoslavia where liberal-minded communists were purged in Serbia, the most important of the republics during the 1970s and 1980s). Through the state media, Balkan communist elites had been able to establish a powerful hold over new social groups that emerged from the nationalization of productive resources. Peasants in collectivized agriculture and workers in heavy industry were the most numerous social groups after nearly two generations of communist rule, and they had grown used to being centrally directed by a state which supervised their attitudes and behaviour.

The state media, which at least in Bulgaria, Romania and Albania was one of the most effective instruments with which the communist leadership could control society, was not a weapon to be discarded lightly. In this chapter I argue that post-communist elites relied heavily on the state media to retain their influence over numerically dominant groups which would provide a strong power-base for the left in the Balkans through the 1990s. It continued to be a rather crude transmission belt with which the left directed ideological messages at its natural constituencies, stressing collectivist themes, identifying a range of external and internal enemies, and insisting that there was no alternative to rule by experienced leaders who had the interests of workers and peasants at heart. The state media was thus seen as a branch of the ruling party. Not only were political challengers denied ready access to it, but their fitness to rule was frequently questioned by it.

For opposition parties unable, at least initially, to rely on a coherent electoral base made up of distinct social groups or classes, this situation was intolerable. Confrontations in tentative democracies, where polarized pluralism prevailed, often consisted of battles to control information sources. In countries like Albania and Croatia where self-styled anti-communists succeeded in winning power, it soon emerged that the tendency to regard the state media as a servile branch of the ruling party and the private media as a potential enemy to be disabled or controlled was not just a reflex of the ex-communist left. More than any other region of the world that has seen a retreat from openly authoritarian rule in the last twenty-five years, South-East Europe has proven most resistant to a culture of free access to information. External vigilance by multilateral organizations, non-governmental organizations (NGO)s, and several of the Atlantic democracies has been vital in shoring up fragile press freedoms. Accordingly, external support for the pluralist media will probably be necessary until political contenders for power in South-East Europe are no longer so ready to push their differences to the point of outright confrontation.

The media's role under communism

The only guaranteed activity enjoyed by the Balkan media under communism was that of supporting the existing political system in prescribed ways. A high degree of political orthodoxy was demanded of journalists in the Balkans. They were seen as defenders of a social system which was promoted more zealously than in other parts of communist Eastern Europe. Even in Yugoslavia, the Official Code of Journalists defined a journalist as 'a socio-political worker who, conscientiously adhering to the ideas of Marxism-Leninism, participates in the development of social self-management society'.[1]

Electronic means of communication were seen as key instruments for socializing the population in the desired political way. To take one albeit extreme example, 'Romanian television under Ceausescu', according to the sociologist Pavel Campeanu, was 'an amazing concentration of ideological messages . . . to transform the television schedule into a pure instrument of political ideology'.[2] Most of the television reporters and editors survived the overthrow of the dictatorship at the end of 1989. Trained to be subservient to the government, 'many viewed their calling in life as keeping Mr Iliescu [Ceauşescu's successor] in power, or at least faithfully reporting his policies'.[3]

In Serbia, communist hardliners mobilizing nationalism in order to retain their monopoly of power found the electronic media to be their most effective tool. The media in Serbia, arguably freer than anywhere else in the communist world up to the late 1980s, was purged of liberals and reformers who refused to promote conflict between Serbs and other nationalities, especially Albanians and Croats. Irresponsible treatment of sensitive national issues wrecked nascent attempts at democratization. As Yugoslavia disintegrated, the media of the major republics bolstered regional elites which, in Serbia and later Croatia, promoted conflicts of identity to preserve their own power-bases.[4] Media pluralism was gravely weakened by the exploitation of nationalism. This was a dangerous portent in an area where the politics of ethnicity had produced numerous inter-state and majority–minority conflicts.

The media during the early transition

The passage from Marxism-Leninism to a form of post-communism with a range of concessions to liberal democracy was a conflict-ridden process. No pacts were arranged between rival political forces and a form of polarized pluralism usually emerged wherever the rulers were prepared to tolerate organized opposition. Often, access to or control of the means of inform-ation was at the heart of the power struggles between communists regrouped as socialists and anti-left-wing forces. Existing newspapers attempted to remain viable by dropping Marxist titles and stressing their fidelity to democracy. Far more new ones materialized which backed the opposition, if not acting as the mouthpiece of a particular grouping. In Romania, up to 900 newspapers sprang up in 1990 alone. Publications flooded on to the market before the law permitted private companies or decreed how the press was to be regulated. It was relatively easy to launch a newspaper; not a lot of capital was required. Publishing proved a magnet for politically minded young people drawn to public affairs but unwilling to subject themselves to the discipline of a political party.

A partisan press contributed to the hate-filled atmosphere which marked the first multi-party elections in Romania and Bulgaria in 1990 and in Albania one year later. Newspaper sales were approaching their peak in the first two countries, purchasing power was greater than it would later become and people, at least in the cities, were curious to read opinions that had previously been censored. But the invective of the press alarmed older generations of citizens who preferred security and a degree of political continuity to experimentation and headlong change. They provided the bulk of the votes for the post-communist parties of the left which won the first elections in Romania, Bulgaria and Albania.

Ruling ex-communists frequently singled out the existence of an uncen-sored, politically diverse press as proof that democracy was safe in their hands. But tolerance of diversity in the media did not extend to the electronic airwaves. Television was the main source of regular news in the Balkans for nearly everyone, especially citizens living in the countryside and small towns where newspapers were only infrequently seen. The provisional governments in Romania and Bulgaria used television to direct reassuring messages to the non-urban electorate which would become their chief electoral reservoir: social protection for the vulnerable during a period of economic restructuring; and defence of national values, parti-cularly in the face of demands from assertive minorities.

The legacy of doctrinaire communism and older traditions of political partisanship left journalists ill-equipped to nurture pluralist values even where media freedoms enjoyed some toleration. Low standards of profes-sionalism resulted in polemical journalism where opinions and rumour masqueraded as analysis and factual reporting.[5] A formula of cheap sensationalism was often followed to carve out a niche in a volatile market. In times of economic hardship such papers often had short-lived appeal and helped to contribute to the political apathy of the masses. Autocratic leaders generally saw a low-circulation and mediocre press as far less of a threat than an electronic media in independent hands. Without exception, television in the region was strictly controlled by the regime of the day and radio only usually enjoyed limited autonomy.

Only in Yugoslavia was there initially an attempt to revamp television in order to strengthen the prospects for democratization in the troubled federation. In October 1990 the reformist federal President, Ante Marković, launched Yutel, a federal television station, in a bid to rally citizens committed to a democratic Yugoslavia and unwilling to espouse narrow nationalism.[6] But Yutel arrived too late to act as a moderating force in a country being torn apart by ethnic and economic conflicts. The federation was on the point of collapse because most of the other republics were refusing to acquiesce in their own domination by Serbia; Slovenia and Croatia preferred to secede rather than unite with moderates in Bosnia-Herzegovina and Macedonia to work in defence of democratic principles.[7]

Yugoslavia's days may have been numbered when in 1987 Slobodan Milošević, the newly installed leader of the communist party in Serbia, broke with the Yugoslav communist tradition that workers should be defended without regard to their nationality and instead began to work towards the goal of a Greater Serbia. From then on, the control and manipulation of the media would be a crucial factor in Milošević's acquisition and retention of political power. In 1986 he had ordered live television coverage of a central committee meeting that was a key stage in his rise to power: 'never before had people . . . seen what went on at closed party sessions . . . When Milošević spoke he addressed the people at home rather than the central committee.'[8]

Milošević was using classic populist techniques to distance himself from the discredited economic policies of the colourless leadership which had succeeded the architect of communist Yugoslavia, Marshal Tito (Josip Broz). He championed the interests of Serbia in the province of Kosovo, which was seen as the cradle of Serb nationalism despite Albanians having been in the majority for over a century. The campaign around Kosovo orchestrated by the media was intended to mobilize a people disenchanted with politics and the political class by convincing them, as Milošević declared in 1987, that '[w]hat we are discussing here can no longer be called politics, it is a question of our fatherland'.[9] Milošević's promise to Serbs in Kosovo that 'no one will beat you again' struck a chord with Serbs who had been encouraged to believe that their interests had been systematically ignored in the decentralized but still very much communist state created by Tito. Dusan Mitević, deputy director of Serbian state television, said later: 'we showed Milošević's promise [in Kosovo] over and over again. And this is what launched him.'[10]

State television became the chief instrument of a propaganda drive which insisted that Kosovo Serbs were facing genocide from Albanian 'terrorist-separatists'.[11] Yugoslavia's Albanian population was criminalized in the minds of many Serbs and television and radio were purged of journalists and editors who refused to accept the new ultra-nationalist orthodoxy. The emphasis in daily news broadcasts of Serbian valour in their struggles for independence, the losses they suffered in the Second World War at the hands of Croatian fascists, and the dangers posed by separatist Albanians, created a sense of 'war psychosis', so that ordinary people came to believe that they were surrounded by enemies prepared to wipe them out.[12] The electronic media enabled an unscrupulous leader to transmit a message of divisiveness and ethnic intolerance into millions of homes on a nightly basis. Later, during 1991–2 when war erupted in Croatia and Bosnia, state-run television devoted hours of prime-time television to war propaganda pitched to keep viewers in a state of patriotic frenzy.[13] A typical item from the state media was the allegation made in 1992 that Macedonia was a place where people played football with the bones of Serb soldiers killed during the First World War.[14] Milos Vasić, the Belgrade dissident journalist, explaining to foreign audiences how the ground had been prepared through television for the 1991–5 wars in Yugoslavia, argued that 'if all American television had been taken over by the Ku Klux Klan, the USA too would have had war in five years'.[15]

Milošević's control of the electronic media was arguably the key factor helping him to stay in power, even though his Greater Serbia strategy fell far short of success and invited retaliation from the international community in the form of economic sanctions which crippled the Serbian economy. At 7.30 p.m. each evening in the first half of the 1990s, an estimated 3.5 million people – more than one in three of all Serbs – sat down to watch the state television newscast. Its content was not journalism but 'propaganda and lies', according to news editor Vlado Mares who was purged in 1990. He reckoned that the state station was so powerful owing to the poor educational standards of the country: 'Half [the Serbs] have completed only elementary school and 12 per cent did not even get that far. Only 6 per cent have any higher education, and a good proportion of these live in Belgrade, a city which is openly anti-Milošević.'[16] In 1993 another wholesale purge of Serbian state broadcasting resulted. Milošević dropped several hundred supporters of the ultra-nationalist Serbian Radical Party as he was promoting his regime as a force for peace and stability in the Balkans. Television had to promote a less embattled image of Serbia as part of a strategy to get UN sanctions lifted and so ease pressure on the collapsing economy.[17]

Henceforth, Serbian television increasingly resembled state television in neighbouring countries where the news was managed in order to diminish the potential for social conflict and encourage depoliticization among viewers and listeners. Writing about Romania after 1990, Henry F. Carey has described how the main evening news show on state television, *Actualitati*, 'socializes *disinterest* in politics'.[18] No investigative reporting on what the government really does ever appeared; the few programmes examining abuses of power in communist times were shown at obscure hours when the potential viewing audience was low; and the opposition's activities were covered in ways that reduced their chances of being seen by viewers as a government-in-waiting.

Restrictions on the media

Article 19, the London-based International Centre Against Censorship, found, in the first half of the 1990s, that nearly all of the Balkan countries fell far short of international standards protecting freedom of expression and information. Perhaps surprisingly, there was no correlation between the strength of neo-communist influence in government and the prevalence of restrictions on the media.

In Romania, where a ruling elite with roots in the communist era held sway till 1996, the press was among the freest in the region and independent private television companies were in operation by 1994 even though they only reached a very small audience. In Serbia, (until 1998) Milošević allowed opposition papers to publish. Their circulation did not extend far beyond Belgrade and this was seen as a gesture allowing the opposition to let off steam while not undermining the basis of his rule since they only circulated among the small liberal intelligentsia and young people.

In Bosnia, despite the conditions of warfare which existed there from 1992 to 1995, there was a huge number of electronic media outlets. The absence of strong governmental authority and the concentration of the Sarajevo government on military survival enabled small private radio and television stations to flourish. By the spring of 1996, there were forty radio stations and seventy-seven television stations in government-held territory, a remarkable concentration in a place where most other conditions of normal life had completely broken down.[19]

By contrast, in Macedonia where the President was Kiro Gligorov, a former high communist official in the Tito era, the media in all its forms remained stunted. Nevertheless, the level of internal democracy was sufficiently high for the EU in 1992 to recommend that Macedonia's independence be formally recognized. Then, and later, Gligorov kept a delicate balance between the parties of the Macedonian majority and the Albanian minority which had sharply diverging interests. But a desperate economic situation, exacerbated by an embargo imposed by neighbouring Greece from 1992 till 1995, as well as UN sanctions against neighbouring Serbia, deprived newspapers of a viable market for their products.[20] Moreover, the government has kept discreet control over information sources. Newspapers from neighbouring countries can only be imported with the permission of the ministry of internal affairs. The leading newspaper publisher is a government company that owns the only modern high-speed printing plant in the country, as well as most newspaper kiosks; in 1996 opposition groups were complaining of being charged high prices for the services of the printing plant. But the state-owned media's reporting of opposition activities is regarded as balanced, at least by the US State Department.[21]

Ironically, restrictions on the media at all levels were most pronounced in two Balkan countries which insisted most loudly on having severed links with communist era methods and having embraced liberal democratic values. Croatia and Albania figure prominently in any review of state interference with the media. State pressure on the media ranged from economic interference to political and legal restrictions, and ultimately to physical intimidation. The concept of a self-limiting state prepared to allow constraints on its powers, which an independent media provided, signally failed to take root in the Balkans during the 1990–5 period and all states furnished examples of government harassment of the media, irrespective of their ideological complexion.

Governments possessed a lot of economic influence over the press and economic pressure was the easiest form to impose on a recalcitrant media. Newsprint remained a state monopoly in countries like Serbia, Albania and Romania well into the 1990s and editors often complained about shortages of newsprint especially at politically sensitive moments. The price of newsprint also determined the price of newspapers and hence their circulation. In 1993 the Romanian press was obliged to increase its prices sharply after the price of newsprint was driven up by the government monopoly; inevitably, the circulation of newspapers tumbled in what was a time of economic austerity.

Throughout much of the region, the state maintained a monopoly over the distribution of newspapers. Complaints were frequent about newspapers never reaching towns or districts where the government was keen to restrict the growth of the opposition. Such interference with the circulation of newspapers was usually discreetly applied. But in Albania in January 1996, armed police prevented twelve daily papers from circulating beyond the capital by impounding distribution vans because they allegedly lacked proper documentation.[22] In Croatia, the internationally recognized weekly *Damas* had to close down in 1992 after the government deprived it of printing and distribution facilities.[23]

Another effective source of government control over the media is the law. New laws, such as that on the Romanian broadcasting media in 1992, made 'defamation of the country and the nation' a criminal offence without specifying how it might be committed.[24] Old laws still in force from communist times could impede the press. In Macedonia, a pre-1989 law authorized imprisonment for spreading false views and slander.[25] Certain things could not be criticized in Skopje, such as the personality of President Gligorov or the wartime anti-fascist struggle.[26]

Where the judiciary was compliant to the government, the media could find itself coming under unexpected legal pressure. In Bosnia, a 1998 report claimed that newspapers suffering harassment for uncovering links between the Muslim political leadership and corruption and crime received little protection from the courts.[27] In December 1994 the only private daily in Belgrade was placed back under government control after a court ruling that it had been 'improperly incorporated'. In February 1995 the same was done with Studio B, the only independent television station in Serbia. Meanwhile, in Croatia the influential newspaper *Slobodna Dalmacija* suffered a similar fate in 1992. In 1991 its employees had organized a buy-out of the shares, all of which had been held by a government-controlled union. The new owners borrowed against the share capital and invested in new equipment. But in 1992 the privatization was declared illegal. A temporary state board was appointed to re-privatize the newspaper. It wrested control from the staff by changing the terms of a bank loan incurred to re-equip the newspaper. Instead of being repaid over fifteen years, the government insisted upon immediate repayment, the banks having recently fallen under its control.[28] The Croatian regional press was also targeted, the ruling Croatian Democratic Union (HDZ) being a sworn enemy of regional sentiment. In 1996 it sought to cripple the Istrian daily *Novi List* when it was fined for allegedly evading taxes and customs duties.[29] Through such measures, the Tudjman regime effectively crippled the independent daily press and re-imposed state control behind a veneer of privatization.

Alternatively, the state could bend the law to reward newspapers which it valued as allies. The pro-government press enjoyed tax-breaks in Albania; and in Serbia it had access to newsprint at much cheaper prices than independent publications.[30] On the other hand, independent papers might be handicapped by the sudden imposition of taxes and tariffs without any explanation being given. The independent media also suffered from outright political interference without any legal sanction behind it. The purging of disobedient journalists from state television, having begun under Milošević in Serbia, was pursued in Croatia as soon as Tudjman came to power in 1990.[31] In Romania, the government blocked the appointment of the noted independent publisher, Gabriel Liiceanu, to the management council of state television even though the staff had elected him to his allotted position. Wherever independent television companies were permitted, there were usually attempts to manipulate the composition of their boards to ensure a large degree of state control. Sometimes, different branches of government might be in conflict over which should exercise control over the media. This happened in Bulgaria during 1996 when a law passed in parliament by the ruling Socialists, allowing for a politically appointed board to oversee the electronic media, was blocked by the President and also met resistance in the Constitutional Court.[32] Arguably, the Bulgarian media escaped many of the restrictions faced by counterparts in the former Yugoslavia because of the frequency of such conflicts between 1990 and 1997.

The state could also exercise influence over the private media if the latter was owned by economic interests that enjoyed a privileged relationship with the regime in power. In Romania, some of the leading dailies in the capital were controlled by ex-nomenklatura businessmen who ensured that there was little or no coverage of the way in which state assets had been sold off to the regime's political clients in dubious ways. The government itself did not hesitate to subsidize directly several newspapers which became mouthpieces for President Iliescu.

In Serbia, the regime finally dropped any remaining pretence about being a functioning democracy under Milošević by passing a new media law in 1998 which allows the authorities to close down periodicals and independent radio stations the ruling elite doesn't like. It gives extensive discretionary powers to the Ministry of Culture, including the right to impose massive summary fines on managements, editors and journalists with no process for an appeal being allowed.[33]

When all else failed, a regime might use physical intimidation to deter the independent media from reporting critically on its activities. In January 1994 Victor Ivancić, the editor of Croatia's satirical weekly *Feral Tribune*, became the only editor out of two hundred to be conscripted into the military by the authorities.[34] In Romania, when a beleaguered government mobilized vigilante coal-miners and members of the secret police to sweep its opponents from the streets in June 1990, opposition newspaper offices were systematically wrecked in the process. But it was in Albania that physical coercion was taken furthest. One of the biggest thorns in the side of President Berisha's regime was the independent daily *Koha Jone*. Between 1993 and 1996, its owner and his staff experienced 'repeated police raids, arrests, and attacks by unidentified assailants'.[35] On the eve of the 1996 elections, widely believed to have been fixed by the government, the newspaper's property was seized by the state. The paper's offices were finally burnt to the ground, apparently by the security police, the Shik, on the night of 2–3 March 1997 during the first stages of a popular uprising against Berisha.[36] *The Times*, in an editorial, was one of many Western papers which condemned the actions of 'Shik plainclothes thugs [who] have been threatening foreign and domestic journalists, smashing their cars, and inciting crowds to turn on those suspected of reporting the violence'.[37]

Resistance to state interference

Independent local media in the Balkans are not absolutely powerless in the face of a hostile state intent on restricting their activities. They can organize themselves into associations in a bid to survive; or they can take collective action to publicize their problems, as most of the Bucharest daily press did in the early 1990s to protest at the difficulty in obtaining newsprint and reliable forms of distribution.

But autocratic governments are not usually deterred by such gestures of solidarity. To survive in a hostile political environment, media outlets in the Balkans have found mobilizing external backing to be more effective.

NGOs, some of which have close links with Western policy-makers, have championed the cause of the free media in the Balkans. Freedom House, which promotes an engaged US foreign policy determined to strengthen democratic values where these are under threat, closely monitors state treatment of the media in the Balkans and has lobbied actively to ensure that the guarantee of press freedom is a precondition that has to be met before the ex-Yugoslav states in particular benefit from Western assistance.[38] Through its journal *Warreport* (1991–7) the London-based Institute of War and Peace Reporting tracked media developments, provided training for journalists from ex-Yugoslavia, and launched a range of initiatives to champion media pluralism in Bosnia. Over the longer term, Radio Free Europe and the BBC World Service have broadcast to South-East Europe and provided alternative news sources for local populations when state censorship has been particularly intense.[39]

A remarkable degree of financial assistance for the pluralist media across the whole of the former communist bloc has been provided by the billionaire philanthropist George Soros. His Open Society Foundation is committed to creating open and inclusive political and economic systems from the rubble of communism, ones that are guaranteed by the free flow of information. The foundation has centres in each of the Balkan states and without Soros's money the independent media would find it impossible to survive in a number of them.[40] Whatever their ideological complexion, authoritarian-minded governments have railed against Soros's interference. In 1996 the Albanian government was accusing Soros's local officials of trying to take over the Albanian press and subsidize opposition to the government at a time when the Serbian authorities were trying to shut down the foundation's operations completely and Croatia was complaining about Soros's interference.[41]

The Council of Europe, membership of which is seen as an important badge of political respectability, assisting ex-communist states to integrate with Western institutions, has closely monitored the record of Balkan states towards the media. In 1993 it urged parliamentary control of the state broadcasting media before Romania could gain admission. But in 1996 it proved irresolute towards Croatia, granting it admission even though it was clear that the media there enjoyed very few of the freedoms taken for granted in Western Europe. Sometimes the actions of the international community compounded the difficulties of the pluralist media in the region. The failure of the EU to recognize Macedonia between 1992 and 1995 left its journalists unable to gain membership of international media organizations, and they had difficulty travelling owing to their 'unofficial' nationality. Sanctions imposed on Serbia and Montenegro also led to similar problems.[42]

Prominent individuals with good lines of communications to key Western governments have been able to intercede on behalf of beleaguered journalists. One of these was Kati Marton, the Hungarian-born wife of

Richard Holbrooke, the US State Department official who masterminded the US-led NATO intervention which brought the Bosnian conflict to an end and who oversaw the subsequent peace negotiations at Dayton in the USA. In her capacity as President of the US Committee to Protect Foreign Journalists, Marton visited Croatia and Serbia in 1996 to monitor the state of the media in both countries.[43] She reminded Croatia's Franjo Tudjman of the commitment he made to protect the independent media when he signed the Dayton Peace Accord. Unimpressed, an angry President showed her a copy of the *Feral Tribune* and said: 'It's me who needs protection from such a newspaper. Not the other way round.'[44] Over a dozen representatives of NGOs for the protection of media freedom attended the trial of *Feral Tribune* journalists accused of defaming Tudjman in an article criticizing his proposal to place the graves of Second World War fascists alongside those of their victims at the former Jasenovac concentration camp in Croatia.[45] The high degree of foreign interest the trial attracted probably resulted in the charges being temporarily dropped.

Serbia's desire to rejoin the international community, albeit on its own terms, has enabled prominent Western officials to warn Milošević about going too far in his drive to obtain media conformity. Hans Van den Broek, the EU Commissioner for Foreign Affairs, issued a demand to Milosevic in 1996 that 'measures be taken to preserve the independence of the television station, Studio B'. In 1993 the UN's special rapporteur in Bosnia, Tadeusz Mazowiecki, urged that 'the information blockade which prevails in the region should be broken. Support should be given to initiatives which aim to provide objective information.'[46] There was particular concern about the 'hate speech' emphasized by the media in the Republic of Srpska, the part of Bosnia controlled by hardline nationalist Serbs which branded Muslims, Croats and other Serbs committed to rebuilding a multicultural Bosnia as the enemy within. Here during 1997, the NATO-led stabilization force knocked out of action several transmitters in the hands of extreme nationalists at a time when it was throwing its weight behind more moderate Bosnian Serb leaders.

Until 1998, Balkan regimes were hesitant about coercing or restricting foreign media outlets, but several such attempts have been made. In Albania, RadioTirana ended all re-broadcasts by Deutsche Welle's Albanian language service from local transmitters in 1996, one year after the Romanian government prevented state television from airing the BBC's news programmes in Romanian. During the early stages of the 1997 rebellion against President Berisha, a blackout was even attempted on the transmission of satellite television pictures from Tirana so as to prevent the outside world learning about what was happening.[47] Far more stringent was the law passed in Serbia in October 1998 which bans the re-broadcast of foreign news services

In November 1998 the Belgrade independent radio station B92 was denounced as being a mercenary working for foreign interests hostile to

Serbia by the Deputy Premier, Vojislav Šešelj.[48] The speed of change in the world of information technology and the opportunities it affords for liberals struggling to be heard in despotic countries may account for the virulence of this outburst. Even relatively backward countries like Albania have a surprising number of Internet users who were able to relay information about the crisis in the first months of 1997 right across the world. High levels of technical expertise exist in many parts of Eastern Europe which makes the Internet an effective means of relaying political information. Countries like Croatia which have largely silenced the independent press, have not so far tried to impose their will on cyberspace and it may largely be beyond the control of authoritarian leaders. In Serbia, it was even claimed by Veran Matić, editor-in-chief of the independent Belgrade Radio station B92, that mobilization of international support on the Internet thwarted the Serbian government when it consistently jammed B92 broadcasts in the winter of 1996–7.[49]

The crisis of post-communism and the media

In 1996–7 much of the region was shaken by large-scale protests as citizens rose up against governments whose nationalist posturing or promises of social protection had earlier been attractive, but whose record of misrule eroded much of their remaining legitimacy. In several countries protests were fuelled by government attempts to further limit citizens' access to a free press.

Tightening control over the media was as vital for semi-despotic leaders seeking to preserve their authority in difficult times as it had been when they first came to power after 1989. Veran Matić, of the Belgrade radio station B92, remarked in January 1997 that state television 'will be the last thing Milošević will give up. He's the first east European leader who understood the power of TV. He realised he can control society better with TV than with the police.'[50] Matić's remarks followed two months of protests over electoral fraud which prevented the opposition taking possession of town halls they had won in the 17 November poll. One of the reasons it was widely assumed that the opposition victories had been annulled was to prevent local broadcasting facilities controlled by town halls falling into the hands of Milošević's opponents. A study of media coverage of the election campaign found that 95 minutes out of 100 on state television were devoted to a favourable portrayal of the ruling political alliance.[51]

The government-controlled media attempted to impose a news blackout on nightly demonstrations in Belgrade which drew hundreds of thousands of people on to the streets. Steve Crawshaw of the London *Independent* described the surreal nature of television news as the marathon Belgrade protests stretched into their third month, with middle-class and working-class Belgraders making common cause with Milošević's political opponents for the first time, and the action winning widespread international backing:

> Watch the television evening news and you will learn: the economy is booming; international links are flourishing; the President is a calm and confident hand on the tiller, bringing peace and prosperity to his country . . .. The style of television news is reminiscent of old-style communism: lots of meetings and ceremonies and few glimpses of reality.[52]

Eventually, the controlled media itself became a focal point of protest. Each night around 7.30 p.m. during the first part of 1997, the Belgrade air echoed to clangs and whistles for a full half-hour as thousands of residents hung out of their windows banging pots and pans to drown out the news.

At the start of the crisis, Milošević had attempted heavy-handed forms of intimidation against his media critics. *Blic*, the only daily paper to report the demonstrations, was told on 26 November by its state-owned printers that due to previously unannounced repair work on the presses, its print-run would be reduced from 200,000 to 80,000.[53] Protests were in fact fuelled by the government's unsuccessful attempt to take the B92 radio station off the air. Its output could only be heard in part of the capital but within that limited area its audience tripled from 300,000 to more than a million during the last weeks of 1996. The opposition news magazine *Vreme*, the most authoritative current affairs weekly in the Balkans, and once read only by a tiny minority, doubled its circulation to 60,000 during the same period.[54] In February 1997 the protests ended when the November election victories for the opposition were re-instated. Zajedno, the opposition alliance, took possession of town halls in Serbia's main cities. Technically, this victory also gave them control over local radio and television stations, power which Milošević in the end did not have to cede owing to the infighting in the second half of 1997 which blunted the opposition's challenge to his rule. The media was therefore at the very heart of democratization struggles in Serbia and it is likely to play a similar role if and when the opposition is able to recover the initiative.

In Bulgaria, state attempts to tighten control over broadcasting media were the background against which mass protests over the economic policies and corruption of the left-wing Bulgarian Socialist Party (BSP) government got underway in late 1996. Radio Free Europe proved to be an important source of reliable information for many Bulgarian citizens during this confused time.[55] One of the first acts of the reformist government which won elections in April 1997 was to annul the law passed by its predecessor which would have subjected the broadcasting media to the close supervision of the party in power.[56]

In Croatia, government restrictions on the remaining independent branches of the media acted as a catalyst for mass protest. In November

1996 more than 100,000 people protested in Zagreb in support of Radio 101, a beacon of free expression which the government tried to exclude from the airwaves. It was the largest anti-regime protest seen since Croatia became independent in 1991. Combined with pressure from Western governments, it resulted in the station's licence being renewed for five years early in 1997.[57]

In Romania, the media undoubtedly played a role in securing the electoral defeat of the ruling ex-communists in November 1996. By 1996 fifty-three private television stations were broadcasting, with the largest reaching approximately 46 per cent of the country and 72 per cent of the urban market; these stations were far less restrictive than state television in their political coverage and increasing access to them may have contributed to the large swing to the opposition in urban areas.[58] A vigorous independent press had emerged in previous years which harried the government more successfully than the opposition parties managed to do. It campaigned against the pyramid schemes – pseudo-banks based on fraud or organized crime that offered astronomical rates of interest – which flourished in Romania during 1992–4 without interference from the government before the inevitable crash robbed hundreds of thousands of small investors of their savings. The most successful newspaper, *Evenimentul Zilei* (News of the Day), acquired a large circulation by mixing a diet of sensationalist news with hard-hitting criticism of the Iliescu regime. Its ownership structure made it immune to economic pressure from the government and its revenue was acquired through circulation (which unusually for the Balkans extended nationwide) rather than advertising. During the election period, it campaigned for a change of government and its growing influence in parts of the country where the opposition previously had been weak may have played a key role in deciding the result. Interestingly, it was not dependent on foreign support to remain viable which was the case with *România líberă*, the chief opposition daily which lost readership owing to its failure to adapt to the growing demand for less polemical and more factual coverage of events.[59] Gheorghe Dumitrascu, a deputy for the ruling party, declared after the voting that one of the government's greatest mistakes had been its refusal to institute a media clampdown during its years in power.[60] But the Romanian post-communists depended on external backing to sustain a failing economy and they were nervous about attracting invidious comparisons with the notorious regime of Nicolae Ceauşescu in which many had served.

Rather than harass or shut down its press critics, the Iliescu regime promoted ultra-nationalist press outlets in the hope that chauvinist attacks on minorities or neighbouring states like Hungary might bring it political benefits at home. The most influential extremist newspaper editor, Corneliu Vadim Tudor, was even able to launch a successful political career after his incendiary weekly, *România Mâre*, acquired a circulation that may have approached half-a-million weekly sales in the early 1990s.[61] Various forms of support from unreconstructed sections of the state bureaucracy assisted its rise, but the ultra-nationalist press fell on hard times as the economic troubles of the country deepened after 1992. Tudor remains a powerful figure but newspapers do not play a key role in sustaining his appeal. Generally, the influence of chauvinist newspapers in the Balkans receded as the manipulation of nationalism by ruling ex-communists started to fail as an effective control strategy.

Conclusion

There are serious obstacles preventing the electronic and print media from supporting democratic development in the Balkans. The legacy of Stalinist one-party rule and older traditions of political partisanship left journalists ill-equipped to encourage political pluralism. Partisan journalism was more likely to spread apathy among the mass of the population or play into the hands of ex-communist leaderships than to promote sustained interest in political affairs; alternatively, the irresponsible treatment of sensitive nationalist issues could inflame passions and wreck nascent attempts at democratization as happened in Serbia.

The scale of the economic crisis in the Balkans has perhaps been as crucial as state victimization in impeding the rise of serious and profes-sional publications with a large readership and a demonstrable impact on public affairs. Outside assistance provided by the EU through its PHARE programmes as well as the Soros Foundation and the Institute of War and Peace Reporting has in some countries enabled a new generation of journalists to emerge capable of sustaining a vigorous free press. But the recession induced by the legacy of communist misrule, combined with the plundering of the most productive parts of the economy by former communist officials and economic speculators, has eroded the market for high-quality and profitable print journalism. The decline of the middle classes in the region, and the shortage of advertisers willing to promote their goods and services via the press, forces down quality. There is little likelihood of a paper like the independent quality *El Pais* emerging, as happened in Spain after Franco's death in 1975, to play a vital role in strengthening a democratic political culture. It is perhaps more likely that criminal elements seeking political respectability and influence might, as a first step, acquire control of newspapers or even private television stations in one or more countries.

Where newspapers do provide a distinctive liberal message which finds an appreciative audience, severe restrictions on their freedom of action are often not long in following. This has proven to be the case in most of the countries surveyed here.[62] Control of information is seen by many rulers as essential for their survival in office. In Serbia and Croatia, it was also necessary to enable militaristic leaders to pursue their war aims. Even those leaders in Albania and Croatia who disavowed communism possessed the communist-era mentality under which political power was seen as the private possession of a small governing elite; therefore the attempt of journalists to pose as a Fourth Estate entitled to investigate and criticize the deeds of the powerful was viewed as an affront not to be tolerated. State-ownership, particularly of radio and television, is viewed as government ownership; the government is therefore entitled to dictate the editorial content of programmes and allow censored and propagandized news reports to pass as normal.

The emergence of internal conflicts in a region so diversified in ethnic, cultural and religious terms made it difficult for the media to report identity conflicts in balanced and unemotive terms. Although there are genuine conflicts of interest in the Balkans over the allocation of cultural or educational resources on an ethnic basis, many of the conflicts that did erupt were artificially stoked up and the media often played a key incubating role. In Serbia state television was used to put the population on a war footing and promote a series of European wars unprecedented in their viciousness since 1945. In other countries affected by majority–minority tensions, the media played a more responsible role (Macedonia in particular), but nevertheless the circulation of rumour and stereotypes was often regarded as less problematic than carrying out investigative reporting to discover the origins of local ethnic disputes or the way they were being manipulated from above.

The emphasis placed in the 1995 Dayton Accord on challenging the politics of ethnicity in states adjacent to Bosnia, so as to strengthen a tenuous peace in that shattered country, briefly strengthened the forces of liberalism in a region where they have been historically enfeebled. The Dayton signatories, despite the authoritarian reputation of some of them, undertook to respect media freedom in their respective countries. In the mid-1990s, with Western governments more attentive to Balkan develop-ments than at any time since the Cold War, authoritarian leaders in Serbia and Croatia relaxed their grip slightly and the media was a beneficiary. In 1996–7 they were even thrown on the defensive owing to chronic failure of their economies, the waning appeal of nationalism, and the shifting balance of power in the region.

The independent media used the space permitted to it to expose the contradictions of undemocratic post-communist rule in the Balkans. Issues of media freedom are likely to play a central role in Balkan politics in the time to come. Illiberal governments have probably expended more time and energy in trying to muzzle the independent media than in thwarting the opposition parties. These parties are often moribund between elections and may hardly exist outside parliament. The organizations making up civil society often remain dependent upon foreign support. Thus, in the institutional wasteland that still exists after communism, independent media outlets often play a crucial role in shaping public opinion (even though their circulations are smaller than equivalent press outlets in

Western Europe). They thus have a major responsibility not to abuse their role as a watchdog for society, nor to discard professional attitudes towards facts and news values.

In South-East Europe, the legacies of inter-ethnic conflict and chronic economic mismanagement, which no government can easily overcome, give the media an unusual degree of power to exacerbate or pacify resulting conflicts. In ethnically mixed states, democratization prospects will be strengthened if the media strives to show that complexity and even conflicts of interest are normal and that the state can devise rules and conventions to manage such tensions.[63] Where the shallow performance of reform parties confronted with a disastrous economic situation breeds despair or alienation, the media's restraining and educative roles are often crucial in order to prevent an authoritarian resurgence. It is not difficult to envisage a situation where a demagogic press undermines a weakly placed democracy (Romania in the late 1990s perhaps being the closest approximation). But for now the free media are usually the victim rather than the scourge of Balkan rulers.

Serbia has shown that cornered despots will not lightly give up the control of the airwaves, which is crucial for the maintenance of authority, while it remains to be seen if democratic leaderships in countries that have seen recent changes of government through the ballot box will encourage the growth of a free media.[64] For some time to come, it is likely that the acid test of whether democratic regimes in South-East Europe are slowly moving towards consolidation will be how they respond to criticism and searching investigation of their activities by the press and broadcasting system.

Notes

1 Mark Thompson, *Forging War: The Media In Serbia, Croatia and Bosnia-Herzegovina*, London: Article 19, 1994, p. 14.
2 Henry F. Carey, 'From big lie to small lies: state mass media dominance in post-communist Romania', *East European Politics and Societies*, 10, 1, 1996, p. 25.
3 Jane Perlez, 'Legacy of controlling the press dies hard in Bucharest', *International Herald Tribune*, 6 May 1997.
4 Christopher Bennett, *Yugoslavia's Bloody Collapse: Causes, Course and Consequences*, London: Hurst, 1995, p. 5.
5 A good example of polemical journalism based on rumour and personal defamation is the long-running controversy in the Romanian press about the bloody events accompanying Ceauşescu's downfall in 1989. see Richard A. Hall, 'The dynamics of media independence in post-Ceausescu Romania', *Journal of Communist Studies and Transition Politics*, 12, 4, 1996, pp. 102–23.
6 Thompson, *Forging War*, p. 18.
7 Ibid., p. 21.
8 Tom Gjelten, *Sarajevo Daily: A City and its Newspaper Under Siege*, London: Harper Collins, 1995, p. 53.
9 Thompson, *Forging War*, p. 53.
10 Laura Silber and Alan Little, *The Death of Yugoslavia*, London: BBC/Penguin, 1995, p. 38.

11 Thompson, *Forging War*, pp. 55–6.
12 Bennett, *Yugoslavia's Bloody Collapse*, p. 248.
13 Marcus Tanner, *Independent*, 24 May 1993.
14 Ursula Ruston, 'The war of words', *Index On Censorship*, 9, 1992, p. 10.
15 William Shawcross in Thompson, *Forging War*, p. x.
16 Petar Hadji-Ristic, 'Holding on to the home front', *Index On Censorship*, 9, 1992, p. 11.
17 Stan Markotich, 'Milošević's renewed attack on the media', *Transition*, 1, 3, 15 March 1995, p. 28.
18 Carey, 'From big lie to small lies', p. 29.
19 R. Budalic and M. Wheeler, 'Press war by other means', *Warreport*, 42, 1996 , p. 17.
20 Branko Geroski, 'Waiting for a second chance in Macedonia', *Transition*, 1, 18, 1995, pp. 44–5.
21 See US Department of State Human Rights Report 1996, 'Macedonia', Washington, Bureau of Democracy, Human Rights and Labour, 1997.
22 Fabian Schmidt, 'Party politics rules the Albanian press', *Transition*, 2, 21, 1996, p. 37.
23 J. Lovric, 'Croatia: edging towards a one-party state', *Warreport*, 16, 1992, p. 4.
24 Dan Ionescu, 'Romanian media's independence struggles', *Transition*, 1, 18, 1995, p. 52.
25 Miklos Biro, 'Is anybody out there?', *Warreport*, 39, 1996, p. 17.
26 Information from Kyril Drezov, a contributor to this volume.
27 Patrick Moore, 'Taboos in the Media', *RFE/RL Balkan Report*, 2, 26, 1 July 1998.
28 V. V. Janekovic, 'A privatization to make the IMF proud', *Warreport*, 18, 1993, p. 9.
29 Biljana Tatomir, 'Croatian government calls certain media "Enemies of the state"', *Transition*, 2, 21, 1996, p. 25.
30 Biro, 'Is anybody out there?', p. 17.
31 Lovric, 'Croatia', p. 3.
32 Stefan Krause, 'Bulgaria's controversial electronic media law', *Transition*, 2, 21, 18 October 1996, p. 32.
33 'Serbia throttle free media', *RFE/RL Balkan Report*, 2, 42, 28 October 1998; B92 Open Yugoslavia, Daily News Service, 15 October 1998, at Internet address http:// b92eng.opennet.org/
34 Drago Hedl, 'Feral Tribune on trial', *Warreport*, 43, July 1996, p. 22.
35 Schmidt, 'Party politics'.
36 See Ben Blushi, 'Curse of the last dictator', *Guardian*, 12 March 1997.
37 *The Times*, Editorial, 5 March 1997.
38 The Internet address for the Freedom House organization is http://www.freedomhouse.org
39 The Internet address for Radio Free Europe/Radio Liberty is http://www.rferl.org
40 In 1994, almost $12 million were given to media and communications projects in the Balkans, particularly in Serbia, Romania and Macedonia, by Soros. Important financial assistance to the independent media in Serbia, Croatia, Bosnia and Montenegro has also been provided by the International Federation of Journalists and by the Federation Internationale des Editors de Journaux, 'some of which owe their very existence to this support'. See *Unfinished Peace: Report of the International Commission on the Balkans*, New York: Aspen Institute/Carnegie Endowment For International Peace, 1996, p. 154.
41 Schmidt, 'Party politics', p. 37.
42 Ruston, 'The war of words', p. 9.
43 See Kati Marton, 'Put a free press atop the agenda of the former Yugoslavia', *International Herald Tribune*, 3 June 1996.
44 Hedl, 'Feral Tribune on trial', p. 22.
45 See 'Good Morning Mr Tudjman', editorial in the *Washington Post*, 2 August 1996.
46 *International Herald Tribune*, 28 July 1995.
47 Schmidt, 'Party politics', p. 37; Ionescu, 'Romanian Media', p. 53. For Berisha's 1997 move, see *The Times* editorial, 5 March 1997.

48 B92 Open Yugoslavia, Daily News Service, 16 November 1998.

49 Natasha Borchanin and Julie Moffett, 'Serbia: Internet play key role in Belgrade politics', *Radio Free Europe*, 14 April 1997.

50 Steve Crawshaw, 'Protestors pull the plug on Milosevic's cosy vision of Serbia', *Independent*, 24 January 1997.

51 Julian Borger, *Guardian*, 2 November 1996.

52 *Independent*, 24 January 1997.

53 Julian Borger, *Guardian*, 27 November 1996.

54 *Independent*, 24 January 1997.

55 Information from Kyril Drezov.

56 'Bulgaria-human rights', RFE-RL, 1997, http://www.rferl.org/bd/bu/info/Bu-hr.html

57 Tony Barber, *Independent*, 25 January 1997.

58 See US department of State Human Rights Report 1996, 'Romania', Washington, Bureau of Democracy, Human Rights and Labour, 1997.

59 See Thomas Carrothers, *Assessing Democracy Assistance: The Case of Romania*, New York: McArthur Foundation, 1996.

60 *Evenimentul Zilei*, 7 November 1996.

61 Tom Gallagher, *Romania After Ceauşescu: The Politics of Intolerance*, Edinburgh: Edinburgh University Press, 1995, p. 205 .

62 The human rights watchdog Freedom House carries out an annual survey of press freedom worldwide. South-East Europe fared significantly worse than other regions, such as Central and South America which have moved away from fully authoritarian rule. In four out of the seven countries (Bosnia, Albania, Croatia and Serbia) the media was described as 'Not Free' in 1997. In Bulgaria, Romania and Macedonia the media was seen as 'Partly Free' (a category to which Croatia had belonged till 1996). While the media in all of ex-communist Central Europe (with the exception of Slovakia) was seen as completely free, not one Balkan state belonged in that category. For more details, see Freedomhouse.org/Press/Press97/ratings97.html

63 The 1998 decision of two Romanian daily papers, *Ziua* and *Monitorul* to publish Hungarian-language papers may help to persuade their readers from the Romanian majority that it is normal for Romanians to contribute to the minority language press. See Monitorul, 12 December 1998, http://www.monitorul.ro/

64 In Bulgaria, President Stoyanov vetoed a new radio and television law on 28 September 1998 out of concern that it fell short of guaranteeing the political independence of the broadcasting media and could create divisions between ethnic groups. See Reuters, 28 September 1998, quoted in *Central Europe Online*, 29 September 1998, at website, http://www.centraleurope.com/.

6 Economic transformation and democratization in the Balkans

Will Bartlett

Introduction

A central question in the study of democratization has been the relationship between the level of economic development and the level of support for democratic institutions. In a classic work, Lipset argued that the more prosperous a nation is, the more likely that it will be able to sustain democracy.[1] A key role was played in Lipset's theory by the assumption that economic development would be associated with a reduction in the economic role of the state. This would further increase the chances for democracy through the growth of a middle class with interests independent of the state; through a reduction in clientelistic relations, nepotism and corruption, as income-earning opportunities outside the state become more abundant; and through the development of civil society in which voluntary and intermediary associations play an increasing role, and through which a pluralistic competition of interest can develop.

Even in societies in which the role of the state does diminish as economic development takes place, this virtuous relationship may be interrupted. In the extreme, in what Diamond refers to as 'statist' societies in which the state plays a predominant role in economic affairs, democracy may be undermined as individuals seek to manipulate state resources in order to enhance their personal wealth.[2] In statist societies, political corruption becomes the chief vehicle for upward social mobility which drains democratic institutions of both economic resources and political legitimacy. Diamond argues that the consequences of such statism are likely to be corruption, abuse of power, economic stagnation and crisis, ethnic conflict, electoral fraud and political violence. As a result of these effects, statism can lead to the breakdown or interruption of democracy. These types of effects, including both the perverse economic and political consequences of statism, have become familiar hallmarks of the transition processes in the Balkan states.

In an extensive review of the literature since the publication of Lipset's work, Diamond found substantial support for this proposition, but highlighted the importance of a set of intermediary factors which, supported by economic development, lead directly to democratization. These inter-mediary factors include improvements in education which lead to and support the development of a democratic political culture; the inter-nationalization of elites which exposes them to Western democratic values and beliefs; and improved living standards which increase the time horizon for change and induce a more gradualist democratic approach to politics.

Since the relationship between economic development and democratiz-ation in Lipset's theory was posited to operate through a variety of inter-mediary factors, there was no necessary direct link between the two, and many counter-examples have been found. The most obvious of these was the persistence of authoritarian regimes for many years in Eastern Europe despite their relatively high level of economic development. But even here the events of 1989 seemed to support the Lipset theory, as the totalitarian regimes were swept away and the predicted process of democratization began. However, in South-East Europe (which we will refer to as the 'Balkans') the old statist political systems were not transformed by popular revolutions as they had been elsewhere in Eastern Europe. Only in Slovenia did popular social movements play a key role in the overthrow of the old regime. In many cases, the old elite continued to hold on to power even after the introduction of democratic political systems.[3] In several of the Balkan states, the communist parties, renamed the Socialist Party (in Bulgaria and the Federal Republic of Yugoslavia), the National Salvation Front (Romania), or the Social Democratic Union (Former Yugoslav Republic of Macedonia), won elections outright.[4] Elsewhere, genuine anti-communist opposition parties came to power.[5] But these opposition parties did not fundamentally transform the statist approach to national govern-ance, and in most instances co-opted members of the former ruling elite.

In general, therefore, in the Balkan region, there has not been a significant transformation of the political and economic elite, nor has there been a significant reduction in the economic role of the state. These societies have retained much of their previous character of statist societies, despite nearly ten years of economic and political transition. An extreme version of this perspective can be found in the work of Diamandouros, who, drawing on the work of Max Weber, refers to the Balkan states as being characterized by 'sultanism'.[6] By this he means an ideal type regime distinguished by 'the highly personal and arbitrary nature of rule, by the absence of the rule of law, the unmediated and despotic exercise of power, low institutionalization, the absence of intermediary structures, and hence the weakness of civil society'.[7] These characteristics can to some degree be found in many of the Balkan states. The lingering role of this type of state imposes in many cases a formidable obstacle to the development of democracy.

This chapter will discuss comparatively and in some detail the impact of economic developments directly on the chances for democratization in the Balkan countries. The strong role of the sultanistic state will serve as a background to explain some of the choices which have been made in the field of economic policy. For example, Smith emphasized the gradualist policy orientation in Romania, Bulgaria and Albania, as opposed to the more rapid and effective approach adopted to economic reform in Poland, the former German Democratic Republic and elsewhere.[8] Smith noted the lack of a clean political break with the past, and the way in which communist parties retained significant power and influence in the transition period. In this view the Balkan states have become nomenklatura-dominated economies characterized by soft-budget constraints; subsidies to loss-making industries; a lack of genuine privatization; extensive bribery and corruption; protection from foreign competition; hostility to foreign investment; and a tendency towards import substitution rather than export promotion.[9] This has imposed constraints on the speed of reforms, and also on the willingness of international financial institutions to provide support to the process of economic transition. Stalled economic transition has been characterized by severe economic downturns in some states, and by slow growth in others. The resulting absence of significant improvements in economic conditions has reduced the chances for a successful transition to democracy. A vicious downward spiral of low economic growth and reduced democratic political culture is in danger of spinning out of control in a region which has seen more than its fair share of crisis and social collapse.

Continuities and discontinuities in the post-communist Balkan states

In the context of South-East Europe one can identify two distinct groups of countries with quite different sets of preconditions for economic and political transition. The first group is composed of the former centrally planned economies of Albania, Bulgaria and Romania. These economies operated on the classic pattern of Stalinist central planning, implemented far more rigorously than in some other more developed East European economies to the north.[10] Economic development was promoted on the basis of extensive state ownership of the means of production. There was an emphasis on extremely large-scale enterprises focusing on the priority given to heavy industry at the expense of consumer goods. In each country the political system was highly centralized and based on the elimination of all political opposition. Within this group an important distinction can be made between Bulgaria and Romania, which were previously within the Soviet bloc, and Albania, which had pursued an independent and isolationist policy outside the bloc. Political change in Bulgaria and Romania has been characterized as one of preventive reform or compromise, through which the ruling elite from the previous communist period retained political power during the first half of the 1990s (or in the case of Bulgaria regained power after an initial period of coalition government).

In contrast, anti-communists came to power in the 1992 elections in Albania, but the nature of the ruling party under Sali Berisha remained highly authoritarian.

The second group is composed of the successor states of the former Yugoslavia in which central planning had been abandoned in the early 1950s and replaced with a unique form of market socialism. Although a one-party system had been in operation, there was some space for independent social movements, especially in the northern republics. There was also competition between the decentralized republican communist parties. Yugoslavia was furthermore significantly more prosperous than its centrally planned neighbours throughout the post-war period. Elections held in 1990 saw the emergence of nationalist parties, either as transformed communist parties as in Serbia, Montenegro and Macedonia or as anti-communist parties as in Croatia and Slovenia. Following the break-up of Yugoslavia the political transition in the Federal Republic (FR) of Yugoslavia and Macedonia was therefore similar in some respects to that in Romania and Bulgaria, owing to the elements of continuity in the political make-up of the governments from the previous regime. In Croatia and Slovenia there was a discontinuous break with the political past. However, there was a more broadly based civil society and democratic culture in Slovenia than elsewhere in former Yugoslavia, and the prospects for genuine democratic reform were correspondingly greater.[11] In Bosnia-Hercegovina, the elections brought to power nationalist parties based around ethnic divisions, but the slide to civil war quickly arrested any prospects of democratic transition.

In general, therefore, in all the Balkan states, there was a lesser challenge to the position of the ruling economic elites than occurred in the northern tier of East European states. With the exception of Slovenia, the new democracies were governed by rulers with authoritarian tendencies, and with extensive links to the economic elites comprised of managers of state enterprises, or of 'socially owned' enterprises in the case of the former Yugoslavia. In several cases the new political regimes displayed characteristics which can be categorized as sultanistic, especially in those countries in which a dominant presidential figure has a large amount of power and influence as in Albania, Croatia, Serbia and Romania. But it also characterized the political regime in other countries which had for long periods in their history been under Ottoman rule, such as Bulgaria and Macedonia. The results of sultanism have been, to various degrees, corruption, abuse of power, economic stagnation and crisis, electoral fraud and political violence.[12]

Political economy of privatization: preserving the old elite

The economic policies adopted in the Balkan states reflected the continuities and discontinuities in the composition of political elites. In contrast to the shock therapy approach adopted in the northern tier of East European countries, the dominant approach to economic transition was one of gradualism. This was reflected in the generally slow pace of privatization. Although privatization is normally conceived as a primary means of creating a market economy, in the Balkan context privatization has provided ample opportunities for the ruling elite to maintain its grip on power. Four distinct modalities of privatization can be identified: stalled privatization, 'wild' privatization, insider privatization and politicized privatization.

Stalled privatization

In Bulgaria, Romania and Albania privatization has proceeded slowly, and has not occurred at all in FR Yugoslavia. Economic elites have held on to power through the preservation of state-owned enterprises, and close links between the political and economic elites have been retained. In Bulgaria, although a privatization law was passed in May 1992, in practice it was implemented half-heartedly by different governments over the next five years. The early non-socialist governments of 1991–4 hesitated to implement privatization because they suspected that the process would be captured by former communists who had amassed fortunes from corruption and semi-legal dealings.[13] But when a socialist government was elected in 1994 it turned out that it had little interest in pushing privatization forward. Enterprise managers, state officials, as well as the government itself, all sought to block or delay the privatization process.[14] In Romania there were two rounds of mass privatization, but these covered mainly smaller enterprises. During this period the government failed to break the links between the enterprises, the state bureaucracy and the political establishment.[15] Nearly 500 small and medium sized enterprises were privatised up to 1994, mainly through management and employee buy-outs. Many of the larger enterprises and public utilities were converted into autonomous public enterprises and were never included in the privatization process. As many as 2,700 enterprises were entered into the new privatization programme in 1997, but by the end of the year only half were on target for privatization. In Albania a mass privatization programme was begun in 1995, using a voucher scheme. However, the vouchers were viewed with great scepticism by the public and soon became heavily discounted. The privatization process was extremely slow and only twenty enterprises were privatised in the first year and a further fifty in 1996.[16]

In FR Yugoslavia many formerly independent self-managed firms were nationalized especially in public utilities such as electricity, railways, airlines, oil, forestry, water supply, communications, radio and television. In other sectors enterprises were converted into so-called 'mixed ownership' but in which the state has effective control in steel, metal industries and electronics.[17] Even among firms which were formally privatized, in practice many were controlled by the banks which often had a dominant share-holding, and the big banks in turn were controlled by the state. The other major shareholders were very often the managers who had managed to buy large shareholdings at heavily discounted prices, while 'employees were unable to participate in the process because of their total pauperization'.[18] Furthermore, under a law designed to revalue the assets of privatized companies passed in 1994, most of the previously privatized enterprises were effectively returned to state ownership, as their non-privatized 'social capital' was increased in value.

In these four countries, therefore, the bulk of industrial assets remain under state ownership and control and the old managerial elite has maintained its grip on power. The state-owned companies typically operate at a loss with huge state subsidies, draining the budget which could be used to support more productive activities. In Bulgaria, for example, out of a total of 5,890 state enterprises as many as 2,130 were making losses in 1996. Less than one-fifth of the loss-makers accounted for 90 per cent of the losses.

Wild privatization

In countries in which formal processes of privatization were not introduced, or were stalled, there have nevertheless been ample opportunities for various forms of unofficial or 'wild' privatization. This has enabled members of the ruling elite to appropriate the economic surplus from the state-owned enterprises. Methods have included the setting up of 'by-pass' companies by enterprise managers.[19] These private companies operate in parallel with state-owned companies, and the most profitable contracts are offered to the bypass companies, to the benefit of the managers. This has been taken to further extremes in Bulgaria where private conglomerates (so-called 'groupings') have established joint ventures with state-owned firms. The groupings supply the partner state-owned firms with raw materials at high prices, and buy back the products of the state-owned firms at low prices, syphoning off the profits of the state-owned firms. The groupings have been notoriously active in the semi-legal production of pirated compact discs, but have also entered more legitimate areas of business such as the energy sector. Needless to say, the groupings also have close links with organised crime.[20] Elsewhere, enterprise managers have been able to strip the asset base of state-owned companies prior to privatization, reducing their valuation and purchasing shares at low prices, often on the basis of privileged unsecured loans from the state-owned banking system.

Insider privatization

The privatization process has been formally completed only in Slovenia and Macedonia. But in both those countries, most privatized companies are dominated by insiders. In the case of management buy-outs privatized companies have often been transferred to the managers at knock-down prices, while in the case of employee buy-outs the transfer of ownership to employees has often taken place at inflated prices.

Privatization legislation was passed in Slovenia in 1992, but implement-ation did not begin until much later in 1994. The overall share of the private sector in the Slovenian economy was already estimated at 50 per cent of GDP by the end of 1995, providing 47 per cent of total employ-ment. By the end of 1996 around 90 per cent of privatization plans had been approved and privatization was virtually completed by the end of 1997. Privatization to employees and managers formed a significant element of the Slovenian privatization process, but there was also a signi-ficant transfer of assets to three state funds: the Development Fund, the Pension Fund and the Compensation Fund. By the end of 1997, two-thirds of privatized companies had majority insider control (i.e. by managers and employees). These represented one-third of assets of enterprises eligible for privatization.[21] A further third of assets were held by the various state funds, and a further third by outside owners, mainly small shareholders.

Macedonia was also relatively late in implementing its privatization programme. The Macedonian Law on Transformation of Enterprises with Social Capital was introduced in 1993. Little progress was made until early 1995, but once begun it was effectively completed by the end of 1997 by which time over one thousand enterprises had been fully privatized, and only 234 remained in the privatization process. The main method of privatization in Macedonia was through management and employee buy-out.[22] Of these, management buy-outs were the most important form of privatization in terms of both employment and the value of equity involved.[23] The most profitable or potentially profitable enterprises were sold to managers at substantial discounts, often on the basis of severely undervalued asset valuations. Weaker and smaller enterprises were sold to employees often at more inflated valuations of assets. In one case, a mine with over a hundred years of mineral reserves was sold to managers at a ridiculously low valuation of DM 300,000. In another case a struggling tobacco company in a weak market position *vis-à-vis* the monopoly tobacco-purchasing company was sold to employees at a highly overvalued price of DM 1.5 million.[24] In a number of cases managements have acquired further shares from employees by dubious methods, or have appropriated the voting rights of the employee share holdings, consolidating majority holdings to the management group.

In both Slovenia and Macedonia, therefore, the old managerial elite has remained in power, despite the appearance of a radical change of ownership as a result of the completion of the privatization process. Despite this similarity, however, the consequences of insider privatization have been quite different in the two countries. In Slovenia a democratic political culture has emerged and the government is committed to radical market reforms, and effective restructuring of privatized enterprises appears to be taking place. In Macedonia, although the state is ostensibly commited to radical market reform, and has adopted a number of measures to implement reforms backed up by significant amounts of international donor assistance, there is little evidence as yet of significant enterprise restructuring. The dominance of the ruling managerial elite at a political level has resulted in the maintenance of subsidies and soft loans from the banking system to the larger enterprises. Recent elections have brought gains for the opposition parties, but as these parties have a strongly nationalistic orientation, there is a danger of polarization of the social and economic elites along ethnic lines which is likely to delay the implementation of economic reforms for the foreseeable future.

Politicized privatization

The privatization process in Croatia has had mixed results. Substantial sections of the formerly socially owned enterprise sector of the economy have been privatized. However, the process has been highly politicized and privatized companies have been transferred at minimal cost to new managers loyal to the ruling political party on the basis of privileged low cost loans from the banks, which have themselves been under political control. Croatia passed its own privatization law in April 1991. Enterprises which did not submit plans were transformed directly into state-owned enterprises, typically in public utilities. Even enterprises which were formally privatized were often effectively under state control, since in many cases the Croatian Privatization Fund held a high proportion of the shares. By 1994, 386 enterprises covering 40 per cent of total assets had majority state ownership through the Privatization Fund.[25] In some cases, the Privatization Agency replaced existing management teams with managers more closely linked to the ruling party.[26] In other cases, privatization led to management buy-outs at high discounts on undervalued assets.

In all the Balkan countries, therefore, the ruling elite has been able to preserve positions of power and influence in relation to the ownership and control of major economic assets. Where privatization has been stalled, this control is direct through the continuing state ownership of major enterprises. Elsewhere, privatization to managers, or politicized privatiz-ation, has resulted in effective control by the political and managerial elite of the newly privatized companies. In each case, the results of privatization have inhibited the attractiveness of these economies for inward foreign direct investment. This in turn reduces the extent to which the elite can become internationalized (one of Diamond's intermediary factors in the development of a democratic political culture), and so reduces prospects for democratization. It also places limits on the reduction in the role of the state in economic affairs and inhibits the development of an independent middle class, another of the conditions required for the development of a sustainable democracy.

Bottom-up transformation and Small and Medium Enterprises (SMEs): creating a middle class

Under these conditions, privatization alone will not create the middle class needed to produce strong pressure for the development of civil society and to support the transition to democracy. The growth of this middle class is predicated on the creation of a class of small business owners. These new businesses are almost by definition small firms. They serve several functions including job creation, improvement of the competitive environment, the growth of productivity and the spread of innovation. Unfortunately, in few of the Balkan economies has there been a substantial growth of a viable small business sector. One of the key reasons has been the lack of a coherent policy for the development of this sector, despite the consistent engagement of international assistance programmes sponsored by the EU (through the PHARE programme) and the World Bank and a plethora of other bilateral and multilateral economic assistance programmes. Why has this been so? Mainly because, in statist societies such as prevail in the Balkans, it is against the interest of the ruling elites, whose fortunes are closely linked to the economic rents earned by the large state-owned or privatized companies. The development of a vibrant competitive small business sector would be a threat to such interests. As a result, policies are weak and lack effective implementation strategies, or worse, the state in various ways actively creates barriers to the entry and growth of the small business sector.

This process can be traced through in the various Balkan countries in different ways. After 1989 Yugoslavia, and subsequently the successor states spawned by secession, experienced a rapid entry of new small firms in the private sector despite significant obstacles in the form of lack of finance, adverse government regulation and taxation policies and the market dominance of the large firm sector. Entry rates were especially high in Slovenia and Croatia between 1990 and 1995. Increasing unemployment levels were moderated by the growth of employment in the small firms sector. However, obstacles to the start-up of new small businesses remain, especially in the southern successor states. Small firms are required to secure a large number of licences to begin operation, each of which requires the employment of specialized consultants, or at worst under-the-counter payments to bribe officials. In FR Yugoslavia import licences are required to secure needed raw materials, and these are open to political abuse and manipulation by politicians. Entrepreneurs seeking import licences require political protection and opponents of the regime are regularly visited by the financial police. Registration requirements to establish new small firms are also onerous, requiring various payments and lengthy registration processes and documentation. Business taxation imposes a heavy burden on small firms, as there are generally few tax breaks related to size or age of the firm.[27] As a result there is a large grey economy in FR Yugoslavia and Macedonia. The war economy of FR Yugoslavia was based on smuggling and sanctions-busting, money-laundering and narcotics – and linked to mafia connections through Montenegro. In Macedonia the mafia even extended its influence into specific ministries, on occasion with the assistance of Italian representatives of international donor programmes.

There are also many obstacles facing the new entrepreneurs as they try to develop their businesses. One of the principal obstacles to growth of the small firms sector is a lack of affordable finance provided through the banking system. In most of the successor states, the banking system has still not recovered from the aftermath of the break-up of the country. In FR Yugoslavia and Macedonia in particular there is a widespread lack of confidence in the banks, and individuals are reluctant to entrust their savings to them. What limited bank finance is available is still largely oriented to the provision of credit to the large enterprise sector. In Macedonia, an influx of foreign assistance geared towards the promotion of small and medium sized firms has begun to ease this constraint. The banking system in Croatia, FR Yugoslavia and Macedonia is also still burdened by a large amount of non-performing debt held by the large companies. When it comes to financing small enterprises, loans are provided at high interest rates, and with large collateral requirements (often as high as 300 per cent). This has placed severe obstacles in the way of small firm growth in FR Yugoslavia and Macedonia in particular, although there is some evidence that recent entrants in Croatia have managed to expand their activities in the post start-up phase.[28]

Entrepreneurs often seek to avoid these obstacles by operating in the grey economy, taking advantage of informal sources of finance, and avoiding the burden of state regulation and taxation. As a result much of the new entrepreneurship is unproductive, as effort and resources are devoted to avoiding regulation. Among larger firms also, unproductive entrepreneurship takes the form of attempts to establish and maintain dominant or monopoly positions. There are close connections between the economic and political elites in many of the successor states. Managers and owners of large firms and banks have developed (or retained) close links with the politicians in the ruling parties. In many cases there is a rotation of elites between positions of political and economic power. The break-up of the old Yugoslavia was led by these local elites, who have only benefited from a reinforcement of their local power by the creation of the new mini-states. This convergence of political and economic power makes it relatively easy for the large enterprise sector to establish and maintain monopoly positions, and influence economic policy in a way that is inimical to the development of a new competitive sector of small business. The lack of a coherent strategy towards the development of the small business sector is

not an accident. In practice, the leading political interests, although often
ostensibly in favour of such policies, actually go out of their way to make
life as difficult as possible for small business entrepreneurs, at least for
those who do not support the ruling party. Only Slovenia seems to have
been able to avoid this malaise, and created a small firms sector which is
competitive and innovative and capable of supporting sustainable growth.

The development of the small business sector is far weaker still in the
former centrally planned economies of Bulgaria and Romania. There is
some evidence that a significant small business sector has begun to
develop in Bulgaria, although it has received little support from the state,
which has devoted most resources to subsiding the large state-owned sector
of the economy.[29] Albania is rather different again, with a substantial part
of economic activity now concentrated in the small business sector,
although this is mainly in the area of trade and services. All have benefited
from large inputs of foreign aid and resources into the development of the
small business sector, through bodies such as the EU PHARE programme
and the World Bank. However, the lack of experience with market
economies and with independent business management will take a long
time to overcome. In the meantime the prospects for the development of
the small business sector and the associated development of a middle class
are problematic.

Trajectories of economic development

The economic trajectories in the post-communist Balkan states have been
strongly influenced by the extent to which privatization has taken place,
and by the pace of small business development. According to the standard
economic theory of transition, structural reforms (privatization and the
development of the new private business sector), as well as stabilization of
the macro-economy and liberalization of economic controls over prices,
wages and foreign trade, are required to underpin sustainable growth and
the development of a market economy. The pattern of economic developments in the Balkans mirrors the pace at which such reforms have taken
place. This section therefore outlines the different economic trajectories of
economic development in each of the Balkan states.

In general, countries with stalled privatization, and which have pursued
a gradualist approach to economic transition, have run into economic
crises of various types. Countries which have pushed through privatization,
even where based largely on insider privatization, or where the privatization process has been politicized, have had a more favourable economic
growth outcome. Even among this latter group of countries, however,
sustained growth seems to depend upon the simultaneous development of
a vibrant sector of new small private businesses, which has really only
occurred in Slovenia. Not surprisingly, it is only in Slovenia where the
prospects for a sustained democracy appear to be at all favourable.

Gradualism and the occurrence of economic crisis

In the aftermath of the overthrow of the communist systems in Albania, Bulgaria and Romania there was an initial period of economic disruption and recession, but by the mid-1990s all three countries had emerged from slump and appeared to be entering into a period of economic recovery. However, in the mid-1990s, almost simultaneously, all three countries entered into a sharp and largely unexpected economic crisis, deeper in Bulgaria and Albania than in Romania. This second round of economic crisis and downturn was linked with a lack of economic restructuring, associated with the gradualist approach to economic transition which had been adopted by the governments in these countries.

In both Bulgaria and Romania, governments had supported state-owned enterprises by providing subsidies and by allowing enterprises to default on loans to the banks. As a result the banking sector in Bulgaria became insolvent and collapsed at the end of 1996, leading to a hyper-inflationary spiral culminating in a monthly inflation rate of 200 per cent by February 1997. Between May and November 1996 fourteen banks were closed, and the surviving banks ceased to lend money.[30] A number of pyramid savings schemes collapsed. People soon lost confidence in the lev as a unit of currency and began to convert their leva into dollars on a mass scale. Transactions were increasingly made on a barter basis or for dollars. There was an outflow of foreign currency and the official reserves fell from $1.2 billion to just $0.5 billion. The exchange rate fell from 70 lev to the dollar in February 1996 to 3,000 lev to the dollar by February 1997. As a result of the collapse of the lev, wages in the public sector fell to the equivalent of $10 per month and pensions fell to $5 per month. In Romania, subsidies to state-owned enterprises amounted to 10 per cent of GDP in 1993. Output growth was dependent on heavy industries which absorbed huge amounts of imports. Since exports were uncompetitive, a balance of payments crisis developed which eventually led to a currency devaluation in November 1995. During 1996 the budget deficit rose to over 10 per cent of GDP and inflation increased from 28 per cent at the end of 1995 to 57 per cent at the end of 1996. Although the Romanian economy did not enter as deep a crisis as occurred in Bulgaria, the International Monetary Fund (IMF) and the World Bank became dissatisfied with the progress of the gradualist policies and withdrew their support.

The onset of the economic crisis in both countries led to significant changes in government and an opening for the opposition to pursue more radical economic policies. Violent demonstrations took place in Bulgaria against the government in January 1997 and a new caretaker government took over in February. The government quickly reached an agreement with the IMF in April on the implementation of a new programme of stabilization and structural reform involving the closure of the largest sixty-four loss-making firms and an increase in IMF credits.[31] General elections were held in May which returned the opposition Union of Democratic Forces (UDF) coalition to power with a substantial majority. The new government took urgent steps to stabilize the economy, ending the subsidization of state enterprises, reducing inflation and introducing a currency board – a drastic measure to stabilize the exchange rate. The policy brought about a rapid drop in the rate of inflation to 19 per cent per annum by June 1998, the lowest rate since 1991. Privatization was relaunched, but it appears that so far mostly smaller enterprises have been privatized, and largely to managers rather than outside investors. In Romania, a new centre-right government was elected at the end of 1996 which re-established links with the international financial organizations and introduced a 'shock therapy' programme. The new policy involved price liberalization, a reduction of import tariffs, and a removal of subsidies. Price liberalization resulted in a further surge in inflation which rose to 160 per cent in 1997. A restrictive monetary policy was designed to reduce the budget deficit to below 5 per cent of GDP. The National Bank raised its discount rate from 35 per cent to 50 per cent in January 1997. The major loss-making industries were to be closed down or privatized, and in general the process of privatization was to be speeded up. However, as a result of the restrictive nature of the stabilization policy, output began to decline, and unemployment increased from 6 per cent in 1996 to 10 per cent in 1997, due to the closing down of companies and an increase in lay-offs.

In both countries, therefore, the gradualist approach to economic policy led to economic stagnation and crisis, which provided an opportunity for opposition parties to gain power. However, the ability of these new governments to bring about effective reform is limited by the entrenched positions of the managerial elite, and prospects for fundamental structural reform appear bleak. Nevertheless, it is clear that the crisis has brought about a significant break with the past and a new opportunity for the consolidation of democratic reforms.

The Albanian case has developed along a rather similar path, despite the position in power of an anti-communist party committed to the development of a market economy. After a sharp decline in economic activity in Albania in 1991 and 1992, economic recovery was led by a rapid growth of agricultural output as well as a construction boom and a growth of the service sector. From 1993 to 1996 Albania achieved one of the highest growth rates of Eastern Europe. In 1993, and again in 1995, GDP increased by 11 per cent. However, these rapid rates of growth should be seen in the context of a dismally low starting point. Moreover, economic growth was supported by large inflows of foreign aid and remittances of earnings of Albanian migrant workers abroad, rather than being an outcome of significant economic reforms. By 1995 unemployment began to decrease from extremely high levels of around 30 per cent, and wages almost doubled from $37 per month in 1993 to $70 per month in 1996. The small-scale private sector developed rapidly, although it was dominated by small-scale retail firms. By 1996 the private sector accounted for 65 per cent of output and employed two-thirds of the workforce. In May 1996 the ruling Democratic Party was returned to power with a huge majority, but the elections were marked by extensive violations of electoral law and intimidation of voters. The rapid economic growth had fuelled an enormous increase in the demand for credit which was met by a growth in informal sector financial institutions including pyramid savings schemes. These schemes collected an enormous amount of money from the population, estimated at more than $1.2 billion, before eventually going bankrupt in 1997. Savings banks were also established on the basis of black market operations linked to smuggling and sanctions-busting, mainly involving the supply of oil to Yugoslavia. Italian Mafia organizations were allegedly involved in these illegal activities in Albania. The pyramid savings schemes were tolerated by the government as a populist measure but also because they supported the ruling party's election campaign.[32] When sanctions against Yugoslavia were lifted in 1995, this source of profit evaporated. Interest rates were raised dramatically to attract depositors, in some cases to as high as 30–100 per cent per month. This proved un-sustainable and the pyramid saving schemes collapsed in 1997, bringing about the impoverishment of large sections of the population. It was revealed in April 1997 that one such company, Vefa, owed $400 million in lost deposits to 86,500 creditors. No one knows where or to whom these funds went. In the ensuing chaos, many of the economic gains achieved over the previous five years were lost.

Yugoslav successor states: transition from self-management

By the mid-1990s the northern states of former Yugoslavia had recovered from the initial transition shock and from the effects of war. Slovenia registered economic growth in 1993 and the Croatian economy began to recover in 1995. Their economies have taken off into sustained growth. The southern economies of former Yugoslavia have fared far worse. Economic disaster has beset Bosnia-Hercegovina as a result of the war, while FR Yugoslavia has been severely affected by economic sanctions. In both cases the economies have been severely affected. Macedonia has also been badly hit and is only just beginning to come out of a sustained period of economic decline.

In the immediate aftermath of the break-up of Yugoslavia, all the former republics experienced a sharp deterioration in their economic positions. This was partly linked to the break-up of the single Yugoslav market, although in any case trade and capital flows between the former republics had already fallen to very low levels. In the case of Croatia and FR Yugoslavia, the fall in production was closely associated with the war between those two new states in 1991–2. The subsequent war in Bosnia from 1992 to 1995 brought about the destruction of the Bosnian state, and a disastrous decline in the economy. FR Yugoslavia suffered further from the imposition of international sanctions during the period of the war in Bosnia. Macedonia to the south was also in a parlous position, cut off from the Yugoslav market and in addition badly affected by a Greek trade embargo imposed in protest against the supposed aggressive symbolism of the Macedonian use of the star of Vergina on the new national flag, and even objections to the name of the new state. Slovenia was easily in the most favourable position, and quickly recovered from the economic slump of the early 1990s to become one of the most prosperous of the Eastern European post-socialist economies, and the only 'Balkan' country to be included in the list of countries forming the first wave of eastward expansion of the EU.

The economic development of independent Croatia was strongly influenced by the impact of war with Serbia between 1991 and 1992. During this war enormous amounts of damage were caused, and large parts of the national territory were effectively lost to rebel forces in the Krajina regions. Real GDP fell by 21 per cent in 1991 and a further 11 per cent in 1992. Unemployment reached 15 per cent and inflation began to increase reaching hyper-inflationary levels in 1993. At this point, with the ending of the war the previous year, Croatia introduced a stabilization programme in October 1993 which was surprisingly successful in eliminating inflation. The programme involved a tight monetary policy, limits on public sector wages and full currency convertibility[33]. There was an initial appreciation of the exchange rate which has been subsequently pegged to the Deutsche Mark. Inflation was more or less eliminated, but it was a further two years before the policy provided any benefits in terms of renewed economic growth. Further fighting took place in 1995 with the bombardment of Zagreb in May and the Oluja ('Storm') offensive against the Krajina Serbs in August. This hindered the revival of the key tourist industry on the Croatian coast, but by 1997 the tourist industry had begun to revive and economic growth of over 4 per cent per annum was recorded. However, the politicized nature of privatization and the lack of an effective policy for the development of the new small-scale private business sector have meant that economic growth has been based upon very insecure foundations. The banking system is under severe strain as large loss-making enterprises, even those which have been formally privatized, continue to attract privileged soft loans from the banks, on the basis of political connections. It seems unlikely that growth can be sustained under the present political regime.

The economy of the FR Yugoslavia was also seriously affected by the war with Croatia, but it was not until the imposition of sanctions against Yugoslavia in May 1992 that the economic impact was felt in a serious way. In 1992 Yugoslav GDP fell by 26 per cent and again in 1993 by a further 28 per cent, the largest recorded annual decline in GDP in any of the Balkan countries in the 1990s. A vicious hyper-inflation developed linked to the contraction of supplies. By December 1993 inflation had reached a

monthly rate of 1,000,000 per cent, bringing about a virtual demonetiz-
ation of the economy, and an enormous growth in the shadow (or 'parallel')
economy, which accounted for more than 50 per cent of economic activity
in 1993.[34] Unemployment growth was restrained by subsidies to loss-
making enterprises, so that the official unemployment rate was 'only' 25
per cent. However, real unemployment, taking into account surplus labour
in enterprises, was undoubtedly far higher. Real incomes fell dramatically
among the mass of the population, while the ruling elite enjoyed enormous
wealth derived from war profiteering. It is estimated that by 1993 the
average wage had fallen to the equivalent of 5DM, and the average pension
to 1DM per week, resulting in an elimination of the middle class and a
pauperization of the population.[35] By the end of 1993 industrial
production had fallen to 35 per cent of its 1989 level. Remarkably, partly
due to the tight control of the state over the mass media, the ruling
Socialist Party of Serbia was returned to power in elections held in
December. An anti-inflation policy was introduced in January 1994. This
involved the introduction of a new currency (the 'new dinar') pegged at a
ratio of 1:1 to the Deutsche Mark. New money creation was to be
completely backed by foreign currency reserves, and fully convertible.
Industrial production began to recover as inflation was eliminated and real
GDP increased by 6 per cent or more for the next three years.

In Macedonia there was a serious economic decline in the immediate
aftermath of independence, partly due to the disruption of trading links
with the former Yugoslav republics to the north, and as a result also of UN
sanctions against Serbia and the Greek trade blockade. Social Product fell
by 14 per cent in 1992, and by a similar amount in 1993. A stabilization
policy was introduced and backed up with a restrictive monetary and fiscal
policy to control inflation. This was accompanied by attempts to control
wages of public sector workers to restrain domestic demand to non-
inflationary levels. The restrictive monetary policy increased interest rates
and reduced the ability of local enterprises to access credit from the
banking system, which in any case was in chaos as a result of bad loans to
large socially owned enterprises and the freezing of foreign currency
accounts. The rate of decline slowed to 8 per cent in 1994 and 5 per cent in
1995, but recorded unemployment reached 32 per cent with heavy
concentrations among young people and the Albanian ethnic minority. It
was only following the lifting of trade sanctions and the Greek embargo
that the economy has begun to recover with a growth of 1 per cent in 1996
and 5 per cent in 1997. However, as in Croatia, it seems unlikely that
growth can be sustained in the context of continued subsidies to loss-
making enterprises, a lack of radical enterprise restructuring and the slow
development of the institutional support structure for small business
development.

It is only in Slovenia that sustained economic growth has taken place.
Five years of continued economic growth reached a peak in 1998 with

expected growth of GDP of 6.5 per cent per annum. The genuine restructuring of the Slovenian economy, and the close links made with Western European export markets, have underpinned the favourable economic performance. Slovenia is also the only Balkan state to be included among the group of countries scheduled for early EU membership, which may be a factor contributing to its developing economic integration into Western markets. However, it also appears that in the context of a democratic political culture, insider privatization has resulted in effective restructuring of enterprises. The introduction of effective bankruptcy laws has enabled loss-making enterprises to be closed down. Nevertheless, there are still significant numbers of enterprises under state ownership, which account for 44 per cent of total enterprise assets, and which are responsible for the bulk of economic losses in the enterprise sector. The government has implemented a consistent policy to support the development of the small business sector, and a middle class has begun to emerge. This, together with sustainable economic growth, suggests that Slovenia, unlike the other Balkan countries, is well positioned to achieve democratic consolidation.

Conclusion: the interrelationship between economic and political transitions in the Balkans

In the Balkan economies political elites have to a greater or lesser extent been able to manipulate the privatization process to their own ends. In the former centrally planned economies of Bulgaria, Romania and Albania, privatization has been slow as elites have pursued a policy of gradualism in relation to economic reform. The elites refused to relinquish their power which was linked to the continued existence of state-owned enterprises. In the northern republics of former Yugoslavia privatization was pushed through by the new non-communist governments. However, in Slovenia insider privatization prevailed, while in Croatia a large part of the former socially owned firms was nationalized, and another part handed over to the associates of the new elite. In the southern republics, privatization in FR Yugoslavia has not yet taken off, while in Macedonia enterprises were mainly privatized to the managers.

As we have seen, these defects of privatization would be less problematic in cases where a new middle class has emerged which could support the transition to democracy. In most Balkan states there has indeed been a rapid growth of the private small business sector, but these new small firms are mainly family operations based on trade, and are not yet in a position to become a new driving force of economic growth. In the worst cases as in Serbia entrepreneurs who do not support the ruling party are obstructed by denial of import licences, tight financial control and discriminatory taxes, and the development of the middle class has been frustrated, or at least driven underground into the shadow economy. In a more democratic political climate such as Slovenia, small businesses are beginning to play an important role in the economy, and an independent middle class is beginning to emerge. Elsewhere, the development of a competitive small business sector is seen as a threat to the monopoly position of elites linked to big business and the development of the middle class has been discouraged.

The Lipset theory suggests that the prospects for democratic consolidation are greatest where economic development takes place. With the exception of Slovenia, the prospects for sustained economic growth which would underpin the regime change in the Balkans look bleak. In Bulgaria and Romania it is possible that the newly elected non-communist governments could effect a real economic and democratic breakthrough. In the northern ex-Yugoslav states economic growth can be expected to lead to a democratic consolidation (Slovenia) or transition (Croatia). In Macedonia some growth is taking place, but it remains a statist society and this interferes with the prospects for democratic consolidation. But in the FR Yugoslavia, economic isolation and decline hinders the transition to democracy. And in Albania and Bosnia-Hercegovina the preconditions for democratic transition have altogether broken down. It therefore appears that there is considerable variation in the prospects for democratization in the Balkan states.

Statism, although taking a different form in different countries, has interrupted the causal link between economic growth and democratization, and in several cases interrupted economic growth itself as it prevents radical restructuring. In turn the lack of growth inhibits the development of an independent middle class which would support democratization. The key to breaking this vicious circle lies in the promotion of inward investment to internationalize the elite, and in real progress with privatization, enterprise restructuring and small business development which would stimulate economic growth and lay the basis for the consolidation of the fragile democracies in the Balkans.

Notes

1 S. Lipset, 'Some social requisites of democracy: economic development and political legitimacy', *American Political Science Review*, March 1959, pp. 69–105.
2 L. Diamond, 'Economic development and democracy reconsidered', in G. Marks and L. Diamond, eds, *Reexamining Democracy: Essays in Honour of Seymour Martin Lipset*, London: Sage, pp. 93–139.
3 See T. Gallagher, 'Democratization in the Balkans: challenges and prospects', *Democratization*, 2, 3, 1995, pp. 337–61.
4 In Bulgaria there was a brief interregnum of opposition parties within the Union of Democratic Forces.
5 In Croatia the Croatian Democratic Union (HDZ) won the elections in 1990, and in Albania the Democratic Party of Albania won the elections under Sali Berisha in 1993.
6 See chapter 2 by Diamandouros and Larrabee in this volume.

7 P. N. Diamandouros, 'Prospects for democracy in the Balkans: comparative and theoretical perspectives', in F. S. Larrabee, ed., *The Volatile Powder Keg: Balkan Security After the Cold War*, Washington, DC: American University Press, 1994.

8 A. Smith, 'Problems of the transition to a market economy in Romania, Bulgaria and Albania: why has the transition proved so difficult?', in I. Jeffries, ed., *Problems of Economic and Political Transformation in the Balkans*, London: Pinter, 1996, pp. 111–130.

9 Ibid., p. 129.

10 For example in Poland private ownership of land had been permitted; in Hungary state enterprises operated with some autonomy from the planners.

11 S. P. Ramet, 'Slovenia's road to democracy', *Europe-Asia Studies*, 45, 5, 1993, pp. 869–86; T. Mastnak, 'From social movements to national sovereignty', in J. Benderly and E. Kraft, eds, *Independent Slovenia: Origins, Movements, Prospects*, New York: St. Martin's Press, 1993, pp. 93–111.

12 Instances of electoral fraud have been most well documented in the Albanian elections of 1996. In Croatia, the election of the mayor of Zagreb was vetoed by President Tudjman in 1996, and local elections in Serbia were vetoed by President Milosevic in the same year. Abuse of power is commonplace in most of the Balkan countries. For example in an economic context, the socialist government in Bulgaria presided over an 'impudent plundering of the state, and a de-capitalization of the Bulgarian economy'. A. Ivanov, 'From collapse to stabilization: through what?', paper presented at the workshop 'Is There a Southern Tier?', Central European University, Budapest, July 1997. Economic stagnation and crisis have been endemic throughout the region.

13 C. Rock and M. Klinedinst, 'Employee ownership and participation in Bulgaria, 1989 to mid-1996', in M. Uvalic and D. Vaughan-Whitehead, eds, *Privatization Surprises in Transition Economies: Employee-Ownership in Central and Eastern Europe*, Cheltenham: Elgar, 1997, pp. 80–119.

14 H. Pamouktchiev, S. Parvulov and S. Petranov, 'Process of privatization in Bulgaria', in D. C. Jones and J. Millar, eds, *The Bulgarian Economy: Lessons from the Early Transition*, Aldershot: Ashgate, 1997, pp. 205–30.

15 P. Ronnas, 'Romania: transition to underdevelopment?', in I. Jeffries, ed., *Problems of Economic and Political Transformation in the Balkans*, London: Pinter, 1996, pp. 13–32.

16 M. Muco, The impact of informal financial sector in Albanian 1996–1997 crisis, paper for the workshop 'Is There a Southern Tier', Central European University, Budapest, July 1997.

17 M. Lazić and L. Sekelj, 'Privatization in Yugoslavia (Serbia and Montenegro)', *Europe-Asia Studies*, 49, 6, 1997, pp. 1057–70.

18 Ibid., p. 1067.

19 A process which had also occurred extensively in Slovenia in the early 1990s.

20 R. D. Kaplan, 'Hoods against democrats', *Atlantic Monthly*, December 1998.

21 OECD, *OECD Economic Surveys: Slovenia 1997*, Paris, Organization for Economic Cooperation and Development, 1997, p. 93.

22 Enterprises could select from a variety of methods of privatization including management buy-out, employee buy-out (provided at least 51 per cent of assets are bought), leveraged buy-out (for a minimum of 20 per cent of assets), commercial sale of the enterprise, issue of shares to outsiders (of at least 30 per cent of the shares), debt equity swaps, leasing, or liquidation and sale of assets. In the case of employee buy-out, employees were offered discounts of 30 per cent plus a further 1 per cent for each year of employment in the enterprise. The maximum amount which could be bought by any employee was restricted to DM 25,000.

23 Management buy-outs accounted for DM 1.3 billion of assets out of a total value of assets of privatized enterprises of DM 3.5 billion.

24 These examples are taken from the author's field research in eastern Macedonia in February 1998.

25 M. Uvalić, 'Privatization in the Yugoslav successor states: converting self-management into property rights', in Uvalić and Vaughan-Whitehead, eds., *Privatization Surprises*, Cheltenham: Elgar, 1997, pp. 266–300.

26 I. Bićanić, 'Privatization in Croatia', *East European Politics and Societies*, 7, 3, 1993.

27 A. Denda, 'Current position of private SMEs and an analysis of the environment supporting the development of private SMEs in Yugoslavia', in J. Minic and A. Denda, eds, *How to Support SMEs in Yugoslavia*, Belgrade: European Movement in Serbia, 1998.

28 Z. Kovačević, 'Comparison of post-entry performance of new small firms in Croatian economy and in some West European countries', *Ekonomski Pregled*, 48, 5–6, 1997, pp. 391–404.

29 W. Bartlett, and R. Rangelova, 'Small firms and economic transformation in Bulgaria', *Small Business Economics*, 9, 1997, pp. 319–33.

30 A. Ivanov, 'From collapse to stabilization'.

31 G. Minassian, 'The road to economic disaster in Bulgaria', *Europe-Asia Studies*, 50, 2, 1998, pp. 331–49.

32 Muco, 'The impact'.

33 V. Franičević and E. Kraft 'Croatia's economy after stabilization', *Europe-Asia Studies*, 49, 4, 1997, pp. 669–92.

34 S. Adamović, 'Efforts towards economic recovery and monetary stabilization in FR Yugoslavia', *Communist Economies and Economic Transformation*, 7, 4, 1995, pp. 527–42.

35 Ibid.

7 Influencing regime change in the Balkans

The role of external forces in the transition

Valentin Stan

Introduction

The newly emerging democracies in the Balkans are generally confronted with two basic difficulties stemming respectively from the political pattern of their recent past and from the long-lasting paradigm of their historical evolution. These difficulties account for the inherent instability of their political systems, highlighted by post-communist developments in some of the Balkan countries, and they raise questions about international factors in regime change in the region.

The first major difficulty derives from the problem as expressed in an official report that 'democracy is not firmly rooted; this shows in the continuing presence of a "rearguard" holding the reins of power, whose methods of locking up the system (muzzling the media and the press, controlling access to jobs and positions of responsibility, monopolizing resources) have not changed since the communist era'.[1] Even if the overall situation is beginning to improve, the transformation of post-communist countries in the Balkans involves a complex process of accommodating old structures to new realities. For many Balkan countries the democratic experience of the non-communist past is very controversial with very scarce evidence of viable democracy despite the rhetoric of 'returning to democracy' (which is portrayed as a 'return to Europe' in some cases) which features in the political discourse in some of these countries. Moreover, the collapse of communism was the result of accumulated tensions illustrating the need to regain national identity thwarted by an internationalizing ideology in the service of Moscow's interests or of a leading nationality (as in the case of Yugoslavia). What seems to be the inner trend of the transformation process is coming to terms with both the re-emergence of national identity with no roots in a traditional Western-type democracy and the need to connect the newly born Balkan society to the exigencies and requirements of the prosperous civic nations of the West. All this has very little to do with the traditional pattern of state-building in South-East Europe.

The second major difficulty encountered by the Balkan countries on the path towards democratization, other than the damage caused by communist rule and by social and economic underdevelopment, has been produced by conflicting ethnic aspirations. These are the difficulties that 'various ethnic and/or religious groups find in coexisting on the same national territory, such as in Bosnia, Croatia, Serbia, the Former Yugoslav Republic of Macedonia and, in more or less acute form, depending on the period, in Bulgaria (with its substantial Turkish minority)'.[2] As far as Romania is concerned, inter-ethnic relations between the Romanian majority and the Hungarian minority are really the litmus test of democracy. Despite recent improvements, the dispute about the nature and the extent of minority rights in Romania still continues, sometimes with high emotional overtones. The real problem here is the clash between Western civic and territorial conceptions of the nation and ethnic concepts of the nation found in Balkan countries.[3]

On the other hand, these new democracies fear the potential security threats coming from the high volatility in the region. Accordingly, they are striving for some kind of security guarantees which can be provided especially by interlocking institutions such as NATO, the Western European Union (WEU) or the European Union (EU) – the last two in spite of the fact that the WEU still lacks effective operational capabilities and the EU has not come yet to a final agreement concerning its Common Foreign and Security Policy (CFSP).

The North Atlantic Treaty aimed at safeguarding the civilization of NATO peoples 'founded on the principles of democracy, individual liberty and the rule of law'. As a result, for many politicians in the Balkans, democratizing means only fulfilling criteria for acquiring the NATO security umbrella, which, in some cases, may only amount to a peculiar form of enlightened despotism. For example, Albania was the first ex-communist country to make a formal application to join NATO, as early as December 1992. It concluded in June 1992 a treaty of assistance with Turkey, strengthening its ties with NATO, and military agreements with the USA and Britain.[4] A few years later, in 1997, however, the country was beset by political disruption, corruption, state institutions collapsing and starvation caused by the failures of so-called democratic governance, which was supported by the West as an alternative to neo-communist rule. As underlined by Tom Gallagher, 'EU states have backed local despots because there is great scepticism about the ability of their peoples to aspire to any better form of government'.[5]

The possibility of improving the human rights record, building up a market-oriented economy and developing the democratic framework of Balkan societies is very much dependent upon Western aid. However, local rulers' political motives behind these programmes of transformation can be misleading. Some of them have acted in a resolute manner benefiting from clear cultural affinities with the West and European integration, as in the case of Slovenia. Others have to cope with immense economic hardship against a background of weak popular enthusiasm for integration with European and Euro-Atlantic institutions, as in the case of Bulgaria.

External support has sometimes been important in previous transitions to democracy elsewhere in Europe. In the case of Eastern Europe, the magnitude of change makes external support quite crucial, and this point may be stressed all the more for countries in the Balkans where the aforementioned problems present serious obstacles to democratization. In any of these cases the West can contribute in two ways to achieving this: by providing economic aid and co-operation; and through political support and advice.[6] These forms of support will be examined and so will the prospects for a security network to stabilize the region. But first we examine the scope for actors to influence transformation in the Balkan countries.

External governmental and non-governmental actors and their scope for supporting democracy

The external contribution to democratization in the region has been enhanced by an extraordinary readiness of governments in Balkan countries to seek the direct assistance of Western governments. These countries set their goal of integrating with the Western international institutions and agreed to adapt their political systems to meet the criteria and requirements of Western democracy. Thus, they invited foreign factors to play an important role in what was considered until recently a domain of internal affairs and sovereignty, jealously guarded and often the subject of international quarrels and anxiety.

This is an entirely new feature of the political environment in the Balkans. It is now the rule rather than the exception to witness reactions from a Western government to internal political developments in a country of the region, followed by the positive response from the government concerned, which does not consider foreign 'pressure' as interference in its internal affairs. This is particularly true of those countries which are EU associates like Slovenia, Romania and Bulgaria. For example, in June 1995 a new criminal code was adopted by the Romanian Senate and presented to the Chamber of Deputies. When it was evident that this meant instituting respect for the state symbols and curbing the hoisting of foreign flags and the playing of foreign national anthems, the United States embassy in Bucharest reacted publicly through an open letter addressed to the Chairman of the Chamber of Deputies.[7] This rather unusual gesture occurred even before the bill was passed by both chambers of the parliament. The message was clear and unequivocal, stressing that the amendments proposed by the Senate would violate the freedom of speech guaranteed in the constitution, particularly as they provided for incongruously harsh punitive measures. The Romanian authorities were asked to assess the consequences of this kind of legislation for Romania's image at home and abroad, at a time when Romania was trying to strengthen its democratic institutions and harmonize its human rights policy with Western practices and norms. This protest had the direct effect of the harsh punitive measures being excluded from the final version of the criminal code. In Romania, this intervention was not generally considered an unfriendly act by the USA, but rather as a sign of good US intentions.

The newly formalized relationship between Balkan countries and Western ones accounts for many actions by Balkan players, reflecting the intricate game of European integration and the powerful influence of national actors on the European level. Such actions tend to bear the imprint of Western democratic standards. For instance, Italy blocked the signing of the Association Agreement between Slovenia and the EU after negotiations between Italy and Slovenia on the return of former Italian property failed in 1994. Immediately after a compromise, regulating the way foreigners could acquire property in Slovenia, was reached in accordance with the democratic principle of liberalising the acquisition of property, the Slovenian–Italian relationship began to improve.[8] This improved bilateral relationship has steadily continued to the point when in 1996 Italy signed an agreement with Slovenia and Hungary instituting trilateral co-operation, the priority of which was to bring Slovenia and Hungary into the EU. Thereafter, Italian support played a major role in nominating the two countries for the first wave of EU enlargement at the Luxemburg EU summit in December 1997 and supporting Slovenia as a reliable candidate for NATO membership in Madrid in July 1997.

At another level of co-operation, the relationship between political parties in Balkan countries and their ideological equivalents in West European ones has opened up a parallel channel for furthering the democratic process because political parties form a crucial component of new liberal-democratic systems as guarantors of political pluralism.[9] As pointed out by Geoffrey Pridham, the possibilities for influence may cover party identity and early programmatic development, the acquisition of political experience and expertise, and building up organizational mechanisms.[10] Such transnational party linkages are fully operational as a means for helping to streamline strategies for European and Euro-Atlantic integration of these countries. The majority coalition party in Romania after 1996, for instance, the Christian-Democratic National Peasants Party (CDNPP), represents the Christian Democratic orientation there as part of the European People's Party, the second major political family represented in the European Parliament. Following the 1996 elections, the democratic process in Romania has been accelerated due among other things to the new and increased support for economic and political reform provided by Western democracies governed by Christian Democratic parties such as Germany.

Aid for democracy development has come also from important private philanthropic actors such as the Soros Foundation, which has made a significant contribution to the democratic trend supported by the European institutions in the Balkans. Moreover, in countries such as Romania, the

Soros Foundation for an Open Society has been by far the most important private philanthropic actor against the background of the absence of most major US foundations, which have been more active in some other countries like Bulgaria.[11] Its annual programme budget for Romania amounting to around $10 million since 1990, the Soros Foundation has placed less emphasis on visiting foreign experts in providing skills in different fields than on supporting local expertise and helping Romanians improve their knowledge through study visits abroad.[12] In 1995 the Soros Foundation in Romania had a very broad agenda comprising: education; conference and travel; the English language; library training, e-mail and communications; research; children and youth; civil society; medicine and health; economic reform and management; the media; publishing; public administration; arts and culture; and special projects. Some 51 per cent of the total expenditure (amounting to $9.66 million) took the form of grants.

This huge amount of activity represents a very important factor influencing public consciousness in different ways. Together with other levels of Western support, it constitutes a salient feature of the democratization process in all the countries of the region.

The EU's support for economic reform through PHARE

The most important aid programme for the area is provided by the EU through PHARE, initially covering only Poland and Hungary.[13] Since September 1990, PHARE has continuously extended its range to other democratising countries including those not only in Central and Eastern Europe, but also Balkan countries such as Bulgaria, Yugoslavia, Albania, Romania (which many political analysts do not regard as a Balkan country[14]) and Slovenia. The PHARE share of aid per country is determined by population, GDP and qualitative criteria. During 1990–4 the EU allocated from its budget ECU 4,248.5 million to finance the PHARE programme (for eleven partner countries) of which 541.7 million went to Romania, 393.5 to Bulgaria, 244 to Albania, 141.1 to the former Yugoslavia, and 44 to Slovenia. The most important target sectors benefiting from the PHARE Programme were: private sector development and enterprise support; education, health, training and research; infrastructure (energy, transport and telecommunications); environment and nuclear safety; agricultural restructuring; humanitarian and food aid; public institution and administrative reform; and social development and employment.

PHARE works in close co-operation with the International Monetary Fund, the World Bank and the European Bank for Reconstruction and Development. The Programme makes a great contribution to the reform process in the target countries in the field of know-how, investment support, and investment in infrastructure. For example, it financed seven agencies assisting small business in Albania in 1994 and made more than 2,000 loans. In Romania, since there was lacking a nationwide land information system, including a modern land registry, PHARE inaugurated an ECU 4 million programme for funding hardware, consultancy for modernizing the land registry system and ensuring legal advice and the establishment of a land information system.

PHARE is fundamentally important for furthering the process of privatization and contributes in a significant manner to the consolidation of the trend toward free market-oriented economies. In Romania PHARE 'provided extensive institutional support for a mass privatization scheme and also contributed to policy and strategy formulation, the creation of basic institutions, screening enterprises and supported active privatization involving foreign investment'.[15] A similar preoccupation with the establishment of a regulatory framework for privatization and developing accounting systems is worth mentioning in the case of Bulgaria, where PHARE organized a roundtable to give impetus to the process of drafting the privatization law.[16]

After the Essen EU summit (December 1994), PHARE is no longer concerned with merely supporting the transformation process. Its dimensions were reframed, the main task being to contribute to the preparation of the candidate countries of the area for accession to the EU.[17] The economic recovery of the above-mentioned countries, which is an important goal to be achieved for fulfilling the economic criteria for EU membership, should be assessed before initiating negotiations for accession to the EU. Romania, Bulgaria and Slovenia have already concluded their Association Agreements, which offer a firm basis for deepening co-operation with EU countries through a wider access of the candidate countries to European markets and a preferential system of trade, although significant limits on the agricultural goods, textiles and steel exports to the EU were specified. Some of the candidates have been able to improve consistently their economic record. This allowed Slovenia, for instance, to have a budget deficit even lower than the Maastricht threshold, while Romania and Bulgaria have been in a much less favourable position.[18]

At the Luxemburg EU summit of December 1997, which included Slovenia in the first wave of forthcoming enlargement negotiations, it was decided that the PHARE Programme, already refocused on accession priorities, should from the year 2000 become a 'structural instrument which will give priority to measures similar to those of the Cohesion Fund'.[19] The European Council defined two priority aims: 'Without prejudice to decisions on the financial perspective for 2000–2006, the PHARE programme will focus on accession by setting two priority aims: the reinforcement of administrative and judicial capacity (about 30% of the overall amount) and investments related to the adoption and application of the *acquis* [i.e. the EU's body of treaties, laws and practices] (about 70%)'.[20]

PHARE is by no means limited to economic matters, for it also contributes to the development of democracy through non-governmental activities. In this vein, the European Parliament launched the PHARE

Democracy Programme in 1992 to assist the development of democratic societies by inaugurating East–West partnership projects involving non-governmental organizations. Over fifty projects focused on specialized support in the field of parliamentary practices, promoting and monitoring human rights, developing independent media and promoting trade union democracy.

The framework of European and Euro-Atlantic organizations: monitoring democratization

Organizations like the Organization for Security and Cooperation in Europe (OSCE), the Council of Europe, NATO, the WEU and of course the EU provide with much overlapping membership a supportive framework for transition to democracy, utilizing a system of encouragement, incentives and pressures. However, these different organizations operate with some-what different priorities and clearly vary in the degree of weight and influence they can exert.

The OSCE (formerly called the CSCE) and the Council of Europe are not so influential in the region as is the EU, due to their lack of mechanisms and procedures for monitoring crises or furthering economic development. As a collective security organization, OSCE is somewhat ineffective despite its huge Euro-Atlantic membership, being incapable of defusing tension or deterring aggression. Despite mechanisms such as 'consensus-minus-one' for responding to 'gross' violations of OSCE commitments, the organization largely remains a 'reaching consensus' structure with no coalition of the willing among its member states.

The problem of the OSCE originates with the lack of political will among member states to address resolutely demanding crisis situations. The poor OSCE record in the former Yugoslavia is but one albeit major example of its ineffectiveness as a collective security organization. The main problems are 'the lack of sufficient structures for running the opera-tions, the lack of personnel at the disposal of CSCE and the problems associated with the financing of CSCE operations'.[21] The Czech Foreign Minister, Josef Zieleniec, recognized this reality in December 1993 when he said: 'the original, rather unrealistic, ideas on the CSCE becoming the backbone of the security structure have been considerably reduced'.[22]

Yet a potentially significant contribution to developments in the Balkan region was made by the OSCE (the Conference on Security and Co-operation in Europe became an organization in January 1995) when it declared that human rights were part of the comprehensive idea of security. The 1994 CSCE Budapest Document, *Towards a Genuine Partnership in a New Era*, highlighted in Chapter VIII on the human dimension: 'The protection of human rights, including the rights of persons belonging to national minorities, is an essential foundation of democratic civil society'. Thus, not only does OSCE put human rights in close relation to security issues but it also evinces the consequences of human rights infringements for regional stability and security.

The OSCE has a fairly praiseworthy record of monitoring the democratization process in the Balkan countries through its involvement in encouraging democratic standards in free elections and in assessing their outcome. The activity of the OSCE observation mission in the Republika Srpska, during the occasion of the National Assembly election in November 1997, is very relevant. As underlined by Javier Ruperez, special representative of the OSCE for the assessment of these elections in Republika Srpska, the technically correct electoral process 'has been grafted onto a political environment which falls far short of democratic standards'.[23] This is a typical feature in some of the new Balkan democracies, where simply staging free elections does not solve the problem of democratization. Hence, the involvement of organizations such as OSCE is so badly needed despite their weaknesses. However, better co-ordination between OSCE and the Council of Europe is necessary in tackling these aspects of supporting democratization in the Balkans. This might help to overcome the 'OSCE's current situation of having to call upon voluntary contributions to cover a large part of its operations'.[24] The view is held that member states and the EU should provide sufficient funding for these operations.[25]

The OSCE line that human rights are a matter of legitimate international concern is connected to the broad security concept promoted by NATO, the WEU and the EU. The new strategic concept agreed by the leaders of NATO countries at the summit in Rome in November 1991 identifies as an important risk to Allied security 'the ethnic rivalries which are faced by many countries in Central and Eastern Europe'.[26] The Balkan countries are indirectly referred to in these paragraphs. Thus, NATO emphasizes the importance of following the strict observance of human rights and especially rights of minorities (without which ethnic rivalries are likely to develop into raging conflicts spilling over into neighbouring countries) in the process of ensuring security and stability in the Euro-Atlantic area. The Alliance's New Strategic Concept stresses the idea that 'it is now possible to draw all the consequences from the fact that security and stability have political, economic, social, and environmental elements as well as the indispensable defence dimension'[27] and places this in the context of achieving the main purpose of the alliance of achieving 'a just and lasting peaceful order in Europe'.[28] The WEU (as in its declaration of the extraordinary meeting of the Council of Ministers with states of Central Europe in Bonn in June 1992) supports NATO's view concerning the broad dimensions of security as encompassing 'not only military but also political aspects, respect for human rights and fundamental freedoms, as well as economic, social and environmental aspects'.

The European Union is motivated by the same democratic principles, making the respect for human rights the basic underlying value of the

European Union and its Common Foreign and Security Policy as specified in the Maastricht Treaty (Title V, Article J.1). The first *Report on European Security Policy towards 2000: Ways and Means to Establish Genuine Credibility* pointed out: 'the CFSP would be limited to defending the interests of the Union, reducing international relations to a simple question of power politics, if it were not for the influence of fundamental and universal values like liberty, justice, solidarity, and democracy guided by the primacy of human rights and the rule of law'.[29] The idea has been voiced that the democratic structure, social stability and the cultural and political identity of institutionalized Europe 'could be threatened by a failure to respect democratic principles or human rights outside the European Union'.[30] Thus, linking broad concerns in the EU with those unfolding in the Balkan area gives added force to European pressure and makes it easier for local political circles in the region to understand EU requirements concerning human rights and the observance of democratic principles.

For example, Romania accepted that the governing principle of its association with the EU was 'respect for the democratic principles and human rights established by the Helsinki Final Act and the Charter of Paris for a New Europe' (Title II, Article 6, of the EC/Romania European Agreement). Thus, the EU has a right of *regard* over the regime of human rights protection in Romania, which cannot be considered an internal affair of the Romanian state. As the European Parliament pointed out in 1993: 'The Community must help Romania to complete its transition to democracy and a market economy but, at the same time, has a right to demand that Romania respect fundamental freedoms as well as human and minority rights. It must be made very clear that failure to respect these two conditions could have negative repercussions with regard to the European Parliament's assent to the European Association Agreement'.[31]

This has combined with pressure from the Council of Europe on achieving democratic reforms. When Romania joined it in 1993 and signed the European Convention for the Protection of Human Rights and Fundamental Freedoms, the Romanian state agreed to transfer some of its sovereign rights. Romania agreed to Articles 25 and 26 of the Convention which clearly stipulate that the European Commission on Human Rights may receive petitions addressed to the Secretary General by individuals and groups claiming to be the victims of violations by the contracting state. Thus, the Council of Europe became a potential source of positive influence on internal developments concerning the protection of human rights.

The preoccupation with maintaining stability and democratization in the Balkans has led to new initiatives in regional co-operation. One of the most important is the South-East European Co-operation Initiative (SECI), which was seen by the USA as a way of strengthening peaceful relationships among the Balkan countries. It was jointly launched with the EU in December 1996. This initiative for regional co-operation on the basis of concrete projects is placed under the aegis of OSCE.[32] Yet, paradoxically, the competition for integration with NATO and EU is a kind of a deterrent to regional co-operation in the Balkan area due to political considerations. There is a fear that this kind of institutionalized relationship might jeopardize the final goal of integration with Europe which these countries are jealously striving after. As pointed out by Peter Schmidt, 'Instead of betting on regional co-operation, every Central and East-European country tries to be better placed for integration with EU and NATO and consequently it finds itself in direct competition with its neighbours'.[33] Countries such as Slovenia and Romania fear the possible consequences for their European future of getting entangled in some unpredictable institutionalized relationship in such a volatile area in terms of security, overladen with national prejudices and simmering conflicts. In this particular case, the 'return to Europe' theme seems rather to coincide with the 'escape the Balkans' theme. Thus, Slovenia refused to take part in a Balkan summit organized in Crete in November 1997 to devise new forms of institutionalized co-operation. In spite of his taking part in the summit, Victor Ciorbea, the Romanian Prime Minister, refused to participate in a proposal for institutionalized Balkan co-operation made by the Greek Prime Minister Simitis.[34] This position reflected the prevailing attitude in Romania which gives overriding attention to integration with the Western world.

Interlocking security institutions and the Balkans: NATO, the EU and the WEU

None of the Balkan candidate countries was mentioned as part of the first group of states to be nominated for NATO enlargement by the North Atlantic Council in Madrid in July 1997. The NATO Heads of State and Government invited only the Czech Republic, Hungary and Poland to begin accession talks.[35] The best explanation for this outcome was given by British Prime Minister, Tony Blair: 'This is a military guarantee that we are giving to these countries that come into NATO. Particularly, if you have got fighting forces as professional and of such quality as ours you have to be very careful in giving these military guarantees . . . we have got to make sure that NATO remains a strong defence security for us'.[36]

The Madrid Declaration on Euro-Atlantic Security and Co-operation, despite reiterating the NATO 'open door' policy, made no reference to a new round of enlargement and refrained from making nominations for it. Yet some excluded candidate countries (including Balkan ones) were mentioned in the Declaration, for political reasons, but only to commend their efforts towards democracy and without any guarantees that they would join the alliance in the future.[37] However, speculation about possible further enlargement triggered reactions from the NATO leading members. Marc Grossman, Assistant Secretary of State for European and Canadian Affairs, clarified the matter before the US Congress in October 1997,[38] as did Madeleine Albright, US Secretary of State, in December 1997: 'There is no need to raise expectations by playing favorites, or to assume that our parliaments will always agree'.[39] Similarly, the British Defence Secretary, George Robertson, commented: 'The key priority now is to ensure that this round of enlargement succeeds. Until we know from experience that it has, we cannot responsibly take decisions about the timing, still less the composition, of any further rounds. We should be very cautious about what we can achieve by 1999'.[40] Nevertheless, some Western analysts or NATO member states' officials stressed, before the Madrid summit, the need to enlarge NATO in order to include some Balkan states which badly need strengthened security. According to William Pfaff: 'If NATO must expand, it is senseless not to use expansion to strengthen security where it is most needed, the Balkans'.[41] At the same time, the Turkish Deputy Prime Minister Oriur Oymen in Sofia took the line that NATO should start its enlargement with Romania, Bulgaria and Macedonia in order to strengthen security in the Balkans.[42] However, it is clear that NATO is not expanding to build up security in troubled or threatened zones by including those zones in the NATO area, but rather to extend security in Europe by adding to the present stable and safe NATO area other stable and safe European zones. In the view of Madeleine Albright: 'the enlargement of NATO must begin with the strongest candidates . . . we expect the new members to export stability eastward, rather than viewing enlargement as a race to escape westward at the expense of their neighbours'.[43]

Linkage made by Turkish officials between NATO enlargement and Turkey's accession to EU[44] reminds us of the interlocking relationship between NATO, the EU and the WEU. But this is a complex question due to the need for internal reform of these structures so as to respond to new challenges. To this may be added the new dimension of their own interrelationship making them even more complementary to each other. The first challenge to be addressed is that of adjusting the machinery of European institutions to a changed pattern of collaboration with the American allies, such as building up a European Security and Defence Identity (ESDI) within NATO as a basis for European initiatives in the field of peacekeeping or humanitarian operations (the so-called Petersberg operations) against the background of proliferating crises on the European continent. Moreover, Title V of the Treaty of Maastricht establishes a formal link between the EU and the WEU, the latter being envisaged as part of the development of EU. What is most important, in terms of political integration, is the fact that the declaration attached to the Treaty provides for WEU membership of EU member states: 'States which are members of the European Union are invited to accede to WEU on conditions to be agreed in accordance with Article XI of the modified Brussels Treaty,[45] or to become observers if they so wish'.

Bearing in mind that all WEU member states are also NATO members and in a close collective defence relationship with the USA through the Treaty of Washington, it is evident that by entering the EU and afterwards the WEU, a state could enter a security relationship with the USA without being a NATO member. Moreover, the modified Brussels Treaty that governs the WEU establishes a juridical link between the WEU and NATO through which it is clearly understood that the collective defence of the WEU member states is NATO's duty and would not be duplicated by any prerogatives or self-assumed new missions by the WEU under the Treaty.[46] Such a reality is acknowledged by American security experts who point out that: 'Some US State and Defense officials express the additional concern that EU expansion, proceeding without a decision to enlarge NATO, carries with it a "back-door" US involvement in the security of Central European states', including their would-be conflicts with neighbouring states such as in the Balkans.[47] It is very interesting to note that Serbia (which is clearly a Balkan country) and Romania (which nevertheless signed an Association Agreement with the EU) were portrayed as potential enemies of some would-be NATO members. That casts doubt on Balkan countries being considered reliable allies in the near future. In order to reduce the complexity of this problem, NATO has adopted the line that 'its own enlargement and that of the EU are mutually supportive and parallel processes which together will make a significant contribution to strengthening Europe's security structure . . . while no rigid parallelism is foreseen, each organization will need to consider developments in the other'.[48] However, while taking the same line, the European Commission admits in Agenda 2000: 'the issue of congruence in membership of the EU, Western European Union (WEU) and NATO remains an open and delicate question, the outcome of which may also affect the objective of integrating the WEU into the EU'.[49]

Nevertheless, Klaus Kinkel, the German Foreign Minister, firmly emphasized that EU enlargement has priority and not that of NATO, despite the two enlargements being parallel processes.[50] In this context, the idea of the so-called 'Royal Road' (EU–WEU–NATO) was presented by the German Defence Minister Volker Ruhe as early as May 1993: 'With their forthcoming association with the European Communities, the political foundations have been laid [for EU and WEU membership] and for the Visegrad states – Poland, Hungary, the Czech Republic and the Slovak Republic. I therefore see no reason in principle for denying future members of the European Union membership of NATO'.[51] This applies also to those Balkan countries having signed an Association Agreement with the EU (i.e. Slovenia, Romania and Bulgaria) and having good prospects of becoming EU members.

On the other hand what is still insufficiently understood in countries such as Romania, for example (which is campaigning resolutely for NATO membership, seen as a miraculous security panacea), is the fact that Article V of the modified Brussels Treaty governing the WEU offers much stronger security guarantees than Article V of the Treaty of Washington governing NATO.[52] Even if, at first sight, seeking WEU membership does not seem to be as valuable as seeking NATO membership because the WEU is considered to be a 'soft' organization, in security terms the WEU option might prove itself at least as valuable as the NATO option given that the two organizations are not contradictory but supportive ones. Of course, integration into the EU appears, at first sight, as being a much more complicated process than that of acceding to NATO because of the economic and legislative requirements. Moreover, before effectively expanding eastwards, the EU has to reform its own institutions, which will considerably delay the enlargement as such.

Conclusions

Undoubtedly, the Balkans represent an important but also difficult area in the process of consolidating the Euro-Atlantic security framework. The internal developments within the Balkan societies indicate a regime change which is strongly supported by the Western democracies and their organizations. Yet only a few states have prospects of becoming fully integrated into European and Euro-Atlantic organizations not only because of the qualitative criteria of transformation required for membership but also because of their own priorities set by these organizations. And, as we have seen, differences have emerged between them regarding closer links with Balkan countries.

It is also evident that Western influence in the area covers a wide range of fields such as economic recovery and market-oriented transformation, public institutions and administrative reform, social development and employment, the evolution of parliamentary democracy, monitoring human rights, developing independent media and promoting trade union democracy. All these fields have some bearing on the process of democratization whether direct or indirect, although the role of the West remains one of influence albeit of a rather significant kind. Much depends of course on internal developments in strengthening the course of democratization, despite the tendency to look for help to the West. Admittedly, there are differences among the countries of the region in the way they can develop their relationship with the West. But the clear deepening of this relationship is a major feature of the new Balkan political environment.

The best placed in the struggle for better living standards and competitive economies are the countries associated with the European Union, which is clearly the most important external actor. Unfortunately, the major crisis for the European stability which emerged after 1990 in the Balkans, namely in former Yugoslavia, led to a 'rediscovery' of the 'powder keg' legacy in the Balkans. It is highly unlikely that the North Atlantic Alliance will expand decisively into the Balkans in the foreseeable future due to the need to avoid the security imbalance which might be caused by a Balkans actor becoming a NATO member and thus embroiling NATO in a regional conflict.

Romania and Slovenia are the best placed candidates for NATO membership after the Madrid summit, but obviously Slovenia (given the green light to start accession negotiations with EU) could follow the EU path ('the Royal Road') for joining NATO irrespective of the strong possibility that the alliance will not directly expand again in the foreseeable future. For three of the Balkan countries – Slovenia, Romania and Bulgaria – the EU option seems to be the only viable solution. The European Council decided in Luxemburg in December 1997 to start accession negotiations with six candidate countries, including Slovenia, but excluding Romania and Bulgaria. Nevertheless, the Luxemburg document placed all the candidate countries on an equal footing in the accession process, differentiation being made only with regard to the timing according to the level of preparedness of each candidate.

This decision by the EU has long-term consequences for furthering the democratization process in the region since enlargement will be a 'comprehensive, inclusive and ongoing process, which will take place in stages; each of the applicant States will proceed at its own rate, depending on its degree of preparedness'.[53] Democratic reforms in the Balkan candidate countries should not be hindered by the decision in Luxemburg to start accession negotiations only with a few of them, for the EU emphasized the need to maintain these countries on the path towards European integration and democratization: 'Financial support to the countries involved in the enlargement process will be based on the principle of equal treatment, independently of time of accession, with particular attention being paid to countries with the greatest need. The European Council welcomes in this connection the catch-up facility envisaged by the Commission'.[54] These EU membership prospects are the most important incentives for democratization in the Balkan countries since, by comparison with other European or international organizations, the EU has increasingly stood out as the one with the most comprehensive approach and effective policy in pursuing democratic conditionality.[55]

Of course, this is not to deny the value of other transnational players in the process of democratization in the Balkans. It is only to highlight the weight the EU has acquired here. The presence of the EU in some Balkan countries other than the associate ones, including Yugoslavia, Macedonia, Albania or Bosnia-Hercegovina in terms of economic aid or political support for democratization is an increasingly salient feature. There is an ever-growing awareness that the role of the EU concerning democracy and human rights observance in this region has implications for Europe as a whole. It also underscores the role of the external forces in the Balkan transition as a token of the new democratic age of interdependence and globalization.

Notes

1 Mr Arthur Paecht (France), General Rapporteur, 'Stability in the Balkans: a role for

NATO', Draft General Report, North Atlantic Assembly, International Secretariat, AP 82, CC (97) 5, 4 April 1997, para. 32.

2 Cf. M. Arthur Paecht (France), M. Willem Van Eekelen (Pays-Bas), Co-Rapporteurs, 'La stabilité dans les Balkans: Le role des institutions de sécurité européenne', Projet de Rapport General, Assemblée de l'Atlantique Nord, Secrétariat international, AP 198, CC (97) 14, 1er septembre 1997, para. 64.

3 Anthony D. Smith, 'The ethnic sources of nationalism', in Michael E. Brown, ed., *Ethnic Conflict and International Security*, Princeton: Princeton University Press, 1993, p. 34.

4 See Hans Joachim Hoppe, 'The situation in Central and South-East European countries', *Aussenpolitik*, 45, 2, 1994, pp. 140–1.

5 Tom Gallagher, 'Chance for change in the Balkans must not be lost', *Irish Times*, 22 March 1997.

6 See Adrian G. V. Hyde-Price, 'Democratization in Eastern Europe: the external dimension', in Geoffrey Pridham and Tatu Vanhanen, eds, *Democratization in Eastern Europe. Domestic and International Perspectives*, London and New York: Routledge, 1994, p. 226.

7 See 'De la Ambasada Statelor Unite ale Americii. Scrisoare deschisa adresata dlui Adrian Nastase', in *România libera*, new series, 1574, 1 June 1995.

8 Cf. Joze Mencinger and Reinhard Olt, 'Slovenia', in Werner Weidenfeld, ed., *Central and Eastern Europe on the Way into the European Union: Problems and Prospects of Integration*, Gütersloh: Bertelsmann Foundation Publishers, 1996, p. 230.

9 Cf. Geoffrey Pridham, 'The European Union, democratic conditionality and trans-national party linkages: the case of Eastern Europe', in J. Grugel (ed.), *Democracy Without Borders: Transnationalisation and Conditionality in New Democracies*, London: Routledge, 1999.

10 Ibid.

11 See Thomas Carothers, *Assessing Democracy Assistance: The Case of Romania*, Washington, DC: Carnegie Endowment for International Peace, 1996, p. 24.

12 See ibid., pp. 112–13.

13 PHARE Regulation No. 3906/89, in *Official Journal* L 375, 23 December 1989. It was amended later to include a larger number of new democracies.

14 The Romanian press covered the statements by General Constantin Degeratu, Chief of the General Staff of the Romanian army, according to which Romania 'is not part of the Balkan area, but is extremely interested in maintaining the stability in the Balkans'. Cf. Monica Szlavik, 'Principalul risc la adresa României este instabilitatea' (The main risk Romania faces is instability), *Curierul National*, VIII, 2038, 17 November 1997.

15 Leader Author: Simona Gatti, Editors: Vittoria Alliata and Jonathan Hatwell, *Enterprise Restructuring and Privatization*, European Commission, Progress and strategy paper, Directorate General for External Economic Relations, Brussels, July 1994, p. 16.

16 Ibid.

17 See Martin Brusis and Cornelius Ochmann, 'Central and Eastern Europe on the way into the European Union', 1996 report on the state of readiness for integration, in Weidenfeld, ed., *Central and Eastern Europe on the Way into the European Union*, p. 25.

18 See Jurgen Noetzold, 'European Union and Eastern Central Europe: expectations and uncertainties', *Aussenpolitik*, 46, 1, 1995, p. 17.

19 Luxemburg European Council, 12 and 13 December 1997, Presidency Conclusions, para. 17.

20 Ibid., para. 18.

21 Mr Loïc Bouvard (France), Mr Bruce George (United Kingdom), Co-Rapporteurs, 'The CSCE Forum for Security Cooperation: from Rome to Budapest', Draft Interim Report, Working Group on the New European Security Order, Political Committee, North Atlantic Assembly, AL 91, PC/ES (94) 1, May 1994, para. 3.

22 Ibid., para. 5.

23 'Election Observation Mission, National Assembly Elections in Republika Srpska, 22–23 November 1997', Press Release, in *USIS Washigton File*, Text: OSCE Press Release on Republika Srpska Elections, (Special Rep. of OSCE Chairman assesses elections) (570), 1 December 1997.

24 Cf. Mr Willem van Eekelen (Netherlands), Rapporteur, 'Stability in the Balkans: a role for mutually reinforcing institutions', Draft Interim Report, North Atlantic Assembly, International Secretariat, AP 86, CC/CSC (97) 1, 4 April 1997, para. 32.

25 Ibid.

26 'The Alliance's new strategic concept', agreed by the Heads of State and Government participating in the meeting of the North Atlantic Council in Rome, on 7–8 November 1991, NATO Press Communique, S-1 (91) 85, para. 10, p. 3.

27 Ibid., para. 25, p. 6.

28 Ibid., para. 16, p. 4.

29 See high-level group of experts on the CFSP, first Report at the request of Mr Hans van den Broek, 'European security policy towards 2000: ways and means to establish genuine credibility', Brussels, 19 December 1994.

30 See Luc Stainier, 'Common interests, values and criteria for action', in Laurence Martin and John Roper, eds, *Towards a Common Defence Policy*, a study by the European Strategy Group and the Institute for Security Studies of Western European Union, Institute for Security Studies of WEU, Paris, 1995, p. 17.

31 See Mr Richard Balfe, Rapporteur, 'Report of the Committee on Foreign Affairs and Security on relations between the European Community and Romania', European Parliament, A3–0128/92, PE 202.917, DOC EN/RR/225/225130, 1 April 1993, para. 31, p. 18.

32 See M. Arthur Paecht (France), M. Willem Van Eekelen (Pays-Bas), Co-Rapporteurs, 'La stabilité dans les Balkans: Le role des institutions de sécurité européenne', Projet de Rapport General, Assemblée de l'Atlantique Nord, Secretariat international, AP 198, CC (97) 14, 1er septembre 1997, para. 86.

33 Peter Schmidt, 'Défis et perspectives de la politique de sécurité européenne de l'Allemagne', *Politique Étrangère*, 61, 3, Autumn 1996, p. 579.

34 See 'România s-a opus crearii unui Secretariat Permanent balcanic' (Romania opposed the setting up of a Balkan Permanent Secretariat), in *Ziua*, IV, 1030, 5 November 1997.

35 The accession talks were concluded in December 1997 and the Protocols to the North Atlantic Treaty on the accession of the three countries were signed, in Brussels, on 16 December 1997.

36 Cf. Interview by Prime Minister of the United Kingdom, Mr Tony Blair, Madrid, 8 July 1997.

37 Paragraph 8 of the Madrid Declaration on Euro-Atlantic Security and Co-operation issued by the Heads of State and Government on 8 July 1997 reads as follows: '. . . With regard to the aspiring members, we recognise with great interest and take account of the positive developments towards democracy and the rule of law in a number of South-Eastern European countries, especially Romania and Slovenia . . . At the same time, we recognise the progress achieved towards greater stability and cooperation by the states in the Baltic region which are also aspiring members . . . '.

38 Cf. Opening Statement by Marc Grossman, Assistant Secretary of State for European and Canadian Affairs before the House International Relations Committee, 29 October, 1997, in *USIS Washington File*, 29 October 1997, Text: Asst. Sec. Grossman Testimony to Congress on Europe Oct. 29 (Hearing of House International Relations Committee) (4120).

39 Cf. Statement by Secretary of State Madeleine K. Albright, North Atlantic Council Ministerial Meeting, NATO Headquarters, Brussels, 16 December, 1997.

40 Cf. 'NATO for a new generation', Speech by the Defence Secretary, Mr George Robertson, to the National Conference of the Atlantic Council of the UK, Church House, London, 19 November 1997.

41 William Pfaff, 'If NATO has to expand, Romania has to be one of the elect', *International Herald Tribune*, 11 April 1997, p. 8.

42 See Dan Dragomir, 'Turcia crede ca extinderea NATO ar trebui sa înceapa cu Romania, Bulgaria si Macedonia' (Turkey thinks NATO enlargement should start with Romania, Bulgaria and Macedonia), *Jurnalul National*, V, 1164, 26 March 1997.

43 Madeleine Albright, 'Enlarging NATO: why bigger is better', *The Economist*, 342, 8004, 15 February, 1997, pp. 22–3.

44 See 'Presedintele Turciei ameninta din nou cu boicotarea extinderii NATO' (The President of Turkey threatens again to boycott NATO enlargement), *Cronica Româna*, IV, 1235, 8 February 1997; see also 'Turcia ameninta ca va bloca extinderea NATO daca nu va fi primita în UE' (Turkey threatens to block the Alliance's expansion if it is not accepted into EU), *Adevarul*, 2092, 8 February 1997.

45 Article XI: 'The High Contracting parties may, by agreement, invite any other State to accede to the present Treaty on conditions to be agreed between them and the State so invited . . . '.

46 Article IV of the modified Brussels Treaty reads as follows: 'In the execution of the Treaty, the High Contracting Parties and any Organs established by Them under the Treaty shall work in close co-operation with the North Atlantic Treaty Organization. Recognizing the undesirability of duplicating the military staffs of NATO, the Council and its Agency will rely on the appropriate military authorities of NATO for information and advice on military matters.'

47 Paul E. Gallis, Specialist in West European Affairs, Foreign Affairs and National Defense Division, Congressional Research Service Report for Congress, 'NATO: enlargement in Central Europe', 10 November, 1994, p. 12.

48 'Study on NATO Enlargement', September 1995, para. 18, pp. 7–8.

49 Cf. *Agenda 2000 – Volume II – Communication: Reinforcing the pre-accession strategy*; DN: DOC/97/7; Brussels, 15 July 1997; *Communication: The effects on the Union's policies of enlargement to the applicant countries of Central and Eastern Europe (Impact study)*; Part II. analysis; 1. The external dimension; 1.1 Political.

50 Hans Stark, 'Allemagne-Russie: les aléas d'un parteneriat difficile', *Politique Étrangère*, 61, 3, Autumn 1996, p. 610.

51 John Borawski, 'Partnership for Peace and beyond', *International Affairs*, 71, 2, April 1995, p. 237.

52 Article V of the Treaty of Washington governing NATO reads as follows: 'The Parties agree that an armed attack against one or more of them in Europe or North America shall be considered an attack against them all; and consequently they agree that if such an armed attack occurs, each of them, in exercise of the right of individual or collective self-defence recognized by Article 51 of the Charter of the United Nations, will assist the Party or Parties so attacked by taking forthwith, individually and in concert with the other Parties, such action as it deems necessary, including the use of armed force, to restore and maintain the security of the North Atlantic area . . . '. As very clearly stated, the allies are not obliged to use military force to assist one of them under attack, the military force being only one of many options 'deemed necessary'. Article V of the modified Brussels Treaty governing WEU reads as follows: 'If any of the high Contracting Parties should be the object of an armed attack in Europe, the other High Contracting will, in accordance with the provisions of Article 51 of the Charter of the United Nations, afford the Party so attacked all the military and other aid and assistance in their power'. As very clearly stated, the allies are obliged to use military force to assist one of them under attack.

53 Luxemburg European Council, 12 and 13 December 1997, Presidency Conclusions, para. 2.

54 Ibid., para. 17.

55 Cf. Pridham, 'The European Union, democratic conditionality and transnational party linkages.

8 Light at the end of the tunnel

Romania 1989–1998

Aurelian Craiutu

Introduction[1]

On 3 November 1996, the day of the Romanian general and presidential elections, the *New York Times* published an article (by Jane Perlez) with a striking title: 'Romanians Go to Vote, but Change Isn't Likely'. Less than twenty-four hours later, it became evident that Romanians voted for change; the former opposition came to power for the first time in the history of post-communist Romania, thus marking one of the greatest electoral surprises of 1996. As a result of the elections, the distribution of seats in parliament changed and a new president, Emil Constantinescu, who represented a clear break with the past, replaced the once seemingly invincible Ion Iliescu. The latter duly recognized his defeat and made clear that he would accept the will of the people as manifested at the polls. Thus the country passed the *formal* test of democracy, that is to say regular fair elections and peaceful rotation in power.[2] This was the first time in more than fifty years that a peaceful change in government occurred in Romania, a country which, to many Western observers, appeared to be stuck in a grey zone of stagnancy and irresolution after the 1989 Revolution.

One cannot help wondering at the contrast between the magnitude of electoral change and the false prediction of the *New York Times* journalist who, on the very eve of the elections that radically changed the electoral map of Romania, wrongly believed that former President Iliescu and his ruling coalition led by the Party of Social Democracy in Romania (PSDR) would remain in power for yet another term. Nonetheless Perlez was not the only Western analyst to harbour pessimism regarding the prospects of change in Romania. In order to comprehend where this pessimism came from, we must provide an overview of Romanian politics after 1989 that would enable us to understand why Romanians voted for change in 1996 and whether this change could have been foreseen or not by Western observers.

Like other East European countries, post-communist Romania has offered the spectacle of a cacophonic democracy which often invited hyperbole or simplification. Important issues like nationalism and minority rights have been highly salient, while other equally significant aspects of Romanian politics and society have been overlooked, distorted, or simplified.[3] More importantly, scholars often showed an unjustified tendency to draw sweeping generalizations and predictions based on limited historical and contextual knowledge. In this chapter, I would like to shift the focus of inquiry to more substantive issues bearing on democratic consolidation. The consensus among comparativists is that the notion of democratic consolidation should be linked to a minimalist conception of democracy. In his classic *Polyarchy*, Robert Dahl highlighted eight institutional requirements for the existence of polyarchy that constitute the 'procedural minimum' of democracy: freedom to form and join organizations, freedom of expression, right to vote, eligibility for public office, right of political leaders to compete for support and votes, alternative sources of information, free and fair elections, and executive accountability.[4] While not questioning the validity of linking the notion of democratic consolidation to a minimalist conception of democracy, I shall argue, however, that fledgling democratic regimes like the Romanian one demonstrate that we must take into account the way in which the newly acquired rights and liberties are institutionalized. In other words, one must look for the existence or the lack of perverse elements undermining the aforementioned procedural minimum of democracy. To this effect, I shall concentrate on the emergence of political pluralism, the nature of the new democratic institutions, the challenges faced by the new parties, and the political style which characterized the co-operation between political elites.

The legacy of the past

Eight years after the collapse of communism in Eastern Europe, we have come to realize that the Revolution of 1989 generated a plurality of transitions to different types of political institutions. The nature of the new political institutions and the way in which political elites conceived and engineered the first steps away from state socialism depended to a considerable extent on historical legacies, previous experience with democracy, the strength of civil society, and – last but not least – the mode of extrication from the old regime.

As Daniel Daianu noted, there is little doubt that Romania's poor image and economic performances after 1989 could be linked to the lack of market reforms under communism.[5] Unlike Hungary, Romania did not have a second economy, whose gradual development would pave the way for real market reforms and the transition to a market economy later on. Some attempts at decentralization and self-administration were made in the late 1960s and 1970s, but they were followed by rigid economic policies, which defied the logic of supply and demand and ignored the real needs of economy and population. Thus the Romanian economy entered the highly competitive international market with an oversized and technologically obsolete industry, an inefficient agriculture, and a weak tertiary sector. As a result, the country sank into a deep crisis in the 1980s, when Ceauşescu decided to pay the external debt and opposed any economic reforms; he implemented a shock therapy *sui generis* based on a drastic reduction of domestic consumption, from which the Romanian economy has not fully recovered to the present day. This was the price to be paid for the irrational model of 'immisering growth',[6] which furthered a perverse form of economic development, based on ideology and political arbitrariness. The choice of a repressive and intolerant 'no compromise' politics by the leadership of the party was responsible for both the deep economic crisis of the 1980s and the violent collapse of the communist regime in December 1989.

Furthermore, Romania did not have a strong dissident movement comparable to Solidarity in Poland or Charter 77 in Czechoslovakia, which successfully challenged the former communist elites in those countries. This is not to say, however, that dissenting voices did not exist in Romania, a mistake commonly made by journalists and political analysts who wrongly believe that the communist ideology was never challenged under Ceauşescu's regime. To be sure, a few courageous dissenters voiced their discontent with the authoritarian way in which the country was governed; nonetheless their dissent remained isolated until as late as 1987 and drew the attention of the international media only in the spring of 1989.[7] Due to the strict surveillance of the famous secret police, which attempted to prevent all forms of organized resistance, the nascent 'parallel polis' could not articulate a coherent programme that would successfully challenge the orthodoxy of the communist party[8] and serve as a platform for the country's reconstruction after the fall of the Ceauşescu regime. Equally important was the way in which power was exercised. The Romanian case displayed a mixture of highly personalized and discretionary power, which consolidated personal dependence of office-holders on the leader, while the state was looked upon as a source of personal power and enrichment. As a result, political power was exercised in an unrestrained and un- mediated way, since there were very few mediating structures to protect individuals from encroachment on their rights.

Therefore civil society was weak on the eve of the collapse of com- munism and its fragility did not bode well for the consolidation of the new democratic institutions. Political analysts have explained this weakness by also pointing to Romania's political culture, which traditionally stressed the gap between political elites and ordinary citizens and reinforced collectivist values, paternalism and civic apathy. It is true that, after years of oppression which finally degenerated into the obscene cult of the Ceauşescus, many Romanians adopted a psychology of resignation and found various ways of accommodating themselves with the regime.[9] Moreover the state has traditionally enjoyed a privileged status in the eyes of Romanian citizens, while collectivist ('levelling'[10]) egalitarianism and the absence of social trust have gone hand in hand with other characteristics of the Romanian political culture, such as familial parochialism, little confidence in – and experience with – institutions and impersonal rules, and a reluctance to co-operate with one's equals for the common good.[11] As we shall see in the next section, these elements would have a strong impact upon subsequent political developments in the first years of the transition to open society.

Learning the ABC of democracy: new political parties and institutions

According to the conventional wisdom, the emergence and consolidation of political pluralism are to a great extent dependent on the strength of *civil society*: the stronger the latter, the better the prospects for genuine political pluralism. Equally important for the subsequent crystallization of institutional arrangements is *the mode of extrication from the old regime*. Transitologists like Huntington, Gunther and Higley have pointed out that, for a newly established democratic regime to take root, *elite pacts and settlements* are indispensable, whereas a sudden and violent revolution is not likely to be a good omen for the future of democracy. The fact that in Romania the transition to an open society was initiated not through negotiations like in Poland or Hungary,[12] but through the sudden collapse of the former regime, had a strong impact and placed significant constraints upon subsequent political developments. As a result, there were no institutional arrangements in place capable of providing channels for collective action and bargaining in an uncertain and highly volatile environment. The lack of pacts and negotiations before 1989 could account for the rhetoric of intransigence and the winner-take-all mentality of the main political actors after 1989, which delayed the consolidation of the new democratic regime.[13]

What really happened in December 1989 is still a controversial topic on which not much light has been shed so far.[14] Many political analysts and journalists believe that the Revolution was both a coup staged by intelligence officers and second-rank members of the nomenklatura and a genuine uprising which triggered and eventually changed the plans of the officers.[15] The way in which the Ceauşescus were arrested and executed, the emergence of the National Salvation Front (NSF) who took power on 22 December 1989, disturbing statistics (about a thousand innocent victims), and the alleged presence of foreign mercenaries or foreign intelligence officers on Romanian soil in December 1989 are among the (unsolved) mysteries of the Revolution.[16] Even though the most eccentric scenarios cannot be entirely dismissed, Verdery and Kligman were right to affirm that 'the revolution came from a fortuitous convergence of several elements: superpower interests, events in neighboring countries, some sort of conspiracy at the top, and a long-incubated "movement of rage" culminating in a genuine popular uprising. None of these elements alone would have been sufficient.'[17]

The first half of 1990 was marked by political unrest and violence that triggered an increased polarization and radicalization of the population. The new leaders chose strategies and policies that polarized Romanian society into supporters and opponents of Iliescu and his National Salvation Front. At the same time, they capitalized upon the ideals of the Revolution, while attempting to strengthen their own privileges and power. The perception of most political actors was that an all-or-nothing approach was preferable to a more accommodating policy. On several occasions, the costs of toleration were perceived by authorities as exceeding the costs of suppression, a fact that may account for the high level of violence during the first months of 1990. Ethnic clashes between Romanians and Hungarians (allegedly orchestrated by the newly established Romanian Information Service)[18] occurred in Tg. Mures in March 1990. Demonstrations and protests took place on different occasions (18 and 28–29 January, 18 February),[19] culminating in the two-month student demonstration in the University Square in downtown Bucharest (April–June 1990). Organizations of civil society asked for a quick decommunization of the country and vigorously opposed the authoritarian leanings of Ion Iliescu and his government.[20]

One of the first decree-laws (8/1989) of the Council of the National Salvation Front, constituted on 22 December 1989, created the framework of political pluralism by enshrining the freedom of association as a fundamental principle of the new regime; it also stipulated loose conditions for the organization of political parties.[21] The law provided for a system of proportional representation and did not have a threshold requirement for parliament. Not surprisingly, this liberal provision led to a rapid proliferation of political parties. The result was a weak pluralism, not conducive to a genuine political competition. In 1990 the National Salvation Front competed for power with opposition parties, which, unlike NSF, had neither the time nor the resources to create strong organizations and electoral strongholds. At that time, the opposition was formed by the National Peasant Party Christian Democratic (NPPCD),[22] the National Liberal Party, and the Social Democratic Party, which had played a significant role in Romanian politics before 1948, but were outlawed by the communist regime. Other forces of the opposition came from organizations of civil society, among which the most prominent has been the Bucharest-based Group for Social Dialogue (founded on 31 December 1989). The latter edited an influential weekly, *22*, which published cogent criticisms of Iliescu's government.

The most mature and comprehensive formulation of the objectives of the Romanian revolution was the thirteen-point Timişoara Declaration, adopted on 11 March 1990 by participants in a rally in Timişoara, the city where the Revolution started from in December 1989. The most controversial claim was Article 8 demanding that former prominent members of the nomenklatura be not allowed to run for public office in the future. Signed by almost four million citizens, the Timişoara Declaration pointed out that the true goal of the Revolution had not been the replacement of Nicolae Ceauşescu with second-rank members of the nomenklatura, but a clear-cut break with the communist past. It also stressed the need for the consolidation of genuine political pluralism by means of fair political competition. Had the Timişoara Declaration become law, former President Iliescu and most of his close supporters would not have been allowed to hold any political office because of their communist pasts. Not surprisingly, they opposed and criticized the Timişoara Declaration, which in their view was nothing other than a vendetta. An object of intense political controversy, the Declaration had no tangible consequences in the short run, apart from contributing to the zero-sum mentality which had arisen in the wake of the Revolution.

A poll conducted in April 1990 indicated that only 8 per cent of the electors were affiliated with political parties; to some, this figure may appear as strikingly low, given the politicization of the entire society in the first half of 1990.[23] The poll also demonstrated the fragility of the newly created political parties, which were based on weak constituencies and had few organizations in the territory (most of them were strong only in the capital, Bucharest, and a few other cities). Moreover, they lacked well-defined doctrines and internal discipline. The National Salvation Front initially claimed that it would not run in the May 1990 elections; nonetheless, in January 1990 the NSF made public its decision to compete for political power, a move that worried the nascent Romanian civil society. In fact, Ion Iliescu and other prominent NSF members shrewdly used their exposure to the mass media and claimed that they were the 'emanations' of the Revolution, whose ideals they allegedly incarnated. To many Romanian citizens (mainly in the rural areas), the NSF appeared as the only 'true' exponent of the Revolution, thus acquiring a semi-providential status that was instrumental in securing the electoral allegiance of large strata of the population in the May 1990 elections.

To be sure, the NSF resorted to populist appeals and policies by using large public resources to make the life of the population a bit easier, while knowing, however, that democracy's honeymoon would soon be over. The leadership of the NSF shrewdly played with the population's fear of sudden change and its parochial (passive) political culture, by manipulating information and preventing the opposition parties from reaching out to the country at large. Unfortunately, due to a lack of information, many citizens condoned the attacks on the opposition parties launched by the NSF, while the new leaders of the country resorted to the well-known *divide et impera* strategy, which enhanced confrontational politics and blocked political negotiations. This was one of the reasons why the discourse of the democratic opposition failed to reach larger strata of the population.

This pattern of intolerance was an outcome of the ideological political style whose first manifestations appeared as early as January 1990. The NSF was created from top down with the expectation that it could – and should – control or closely supervise the emergent political competition. It also sought to continue a pattern of politics whose main goal was to elicit popular acquiescence in elite-determined politics, which put a low emphasis on political accountability and responsiveness to one's constituency. Opposition parties were tolerated, but they were not viewed as equal partners in the competition for power. At the same time, the willingness to compromise and power sharing was limited among the new leaders of the country. Iliescu's conception of democracy was an old-fashioned one that assigned a minor place to opposition and did not have great respect for genuine pluralism and political contestation.[24]

Clearly, the parties which competed for power in the first free post-communist elections of the country did not start from an equal footing. The unequal balance of forces that emerged after 22 December 1989 was subsequently reinforced by the unfair way in which seats were distributed in the first (provisional) parliament created in February 1990, when the NSF obtained an absolute majority by means of a weird computation. The victory of the NSF – the most powerful contender – in May 1990 hardly surprised anyone. The NSF ran its electoral campaign by using state assets and the national television to boost its candidates and discredit its political opponents. Ion Iliescu received 85 per cent of the popular vote, while his party obtained a comfortable majority in both the Senate (67.02 per cent) and the Assembly of Deputies (66.31 per cent). In a distant second place came the Democratic Union of Hungarians in Romania, which harnessed 7.2 per cent of the vote. The National Liberal Party received 7.06 per cent in the Senate and 6.41 per cent in the Assembly, while the NPPCD won a modest 2.5 per cent of the popular vote for both legislative chambers. Eighteen parties entered the new parliament, but it was clear that the May 1990 elections led to a highly imbalanced party system. A huge gap – more than 50 per cent of the vote – separated the leading party from its main rivals.[25] Electoral fraud cannot solely account for these electoral results. First and foremost, the landslide with which Ion Iliescu and the NSF won was due to the fact that the country had little or no previous experience with political pluralism and was mired in paternalism and levelling egalitarianism. The NSF's electoral base consisted of former apparatchiks, peasants, and blue-collar workers in large industrial areas; they had few ties to organized political life and preferred protective socialism to market capitalism. The young generation of students, intellectuals and members of liberal professions voted against Iliescu and the NSF, a pattern that would be found in the 1992 and 1996 elections too. The polls also manifested the weakness of the opposition, which did not have a strong foot in the countryside or in small towns.

Thus the upshot of the May 1990 elections was a quasi-pluralist political system characterized by chronic disequilibrium and ideological confusion.[26] The most radical revolution ended in a regime whose new leaders seemed to be reluctantly committed to the principles of constitutional democracy. As Verdery and Kligman noted,[27] the paradox of the first free elections lay in the fact that the December 1989 Revolution had an anti-communist character, while Romanian electors – most of them free to choose for the first time in their life – legitimated at the polls a government that was far from being the true exponent of the ideals of the Revolution. In June 1990 the Romanian political regime was a weird mixture of 'plebiscitary autocracy'[28] and an 'original' democracy. Old regime hardliners competed for power with former communist reformers, radical reformers and staunch anti-communists. From now on, Romanian political life would be polarized between reluctant democrats and prophets of the past supporting Ion Iliescu, and a radicalized but disunited opposition, which wanted a clear break with the past and a more rapid integration of the country into Western organizations.

The configuration of the newly elected parliament was not an incentive for the emergence of a politics based on bargaining, compromise and self-restraint. On the contrary, it generated a winner-take-all mentality that hindered elite pacts and settlements; it also encouraged and rewarded intolerance on the part of the members of the majoritarian party. More importantly, the political events of the first half of 1990 and the distribution of power in parliament reinforced an adversarial pattern of relations and politics based on an 'us versus them' mentality, which over-politicized nearly every issue on the legislative agenda to the point of excluding enlightened pragmatism and co-operation across party lines. This situation became evident in June 1990, when the set of non-negotiable issues proved to be too narrow for a consensus to be reached in due time concerning the outcome of the two-month student demonstration in downtown Bucharest. The NSF leadership's decision to mobilize civilian support (the famous Jiu Valley miners) to end the protests was a strikingly unconstitutional political decision, whose costs outweighed benefits and which set an unfortunate precedent that poisoned the political atmosphere and fostered distrust among citizens and government.[29] The atrocities perpetrated by miners against innocent students and civilians on the streets of Bucharest brutally ended the democratic honeymoon and substantially damaged the international credibility of Romania's new leaders. Six years had to pass until the country would manage to improve its image in the Western mass media. The bloody end of the two-month demonstration in the University Square of Bucharest also demonstrated that the NSF was not fully committed to respecting the principles of constitutional democracy. The way in which the peaceful demonstration was handled also fore-shadowed the existence of divisions within the NSF, which would become manifest in the years to come.

Muddling through the no-man's-land of transition

As already noted, the inexperience of the new political class, in addition to an uninspired form of political crafting, devoid of flexibility, visionary skills or enlightened pragmatism, led to weak and chaotic political pluralism, characterized by the existence of 'conglomerate parties'.[30] They resembled movements uniting a wide variety of individual views, which were not held together by a clearly defined doctrine. As time passed by, political parties devoted excessive time and attention to domestic infighting and developed into internally rigid, elite-oriented organizations, centred around a few prominent personalities. To some foreign observers,[31] Romanian political parties appeared more as vehicles for polarizing polemics than interest aggregation and compromise. This development foreshadowed a characteristic of the Romanian political system that would become more evident in the years to come – the influence of political personalities at the expense of institutions and impersonal rules. Political actors often capitalized upon certain characteristics of the Romanian political culture (paternalism, deference toward office-holders, and the like), and opted for a pattern of politics that left little room for compromise and political learning. Last but not least, inter-party migration became a strategy chosen by political actors in search of short-term gains.

Nonetheless, as George Voicu rightly pointed out, the inter-party migration that occurred after the May 1990 elections was more than a mere expression of individual rent-seeking; it aimed in fact at correcting the serious parliamentary disequilibrium that resulted from the May 1990 elections. If one looks at the Romanian political market of 1990–2,[32] one would be surprised by the great number of dissenters and divisions that occurred during such a short time. The NSF itself, the political party which won two-thirds of the popular vote in May 1990 and enjoyed an absolute parliamentary majority, was incapable of preserving its own unity. Internal divisions were quick to appear, culminating in the rivalry between former President Iliescu and his former Prime Minister, Petre Roman. In the spring of 1992, Iliescu's supporters left the NSF to form the rival Democratic National Salvation Front (later renamed the Party of Social Democracy in Romania). As Steven Roper noted, 'the National Salvation Front was transformed from a catch-all party into two different mass parties, each attempting to create its own image and membership base'.[33] Furthermore, parliamentary migration and ambiguities of the new electoral law[34] were the main factors responsible for the fact that parties which had not participated in the May 1990 elections, like the Greater Romania Party or the Socialist Party of Labour led by Ilie Verdet, a former Prime Minister under Ceausescu, became represented in parliament through defections from other parliamentary parties.

As time passed by, however, political parties began to consolidate and turned into slightly more professional organizations.[35] The spectrum of political parties became more diverse, even if personal animosities between leaders often carried the day at the expense of true deliberations on crucial issues of public and national interest. Parties developed organizations and programmes, and started enforcing stricter discipline rules. 'Catch-all' parties competed with ethnic and historical parties. Less well represented was the category of parties with a specific interest representation. It would take some time until anti-communist cleavages would lose their importance as the main dimension of politics.[36]

The Democratic Convention (later renamed the Romanian Democratic Convention) was formed in November 1991 and consisted initially of thirteen opposition parties and political organizations, ranging from Christian Democrats and Social Democrats to Liberals and representatives of the Hungarian minority in Romania. Pointing to the internal diversity of the Convention, political analysts raised some doubts about its future ability to present a unique, coherent political programme. More specifically, it was unclear whether or not the shared antipathy towards Ion Iliescu and the National Salvation Front (or, later, the PSDR) would be an element strong enough to cement an uneasy electoral alliance and reconcile otherwise different programmes and personal rivalries.[37] The candidates of the Convention fared well in the February 1992 local elections, when they won mayoral elections in the most important cities of the country: Bucharest, Timişoara, Ploiesti, Íasi, Brasov, Constanta, Arad, Sibiu. The 1992 local elections signalled a positive development: electors began to pay attention to the personal qualities of the candidates, even though, in most cases, the vote was still divided along ideological lines, based on black-and-white categories. The results of the first post-communist local elections indicated that Romanian society had become more diverse than in the past, while opposition parties were viewed with more confidence than two years before.

Over one hundred parties competed for seats in the Romanian parliament in the September 1992 elections. While revealing a greater confidence of the population in the opposition parties, the 1992 parliamentary elections consolidated the influence of political parties of collectivist extraction. The Democratic National Salvation Front won 27.7 per cent of the votes for the Chamber of Deputies and 28.3 per cent of the votes for the Senate, while the Democratic Convention came in second place with 20 per cent of the votes for both the Chamber and Senate. Eight parties fulfilled the 3 per cent threshold to enter parliament. Asked to form a new government, the Democratic National Salvation Front allied itself with extremist parties like the Party of National Unity of Romanians (PNUR), the Greater Romania Party (GRP), and the Socialist Party of Labour (SPL). The elections also indicated the two main forces which would dominate the political scene in the years to come: the Democratic Convention and the Democratic National Salvation Front (later renamed the Party of Social Democracy in Romania, PSDR).

The upshot was a fragmented political scene, a 'hybrid multipartidism'[38] in keeping with and reflecting the new economic and political interests. The ideological distance between political parties remained high, in spite of the fact that they did not fit very well into the classical definitions of the left and right.[39] A study conducted in 1992[40] showed that Romanian electors distinguished between collectivist-nationalist and liberal-universalistic parties that espoused different views on issues like economic reform, privatization and minority rights. Nonetheless political parties continued to resemble political elitist clubs, i.e. institutionalized networks of clients or friends, and organizations in which a group of followers surrounds one or several leaders who dictate the rules and the direction to follow.[41] This was true of Ion Iliescu's Party of Social Democracy in Romania, but also of the PNUR, GRP, SPL, and even some former opposition parties.

On a more general level, the party system in Romania began to display characteristics that were found all over Eastern Europe: splits in the camp of anti-communist parties, crystallization of extremist forces, and the absence of working-class parties. The political spectrum was divided between parties strongly committed to Romania's integration into the European structures and centrifugal forces – parties like the PNUR, GRP, SLP – that appealed to their constituencies by overplaying the nationalist card and criticizing international organizations (such as the IMF, World Bank, Council of Europe) for their alleged interference in Romania's domestic affairs.[42] The only characteristic that would set Romania apart from its East European neighbours has been the presence of relatively strong historical parties, which had not been eliminated from electoral competition during the first years of the transition.[43]

The electoral politics of 1992 highlighted yet another characteristic of Romania's nascent democracy. As already noted, political cleavages that emerged after 1989 were ideological rather than economic or social. Ideological conflicts are less negotiable than distributional ones; the latter are of a 'more or less' type, leaving room for accommodation and compromise, whereas the first are of a 'either/or' kind, that doesn't further bargaining. The greater the intensity of ideological conflict, the bleaker the prospects of consensus on the rules of the democratic game. In 1992 values and symbols appealing to emotions and passions played a greater role in delineating the electoral agenda than social interests.[44] The 'us versus them' mentality led to the emergence of a polarized pluralism,[45] characterized by an incompatible bilateral opposition, an ideological political style (as opposed to a pragmatic, consensual one), the central presence of one political party, centrifugal rather than centripetal drives, and an intolerant politics of outbidding and radical contestation. This had been the spirit which had presided over many parliamentary sessions, most importantly over the debates on the new constitutional text in the autumn of 1991.[46]

Perverse institutionalization

The pattern of highly confrontational politics contributed to the consolidation of an ideological political style, in which loyalty to a party or
group was put ahead of loyalty to one's constituency and the responsibility
for one's actions. Efforts to discredit political opponents and characterizing
other parties as representative of narrow and allegedly pernicious interests
have often replaced serious deliberation on important political, social and
economic issues. This polarization was made possible by the low level of
toleration and trust which existed among political actors. In an uncertain
and volatile environment, in which an all-or-nothing approach prevailed
over consensual politics, there were few incentives to practice moderation
and toleration towards political opponents. Political extremism manifested
itself as hostility towards opposition parties or chauvinistic attitudes towards
members of other ethnic communities. Since many political actors came to
understand politics as a zero-sum game that excludes compromise with
one's political opponents, rigid partisan allegiances and mutual distrust
inhibited co-operation across party lines. Not surprisingly, such a view
furthered a politics of passions based upon a rhetoric of intransigence. To
be sure, communication and influence networks rarely crossed party lines,
and distrust among political actors led to a particular form of confrontational politics, which, in turn, reinforced the 'us versus them' mentality and
the image of politics as a zero-sum game. This confrontational atmosphere
had a strong impact on the adoption of many laws and the creation of
important institutions. Important laws regarding issues as diverse as the
restitution of land or privatization were in fact the expression of the
political will of a single party or ruling coalition rather than the outcome of
extensive deliberations, conducted with a view to the common good.

By the end of 1992, it had become clear that a major obstacle to the
consolidation of democracy in Romania was the existence of consensually
disunified elites and the emergence of a certain pattern of elite interaction[47] that was not conducive to political negotiation and compromise. As
Burton, Gunther and Higley pointed out, the stability and prospects of a
new democratic regime are to a great extent dependent on the type of
political elites. In their view, the establishment of an elite procedural
consensus concerning the rules of the democratic game is crucial for the
consolidation of fledgling democracies.[48] The Romanian case buttresses
this conclusion. As already noted, after the elections of 1992, instead of
initiating a true dialogue with the former opposition, the ruling PSDR-led
coalition chose to ally itself with extremist parties that lacked democratic
credentials. And the lack of consensually unified elites and political
moderation became once again evident.[49] While agreeing on the need for
intensifying efforts to promote Romania's membership of NATO and the
EU,[50] political elites continued to disagree on issues like state intervention
in the economy, the power of the President, the independence of the

judiciary, political and administrative decentralization, the restitution of confiscated property to former owners, privatization, and the control over the electronic media.

With the benefit of hindsight, one can argue that the policies pursued by the PSDR-led coalition led to a perverse institutionalization,[51] by which I mean the coexistence of 'virtuous' and 'perverse' institutions. I would like to emphasize here the centrality of this concept to the argument developed in this chapter. In the academic literature, virtuous institutionalization refers to the workings of political institutions that allow the reproduction of the minimal conditions of democracy.[52] On a more general level, the notion of virtuous institutionalization also includes a strictly enforced separation of powers, political accountability, and the protection of citizens' rights. On the contrary, the lack of the aforementioned conditions indicates the existence of vicious or perverse institutionalization, which is often the characteristic of an unconsolidated democracy. Most often, virtuous and perverse institutions coexist in practice; their interplay may account for the obstacles to the consolidation of fledgling democracies. In an excellent study published a few years ago, Samuel Valenzuela pointed out the four main elements that define perverse institutionalization: tutelary powers whose limits are ill-defined, reserved domains of authority and policy-making which are not under the control of elected officials, major discrimination in the electoral process (including electoral fraud), and the lack of centrality of elections in constituting governments.[53] To these elements, I would like to add the existence of clientelistic/patronage networks in the economy, which might lead to the emergence of an oligarchic regime.

A cursory look at Romanian political life indicates the existence of a certain degree of perverse institutionalization, which may explain the country's muddling through the no-man's-land of transition for the last six years. But a caveat must be made right from the outset. The fourth element invoked by Valenzuela – the lack of centrality of elections in forming governments – is not present in the Romanian case; nonetheless its absence does not render the concept of perverse institutionalization irrelevant for our discussion. First, any observer of Romanian politics can note that former President Iliescu and the PSDR-led government enjoyed considerable tutelary powers in that they attempted to exercise broad oversight of all major political decisions, while rejecting in practice some of the principles of constitutionalism. Moreover the limits of their powers were sometimes ill-defined; and this ambiguity created confusion and furthered various forms of patronage and clientelism.[54] Second, key political decisions were insulated to a certain degree from the influence of elected officials, a fact which accounts for the existence of certain reserved domains of authority and policy-making in the Romanian case. A good example was the dismissal of democratically elected mayors by cabinet members of the PSDR in 1993–4. These non-democratic decisions triggered the vigorous protests of the Council of Europe and other international organizations that prompted the Romanian government to reverse its decisions. Discriminations in the electoral process occurred in 1992, when the PSDR enjoyed more access to television than opposition parties. The Iliescu regime also opposed any attempt to create a permanent election commission, thus failing to allay long-standing fears and doubts about its commitment to holding clean and fair elections.[55]

In spite of formal parliamentary supervision over security services, the Romanian political and civil society achieved little control over the intelligence community, which was far from being a monolith, as it had its own factions and divisions.[56] By displaying a disquieting degree of partisanship, the leaders of the Romanian Information Service (RIS) gave the impression that they were serving the interests of a particular group rather than the national interest. On many occasions, RIS officers, including its former controversial director, Virgil Măgureanu (whose role in the Revolution is still unclear), were in fact politically unaccountable to parliament. They enjoyed unlimited access to information (for example, the files of the former Securitate) that had remained inaccessible to the population at large; at the same time, public access to political archives was severely limited.[57] Furthermore, security services disposed of generous financial resources, while parliament was incapable of monitoring the RIS's budget.

The emergence of clientelistic networks and – to use Verdery's evocative phrase – 'unruly coalitions'[58] may explain the slow pace of economic reforms. Like in other East European countries, in Romania the 'natural' outcome of state socialism had been a perverted form of political capitalism, in which managers of state enterprises created parasitic private firms by using state resources and personal influence. To describe this new economic elite which tended to form a new plutocracy, Andrei Cornea coined the term *directocratie* (directocracy).[59] This refers to a system based on corruption and patronage networks, dominated by former state managers with close ties to the old and new regime.[60] It has been suggested that the private sector controls in fact more than official statistics indicate. The size of the grey economy is difficult to ascertain, but one can hypothesize that it reaches up to 40 percent of the GDP. The considerable size of the grey economy not only encourages tax evasion and capital flight; it also affects the state's capacity to extract resources for delivering public services and increasing social spending. Moreover, the emerging financial sector was marred by corruption scandals and proved to be an unreliable means of providing safe channels for saving and investment. Dubious private saving and investment schemes (pyramids) flourished, culminating in the famous Caritas affair in 1992–4[61] and the fall of a few investment funds and private banks in 1996–7. As Verdery rightly noted,[62] unruly coalitions, pyramid schemes and certain parties have established various links that led to the overnight enrichment of a tiny elite and reconfigured the wealth map of the country.

In retrospect, it can be argued that the economic policies of these governments postponed radical reforms and failed to eliminate the chronic distortions in resource allocation that have plagued the Romanian economy in the past few decades. Cheap credits were generously given to bad economic agents, which eventually came to count on the government to clear off their unpaid debts.[63] By failing to place state-owned enterprises under tight budgetary constraints, the government allocated a large proportion of state revenues to subsidizing inefficient units in obsolete industries. Private enterprises were obstructed through heavy taxation and red tape, while the process of privatization based on an inefficient voucher strategy was overbureaucratized and lacked transparency.[64] By using political criteria for nominations in top economic positions, the former PSDR-led coalition retained control over the five Privatization Funds, along with a monopoly over investment information. Despite temporary improvements in the macroeconomic climate in 1994, Romania failed to attract foreign investment on a scale comparable to its neighbours. Rampant corruption and imperfect legislation represented a strong disincentive to potential foreign investors, which explains the low level of foreign investment in Romania, the second largest market in Eastern Europe.[65]

With the benefit of hindsight, one could say that the nascent Romanian democracy was built on shaky foundations in the first years of the transition, which may explain its erratic evolution thereafter. It would be an exaggeration to advance that the Romanian leaders who came to power in December 1989 were (closet) communists whose main goal was to lead the country back into communism. This was a thesis on which too much ink has flowed and on which journalists and academics alike have insisted *ad nauseam*. To ascribe to a group of mediocre politicians visionary abilities, or the capacity to lead a whole country into one – admittedly, heinous – direction, would amount to granting them almost supernatural powers, which they most certainly lacked. The core of the problem lies elsewhere. Iliescu and his party were unprepared for the task with which they were entrusted and were often surprised by events. Their reluctant reformism and preference for gradualism were not immune to the temptation of enlightened authoritarianism. Such policies were certainly inappropriate to a market-dominated world in which socialism (in all its forms) had lost its salvationist appeal. While attempting to consolidate its power, the former PSDR-led coalition fostered a clientelistic regime that threatened to 'Mexicanize' the country, by attempting to perpetuate the rule of a single dominant party and linking the economically well-to-do, the *nouveaux riches*, to the new political elites. Romania could have easily sunk into an abyss of corruption, clientelistic networks, and poverty. Nonetheless it managed to avoid this denouement and voted for change in 1996. What then made possible this 'electoral revolution'?

A new honeymoon and new challenges

The facts are known: the parliamentary and presidential elections of November 1996 changed the power distribution in Romania. The Romanian Democratic Convention won 30.17 per cent of the seats in the Chamber of Deputies and 30.7 per cent in the Senate and formed a new ruling coalition with the Social Democratic Union and the Democratic Alliance of Hungarians in Romania.[66] The PSDR came in a distant second place with 21.52 per cent in the Chamber and 23.08 per cent in the Senate; compared to the 1992 elections, it lost about 10 per cent of its supporters, a quarter of whom seemingly voted for the Convention. For the first time in sixty years, a peaceful change in government occurred in Romania and a new president was elected; Emil Constantinescu, the presidential candidate of the Convention and former rector of the University of Bucharest, defeated Iliescu in a tight run-off.[67] Students and the rising middle class voted for Constantinescu, while peasants and elderly people preferred Iliescu.[68]

The victory of the Convention did not come unexpectedly. To be sure, signs of impending change had already been visible in the local elections of June 1996, when the Romanian Democratic Convention and the Social Democratic Union scored victories in the most important cities of the country, including Bucharest.[69] Yet few believed that by the end of the year Romania would have a new parliament and, above all, a new President. The miracle occurred: why were Western analysts unable to predict it? And, more importantly, how did the new government fare in its first year in office?

To answer these questions one must ask first whether the 1996 presidential and general elections were a mere repudiation of Iliescu – that is to say, only a vote against the former President and his party – or (also) a conscious endorsement of the former opposition and a decisive step in a new political direction. In other words, did Romanians come to the conclusion that the former opposition could be entrusted with power, that their vote could, after all, bring about the much-needed change, by punishing those who had made electoral promises, but never kept them? Have therefore the 1996 elections signalled a change in the political culture of the country toward a more participatory and less parochial (passive) political culture?

There is a case for advancing that political learning did play a significant role in bringing about electoral change[70] and that the outcome of the 1996 local, parliamentary and presidential elections was more than a mere repudiation of Ion Iliescu and the former PSDR-led government. It signalled that Romanian electors have learned from the aborted policies of the past and were ready to put an end to a regime of 'corrupt sycophants'[71] and reluctant democrats. Many Romanians decided to vote for new parties, which suited better their interests and views. Ex-Iliescu voters themselves came to understand that paternalism and cosmetic reforms were not the best recipe for the country and changed their electoral allegiances.[72]

A peaceful rotation in power is a litmus test for any nascent democracy. One could argue that the 1996 elections 'ended' the revolution that had started in December 1989 and paved the way for the consolidation of the new democratic institutions. The lack of anti-system parties and the narrowing of the ideological distance between the major parties seem to buttress this point. November 1996 also demonstrated that Romanian electors had become interested more in down-to-earth than ideological issues. Themes like economic reforms, inflation, unemployment, bureaucracy, corruption, and social assistance loomed large in their minds, while moralizing issues like the trial of communism failed to capture people's attention to the extent they had four years before.[73] As Tom Gallagher noted, 'Romanian political culture was beginning to outgrow the Balkan stereotype dominated by images of partisanship, collectivist values, and nationalism'.[74] The latter seems to have been the greatest loser in the 1996 elections. Extremist nationalist parties – above all, the PNUR – barely passed the 3 per cent threshold; ethnic issues did not loom large in the 1996 electoral campaign. The new government which includes members of the Democratic Alliance of Hungarians in Romania[75] distinguishes Romania among its neighbours for its courageous initiative to invite its largest minority to share in the government of the country. Finally, the elections brought a much-needed concentration in the political arena, even if the liberal camp was substantially weakened by the poor electoral performance of the National Liberal Alliance, which failed to pass the 3 per cent threshold to enter the parliament.[76]

To sum up, the outcome of the November 1996 elections demonstrated that Romanian society has ceased to be monolithic; a diversity of views has replaced the once dominant grey uniformity that was the mark and legacy of communist rule. Western observers seem, however, to have missed this important change. The voting behaviour of the young generation and their support for the new ruling coalition – only one out of ten students voted for the PSDR – demonstrates that the new generations display a greater openness to and willingness to embrace Western values than their parents, while being more capable of adjusting to the challenges of the new economic and social environment. The new class of small and medium entrepreneurs also voted for the Romanian Democratic Convention and the Social Democratic Union, while inhabitants of rural areas and elderly people preferred Ion Iliescu and his PSDR. The independent press and the new cable (private) television (Pro-TV, Tele7ABC, Antena 1) contributed to a large extent to a better dissemination of the information in the whole country, thus ending the baleful state monopoly on electronic media that had prevented former opposition parties from reaching out to the population at large.

The rotation in power is a good omen for the future of Romanian democracy; yet the magnitude of the problems facing the new cabinet is, indeed, daunting. Privatization, industrial restructuring, and integration into the European structures loom large on the political agenda of the new government; while the control of inflation and the budget deficit[77] must go hand in hand with keeping social spending at a reasonable level and preventing a drastic fall in output and living standards. Both President Constantinescu and the cabinet led by Victor Ciorbea launched a widely publicized campaign against corruption and organized crime that is meant to put an end to the misuse of public funds for private enrichment. A wholesale reform of the banking system is supposed to assist the belated restructuring of the economy. Important steps have been made towards strengthening the independence of the judiciary, which has been the weakest of the three main powers in the state. Finally, the new leaders of the country launched a vigorous international campaign for Romania's admission into NATO and the European Union. Even if Romania was not invited to join NATO at the Madrid summit of July 1997, its efforts towards reintegration into the Western world were duly appreciated in the final communiqué, which signalled Romania and Slovenia as two strong candidates for a second wave of admission likely to occur in 1999.

A year after the elections, it became evident that in spite of its reformist agenda the coalition cabinet led by Victor Ciorbea – a 'marriage of convenience', to use Tismaneanu's evocative phrase[78] – has yet to go a very long way in implementing its economic agenda. Its record has been thus far a mixed one. On the one hand, the government managed to reform the mining sector, while the reserves of the National Bank reached a record level of 2.5 billion dollars. On the other hand, in 1997 the inflation rate rose to 151.4 per cent (the highest in the region), while the value of national currency (leu) dropped by more than 50 per cent. GDP fell by 5 per cent, while the privatization process and the reform of the banking system continued to be marred by bureaucracy, red tape and confusion.[79] For the sake of expediency, however, the government used more than 500 ordinances (*ordonante*), a fact that indicates some dysfunctions in the legislative–executive relations, with potentially negative consequences for the separation of powers.[80] This policy pattern may lead to a particular form of delegative democracy, in which the executive authority considers itself delegated the right to do whatever it sees fit for the country.[81]

The slow pace of economic reforms has made Western analysts raise new concerns about the future of the Romanian economy. An overdue cabinet reshuffle took place in December 1997, with key positions being given to independent personalities (Education, Finance, Economic Reform, and Foreign Affairs). The reorganization of the government indicated serious flaws in the functioning of the ruling coalition, which, as Michael Shafir rightly pointed out, has been a 'coalition of coalitions' that united parties with different programmes.[82] The coherence of the government agenda was affected by constant bickering among coalition members, which often led to confusion and an inability to implement radical reforms. Once again, the lack of a tradition of political accommodation and compromise took a heavy toll. Disagreements among the two main members of the coalition, the NPPCD and SDU, resulted in an open confrontation in early 1998, when the SDU decided to withdraw its ministers from the coalition government. The coalition's crisis showed that trust is still a scarce resource in Romanian politics, while conflicts of interest continue to be expressed in mutually irreconcilable terms. Above all, it demonstrated once again that Romania needs a new political style and a 'de-emotionalization' of politics as a means of encouraging substantial debates on issues of public interest. As Vladimir Tismaneanu put it, 'the only solution is to replace a culture of fear, intimidation, and distrust with one of dialogue, procedures, and trust'.[83] A change in political style is, however, likely to occur only when elites finally learn the art of political compromise and perceive themselves as truly equal partners in an endless democratic dialogue that requires flexibility, prudence and political imagination. If democracy is to work in Romania, political accountability must be more than a mere electoral slogan, and politics must not remain an elite game as it has been the case thus far.

In lieu of conclusion

Most litanies on what could go wrong in Eastern Europe were Cassandra-like[84] variations on classic themes to be found in the literature on the prerequisites of democracy (socio-economic structure, political culture and values, civil society, level of modernization, elite compromise, class conflicts, institutional arrangements and the like).[85] As the democratization process unfolded in Eastern Europe, the inadequacies and limitations of this school of thought became evident. Thus we have realized that the standard literature on democratization cannot account for sudden political change, which occurs in those 'moments of madness' (Aristide Zolberg) when time itself seems to be suspended and the realm of the possible is expanded in ways which had been utterly unimaginable only a few years before. More emphasis must be placed on contingency, unique constellations and multiple variation to describe why and how change occurs. Prominent transitologists like Guillermo O'Donnell and Philippe C. Schmitter also expressed doubts about the power of normal science methodology, with its enduring emphasis on socio-economic structures and political culture, to account for swift, large-scale political change. In the highly volatile context of transitions, these structural elements may cease to work as valid predictors of the future. Perceptions of interest evolve in time, political learning takes place, class alliances are suspended, institutional identities and ideological allegiances change, while cultural values can no longer serve as unambiguous parameters for evaluating the prospects of democracy.

In other words, none of the aforementioned prerequisites of democracy appear to be compelling; what we have taken in the past as prerequisites of democracy appear to many of us today as the outcome of democratization. More than two decades ago, Albert O. Hirschman criticized the excessive inclination of social scientists to theorize for the sake of theorizing, and emphasized the importance of the unintended consequences of human action.[86] Changes often arise out of unique economic, cultural and political constellations; this amounts to saying that especially favourable conditions are not required for the emergence of a democratic regime. Hence a lack of familiarity with democratic rules and institutions is no infallible sign that a fledgling democratic regime is *a priori* doomed to failure. Through political learning, individuals can critically revise their old values, strategies and attitudes, and adopt new ones. After all, the ancients got it right: politics is the art of the possible, with probabilities, surprise and luck playing as important a role as structural constraints and past patterns.

The outcome of the 1996 Romanian elections took by surprise those of us who have relied excessively on normal science methodology and worked with its standard concepts. To study consolidated democratic regimes, the conceptual framework provided by the standard literature on democratization and transitions may suffice. Nonetheless to analyse the profile and prospects of fledgling democracies, one should also borrow concepts from sociology, anthropology and history. For example, states do not act independently from society; they are embedded in the latter and interact with it. It would be a mistake to conflate state with state apparatus, public bureaucracy, or the public sector; the state is also characterized by an ideological dimension as well as by a set of social relations which cannot be separated from the legal and the institutional system at large. Sometimes it is not the size of the state apparatus (bureaucracy) that is the most important aspect, but its capacity to enforce order, comply with the rules of the democratic game, and – last but not least – its ability to follow non-particularistic interests. As Guillermo O'Donnell put it, 'the embeddedness implies that the characteristics of each state and society greatly influence which type of democracy will be likely to consolidate and which will merely endure or eventually break down'.[87] Thus society itself appears as a map on which enclaves of parochial political culture, low-interest citizenship and weak horizontal accountability coexist with enclaves of vibrant participatory politics, high-interest citizenship and strong horizontal and vertical accountability.

Revisiting the literature on democratization through post-communist Romania, it becomes evident that we still lack a good analysis of the interaction between state and society. Most studies have relied so far on political elites, and did not offer a detailed analysis of the embeddedness of the state in society.[88] We also need more studies exploring the shift in values and the dynamics of inter-generational relations, two factors that have had a great influence on the outcome of the 1996 elections. Our conceptual tools ought to be revised and adapted to the new world in which we are living.

Notes

1 I would like to thank Michael Shafir, Mary Ellen Fischer, Tom Gallagher, Geoffrey Pridham, Nikiforos Diamandouros, Peter Siani-Davies and Lavinia Stan for their helpful comments on an earlier draft of this paper which was presented at an international conference on the democratization in the Balkans organized by the Centre for Mediterranean Studies at the University of Bristol (1997). I am also grateful to Nancy Bermeo and Princeton University for financial assistance that enabled me to complete this project.

2 This should not be taken as a statement about the degree of democratic consolidation. It goes without saying that a peaceful change in government does not provide in itself an adequate criterion of democratic consolidation, even if it enhances its prospects.

3 One of the most salient examples here is Samuel Huntington, who mistakenly argued that Romania did not have any previous experience with democracy (Huntington, *The Third Wave*, Norman: Oklahoma University Press, 1991, p. 271). In a recent essay, Robert Weiner builds on Huntington's argument and espouses a strongly deterministic approach – no past experience with democracy, no hope for a democratic future – that fails to capture the texture of Romanian politics. See Weiner, 'Democratization in Romania', in Lavinia Stan, ed., *Romania in Transition*, Aldershot, UK: Dartmouth Publishing Company, 1997, pp. 3–23.

4 Robert Dahl, *Polyarchy*, New Haven: Yale University Press, 1971, p. 3. On the procedural minimum of democracy also see Guillermo O'Donnell and Philippe Schmitter, 'Tentative conclusions about uncertain democracies', in Guillermo O'Donnell, Philippe Schmitter and Laurence Whitehead, eds, *Transitions from Authoritarian Rule: Prospects for Democracy*, Baltimore: Johns Hopkins University Press, 1986, p. 8.

5 Daniel Daianu, 'Transformation and the legacy of backwardness: thoughts from a Romanian perspective', *Économies et Sociétés*, 44, 1992, pp. 177–8.

6 The term was originally coined by Jadwish Bhagwati in 'Immisering growth – a geometrical note', *Review of Economic Studies*, 25, 1958. For more detail see Daianu, 'Transformation', pp. 182–5.

7 Many dissidents were writers and academics. I would mention here Paul Goma, Dorin Tudoran, Mihai Botez, Gheorghe Ursu, Doina Cornea, Petre Mihai Bacanu, Gabriel Andreescu, Dan Petrescu, Mircea Dinescu, and the writers who stood by him in 1989. Along with some former prominent communist leaders (Silviu Brucan, Constantin Pârvulescu, Gheorghe Apostol), they publicly opposed the policies of Nicolae Ceaușescu; other protests had been organized by students, workers, and trade unions. The Jiû Valley miners' strike of 1977, the Brasov workers' strike of 1987, and the students' manifestations in Íasi in 1987 are examples of resistance to the communist regime. On this topic, see Michael Shafir, 'Political culture, intellectual dissent, and intellectual consent', *Orbis*, 27, 2, 1983, pp. 393–420, and Vladimir Tismaneanu, 'Romanian exceptionalism?', in Karen Dawisha and Bruce Parrott, eds, *Politics, Power, and the Struggle for Democracy in South-East Europe*, Cambridge: Cambridge University Press, 1997, pp. 403–50.

8 Two exceptions must be acknowledged here. In the 1980s, Mihai Sora, a distinguished philosopher who made his academic debut in Paris in 1947, articulated a vigorous liberal political philosophy that championed the rule of law and an open society. Sora's *Eu & tu & el & ea . . . sau dialogul generalizat* was originally written in 1987–8 and circulated among a group of intellectuals all over the country. Dan Petrescu co-authored with Liviu Cangeopol *Ce-ar mai fi de spus?*, a volume that commented on East European

190   Aurelian Craiutu

politics and the prospects of change in the region; like Sora's book, it was published in Bucharest, in 1990.

9 New studies are required to account for this ideology of compliance, its invisible forms of resistance (foot dragging, pilfering, false compliance, feigned ignorance, slander, and the like), and the difference between on-stage and off-stage behaviour. These individual forms of resistance did not themselves constitute a vibrant civil society, nor did they successfully challenged the symbolic order; nonetheless, they were not devoid of some influence and cannot be simply dismissed as instances of unconditional submission to the *status quo*. James C. Scott's books may serve as a useful model, above all his *Weapons of the Weak*, New Haven: Yale University Press, 1985, and *Domination and the Arts of Resistance*, New Haven: Yale University Press, 1990. One of the main conclusions of Scott's books is that one should not infer ideological support from mere ritualistic compliance. On the other hand, Scott rightly points out that it is very difficult to wear a mask or play a role without acquiring the character that goes with them.

10 I borrow this concept from N. Diamandouros.

11 I have explored this issue in my study 'De la clientelism politic la societatea civila' (From political clientelism to civil society), *Litere, Arte & Idei*, 33, 167, 29 August 1994, pp. 1–3, 8, reprinted in Iordan Chimet, ed., *Momentul adevarului*, Cluj: Dacia, 1997, pp. 453–67. On the Romanian political culture also see Ioan Mihailescu, 'Mental stereotypes in post-totalitarian Romania', *Government and Opposition*, 28, 3, Summer 1993, pp. 315–24.

12 For an account of the pacted revolution and political roundtables in Hungary see Laszlo Bruszt and David Stark, 'Remaking the political field in Hungary: from the politics of confrontation to the politics of competition', in Ivo Banac, ed., *Eastern Europe in Revolution*, Ithaca: Cornell University Press, 1992, pp. 13–55, and Rudolf Tökes, *Hungary's Negotiated Revolution*, Cambridge: Cambridge University Press, 1996.

13 For a comprehensive treatment of this issue see Tismaneanu, 'Romanian exceptionalism?', pp. 403–33. The most recent book co-authored by Juan Linz and Alfred Stepan, *Problems of Democratic Transition and Consolidation: Southern Europe, South America, and Post-Communist Europe*, Baltimore: Johns Hopkins University Press, 1996, has a special chapter on Romania (pp. 344–65).

14 On this issue see Aurelian Craiutu, 'Ucenicia dificila a libertatii: note despre consolidarea democratiei in Romania' (The difficult apprenticeship of liberty: notes on the democratic consolidation in Romania), *Polis*, 3, 2, 1996, pp. 140–62.

15 On the Romanian revolution see Nestor Ratesh, *Romania: The Entangled Revolution*, Washington DC: Center for Strategic and International Studies, 1990; Katherine Verdery and Gail Kligman, 'Romania after Ceauşescu: post-communist communism?', in Banac, ed., *Eastern Europe.*, pp. 117–48; Steven D. Roper, 'The Romanian Revolution from a theoretical perspective', *Communist and Post-Communist Studies*, 27, 4, 1994, pp. 401–10; Peter Siani-Davies, 'Romanian Revolution or coup d'état?,' *Communist and Post-Communist Studies*, 29, 4, 1996, pp. 453–66.

16 Also see Matei Calinescu and Vladimir Tismaneanu, 'The 1989 Revolution and Romania's future', in Daniel N. Nelson, ed., *Romania After Tyranny*, Boulder CO: Westview Press, 1992, pp. 13–45.

17 Verdery and Kligman, 'Romania after Ceauşescu', pp. 121–2.

18 The official founding act of the Romanian Information System coincided with the events of Tg. Mures in March 1990. Tom Gallagher discusses the relation between the RIS and the ultra-nationalist organization Vatra Românească in his article 'Vatra Romaneasca and resurgent nationalism', *Ethnic and Racial Studies*, 15, 4, 1992, pp. 570–98, and in his *Romania After Ceauşescu*. Cornel Ivanciuc argued, however, that the founding of the RIS could be traced back as early as January 1990, when the new leaders felt increasingly threatened by intra-army factions as well as by the politicization and radicalization of the Romanian civil society. For more detail see Cornel Ivanciuc, 'Virgil Magureanu sau modelul exemplar al actunilor SRI' (Virgil Măgureanu or the perfect model of RIS's actions), 22, 1995, p. 12.

19 For more detail see Mary Ellen Fischer, 'Romania: the anguish of postcommunist politics', in Fischer, ed., *Establishing Democracies*, Boulder CO: Westview Press, 1996, pp. 187–8.

20 For more detail see Vladimir Tismaneanu, 'The quasi-revolution and its discontents: emerging political pluralism in post-Ceauşescu Romania, *East European Politics and Societies*, 7, 2, 1993.

21 This characteristic would be reinforced by the Electoral Law adopted in March 1990. Only 251 members were required for forming a political party. For more detail see Michael Shafir, 'The electoral law', RFE, *Report on Eastern Europe*, 1, 4 May, 1990, pp. 28–31.

22 This party was led by Corneliu Coposu who, until his death in November 1995, was considered the uncontested leader of the then opposition. A secretary to Iuliu Maniu, the chairman of the party until 1947, Coposu spent eighteen years in prison or seclusion and was released in 1964. His democratic credentials were impeccable and he succeeded in affiliating the party to the Brussels International of European Christian Democratic parties.

23 The situation was not much different in the other East European countries at that time. See Linz and Stepan, *Problems of Democratic Transition and Consolidation*.

24 In January 1990, Iliescu argued: 'Democracy means freedom and dignity . . . As long as a democratic framework is used for destructive or even anarchical purposes . . . these actions have to be stopped, restricted.' *FBIS-EEU*, 90–011, p. 76.

25 For a good analysis of the May 1990 elections see Voicu, 'Sisteme de partide in Europa de Est' (Political party systems in Eastern Europe), *Polis*, 3, 2, 1996, pp. 116–39.

26 Ibid., p. 129.

27 Verdery and Kligman, 'Romania after Ceauşescu', p. 125.

28 Fischer, 'Romania', p. 190.

29 For an account of the University Square demonstration of 1990 see the *Report on the 13–15 June Events* edited by the Group for Social Dialogue and the Association for the Defense of Human Rights in Romania, the Helsinki Committee (Bucharest, 1990). Also see Mihai Sturdza, 'The miners' crackdown on the opposition: a review of the evidence', *Report on Eastern Europe*, 11 January 1991, pp. 25–33; Verdery and Kligman, 'Romania after Ceausescu', pp. 130–40.

30 I borrow the expression from George Schöpflin, *Politics in Eastern Europe*, Oxford: Blackwell, 1993, p. 258.

31 This is a point made, among others, by Henry F. Carey in his study 'Post-communist radicalism in Romania', published in Peter H. Merkl and Leonard Weinberg, eds, *The Revival of Right-Wing Extremism in the 1990s*, London: Pinter, 1997.

32 This characteristic persisted for a few more years, thus signalling a chronic weakness of most political parties.

33 Steven D. Roper, 'The Romanian party system and the catch-all party phenomenon', *East European Quarterly*, 28, 4, Winter 1994, p. 525.

34 Due to inter-party migration, new parliamentary groups were formed, representing former non-parliamentary parties.

35 For a slightly different view see Katherine Verdery, *What Was Socialism and What Comes Next?*, Princeton: Princeton University Press, 1996, pp. 192–4. In Verdery's view, Romanian politics has been dominated by 'unruly' coalitions, i.e. 'loose clusterings of elites who cooperate to pursue or control wealth and other resources' (p. 193).

36 For a (post-Marxist) theoretical treatment of this issue in the larger Eastern European context see Herbert Kitschelt, 'The formation of party systems in East Central Europe', *Politics & Society*, 20, 1, March 1992, pp. 7–50. Unfortunately, Kitschelt's superficial analysis of Romania is based on limited and outdated information.

37 Within the Convention, there were disagreements on issues like monarchy, nationalism, religion.

38 The phrase belongs to Voicu, 'Sisteme de partide', p. 134.

39 In the western world, the left–right division is understood primarily in terms of economic policies. The left leans towards a stronger welfare state, while the right prefers less state intervention, lower taxes, and more privatization. In Eastern Europe, in the first years after 1990, a strong anti-communist position automatically placed a party on the right of the political spectrum, while the economic dimension was of less importance.

40 William Crowther and Georgeta Muntean, 'Electoral politics and transition in Romania', paper presented at the international conference on national reconciliation, Bucharest, Social Science Center, 4 June, 1994.

41 For a similar argument see Thomas Carothers, *Assessing Democracy Assistance: The Case of Romania*, Washington DC: Carnegie Endowment, 1996, pp. 39–41.

42 Whether or not these extremist parties should be equated with anti-system forces remains an open question. In his study 'Post-communist radicalism in Romania', Henry F. Carey pays extensive attention to these extremist forces and concludes that they posed a real threat to the stability of the regime. Carey's predictions were falsified by subsequent developments.

43 I disagree here with Mary Ellen Fisher, who lists among the characteristics that Romania shared with other East European countries 'weak historical parties' and 'the presence of anti-system parties (red and brown)' ('Romania', p. 200).

44 Again, this is not a specifically Romanian phenomenon; it can be found all over Eastern Europe. See András Körösényi, 'Stable or fragile democracy? Political cleavages and party system in Hungary', *Government and Opposition*, 28, 1, Winter 1993, pp. 87–104.

45 I borrow this phrase from Juan Linz, *The Breakdown of Democratic Regimes: Crisis, Breakdown, and Reequilibration*, Baltimore: Johns Hopkins University Press, 1978. On the political style of the Romanian elites see Fischer, 'Romania', pp. 189–90, Michael Shafir, 'Guvernarea Ciorbea si democratizarea: bilant intermediar,' (Ciorbea government: an assessment), *Sfera Politicii*, 55, 1997, pp. 6–24, and my essay 'Despre pacte si negocieri politice' (On pacts and political negotiations), *22*, 43, 23–29 October 1996, pp. 11–12.

46 Due to space constraints, I cannot elaborate on this topic here. For a good analysis of the Romanian constitution see Fischer, 'Romania', pp. 193–6; Cristian Preda, 'Ce e Romania? Filozofia politica a Constitutiei de la 1991' (What is Romania? The political philosophy of the 1991 constitution), *Polis*, 3, 2, 1996, pp. 25–47. Also see Craiutu, 'Ucenicia dificila a libertatii' (The difficult apprenticeship of liberty), pp. 147–9.

47 I define elites as groups who, by virtue of their political position, are able to affect regularly and substantially parliamentary decisions and public policies.

48 Michael Burton, Richard Gunther and John Higley, 'Introduction: elite transformations and democratic regimes', in John Higley and Richard Gunther, eds, *Elites and Democratic Consolidation in Latin America and Southern Europe*, Cambridge: Cambridge University Press, 1992, p. 3.

49 For a good analysis of Romanian political elites see George Tibil, 'Conflictul elitelor si instabilitatea politică in evolutia moderna şi contemporana a României' (Elite conflicts and political instability in modern Romania), *Polis*, 2, 4, 1995, pp. 85–112.

50 GRP, PNUR and SPL often opposed this policy, criticizing international institutions for their alleged interference in Romania's domestic affairs.

51 I borrow this term from J. Samuel Valenzuela. For more detail see his excellent study 'Democratic consolidation in post-transitional settings', in S. Mainwaring, G. O'Donnell and J. S. Valenzuela, eds, *Issues in Democratic Consolidation*, Notre Dame: University of Notre Dame Press, 1992, pp. 57–104.

52 These are: freedom to form and join organizations, freedom of expression, right to vote, eligibility for public office, right of political leaders to compete for votes and support, alternative sources of information, and institutions for making government policies depend on votes and other expressions of preference.

53 For more detail see Valenzuela, 'Democratic consolidation', pp. 62–8.

54 The existence of tutelary powers in the Romanian case must be taken, however, with a grain of salt, since Iliescu's power was entirely different from, say, Chile's Pinochet. The latter unambiguously placed himself in a tutelary position over the democratic process, whereas Iliescu had to abide by the rules of the democratic game, even if he fostered an oligarchic regime.

55 For an account of irregularities in the 1992 parliamentary elections see Henry F. Carey, 'Irregularities or rigging: the 1992 Romanian parliamentary elections', *East European Quarterly*, XXIX, 1, 1995, pp. 43–66.

56 I address this issue in Craiutu, 'Ucenicia dificila a libertatii', pp. 142–7.

57 See Marius Oprea, 'Culisele puterii comuniste' (Behind the closed doors of the communist power), *Sfera Politicii*, 31, 1995, pp. 23–5.

58 Verdery, *What was Socialism?*, p. 193ff. 'What defines unruly coalitions in contrast to political parties', writes Verdery, 'is that they are less institutionalized, less visible, less legitimate, and less stable than parties, and their territorial base is primarily regional or local rather than national' (p. 194).

59 Andrei Cornea, *Masina de fabricat fantasme*, Bucharest: Clavis, 1995. Also see *Eastern European Newsletter*, 10, 2, pp. 5–7.

60 The business elite included a number of expatriates who returned and invested in Romania after 1989; they benefited from their Western contacts and capital at a time when most Romanian citizens had neither Western experience nor money to invest. Many statistics demonstrate that the private sector now accounts for 35–40 per cent of the GDP, with agriculture, retail trade, and construction as leading sectors.

61 On Caritas, see Verdery, *What was Socialism?*, pp. 168–203.

62 Ibid., pp. 196–203.

63 On inter-enterprise arrears see Daniel Daianu, 'Macroeconomic stabilization in post-communist Romania', in Stan, ed., *Romania in Transition*, pp. 93–126.

64 On privatization see Lavinia Stan, 'Romanian privatization program', in Stan, ed., *Romania in Transition*, pp. 127–62.

65 Foreign investment in Romania amounted to $3 billion at the beginning of 1998; Hungary has already attracted $17 billion.

66 The Social Democratic Union came in the third place with 12.93 per cent in the Chamber and 13.16 per cent in the Senate, while DAHR received 6 per cent of the electoral vote. Only two other parties, PNUR and GRP, passed the 3 per cent threshold. Four small parties that were represented in the previous Parliament failed to pass this requirement: the Party of Civic Alliance, the Liberal Party-93, the Socialist Labour Party, and the Agrarian-Democratic Party.

67 Constantinescu received 54.41 per cent, Iliescu 45.59 per cent of the popular vote.

68 For a good analysis see Shafir, 'Romanian elections', *Journal of Democracy*, 8, 2, April 1997, pp. 144–58. The Bucharest-based journal of political science, *Sfera Politicii*, devoted two issues (44 & 45, 1997) to the November 1996 elections, featuring important contributions by Michael Shafir, Vladimir Tismăneanu and Virgil Nemoianu.

69 In the local elections of June 1996, the Party of Social Democracy in Romania (PSDR) won 26.49 per cent of the votes, while the Democratic Convention of Romania received 26.45 per cent of the popular vote. The Social Democratic Union led by former Prime Minister Petre Roman came in third place with 13.15 per cent. While the PSDR maintained its grip on rural areas, the Democratic Convention and SDU scored important victories in urban areas, including the most important cities of the country (with the exception of Cluj-Napoca).

70 By political learning I mean here a change in beliefs, attitudes and behaviour. For a seminal study on political learning see Nancy Bermeo, 'Democracy and legacies of dictatorship', *Comparative Politics*, 24, 3, 1992, pp. 273–92. I am not making here any claims about sweeping changes in the political culture; the latter is a collective concept and we must have reliable and extensive data before we hypothesize about the

'Romanian political culture' as a whole. I prefer to disaggregate it and work with the instruments of the new culture theory (Douglas, Wildaawski, Ellis) that focuses on competing ways of life within a national political culture.

71 The expression belongs to Vladimir Tismăneanu, 'Romanian exceptionalism', p. 405. Tismaneanu also writes that 'the vote was as much a protest against social and economic crises as an expression of the mass expectations for change' (pp. 440–1).

72 For an analysis of the November 1996 elections also see Liliana Popescu, 'A change of power in Romania', *Government and Opposition*, 32, 2, Spring 1997, pp. 172–86.

73 Ibid., p. 182.

74 Tom Gallagher, 'Conclusion', *Nationalism si democratie in Romania contemporana*, Bucharest: ALL Publishing House, 1999. Gallagher notes: 'As people increasingly make individual choices about issues important to their lives, social pluralism is likely to raise in importance . . . The rise of debates about lifestyle and personal behaviour is a sign of the decline in a submissive mentality. State institutions are being forced to account for their behaviour.'

75 DAHR received two positions in the Ciorbea cabinet (tourism and minorities), along with positions of prefect.

76 On this last topic see Laurentiu Stefan-Scarlat, 'ANL sub tavalugul alegerilor' (The National Liberal Alliance under the impact of elections), *Sfera Politicii*, 44, 1997, pp. 26–8.

77 In 1996, the real deficit amounted to about 10 per cent of GDP. Cutting down the deficit requires ending the inefficient policy of granting subsidies to loss-making enterprises.

78 Tismăneanu, 'Romanian exceptionalism', p. 441.

79 In 1997, only 1,304 state companies were privatized, most of which were small- and medium-size enterprises. In 1998, the government plans to cut down the inflation rate to 30–40 per cent and the budget deficit to 4–4.2 per cent; its scenario also includes a zero economic growth, the creation of a more investment-friendly environment, tax cuts, and speeding up the privatization process. The 1,600 state enterprises that will be privatized are expected to bring $1–2 billion in state revenues.

80 For more detail see Shafir, 'Guvernarea Ciorbea' (The Ciorbea government), pp. 11–13.

81 I borrow this concept from Guillermo O'Donnell, 'Delegative Democracy', Kellogg Institute Working Paper No. 172, University of Notre Dame, 1992. He argues that delegative democracies are inherently hostile to the patterns of representation normal in established democracies, to the creation and strengthening of political institutions, and to horizontal accountability.

82 Shafir, 'Guvernarea Ciorbea' (The Ciorbea government), pp. 6–24.

83 See Tismăneanu, 'Romanian exceptionalism, p. 440.

84 For an analysis of the rhetoric of academic discourses see Aurelian Craiutu, 'Perversity, futility, and jeopardy revisited: notes on the rhetoric of the great transformation in Eastern Europe', paper presented at the 1996 Annual Meeting of the American Political Science Association, San Francisco, California, August 1996.

85 In his *Polyarchy*, Robert Dahl stressed seven factors of democratization: historical sequence, levels of socio-economic development, concentration of power, socio-economic inequalities, subcultural cleavage patterns, political beliefs, and foreign domination.

86 Albert O. Hirschman, *A Bias for Hope*, Boulder CO: Westview, 1971.

87 Guillermo O'Donnell, 'The State, democratization, and some conceptual problems (a Latin American view with glances at some post-communist countries)', in William C. Smith, Carlos H. Acuña, and Eduardo A. Gamarra, eds, *Latin American Political Economy in the Age of Neoliberal Reform*, New Brunswick: Transaction Publishers, 1994, p. 158.

88 The writings of two American academics, Katherine Verdery and Gail Kligman, have opened new avenues which are worth exploring by political scientists.

9 Bulgaria

Transition comes full circle, 1989–1997

Kyril Drezov

Introduction

Living through a 'transition' is nothing new for Bulgarians. Before the present 'transition to democracy' they experienced perestroika, which was a transition to what Gorbachev wishfully described as 'more democracy, more socialism'. Until the mid-1980s Bulgarians were busy building the Brezhnevite 'developed socialism' as an intermediate transition stage between socialism and communism, and previous to that they were locked up in a 'transition period from capitalism to socialism'. Socialism, of course, was only the first, transitory stage towards full communism. In short, since 1944 Bulgarians were always transiting to something.

Apart from unfortunate similarities between communist and Western usage of the term 'transition' to describe pre-ordained adoption of their respective models, the term itself is far too vacuous to convey anything specific, as in every moment every society can be described as being in some sort of transition. However, since 1989 the concepts of 'transition to' and 'consolidation of' democracy, initially formulated to capture experiences of democratization in the Mediterranean and Latin America, have successfully colonized both post-communist studies and political discourse in Eastern Europe, and some use of them is unavoidable. This chapter is mainly focused on what can be described as Bulgaria's first 'transition to democracy' (1989–97), dominated by the former regime party; and it examines the factors that shaped the policies of the Communist/ Socialist party in this period. Only in the last section is a set of hypotheses formulated concerning the emergence by the late 1990s of a stable polity rooted in Bulgarian traditions. These hypotheses reject the notion of an imminent transition to a Western-style liberal order in Bulgaria: the latter notion seems destined for long life only in the propaganda activities of Bulgarian and Western governments.

After Zhivkov's downfall in November 1989 the impressions both in Bulgaria and abroad were that Bulgaria was moving largely in the same direction as the rest of the former Soviet satellites in Europe – towards multi-party politics, free elections, economic liberalization, privatization, albeit with some delay in comparison with the Central European countries. At the same time, there were some peculiarities: a palace coup rather than popular demonstrations marked the beginnings of transition in Bulgaria, and the renamed communist party won the first multi-party elections. Still, by the end of 1994 Bulgaria had already experienced three parliamentary elections and one presidential election, of which all but the very first parliamentary election in 1990 could be unequivocally described as free and fair. There were several peaceful transfers of power between governments of very different political orientation, and Bulgaria became the first of the former satellite countries to adopt an entirely new non-communist constitution in June 1991. By the mid-1990s constitutional governance in Bulgaria looked both stable and securely established – all major political players were committed to competitive elections, and the country had a functioning two-party system down to the last village. The decisions of the independent judiciary and of the Constitutional Court were accepted and implemented no matter how large was the parliamentary majority of the ruling party.[1]

Yet in the second half of 1996 Bulgaria's seemingly successful democracy underwent severe strain. An unstoppable depreciation of the lev *vis-à-vis* foreign currencies removed a major plank of stability that had been in place since early 1991, and led to spiralling inflation and rising discontent. By the end of 1996 the non-government Bulgarian media would routinely describe the country as 'the first failed transition'. The perceptions that the country needed 'a repetition of 1989' to put it back on the track of reform led first to the mass rallies of January 1997, and then to voluntary abdication from power of the Bulgarian Socialist Party (BSP) on 4 February of the same year.

In its outward features what happened in Bulgaria in early 1997 looked like an extraordinary Bulgarian repetition of '1989' in Central Europe: the economic collapse in Bulgaria was as severe as the one in Poland in the 1980s; there was a united opposition riding the wave of popular discontent; mass rallies began in the capital and some of the big cities, and one bloodied demonstration served as a catalyst for nationwide explosion of demonstrations; 'a sea of national flags' and resistance songs from the nineteenth century engulfed the country in four weeks of daily protests, with people from all social strata and ethnic groups – intellectuals, workers, peasants, Bulgarians, Turks – marching together against the rulers;[2] and 'social-democratic' reformers abandoned what they perceived as an essentially unreformed communist party. While the main pressure for change in 1989 came from outside – from Western countries, worried by the mass exodus of Bulgarian Turks after May 1989, and most importantly from Gorbachev's USSR – the main pressure for change in February 1997 was internal, with sustained mass rallies throughout January 1997 forcing an initially reluctant opposition to create an interim administration and organize early elections.

To sum up, '1997' in Bulgaria was closer in its external forms to '1989' in Central Europe than to the 1989 experience in Bulgaria. Yet this belated revolution occurred in a country that only six months before that could be described as a stable constitutional democracy. The parliament that agreed to be disbanded in February 1997 was elected in free and fair multi-party elections only two years before that; moreover, the country had had pluralistic media, politics and elections since 1990, and a non-communist constitution since 1991.

The fact that a repeat '1989' revolution swept a country that looked so advanced in its democratization points at least to two conclusions: first, that something must have gone terribly wrong between 1989 and 1997 in Bulgaria, and second, that as far as democratization is concerned, this period was not entirely wasted. Moreover, it can be argued that the factors that were crucial for the success of the 1997 'winter revolution' – such as the united nationwide opposition that channelled popular discontent into mass protests, the 'us against them' mentality that united practically the whole nation against a minority group holding on to power, the paralysis and disintegration of the ruling party – owed their existence precisely to the advanced democratization of Bulgarian politics between 1989 and 1997.

The main difference between Bulgaria and the successful post-communist countries of Central Europe was the dominance of Bulgaria's democratization by the largely unreconstructed former communist party. Between 1989 and 1997 the Bulgarian Communist Party (BCP) (from 1990 the Bulgaria Socialist Party) played a decisive role in the Bulgarian transition to democracy. After February 1997 Bulgaria seemingly entered 'a second transition', which resembles the post-1989 'transitions' in Central Europe at least in the very limited role played by the renamed but largely unreconstructed communist party.

The main influences on the policies of the Bulgarian Communist Party before 1989

Three main factors shaped the policies of the BCP before 1989: a deeply rooted egalitarian and 'leftist' tradition, the gradual Westernization of Bulgarian society under Zhivkov, and the impact of Gorbachev's policies of glasnost and perestroika.

The legacy of communist egalitarianism

Before the advent of Gorbachev the Bulgarian Communist Party was a solid Leninist organization with no traditions of 'social-democratising' revisionism. This made the BCP very different from communist parties in Poland, Hungary and Czechoslovakia. In the 1960s–1970s there were many instances of opposition to Zhivkov in the communist party, but almost without exception these oppositionists were criticizing Zhivkov and his policies from Stalinist and Maoist positions. The main emphasis was on the luxurious lifestyle of Zhivkov's party elite, and on its growing 'embourgeoisement' – in contrast to the alleged communist asceticism of the first post-war years. In early 1965 pro-Chinese conspirators in the top echelons of the communist party and the army (among them were three generals and a member of the Central Committee) were planning a coup against Zhivkov, who in their opinion had betrayed Marxism-Leninism and was leading the country to a 'restoration of capitalism'. When this plot was uncovered by Zhivkov's secret services in April 1965, its leaders decided to escape to 'pro-Chinese' Romania, but were arrested before that (one of them committed suicide to avoid arrest). Nine of the leading plotters were given long prison sentences, and a further 192 were expelled from the communist party or suffered administrative penalties.[3] Despite these measures a new pro-Chinese conspiracy was uncovered in 1968, which involved about 100 people with communist party or army backgrounds, organised in a 'Marxist-Leninist Bulgarian Communist Party'. The five leaders of this conspiracy were given long prison sentences.[4]

According to Ivanov, for the period 1963–74 the Bulgarian State Security opened files on 1,200 communist party members who were involved in opposition activities against the Zhivkov regime. Of these about 600 were interrogated, 70 were given prison sentences, 100 suffered internal exile, and six were expelled from the country.[5] The last trial of 'leftist' conspirators in Bulgaria was in 1983.[6]

The popularity of crude egalitarianism among Bulgarian communists corresponded to a regional trend – in 1961–78 Albania was allied to Maoist China, and Ceausescu's regime in Romania sought inspiration in China and North Korea. Whatever the origins for this trend (perhaps rooted in the agrarian and largely 'pre-modern' character of pre-1944 Balkan societies), it certainly was a very different phenomenon from the 'right-wing revisionism' that menaced the communist leaderships of Poland, Hungary and Czechoslovakia. In comparison with his numerous 'leftist' critics in the Bulgarian Communist Party, Zhivkov looked almost like a Westernizer.

Western influences

In the 1970s and 1980s Zhivkov presided over a gradual expansion of contacts between Bulgaria and Western societies – through mass tourism, and through a gradual increase in access to Western publications, films and music. This was in marked contrast to the isolationist and Stalinist policies pursued in Albania and Romania at the same time, and the lack of organised pro-democracy dissent until 1988 showed the acceptance of such policies even by those Bulgarian intellectuals who were critical of communism.

Westernization of Bulgarian society in those years was so gradual and imperceptible that it was almost entirely neglected by Western observers.[7] Yet by the mid-1980s the state had given up on punishing ordinary Bulgarians for following Western ways in their personal lifestyles – like fashion and music. Records of Western pop and rock groups were widely available on the state radio and in music shops, and were avidly bought by visiting Czechoslovaks and East Germans. In the 1980s Romanians preferred Bulgarian television to their own, in contrast to the 1960s when Bulgarians followed Western films on Romanian television. Richard Pipes's books against détente, and avowedly anti-communist magazines like *The National Interest*, *Commentary* and *The New Republic*, were available to all users of the National Library in Sofia (however, access to works of Bulgarian and other East European *émigrés* and dissidents remained strictly controlled until the fall of Zhivkov). In short, Bulgaria of the mid-1980s was far more tolerant of Western ways than Bulgaria of the early 1960s, when 'decadent behaviour' could easily lead to administrative exile and hard labour in 'labour-corrective camps'. Yet this was a controlled Westerniz-ation, and it did not lead to any instances of open dissent against the system. In the 1980s communist party control of Bulgarian society was as unchallenged as in the 1960s, and the same was true of Bulgaria's dependence on the Soviet Union. Gorbachev's coming to power changed all this.

The role of glasnost[8]

Bulgaria is unique among all former Soviet satellites in the fact that a political campaign in the hegemonic state – Gorbachev's glasnost and perestroika policies in the USSR – created the basis for the first open opposition to the communist regime in Bulgaria since the 1940s. The very thoroughness of Bulgaria's Sovietization had inadvertently created chan-nels for a massive influx of subversive ideas from the USSR – universal knowledge of Russian, an extensive set of Russian bookshops and wide availability of Soviet press (with books and printed media much cheaper than Bulgarian ones), and one Russian television channel together with the two Bulgarian ones. Previously the Russian media was considered utterly boring, but in 1987–90 ordinary Bulgarians and communist party members alike massively subscribed to Soviet newspapers and magazines, and avidly watched Soviet television. Overall, the impact of Soviet glasnost on Bulgarian society was far greater than its impact on all other satellite countries: one year of feverish digestion of Soviet glasnost imports was enough to break down forty years of enforced silence in Bulgaria. As a result of these glasnost-induced changes in Bulgarian society, the first openly dissident groups emerged in early 1988 and immediately attempted registration. The names of two of the most popular groupings founded in 1988–9 clearly show the inspiration behind them: 'A Discussion Club in Support of Glasnost and Perestroika' and 'Ecoglasnost'. Another feature similar to the Soviet Union was that communist party members, or people with strong communist and secret police connections, predominated among the organizers and activists of the glasnost-inspired independent associations in Bulgaria.[9]

The spread of pro-reform sentiments in the BCP influenced even some of Zhivkov's erstwhile protégés in the Politburo. It seems that the conspiracy to remove him swung into action in the summer of 1989 (its two most influential members were Defence Minister Dobri Dzhurov and Foreign Minister Petar Mladenov), and it was co-ordinated with Moscow from the very beginning. It was part of a Soviet push to get rid of anti-Gorbachev leaders in the Soviet bloc, and the Soviet ambassador in Sofia Viktor Sharapov (a KGB general) was directly involved in 'persuading' Zhivkov to resign in November 1989.[10] After Zhivkov's removal the Bulgarian communist Party was headed by people who were committed to Gorbachev's policies of glasnost and perestroika. Many of the activists of the pro-perestroika groups welcomed these changes, and returned *en masse* to the communist party.

By the end of 1989 the BCP was a party with a small reformist elite inspired by Gorbachev's policies, which uneasily co-existed with a large conservative membership (by November 1989 the BCP numbered one million members – one-eighth of the total population of the country) shaped by years of Stalinism and lacking indigenous 'social-democratising' traditions.

To sum up, the main consequence of the BCP's thirty years of undisputed dominance over Bulgarian society – between the completion of the forced collectivization of the peasantry in the mid-1950s and the beginning of the forced renaming of the ethnic Turks in the mid-1980s – was that in the beginning of the transition the BCP was virtually unchallenged by pro-democracy opposition forces. This was a situation very different from the mass anti-communist revolutions in Central Europe. While in Poland, Hungary and Czechoslovakia 1989 symbolized the end result of mass opposition against 'the system', in Bulgaria the same 1989 heralded the beginning of mass opposition against 'the system'. This fact alone would give the BCP enough opportunities to dominate the transition.

The formation of a communist-dominated two-party system in 1989–1991

Some of the key elements of the new democratic political system manifested themselves as early as November 1989, and most crucially in the roundtable talks of early 1990. The elaboration and adoption of the 1991 constitution itself was a product of an already well-established power balance. Thus the defining feature of Bulgarian political life since the roundtable talks of early 1990 could be described as a two-party system in which one of the parties ultimately seemed to dominate the system. The parties in question were the Bulgarian Communist (later Socialist) Party, and the Union of Democratic Forces (UDF). The Bulgarian party system has known other parties apart from those two – the Agrarians, the mostly Turkish and Muslim Movement for Rights and Freedoms, and numerous smaller organizations, most of which never stood any chance to enter parliament. Still, in the seven years of the transition only the BSP and UDF would invariably hold between themselves more than two-thirds of the seats in every parliament, and thus the description of the system as a two-party one is justified.

The BSP's domination of the system

From the very start of the transition the BSP had some natural advantages over its main rival – the pro-democracy groups united in the UDF. First, it had a disciplined and smoothly running organization that compared favourably with the anarchic half-party, half-coalition UDF, and second, it exercised a disproportionate influence in the country's administration, management and security apparatus. The BSP managed to democratize itself (by officially allowing 'ideological currents and associations' within the party since January 1990) without a major split or mass desertion of the previously communist membership. Later in the transition the BSP developed symbiotic links with the most powerful economic groupings of nomenklatura origin.

The real advantages that the BSP enjoyed over its main rival were augmented by a popular belief that the BSP leadership was an all-powerful puppeteer that could reshape the Bulgarian political scene at will. A residual deference to the power of 'the communists' ingrained in the minds of several generations of Bulgarians certainly played a role in popularizing this belief. However, the tendency to see the BSP as all-powerful even when it was clearly on the defensive – after the fall of Lukanov's government in the autumn of 1990, and again during UDF's one year in power – certainly mixed the real with the mythical. It is interesting to note that this perception of an omnipotent BSP was actively propagated by people who saw themselves as leading anti-communists. Throughout the 1990s Edvin Sugarev's regular articles in the UDF's daily *Demokratsiya* – always unmasking yet another perfect BSP conspiracy – were religiously read by opposition supporters, and they contributed in no small measure to the fact that in the first seven years of the transition the BSP's perceived power was far greater than its real power.[11] The myth of the all-powerful BSP, and the stranglehold that this myth exercised over the imagination of millions of Bulgarians, were broken only in the mass protests in January–February 1997. Only then the flawed humanity and very real impotence of BSP leaders became obvious to the public, and they turned from objects of awe into objects of ridicule.[12]

In discussing the post-1989 political system one should avoid the temptation to ascribe some grand plan to the BCP/BSP leadership. What with hindsight would seem as a logical and cleverly designed system to ensure BSP domination, was in fact the end result of a long process of trial and error.

The perestroika period

Immediately after the overthrow of Zhivkov the new BCP leadership was contemplating only a limited Soviet-style perestroika, which would allow the formation of autonomous organizations outside BCP control, and yet would stop short of legalizing opposition parties. Everything was to be kept within the confines of 'socialist pluralism'. But the BCP underestimated the strength of opposition feelings in Bulgarian society.[13] The first legal opposition rally on 18 November 1989 was far more numerous than the rival BCP rally held on the previous day, and this event had a truly catalytic effect on Bulgarian society. By the end of November the Agrarian and Social Democratic parties, violently suppressed in the 1940s, had reappeared; on 7 December an umbrella organization of most opposition groupings – the Union of Democratic Forces – was created, and on 14 December an angry mass rally besieged the communist leadership in parliament demanding the immediate repeal of the constitutional clause that guaranteed 'the leading role of the BCP'. By the end of 1989 the BCP's perestroika had become ungovernable.

The roundtable talks

In January 1990, fearful of a comeback of Zhivkov's closest associates on the wave of mass protests of Bulgarians living in mixed population regions, the BCP leadership agreed to roundtable talks with the nascent UDF. What made these roundtable talks different from the ones in Central Europe was that while in the latter 'the push' for talks came from the democratic opposition, in Bulgaria it was a push from another quarter – the mass anti-Turkish rallies that in early January 1990 engulfed a third of the country, and by 7 January had descended by force on the capital. These rallies were no less genuine than the November and December rallies of the democratic opposition in Sofia, and commanded the allegiance of a far wider area.[14] If anything, they were more representative of the 'common people' – of the country rebelling against the capital – being angrier and more anarchic. At that point the BCP leadership made a conscious decision to build the UDF up into a nominally equal partner in Polish-style roundtable talks. This served several purposes: (a) the UDF posed less of an immediate threat to the post-Zhivkov BCP leadership than the anti-Turkish protest, with the added benefit that as an officially designated 'enemy' it could easily unite all BCP supporters behind the new leadership;

(b) by granting 'official' opposition status only to a seemingly pro-Western and liberal grouping like the UDF, all other opposition groups could be demoted in importance in propaganda terms, thus countering the negative effect of mass anti-Turkish rallies on Western opinion; (c) nationalist anger could be diverted to a new and seemingly powerful bogey (the UDF was only too happy to serve for that purpose: it defined itself as anti-nationalist even before it became anti-communist), thus reclaiming the 'nationalist' card for BCP.[15] In short, the BCP needed a credible anti-communist opposition to mobilize its own dispirited supporters, and it also needed a credible non-nationalist opposition to mobilize the anti-Turkish vote for itself. Thus the roundtable talks between January and April 1990 laid the basis for the future two-party system in Bulgaria, in which, however, the UDF was designed to remain the weaker partner.

The successful subordination of the nationalist factor to BSP interests, and the way roundtable talks were organized, also helped the BSP to control the potentially explosive 'Turkish factor'. In January 1990 Medi Doganov (later Ahmed Dogan), at that time a little known former political prisoner, founded together with his ethnic Bulgarian girlfriend a 'Movement for Rights and Freedoms of the Turks and Moslems in Bulgaria' (later shortened to 'Movement for Rights and Freedoms' (MRF) to avoid the ban on ethnically based parties that was included in March 1990 in the new Bulgarian law on political parties, and also in the constitution adopted in June 1991). Dogan was not one of the organizers of the mass rallies of ethnic Turks in 1989 (he was in prison at the time). All leaders of Bulgaria's ethnic Turks having either been expelled or having emigrated from the country under Zhivkov, from January 1990 Ahmed Dogan faced little competition in his bid for the leadership of Bulgaria's ethnic Turks and Turkish-oriented Pomaks (Bulgarian-speaking Muslims). In early 1990 his leadership ambitions were discreetly supported by the Bulgarian Committee for State Security (KDS), and hence by the ruling Bulgarian communist (later Socialist) Party. Apart from behind-the-scenes mediation between the leaders of the anti-Turkish demonstrations and the nascent MRF (which significantly boosted Dogan's prestige as the only Turkish leader who could 'deliver' concessions from both the official authorities and the anti-Turkish protesters), the KDS also guarded Dogan against the emergence of potential competitors from within the Turkish and Muslim community (such people were helped to emigrate to Turkey). In preparation for the first multi-party elections the BSP first ensured Dogan's exclusion from the UDF side of the roundtable talks (thus creating a rift between UDF and MRF), and then helped the MRF to register separately from the UDF for the first multi-party elections scheduled for June 1990 – in violation of the law on political parties drafted by the same BSP in March 1990 (which banned ethnically based parties), but conveniently splitting the opposition vote for the June 1990 elections. By mid-1990 Ahmed Dogan had achieved practical monopoly over political representation of Bulgaria's Turks and Muslims, and his MRF was destined to play a key role in Bulgaria's 'transition', at times commanding influence and importance incommensurate with its stable 6–7 per cent share of the national vote in all elections in the 1990s.[16]

The founding elections

By April 1990 the leadership of the newly renamed BSP was panicking again that UDF influence was spilling out of control. For the first time its response was to seek a constitutional guarantee against a future UDF government. Thus on 3 April enhanced presidential powers were voted through by the communist-dominated parliament (these went beyond the final roundtable agreements that were signed in March by both the BSP and UDF), and later on the same day Petar Mladenov was elected President for a four-year term – well before the multi-party parliamentary elections due in June.

The first free multi-party elections in Bulgaria since 1931 were held in two rounds on 10 and 17 June 1990. With 47.15 per cent of the vote the BSP won 52.75 per cent of all seats in the Grand National Assembly that was entrusted with the preparation of a new constitution, and the UDF came second with 36 per cent of vote and seats.[17] UDF leaders protested about manipulations, and the BSP certainly used to the full all its advantages. Yet the June elections merely confirmed the BSP's domination of Bulgarian society. These elections were most important in determining the shape of the first Bulgarian non-communist constitution.

The BSP's retreat from power

After the June elections the BSP enjoyed more power than at any time since the beginning of the roundtable talks. It had received a democratic mandate, the President was from its ranks, and it had a solid parliamentary majority. Yet for the BSP it was much easier to win elections than to rule the country. Its inadequacy for the new post-communist era was soon exposed: President Mladenov was forced to resign in July for a seemingly trivial reason (a filmed replica about 'calling the tanks' during a UDF rally in December 1989), and after some horse-trading the BSP was forced to accept the UDF's leader Zheliu Zhelev as the new President of Bulgaria.

The second retreat concerned the government. The BSP had signalled its willingness to form a coalition government with the UDF even before the June elections, and this was again on offer after the BSP's victory in the elections. Although BSP propaganda would present such offers as dictated solely by the national interest, a coalition government responsible to a BSP-dominated parliament could only serve the BSP interest, first and foremost by diluting responsibility for painful economic reforms. Thus the BSP offers were declined, and by November 1990 the purely BSP government of Andrey Lukanov had brought the country to hyper-inflation, a system of rationing and mass discontent. When Lukanov resigned in November the UDF rating had shot up to 60 per cent in opinion polls, and it would have surely won early parliamentary elections. Instead a coalition cabinet was formed pending new parliamentary elections in 1991.[18] This gave the BSP enough time to recover, and for the remaining six months the BSP leadership concentrated its efforts on devising the new constitution.

The July 1991 constitution

The effect of the new constitution on the political system was to limit the powers of the President (mostly by allowing presidential vetoes to be overruled by absolute rather than two-thirds majorities), to keep government weak (by not providing for a German-style constructive vote of no confidence which was adopted in Hungary and Poland), and to strengthen the judiciary and the Constitutional Court. The constitution also banned ethnically based parties, but Dogan's MRF escaped this ban partly as a result of its registration before the constitution was adopted and partly as a result of Western pressure.[19] The MRF's 'exception', combined with the existing ban on ethnic parties, made this party the only possible representative of Bulgaria's ethnic Turks. 'Any attempt to establish a second Turkish party could now be declared unconstitutional . . . The MRF was transformed into the only possible outlet for the political representation of the Bulgarian Turks.'[20]

Apart from its effect on the political system, the 1991 constitution preserved a major role for the state in the economy and in society in general. In doing so it followed closely the model of the communist constitutions of 1947 and 1971 rather than that of the liberal Turnovo constitution (in force 1879–1947) with its minimalist role for the state. According to the 1991 constitution the state guarantees a minimal wage (Article 48), has an obligation to protect the family (Article 14), to secure paid maternal leaves and free midwifery to every pregnant woman (Article 47), and to create conditions for a balanced development of all the regions of the country (Article 20). Article 22 forbids foreign citizens and foreign legal persons from acquiring property rights on land; however, they can acquire rights of usage for an indefinite period. The detailed obligations of the state towards the welfare of its citizens, and the constitutional ban on foreigners acquiring private property on land, seem at variance with the needs of a nation with a huge foreign debt and in dire need of foreign investment.

Moreover, the new constitution was made extremely difficult to change – some clauses could be changed only by another Grand National Assembly (like the ones relating to the form of government), and all the rest required either a three-quarters majority for a speedier change, or a two-thirds majority in two votes separated by a period of at least two months, but within the span of five months.

Overall, the adoption of the 1991 constitution was a major victory for the BSP. By enshrining the republican form of government and state intervention in the economy and in society in general, the new constitution implicitly legitimated the most important changes brought about by the communist take-over in 1944. But the main aim of this inflexible constitutional arrangement was to perpetuate BSP influence in all spheres of life even in a situation when both the President and the government would be controlled by the opposition.

Such a situation emerged after the October 1991 parliamentary elections (when the BSP won a minority of votes, 33.14 per cent, in comparison with the combined vote for the UDF and the MRF, respectively 34.36 and 7.55 per cent, who formed a coalition government after the elections), and the January 1992 presidential elections, which were narrowly won by the incumbent President Zhelev, who got 53 per cent of the vote while the BSP candidate Velko Valkanov received 47 per cent (the support of MRF and the ethnic Turkish vote – a stable 6–7 per cent of the electorate in all elections – were decisive for Zhelev's victory).[21]

Paralysis and implosion of the Bulgarian political system

The constitution as an obstacle to BSP power

The 1991 constitution served the BSP well when it was in opposition (from November 1991 to December 1992), and when it was the major force behind Berov's government (December 1992 to September 1994). Then the BSP's aim was to preserve whatever influence it still had in society, and an inflexible constitution with a strong role for the judiciary could only be of help. Similarly, the ineptitude of the allegedly pro-UDF prosecution to control the post-1991 explosion in crime helped the BSP in its successful election campaign in 1994.

The situation changed dramatically when the BSP itself came to power in January 1995, following a victory in the December 1994 parliamentary elections. Then the BSP tried in vain to change the *status quo*, and all these attempts were repeatedly frustrated by the Constitutional and the Supreme Courts, and by the judiciary in general. Preserving the *status quo*, whatever it was, was the one rationale behind the decisions of the courts. In 1995 they prevented changes in the Land Act that were deemed regressive by the non-communist parties, while in 1996 they would delay for months the liquidation of bankrupt banks demanded by the IMF.

The prosecution similarly frustrated the expectations of the BSP leadership that it would be able to combat crime effectively. In Bulgaria 'the prosecution is the body that administers law, not the courts. The prosecution is set up on the principle of hierarchy, and high-ranking prosecutors can suspend the decisions of lower ranking ones. In this way, offenders may be released without prosecution.'[22] Chief Prosecutor Ivan

Tatarchev (in power 1992–8) became notorious for his tough anti-communist and anti-crime statements, in stark contrast to his failure to bring to justice even one of the publicly condemned 'criminals'; moreover, he repeatedly released major criminal bosses without trial.

The police force itself was demoralized, and under the inept leadership of Interior Minister Lyubomir Nachev it remained a largely passive onlooker *vis-à-vis* the crime wave engulfing the country. In comparison with 1994 gang warfare actually intensified in 1995 – the BSP's first year in power – culminating with the murder of the President of the most notorious 'insurance company' VIS-2, Vassil Iliev, in the spring of 1995.

In short, the unchecked independence of the judiciary and prosecution developed into a huge problem for all governments after 1991. The judges and the prosecution discovered that their independence was not checked by any other power, and behaved accordingly.[23]

The temptations of government

While prime ministers could do very little to challenge the 1991 constitutional arrangement, they had plenty of opportunity to enrich themselves – or enrich their friends and loyal supporters. All post-1989 Bulgarian prime ministers have enjoyed extensive powers of patronage – the temptations offered by a huge state sector in Bulgarian industry. This proved detrimental for BSP unity under the Videnov government, when a veritable 'economic civil war' raged within the ruling BSP. From mid-1995 the BSP was badly divided between the economic groupings that grew rich under the 1990 Lukanov governments and afterwards, and groupings close to some of Videnov's advisers (the Orion 'circle of friends').

The basic precondition for BSP domination of the Bulgarian political system was the preservation of internal BSP unity at all costs. The internal balance between the Lilov and Lukanov factions survived intact until the end of 1994, but this changed irrevocably under Videnov. Throughout 1995 and 1996 Videnov worked frantically to create his own power base in the BSP (on a par with similar attempts to control the state administration and the economy). This pitted him against leading party ideologue Alexander Lilov in the wake of the parliamentary elections in December 1994, and from the summer of 1995 Videnov openly quarrelled with the Lukanov faction as well. The result by the end of 1995 was a near complete paralysis of the BSP, of the government (staffed at least partly by Lukanov supporters) and of the economy – in the sense that no important decisions could be taken and implemented. By the end of 1996 Bulgaria was inexorably sliding into chaos and economic crisis reminiscent of the end of 1990. And while the BSP was descending into mutual recriminations, the UDF under its post-1994 chairman Ivan Kostov was successfully evolving into a coherent party. By February 1997 the BSP was deserted by its reformist wing and remained internally divided between pro-Videnov and anti-Videnov factions, thus paving the way for a UDF take-over. The UDF dislodged the previously dominant ex-communist BSP from power in three stages: first, by Petar Stoyanov's victory in the presidential elections in November 1996; second, by heading the mass demonstrations against BSP power in January and February 1997 that paved the way for a UDF-controlled caretaker government headed by Sofia mayor Stefan Sofiyanski; and finally by winning an absolute majority in the parliamentary elections held on 19 April. Altogether five coalitions and parties passed the 4 per cent threshold on these elections – the United Democratic Forces (a UDF-dominated coalition between UDF and the Popular Alliance) got 52.26 per cent, the BSP 22.07 per cent, the MRF 7.6 per cent, the Euroleft (formerly the reform wing of the BSP) 5.5 per cent, and the Bulgarian Business Bloc 4.93 per cent. In the April 1997 parliamentary elections the UDF won almost the same share of votes and seats as did the BSP in the first multi-party elections in June 1990. Seven years later the roles of these two parties were completely reversed: it looked as if this time it was the UDF that was destined to become 'the natural party of government' for years to come. The hope of the millions of Bulgarians who voted for the UDF in 1996 and 1997 was that this party would finally lead Bulgaria out of the misery of the first post-communist years, and propel it into the modern era – at least to the extent that this had already happened in the relatively successful transitions in Central Europe.

Second transition or 'the Bulgarian model'?

The historical setting

Throughout the centuries Bulgarian state formations were not noted for implementing fundamental economic change of their own free volition. Despite Bulgaria's achievement of a 'superpower' status and parity with Constantinople in the ninth and early tenth centuries, the money economy did not arrive there until after its conquest by the Byzantines.[24] Crafts and guilds as a mass phenomenon emerged with the Turks, and industrializ-ation happened under Soviet tutelage.

Moreover, the establishment of multi-party democracy after 1879 may have in fact slowed down economic growth achieved in the late Ottoman empire. By giving the vote to millions of illiterate peasants it certainly conserved a system of subsistence agriculture for decades – until it was destroyed by communist industrialization and collectivization.[25]

In a similar way, the re-establishment of democracy after 1989 has effectively conserved an inherited industrial system. Simplifying a great deal, the single most important result of BCP rule (1944–89) was the creation of a state-owned industry entirely dependent on the importation of energy, and in most cases of raw materials as well. While such dependence is by no means unique to Bulgaria, in the Zhivkov period it required political acrobatics to secure cheap Soviet energy, and in later periods it required hard currency exports. Effectively since 1986 the country has been living beyond its means, amassing a foreign debt of more than $11 billion.

Between 1989 and 1997 industry was neither restructured nor privatized; it existed almost unchanged on its pre-1989 scale – wasteful of energy and often generating losses rather than profits. In fact, the pre-1989 legacy has been exacerbated in at least two ways.

First, while industry remained largely state-owned after 1989, it was actually managed far worse than in the Zhivkov period – with asset-stripping, privatization of profits and nationalization of losses. An elaborate system for milking the state industry has emerged after 1989 – starting at micro-level (the state enterprise with private firms controlling its imports and exports), and moving to macro-level (a banking system financing enterprise losses and creating 'credit millionaires'). 'Industrial conglomerates, such as Multigrup, Orion, and Tron, emerged in the shadowy world between the public, private and illegal economic sectors. Many of the productive assets of the economy passed into private hands while the state was left with the inefficient and debt-ridden ones and often continued to subsidize the new private enterprises.'[26]

Second, ill-conceived restitution schemes replaced a wasteful but functioning system of agricultural co-operatives with a chaos of conflicting restitution claims and new power relations. The 1992 Land Act aimed to re-establish the *status quo* of 1946. However, the majority of owners had no intention of cultivating their property; lacking the right to sell it (because of the unfinished process of restitution), they tended to lease it for periods of one to three years to large-scale tenant farmers (usually belonging to the previously socialist ruling elite), or to co-operatives. However, while the tenants hold a strong position over the land-owners, they themselves are in a weak position *vis-à-vis* the already mentioned economic conglomerates based in the big cities, who control the input and output of agriculture.[27]

Such an economic system could be penetrated, exploited, manipulated, even taken over by a determined Prime Minister (as almost happened under Videnov), but it could not be changed.

The weight of Bulgarian traditions does not favour a radical overhaul of the system that emerged in the 'first' transition. A basic understanding, or even an interest in the workings of the modern market economy did not sink easily into Bulgarian minds either before or after 1989. All important discussions about 'market socialism' in the 1960s to the 1980s have completely bypassed Bulgaria. And all crucial economic reforms of the post-1989 period in Bulgaria were invariably implemented under pressure from the IMF and the World Bank, never by Bulgaria's own choosing.

This aversion to change goes hand in hand with a deep distrust of the foreigners 'who would come and buy us lock, stock and barrel'. That the 1991 constitution would ban the sale of land to foreigners, and that

Bulgaria would rank lowest for foreign investment among the former Soviet satellites in Europe, clearly reflect a well-established pattern. While political nationalism is not an important force and vote-winner in Bulgaria (unlike Serbia, Romania, Slovakia and Croatia), a particularly primitive form of economic nationalism has traditionally enjoyed widespread support among all sections of the population, and left- and right-wing parties.

While not as statist or xenophobic as the BSP rank-and-file, the UDF's brief period of governance in 1991–2 was not a showcase for economic reform. Under present UDF leader Ivan Kostov (Finance Minister in 1991–2) funds were routinely diverted to loss-making enterprises to the benefit of the shady 'economic groupings' that are the curse of Bulgarian 'transition'; relations with international financial institutions were bad, and Lukanov's 1990 moratorium on foreign debt obligations was effectively upheld (a rescheduling agreement with the London club was achieved only in 1993, under Berov). One of the first acts of the new UDF government in November 1991 was to abolish the Ministry of Foreign Economic Relations, thus destroying all documentary evidence about syphoning out of resources under the previous governments (again, directly benefiting the already mentioned economic groupings). The one-year of UDF rule changed very little in the predominance of the state in the economy. The UDF was dominated by a lobby with a vested interest in restitution of urban property, which was the only property-related measure that was successfully implemented during its stay in power. Apart from that, the UDF wasted its energy on a badly designed policy of restitution of agricultural properties (which came to nothing), and on purges in industry in order to create a solid bloc of 'blue directors'.[28]

The consolidation of the UDF power (April 1997 to October 1998)

In the eighteen months between the UDF's victory in the April 1997 parliamentary elections and its first national conference as a ruling party, the main preoccupation of the UDF leadership was not economic reform but consolidation of its power. In a perverse way the installation of a currency board on 1 June 1997 (limiting money in circulation to the foreign currency reserves of the country, and pegging the national currency – lev – to the German mark at a ratio 1000:1), which was supposed to be the first step in a radical overhaul of the economic *status quo* in Bulgaria, was the last radical economic measure of the Kostov government. The inherited approaches to privatization and land restitution were not substantially affected by the advent of the UDF government. Overall there seems to be marginally greater order and efficiency in the machinery of government in comparison with the Videnov period, but no radical change. Foreign investors still do not find Bulgaria particularly attractive,[29] industry is still dominated by the giant public enterprises (whose managing boards were taken over by thousands of 'blue (UDF) activists' keen to supplement their incomes), asset-stripping by private conglomerates continues (although the favourites of the Kostov government are different, and the biggest of the 'old' conglomerates – Multigrup – had suffered financially in 1998 because of previous confrontation with the government), agriculture is hampered by unclear property relations, and corruption remains rampant. The one crucial difference from the Videnov period is the willingness of the IMF to prop up the Kostov government, particularly in acquiescing in September 1998 to sign a three-year agreement with Bulgaria. The securing of this financing would allow Kostov to postpone any painful structural reforms until after the next parliamentary elections in 2001 (earlier in 1998 the IMF extended by further six months – until mid-1999 – the government's deadline to deal with some sixty-odd state loss-making firms, which were first slated for closure under Videnov[30]). The one window that existed for radical reforms was in the year after the April 1997 elections – when the public was willing to accept sacrifices – and it was not used. Local elections are due in the autumn of 1999, and the administering of economic pain one and a half years before the 2001 parliamentary elections is highly unlikely for electoral reasons alone.

That the government, and Kostov himself, consider Bulgaria's economic transition completed with the financial stabilization that was delivered by the currency board (which is the third IMF-supported financial stabilization in Bulgaria since 1991) can be seen from the numerous statements of ministers since the autumn of 1997 that Bulgaria was not only fit for membership of the European Union, but that it was actually close to fulfilling the Maastricht criteria for membership in the European Monetary Union – as if they in any way applied to a country like Bulgaria that is still on the threshold of a functioning market economy.

The consolidation of the UDF's economic position was paralleled by moves to increase the UDF's control over other spheres of social life. A media law passed in September 1998 was so partisan that it was vetoed by President Stoyanov with the explanation that it did not give sufficient guarantees to the independence of the media (this was Stoyanov's first use of veto since his inauguration in January 1997). A lustration law was passed on 20 October 1998 (nine years after the overthrow of Zhivkov), which banned former top communists and agents of the communist-era secret services from occupying senior government and civil service posts for five years.

The tenth national conference of the UDF, held on 17–18 October 1998, adopted important changes in the party statute. First, any mention of the previously existing 'associated organizations' (these were the original founders of the initial UDF coalition in December 1989) was omitted: the UDF was finally transformed into a single party. Second, party discipline was strengthened. From that time onwards party members could express a position different from the leadership only within the structures of the party, and only before the party had adopted a final decision. Otherwise they would be expelled. The deputy chairman of the National Executive Council of the UDF, Ms Ekaterina Mikhaylova, outlined her vision of the obligations of UDF party members: 'Every member has to know his party, he is obliged to work from inside for improvement of its structures, for internal dialogue within the party, against factionalism, to protect the good name of other party members, and to be implacably opposed to all opponents, who should be identified and attacked everywhere'.[31] Thus nine years after the fall of Zhivkov, the UDF 'rediscovered' democratic centralism.[32]

'The Bulgarian model'[33]

The experience of the last nine years of Bulgaria's 'transition' allows for some preliminary hypotheses:

1 *The stability of any government in Bulgaria is crucially dependent on the availability of external financing.*[34] Whether Kostov and the UDF will complete their parliamentary mandate or not is entirely dependent on IMF support. If the IMF consistently supports the Kostov government as a reward for its pro-Western policies, then Bulgaria will experience some growth, a modest rise in living standards, and overall stability until the next parliamentary elections in 2001, and very likely after that. Similarly the survival of Zhivkov was predicated on either Soviet subsidies or Western loans. The 'slow death' of the BSP in the 1990s was a learning cycle for the majority of the adult population, who had to unlearn previous experiences of the BSP's miraculous powers to 'deliver'.

2 *The availability of external financing as 'soft' loans/rewards for political behaviour allows Bulgarian governments to postpone the issue of drastic and painful reform without endangering their own survival.* In-depth moderniz-ation and sustainable development are replaced by the imitation of reforms, implemented solely to satisfy the demands of the external benefactor – 'market' reforms after 1990, and all the variants of socialism tried after 1944.

3 *Major change is forced on a Bulgarian regime only as a result of the collapse/ unavailability of external financing (with time delays caused by tactical behaviour of competing elites), never as a result of political pressure from below. Elections only rubberstamp such cataclysmic changes.* The economic collapse in the autumn of 1990 annulled the June 1990 election victory of the BSP (elite bargaining postponed an immediate UDF take-over, and allowed the recovery of the BSP), and similarly the economic collapse in 1996–7 annulled the December 1994 election victory of the BSP, and was followed by a UDF take-over in February 1997, before the early elections in April.

4 *Multi-party politics in Bulgaria is primarily a competition for 'the right to be corrupt',*[35] *and only to a lesser degree it is a competition of ideas and concepts for securing external financing for the country.* Ideas about in-depth modernization and development within the context of a world economy never really come into the political debate, and remain the preserve of a limited group of intellectuals.[36]

5 *Political democracy in Bulgaria is entirely an elite affair, a competition between 'circles of friends' to milk the public domain for private use. Ideas and ideologies play an important instrumental/ mobilizing role, but survival and enrichment of the competing groups remains their primary objective, allowing for the quick abandonment of principles. Daily politics is usually conducted in a warlike and acrimonious manner, yet when the survival of the individual group is threatened, or a benefit is immediately obvious, then compromise is actively sought and found. Bulgarian politics revolves around dramatic quarrels and quiet compromises.* In the summer of 1991 the 'Group of 39' (the driving force of the hardline faction of the UDF) declared with great fanfare a hunger strike against the June 1991 'communist' constitution, yet shortly after they won the elections in October 1991 they forgot all their opposition to the constitution. The UDF was elected to power in April 1997 on promises of radical economic reform and consensus building: one year later the aim is forgotten, staying in power is all important, and confrontational politics is being resurrected.

6 *Individuals have no autonomous role in Bulgarian politics outside their party, movement, or 'circle of friends'. Everyone anointed by power is popular while either power itself or the aura of power last.* Mladenov and Zhelev were consistently the most popular politicians in the country while in office, yet were immediately forgotten when they lost power. The same is true for all prime ministers for the last nine years. Czar Symeon II is the only 'absentee' politician, who has consistently kept a high, if fluctuating, rating in all opinion polls since 1990 – and this is possible only for someone with a royal aura.

7 *The idea of a national interest above and outside group interests is alien to Bulgarian politicians and the Bulgarian public.* Consensus on some strategic issues of national importance remains elusive in Bulgaria. Significantly, there is substantial cross-party consensus (including both the UDF and the BSP) only on two issues: on the preservation of the present constitution (which perpetuates the existing political class), and on Bulgaria's eventual membership in the European Union (perceived as a future generous source of external financing and general security; in this respect the IMF can be described only as a rather harsh and ungenerous intermediate substitute to the EU). In contrast, there is no consensus on policies towards Bulgaria's immediate neighbours, towards the USA and NATO, and towards Russia.

All these hypotheses are applicable to a large degree to pre-1989, as well as pre-communist Bulgarian politics, with two important caveats: first, under communism the competition between elite groups was far more restricted than under democracy, both pre-1940s and post-1989; and second, the destruction of subsistence farming, and the consequent industrialization and urbanization under Zhivkov, has henceforth made the availability of external financing literally a question of life and death for the majority of Bulgarians, who in previous decades and centuries could eke out a living even in the most severe crises.

Conclusion

In examining the proposition that after 1997 Bulgaria experienced 'a second transition' from communism, one should look beyond the visible similarities of Sofia 1997 and Prague 1989, and beyond the similar career paths of Václav Klaus and Ivan Kostov (in both cases we have a progression from independent expert to Finance Minister, and then from party leader to Prime Minister; plus similar combinations of ambitious wives, arrogance, patronizing attitude to the media, and authoritarian style in party and government). In both societies very different historical traditions were bound to reassert themselves once the stranglehold of their respective communist parties was broken. Even if we assume that in both cases we have a transition to 'normality' (the end of communist domination heralding a return to traditional historical patterns), rather than to some contemporary Western-style liberal model, then such 'normality' would mean very different things in the Czech Republic and Bulgaria.

Concepts like 'transition to democracy' and 'consolidation' are not very helpful in understanding the dynamic of change in Bulgaria after 1989. They put great emphasis on phenomena that have strictly secondary importance in the Bulgarian context. If one takes 'transition to democracy' in Bulgaria between November 1989 and June 1990, it looks remarkably similar in its forms to the 'negotiated transitions' in Central Europe. However, it would be preposterous to conclude from this that both the communist party and the opposition in Bulgaria must have undergone developments similar to the ones in Central European countries. The main reason for the observable similarity is not so much a similarity in internal conditions, but conscious transplanting of Central European forms to a very different context in Bulgaria (for example, mass protests in Bulgaria did not end with the removal of Zhivkov, but rather began after his removal). The 'roundtable period' in Poland or Czechoslovakia corresponds to 'a period of imitation' in Bulgaria, which ended with the June elections 1990, when reality brutally reasserted itself with the victory of the renamed communist party.

If one thinks in terms of 'consolidation', then by mid-1997 Bulgaria had already experienced three parliamentary and two presidential elections that were indisputably free and fair; Bulgaria had also experienced six peaceful transfers of power between governments of very different political orientation – in 1990, 1991, 1992, 1994, 1995 and 1997. However, focusing on the elections would tell us only a small part of the story. The factor most specific to Bulgaria is major change of regime without elections, and often in direct contravention of recent elections, as a result either of parliamentary regrouping as in 1992, or of street pressure organized by one party as in 1990 and 1997. In all of these cases we have public discontent combined with elite bargaining that leads to change, rather than the will of the people expressed through free elections.

To summarize, Bulgaria after 1997 has decisively moved away from communist domination of society, and has come to a stable plateau in its development. This Bulgarian democratic model aspires to, and corresponds in some ways to, the Western liberal model (in early December 1998 the Bulgarian parliament abolished the death penalty), and in other respects (secondary role of elections, pervasive corruption, partisanship) it closely resembles the revolving door cabinets from the turn of the century. One can also find some continuity with the communist period, particularly in the way Kostov's government relates to the media, or utilizes state radio and television for propaganda. Overall, one should analyse eclectic Bulgarian realities in the light of Bulgaria's own history, both communist and pre-communist, rather than try to establish how far Bulgaria has moved along an imaginary Western path.

Notes

1 After the 1994 parliamentary elections the ruling party in Bulgaria was the ex-communist Bulgarian Socialist Party (in power until February 1997). Although BSP had come to power after winning a clear majority in free and fair elections, it had to co-habit with a President with a rival political orientation, and the activities of its government and parliamentary group were closely scrutinized and often overturned by the independent judiciary and Constitutional Court.

2 'In Poland , Hungary, Czechoslovakia, Romania, the crowds were a sea of national flags, while the people raised their voice to sing old national hymns.' Timothy Garton Ash, *We the People. The Revolution of '89 Witnessed in Warsaw, Budapest, Berlin and Prague*, Cambridge: Granta Books, 1990, p. 143. In 1989–90 in Bulgaria 'the democrats' shunned the national flag and the patriotic songs, and these symbols were appropriated by the communist (later 'socialist') rallies, and by the mass anti-Turkish demonstrations in January 1990. People in small towns and villages looked indifferent to the pro-democracy fervour in the capital and the biggest cities, and Turks and Bulgarians in the mixed population regions were bitterly opposed to each other. Only in 1997 did anti-communist rallies in Bulgaria reach 'the quality' of the 1989 rallies in Central Europe – pitting 'the nation' against a tiny clique of rulers.

3 About this plot and other 'leftist' conspiracies see Dimitar Ivanov, *Politicheskoto protivopostavyane v Balgaria 1956–1989* (Political confrontation in Bulgaria 1956–1989), Sofia: Ares Pres, 1994, pp. 23–6. Ivanov is a former head of a section in the secret police department in charge of dissent in the communist party.

4 Ibid., pp. 40–2.

5 Ibid., p. 55.

6 Ibid., p. 59.

7 John Bell links this creeping Westernization with the communist-induced urbanization of Bulgarian society (by the late 1980s two-thirds of the population was urban, as opposed to one-fourth before the communist take-over in 1944), and notes the increased affluence, Western aspirations, and later receptiveness to Gorbachevist ideas of the emergent Bulgarian 'equivalent of a Western middle class' – see John D. Bell, 'Democratization and political participation in "post-communist" Bulgaria', in Karen Dawisha and Bruce Parrott, eds, *Politics, Power, and the Struggle for Democracy in South-East Europe*, Cambridge: Cambridge University Press, 1997, pp. 355–6.

8 This following paragraph is largely based on an analysis of Soviet influences on Bulgaria's transition elaborated by this author in Jan Zielonka and Alex Pravda, eds, *Democratic Consolidation in Eastern Europe: International and Transnational Factors*, Florence: European University Institute (in press).

9 Some 44 of the 81 founding members of the Discussion Club in Support of Glasnost and Perestroika (founded in November 1988) were communist party members – Ivanov, *Politicheskoto*, p. 141. See also Zielonka and Pravda, *Democratic Consolidation*.

10 For the Soviet involvement in the removal of Zhivkov see Dimitar Tsanov, *Smyanata. Kak i zashto se stigna do 10 noemvri* (The Change. How, and why 10th November came about), Sofia: Universitetsko izdatelstvo, 1995, pp. 18–19 ff.

11 A real classic of the genre is a special supplement to *Demokratsiya* entitled 'Who toppled UDF's government. The truth about a case of national treason' – see *Demokratsiya*, 13 January, pp. I–VIII.

12 This process was exemplified best by the colourful daily rallies when thousands of students would 'rock, mock and talk' – and perform different shows every day: ring alarm clocks at BSP headquarters, hold a symbolic burial of the 100-year-old BSP, bring water and towels for the BSP 'clean hands' campaign (for a brief account in English see 'Bulgarian students hold lively rallies for change' – Sofia, 28 January 1997, Reuters).

13 The only mass anti-communist opposition that existed in Bulgaria after the communist take-over in 1944 came from the smallholding peasants and their Agrarian party. As a result of collectivization, industrialization, and rapid urbanization this sort of opposition lost any appeal for the majority of the population by the end of the 1960s. Still, the legacy of this mass opposition, and the fact that the majority of Bulgarians lost some property in the 1940s–1950s meant that the central grievance against communism in Bulgaria was about its expropriation of private properties on a massive scale, and not about the way it eliminated intellectual freedoms. This was important in the evolution of UDF in 1991, when the slogan of the winning faction was 'restitution'.

14 In January 1990 and later the spontaneous character of the mass anti-Turkish protest was questioned – most vociferously by UDF leaders and sympathizers – by pointing out the number of people with BCP and police connections in its leadership, and the support that it got from some local BCP bosses. However, at the very same time the UDF leadership itself consisted mostly of the same type of people (BCP- or police-related), and many of the top UDF leaders in 1989–90 – Rumen Vodenitcharov, Stefan Gaytandzhiev, Petko Simeonov – would later openly side with BSP, and make a career out of it. Yet no one has questioned the spontaneous character of the early UDF rallies because of that.

15 Of all three the last one had the greatest consequence for the future electoral map of the country. From then onwards BSP would be branded 'nationalist' by the UDF, and the UDF would be called 'anti-national' by BSP propaganda. For the next seven years the UDF would be virtually excluded from mixed population regions, with the ethnic Bulgarians there voting for the BSP, and the ethnic Turks voting for the MRF. Only after February 1997 would the UDF pick up in importance in places like Kirdzhali.

16 A decision of the Constitutional Court in the autumn of 1991 (that the existence of the MRF did not violate the ban on ethnic parties enshrined in the June 1991 constitution) turned the MRF's *de facto* monopoly over the Turkish and Muslim vote into a *de jure*

one, and later the MRF played a crucial role in the formation both of the UDF-dominated government of Filip Dimitrov (November 1991 – December 1992), and later of the ostensibly non-party but in practice BSP-dominated government of Lyuben Berov (January 1993 – September 1994).

17 For a detailed table of the results of the June elections see Geoffrey Pridham and Tatu Vanhanen, eds, *Democratization in Eastern Europe: Domestic and International Perspectives*, London–New York: Routledge, 1994, p. 145.

18 For President Zhelev's role in forming this cabinet, and concerning his overall inclination 'to avoid direct confrontation with the Socialists' at the time, see Bell, 'Democratization', p. 372.

19 In September 1991 the central electoral commission quoted Article 11.4 of the constitution to ban the Movement for Rights and Freedoms from participation in the parliamentary elections scheduled for October. After that 'the European Union and CSCE pressured the Bulgarian government in order to compel the Supreme Court to revise the decision of the electoral commission'. Raymond Detrez, *Historical Dictionary of Bulgaria*, New York: Scarecrow Press, 1997, p. 225.

20 Ivan Krastev, 'Poluparlamentarniyat rezhim. Struktura i perspektivi na partiynata sistema v Balgariya (dekemvri 1989–oktomvri 1994)' (The semi-parliamentary regime. Structure and prospects of the party system in Bulgaria (December 1989–October 1994)), in Krasimira Baychinska, ed., *Prehodat v Balgariya prez pogleda na sotsialnite nauki* (The social sciences on transition in Bulgaria), Sofia: Akademichno izdatelstvo, 1997, p. 20.

21 For detailed tables and analysis of these elections see Bell, 'Democratization', pp. 377–8.

22 Judge Rumen Nenkov, Head of the Second Penal Division at the Supreme Court of Cassation, as quoted in the *Sofia Independent*, 10–16 April, 1998.

23 One of the best analyses of the in-built defects of the separation of powers in the present Bulgarian constitution is provided in Velko Valkanov, *Na kolene pred istinata. Politiko-filosofski I lichni izpovedi* (Kneeling before truth. Political, philosophical, and private confessions), Sofia: Bulvest 2000, 1996, pp. 236–42. According to Valkanov, 'the judiciary can control both the legislative and the executive powers, but no one can hold the judiciary responsible for its acts. In this way the judiciary became not only independent but also unchecked.' Ibid., p. 236.

24 See 'Conclusions' in Robert Browning, *Byzantium and Bulgaria: A Comparative Study Across the Early Medieval Frontier*, Berkeley: University of California Press, 1975, pp. 192–8.

25 This argument is best elaborated in Gerschenkron's essay 'Some aspects of industrialization in Bulgaria, 1878–1939', in Alexander Gerschenkron, *Economic Backwardness in Historical Perspective: A Book of Essays*, Cambridge MA: Harvard University Press, 1962, pp. 198–234.

26 Bell, 'Democratization', p. 384.

27 For a detailed analysis of the post-1989 transformation of Bulgarian agriculture see Christian Giordano and Dobrinka Kostova, 'Reprivatizatsiya bez selyani. Za ustoychivostta na edna pagubna balgarska traditsiya' (Reprivatization without peasants. On the persistence of a disastrous Bulgarian tradition), in *Seloto mezhdu Promyana i Traditsiya* (The Village between Change and Tradition), a special issue of *Balgarski folklor*, 3–4, 1997, pp. 130–43.

28 'Blue' is the UDF's party colour: since 1990 colours have played an important role in the symbolic war waged between the UDF ('the Blues') and the BSP ('the Reds').

29 'Foreign investors say lack of coherent legislation, frequent changes, cumbersome bureaucracy and sometimes opaque practices are the main obstacles to investment. The Balkan state of 8.5 million people has one of the lowest foreign investment levels in the region with $1.7 billion invested between 1992 and the end of September this year, of which $302 million was invested in the first nine months of this year.' Reuters, 27 October 1998.

30 Reuters, 29 October 1998.

31 *Kontinent*, 19 October 1998.

32 This is not the only sign of how 'normal' Bulgaria has become under Kostov – in reproducing patterns from its recent history. For example, in the summer of 1997 Kostov repeatedly engaged in symbolic agricultural work in the style of old communist party leaders; in the autumn of 1998 he publicly admonished the journalists for 'inventing' non-existent conflicts between him and President Stoyanov.

33 The title of a popular satire on Bulgaria's transition, which is a collection of essays first published in 1990–1 in the weekly *Kultura* by Stanislav Stratiev. The author defines 'the Bulgarian model' as the opposite of everything that is normally expected: 'Columbus was looking for India and discovered America, we constantly depart for America, and always end up in India – this is the Bulgarian model.' Stanislav Stratiev, *Balgarskiyat model* (The Bulgarian model), Sofia: Ivan Vazov, 1991, p. 5.

34 Pearson makes a similar point about all states in Eastern Europe in the inter-war period: 'Even during the relatively prosperous 1920s, the eastern European states could only survive financially through Western investment . . . In the 1930s, the impact of the world Depression was bound to be severe on an area which combined only modest moderniz-ation with overreliance on external investment.' Raymond Pearson, *The Rise and Fall of the Soviet Empire*, London: Macmillan, 1998, p. 12. The central role of external financing (foreign investment or foreign credits) in Bulgaria's economic development 1878–1944 is analysed in great detail in Rumen Avramov, *Prestrukturirane i privatizatsiya na bankovata sistema – pouki ot minaloto* (Restructuring and Privatization of the Banking System – Some Lessons of History), paper presented at the 7th Banking Conference, Shumen, 29–31 May 1995.

35 'Every cycle of political confrontation becomes a struggle for the right to be corrupt.' Krassen Stanchev, 'Simvolika I pragmatika na prehoda kam pazar I demokratsiya' (Symbolism and pragmatics in the transitions to democracy and market economy), in Baychinska, ed., *Prehodat*, p. 62.

36 Most prominent among these are the already mentioned Rumen Avramov (researcher at the Centre for Liberal Strategies), and Krassen Stanchev (director of the Institute for Market Economics).

10 Democratic despotism

Federal Republic of Yugoslavia and Croatia

Ivan Vejvoda

As power grows security diminishes.

(Montesquieu, *Spirit of the Laws*)

To those who study it as an isolated phenomenon the French Revolution can but seem a dark and sinister enigma; only when we view it in the light of the events preceding it can we grasp its true significance. And similarly, without a clear idea of the old regime, its laws, its greatness, it is impossible to comprehend the history of the sixty years following its fall. Yet even this is not enough; we need also to understand and bear in mind the peculiarities of the French temperament.

(Alexis de Tocqueville, *The Old Regime and the Revolution*)

Despotism alone can provide the atmosphere of secrecy which favors crooked dealings and enables the freebooters of finance to make illicit fortunes. Under other forms of government such propensities exist, undoubtedly; under a despotism they are given free rein.

(Alexis de Tocqueville, *The Old Regime and the Revolution*)

Introduction

The 'interstitial position' of the Balkans, the 'prevalence of conquest and territorial competition', the expansion and contraction of empires in this 'coercion-intensive' region have contributed to the blurring of 'the line between war and revolution more than elsewhere in Europe'.[1] The 'crisis of identity of contemporary Yugoslav society',[2] exacerbating the 'state-seeking' nationalisms[3] in the wake of the demise of communism in the former Yugoslavia, led ultimately to a violent breakdown of the multinational state construct that had come into being in 1918. A war occurred in *fin de siècle* Europe when elsewhere in the nearer and more distant geographical neighbourhood revolution/reform/societal transformation was on the agenda. What kind of regimes have emerged from these wars in former Yugoslavia, and are we witnessing more continuity than change?

It must at the outset be adamantly stated that the infamous 'powder keg' label given to the Balkans has in this latest historical chapter been circumscribed to the territories of the central republics of the former Yugoslavia (with the notable and determining exception of the initial ten-day war in Slovenia in 1991), while the rest of the Balkans have remained free of war and have not been drawn into the vortex of the Yugoslav conflict. This is no minor historical achievement, and should be recognized among other things as a step toward overcoming 'self-imposed immaturity', although it is clearly no guarantee that at some future moment the volatility of the situation in Albania, the tenuous relationships between majority and minority populations in Macedonia, the unresolved situation in Bosnia-Hercegovina or the protracted crisis in Kosovo will not lead to outbreaks of violence. The bout of fever in Greek–Turkish relations over small Aegean islands in 1995–6 only demonstrates the proximity of possible dangers even between members of the same military alliance.

Legacies

The legacy of communist rule is overwhelming. The short-lived experience of incipient liberal democracy at the turn of the last century in independent Serbia and in Austro-Hungarian dominated Croatia, as well as the joint experience in the Kingdom of Serbs, Croats and Slovenes in the years following the 1918 unification, have long been lost. Memories of events and injustices remain, as do histories of certain political parties and their leaders. The nineteenth-century struggle of the intelligentsias of both Croatia and Serbia to create a South Slav state based on a commonality of language and of ethnic fraternity has been dispelled. The centrifugal forces, longtime minoritarian, had their hour of glory and were able to topple at the end of this century the weakened federal communist construct. The absence of any long-lasting democratic political culture, the devastating effect of communist rule in curtailing any form of alternative political expression, its undermining of state and civil society and complete grip on power, have left a political wasteland in which the incumbent rulers or newly elected nationalist-minded politicians had a decisive advantage over the few liberal-minded activists emerging from the oppositional circles in both Serbia and Croatia.

The absence of political accountability and responsibility at the level of the ruling communist party, the legacy of political, social and economic over-experimentation specific to the 'self-managing' brand of Yugoslav socialism have left disabled, fragmented, atomized societies in which individuals had been led to believe that due to a comparatively high standard of living they were already in the vestibule of the West. Little did they know how sparse the middle classes were, and how the total absence of any democratic institutions weakened any meaningful resistance to the onslaught of the power-wielders.

In the case of former Yugoslavia the constitution of 1974 had decentralized decision-making immensely in virtually every field except major political issues. It thus devolved power to the communist leaderships in the six republics and two autonomous provinces, and led to ethnic homogenizing tendencies, identification of the ethnic majority within each republic and province with its territory, and a weakening of the federal bonds. The attempts of the communists to address the national question in this multinational country led to a form of 'constitutional nationalism'[4] which progressively, toward the end of the 1980s, legitimated the existence of constitutionally sovereign proto-states and led to the demise of the federal level of power. The federal construct was dealt a penultimate blow in 1990 with the first free elections in the republics, which gave democratic legitimacy to the elected ruling parties, while simultaneously dispossessing the federal level of government of any significant power. This process was paralleled within the structure of the communist party (League of Communists of Yugoslavia). The monopoly of the communists took the form of a monopoly of each of the six/eight segments of the party within its own territory. The party leadership in each republic thus became the sole representative, interpreter of the collective body, and appeared at the federal level (both party and state) as the defender of the interests of that republic. Communism promoted nationalism and both were against the autonomy of society. One could even say that under communism, borrowing a notorious phrase from a prominent British political leader: 'There [was] no such thing as society, there [were] only men and women and their families'.

The modernization without modernity under communism, which left no scope for the appearance of the autonomous individual, of the citizen endowed with rights and obligations, no free public space for the articulation of interests, created a society without society. People were left to indulge in the benefits of foreign credits that were being poured into their pockets by international monetary institutions, via the communist government, for the sake of social peace and not into productive economic investments. They were thus pushed into the sphere of the private, while being exposed to forced politicization of a ritualistic communist ideology. Militarization of society was an accompanying feature of this 'totalitarian logic'.[5] The experience of the exposure to only the instrumental and manipulative side of politics left a legacy of sentiments of apoliticism or anti-politics, attitudes of cynicism and apathy.

From communism to multi-party politics – diverging paths, similar outcomes

The League of Communists of Yugoslavia (LCY) ceased to exist in January 1990. The last Congress of the LCY failed in its final attempt to reconcile the leaderships of the LC of the different republics. By that time different parties were being formed in Croatia and Serbia, although in Serbia there was great reluctance on the part of the leadership to accept the fact of multi-party elections. Serbia thus isolated itself from the mainstream of East and Central Europe as early as 1989 and 1990. It kept the ideology of communism well in place, supplementing it with a strong nationalism. The party under Milošević's rule advocated through its new ideological front player, Mihajlo Marković (former oppositional intellectual), a political oxymoron named 'non-party pluralism'. In June 1990 the regime held a referendum on whether first to have free elections or to have the outgoing communist Serbian Assembly draft the new constitution. The latter answer received 97 per cent support allowing Milošević to tailor the new consti-tution voted in September 1990 to his own needs. It was a mixed presidential-parliamentary system with a very strong and independent President and a very subordinate Assembly.

In July 1990 the Serbian Assembly passed the Law on Political Organizations, while the LC of Serbia merged with the front organization (Socialist Alliance of the Working People of Serbia) to form the Socialist Party of Serbia (SPS), after the Slovenian and Croatian elections had already been held. Milošević had made the new Serbian constitution for himself as a means to legalize his almost unlimited personal power. He would then only need to hold elections to give democratic legitimacy to his strong position. Serbia was the last to hold its first free elections in December 1990 along with Montenegro. A double ballot majority electoral law was used giving the SPS of President Milošević 46.1 per cent of the votes and 77.6 per cent of the seats (194 seats out of a total of 250).

In Croatia, the ruling League of Communists of Croatia had followed a different path. Without a similarly strong, charismatic, populist leader it sought to produce a majoritarian electoral law which would allow it to acquire a majority in its Assembly (Sabor) with a relative majority of votes. The elections were held in April 1990 but the electoral law played into the hands of the main new opposition party, the Croatian Democratic Union (Hrvatska Demokratska Zajednica, HDZ) led by the former communist army general and then nationalist dissident who had also been imprisoned for his opposition to Tito, Franjo Tudjman.

The HDZ got 41 per cent of the vote but 68 per cent of the seats in the parliament, the League of Communists of Croatia: Party of Democratic Change (SKH-SDP) got 28 per cent of the vote and a minority of fifteen seats, followed by the People's Accord (KNZ) with 10 per cent of the vote and four seats. Tudjman was elected President by the parliament. Com-fortably supported by his two-thirds majority he was able to tailor the new Croatian constitution to his own ambitions. In December 1990 the Croatian parliament voted in the constitution, which was a mixed presidential-parliamentary system with very strong presidential prerogatives.

The result of the first elections were strikingly similar in Croatia and Serbia. So were the electoral laws that yielded those results and the constitutions that had been designed for 'Europe's last strongmen'.[6] The stark reality of the constitutional and political systems that had emerged in

Croatia and Serbia was that two men with complete, unchecked power concentrated in their hands were leading the two biggest and most important republics of the then still existing Yugoslavia.

The relationship between Serbia and Croatia had been, and was still then in the aftermath of 1989, the backbone of Yugoslavia. The importance of leadership, of the role of powerful individuals, in such a crucial historic moment was clear. Milošević's and Tudjman's capacity to act prudently and in the spirit of compromise and tolerance, within a geo-political setting which was of the utmost danger to the well-being of the people in whose name they were supposedly speaking, was non-existent. The two presidents were driven by their own power-seeking and power-conserving agendas. Their goal was not the democratic transformation of the Croatian and Serbian polities, neither was it the abandonment of the practices of the *ancien régime*.

Tudjman with the support of the 'long-distance nationalists' from the Croatian diaspora wished to realize the goal of state independence using all means at his disposal. Milošević wished to preserve all the power that he had and, in the wake of secession by Croatia, to keep the Serbian-populated parts of Croatia in the remaining part of Yugoslavia. While still in a state of peace at the beginning of 1991, but ominously close to the outbreak of violence, Milošević and Tudjman met in Tito's once hunting lodge in Karadjordjevo on 17 March 1991, where by all accounts they planned and agreed upon the partition of Bosnia-Hercegovina among their two republics.

'Europe's two strongmen' are still in power. Milošević came to the leadership of Serbia in September 1987. He was a young leader who to many seemed the epitome of a novel, modern approach, but who to others announced the beginning of a repressive continuation of the communist order. His early arrival may have led some to believe that change would come soon, but in fact it was going to be a retrograde change assuring the continuity of the 'ancien regime in Serbia'.[7] Milošević and his party were forced by the mainstream of events after 1989 to accept the new pluralist political order, but did so on their own terms, giving way to further openings very reluctantly and only when pressured strongly enough (a pattern that would be repeated in all future crises in which Serbia was involved).

Both in Croatia and Serbia the opposition was viewed from the outset, and this still holds true, as an enemy force, traitor to the cause of the Nation, working for foreign interests. There is still a strong identification of both ruling parties with their leaders and more importantly with the national interest. Power is identified as a 'filled up space' to paraphrase Claude Lefort, and not as an empty space which is periodically, through free and fair elections, filled for a set length of time. Both leaders portray a willingness to subsist in power as long as they possibly can regardless of all else occurring in their environment.

Nature of the political institutions, war and politics

Although there was an alternation in power in Croatia in 1990 (the communists having lost to Tudjman's HDZ) it would be more appropriate to say that the character of the present regime resembles the old order. In fact, in Croatia the present state is in many respects worse than the very liberal last stage of communism during the latter part of the 1980s.[8]

All the relevant democratic political institutions have emerged in Croatia and Serbia since 1990 at a formal level. Political parties contest regular elections, parliaments legislate, constitutional courts rule, governments execute; only the substance of democracy is not present. The ruling parties and their two leaders have a propensity to attempt to harness all the means they can for their own purposes, and if they cannot they try to circumvent them and belittle them. Thus parliaments in both Serbia and Croatia have played a minor role in any key decision-making as well as governments. The Constitutional Court in Croatia has in some cases upheld its prerogatives.

War has been a defining feature of both Croatian and Serbian political life in the post-1990 period. War has simply stifled any semblance of a political life. It has enabled the two leaders to rally support around issues of 'collective survival', 'national independence' and 'the national cause', and to avoid any real debate over the war itself or any deliberation over major state policies. Since the outbreak of war in June 1991 in Slovenia until the signing of the Dayton Peace Accord in November/December 1995, political debate has in both Croatia and Serbia centred on the conflict but with no effect on policy. The two presidents with their stable majorities in parliament simply retreated to their highly restrained inner circle of acolytes and ruled far from the public eye more or less single-handedly. President Tudjman has even created a body not stipulated in the constitution, the National Security Council, which is a sort of alternative decision-making body which he calls upon when he needs the endorsement of the influential individual members of the Council.

The peace, or more precisely the cease-fire, that the November/December 1995 Dayton Accords made possible, has again ushered in political competition without the burden of an ongoing war. The voters/citizens are less pressured to rally around the ruling party even though for many in both countries there is still a strong sign of identity between the nation and the ruling party. The scarce strands of civil society that existed throughout the war in Serbia and Croatia have multiplied and their voices have grown stronger but they nonetheless remain weak. However, the protracted demonstrations throughout Serbia from November 1996 to March 1997 have shown there is much latent and active civic energy that has long been dormant and unmobilized. The same can be said of the strong show of 150,000 demonstrators in the centre of Zagreb in November 1996 protesting against the announced closure of the independent radio station, Radio 101.

The emergence of a civil society will be long and slow in both societies. The war, the ensuing economic decline, the generalized impoverishment coupled with the huge brain drain has depleted the future civil society of one of its key elements, the middle classes. The struggle for survival in both republics has left the urban population weak and insecure. Fear, uncertainty and insecurity are still at the core of the political psychology of both Croatia and Yugoslavia. Milošević's share of guilt for the war no doubt outweighs that of Tudjman. Milošević used and abused the fact that the Yugoslav People's Army (JNA) sided with his leadership in attempting to carve out a Greater Serbia from the territories of Croatia and Bosnia. But Tudjman's project of a Greater Croatia carved out from territories in Bosnia-Hercegovina was a defining moment of the wars from 1991 to 1995 and still remains a difficult if not a major issue on the Croatian political scene.[9] Some analysts have suggested that any future democratically elected leaders who will come after 'Europe's last strongmen' should begin their terms in office with a clean slate, by publicly renouncing the Karadjordjevo agreement of March 1991.[10]

Transition, nationalism and the ethnification of politics

Compared to the countries in the immediate neighbourhood (Slovenia, Hungary, Romania, Bulgaria, Macedonia), it seems that not only has there been no alternation in power, but that there has been no substantive change or very meagre change in the character of political power, which remains strongly authoritarian. This does not mean to say that there has been no change whatsoever. On the contrary, change has occurred at different levels. There has been an eruption of nationalism on the scene of political life and, in fact, an ethnification of politics.[11] The former communist ideology was in a variety of ways replaced by the ideology of nationalism, in the name of which purging and ethnic cleansing has occurred, but also in whose name the grip on the levers of power has been maintained by using the framework of democratic institutions. These 'illiberal democracies',[12] which have little regard for liberties and rights so far as the ruling leader's right to power is concerned, have gone down a retrograde path towards a closed society and the maintenance of top-down politics.

The impact of the breakdown of the former Yugoslavia and the accompanying wars have been both the consequence and cause of these processes. War has left an indelible mark on both countries. Croatia suffered and paid a high cost in human lives and a loss of one-third of its territories. This has subsequently with the reintegration of Eastern Slavonia in 1997 now all been recovered; and Croatia is territorially as it was within the former Yugoslavia. Croatia has gained independence and sovereignty through a war and this has been a major difference with respect to FR Yugoslavia (Serbia/Montenegro). The regime in Croatia, President

Tudjman and his ruling party have been spurred on by the legitimacy that the conquest of independence has given them.

The regime led by President Milošević lost in the 1991–5 wars, and although the territory of the country was not itself part of the battlefield, all the consequences of war have been felt: loss of human lives, economic and social devastation, and failure of the regime's and its supporters' project of a Greater Serbia and no 'reward' for all the suffering.

These two former major republics of the former Yugoslavia, in which the populations speak virtually the same language, now called respectively Croatian and Serbian, have parted in a violent manner, but resemble each other in the way they are stifling their societies' attempts to come of age.

Political parties

There has been no manifest will on the part of the ruling HDZ in Croatia or of the ruling SPS in Serbia to sit down at a round table with the opposition and decide the ground rules for the post-communist order. The ruling parties in both countries are centred around their leaders, and are most certainly going to disintegrate once the leader loses in an electoral competition or disappears off the scene (Tudjman is recovering from stomach cancer and his time in office is limited). For the time being these parties are centralized and hierarchical, and they continue to function according to principles of loyalty and obedience with no internal democracy whatsoever. Milošević has several times changed his fellow top-ranking officials, and has most recently had to retrieve some he had discarded nearly two years ago because the supply has dwindled. In the wake of Tudjman's illness there was immediate speculation about how many factions the HDZ would split into as internal fissures became increasingly apparent. The SPS in Serbia ruled in a coalition with a small party New Democracy (ND), rhetorically moderate and Europe- and NATO-leaning until the September 1997 elections. At the level of the federal (Serbia/Montenegro) parliament the 3 November 1996 elections gave a majority to the 'left coalition' composed of the SPS, ND and JUL (United Yugoslav Left), a party headed by Milošević's wife Mirjana Marković, who by all accounts is most influential in public and private family matters. Milošević suffered his first electoral defeat, which was conversely the first major victory for the opposition, in the second round of the municipal elections of 17 November 1996 in the most important urban centres in Serbia (Belgrade, Niš, Novi Sad, Kragujevac, Uzice, Smederevo, Čačak, Kraljevo, Zrenjanin, Pirot, Sombor, Vršac, Jagodina, Kikinda). This meant not only an important political oppositional first, but the taking over of political responsibility which would test its political power and coalition maintenance. It must be stressed that Milošević by initially denying the electoral victory, and thus provoking a massive civic and political movement which respectively lasted four and three months, helped the 'other Serbia', the democratic-minded citizenry that had been laying low in times of adversity, to rise and defend its elementary civic dignity expressed through the ballot box. As has been the case in other circumstances, Milošević bowed to a combination of strong domestic and international pressure and acknowledged the results.

In the September 1997 elections Milošević was once more weakened by losing a further number of seats in the Serbian parliament. It took a record six months for the new Serbian government to be formed – a 'red-brown' coalition consisting of Vojislav Šešelj's ultra-right Serbian Radical Party, JUL and the SPS. In the meantime during the last four months of 1997 there had been two rounds of elections for President of Serbia (since Milošević had had himself elected by the Federal parliament, in a blitz procedural operation, as President of FR Yugoslavia), the first annulled and the second in December 1997 recognized. The crucial feature of these Serbian presidential elections was the sudden rise and near victory of Šešelj. In the second vote he came in a very close second to Milan Milutinović, an acolyte of Milošević who eventually won. In Croatia the ruling HDZ won elections for the lower House of Representatives in April 1995 and rules until the next elections in 1999 with a 75-seat majority in a 128 member House. The HSLS (the Croatian Social Liberal Party) has 13 seats, the HSS (Croatian Peasant Party) 10, the SDP (Social Democratic Party) 9, the rightist HSP (Croatian Party of Rights) 4, the regional IDS (Istrian Democratic Party) 4, and a series of smaller parties including the SNS (Serbian People's Party) 2.

Opposition parties

The oppositions, frail in both countries, have not as yet had a chance to rule except at the local level. They have had to bear the brunt of political dynamics without, until recently, being able to demonstrate whether they are capable of ruling. They had numerous teething problems, but most of all have been unable, due to strong individual vanities among other things, to build lasting and effective coalitions. Coalitions are the only manner in which they can aspire to challenge the rule of those in power.

In Serbia, with the federal and local elections in view, a coalition 'Zajedno' (Together) was formed after many difficulties in the autumn of 1996 and composed of the Serbian Renewal Movement (SPO), the Democratic Party (DS), the Civic Alliance of Serbia (GSS) and the Democratic Party of Serbia (DSS). The coalition was on the crest of a winning wave when the extremely popular former Governor of the Bank of Yugoslavia, Dragoslav Avramović, who had been ousted from his post in May 1996 by Milošević (just after he had proposed an extensive privatization programme), agreed to head the Zajedno electoral list for the federal elections. Most people saw a winning combination. Surprisingly, and contrary to all his prior declarations, Avramović stepped down two weeks before the election, thus literally wasting the potential for electoral victory of the opposition. The reasons most often put forward for his stepping down were threats from the ruling party, advice from Western governments to step down (so as not to destabilize Milošević and consequently the fragile Dayton architecture), and advice from his wife to think of his health rather than a career in politics late in life. The call for a popular, charismatic figure (such as Avramović) speaks much about the problems the opposition has in putting itself 'together' and presenting a coherent alternative programme. There was and is much vanity and bickering among the two then major Serbian opposition leaders Vuk Drašković (SPO) and Zoran Djindjić (DS), the first elected oppositional mayor of Belgrade. It seems though that Djindjić was more seriously committed to a democratic alternative than Drašković. After the September 1997 elections, Drašković broke ranks from Zajedno and offered his services to Milošević in view of a possible coalition government. As a consequence Drašković's SPO aligned with the ruling SPS, ousted Djindjić from his post of mayor of Belgrade, and took control of the only independent television station in Belgrade, Studio B.

The opposition parties in Serbia are not as strongly implanted as the ruling SPS. The Democratic Party has accomplished most in this direction over the past five years since Djindjic took over the helm of the party. The SPO is a much less structured party heavily dependent on its strong leader Vuk Drašković and implanted more in smaller towns. The GSS is a small and weak but politically important party because its leader Vesna Pešić, the most liberal-democratic minded of the three Zajedno leaders, played an extremely important moderating and balancing role in the coalition.

The extreme nationalist, even proto-fascist party of Vojislav Šešelj, the Serbian Radical Party (SRS), has a long history since 1990 of love and hate with the ruling SPS. An extremely militant party, which was involved heavily in paramilitary activities in the wars in Croatia and Bosnia, it won 17.9 per cent of the vote (Zajedno got 22.2 per cent) in the 3 November 1996 federal elections. It won also the municipality of Zemun where Šešelj, along with being Vice-president of the Serbian government, also reigns as mayor, trying to demonstrate that he can be the man of new beginnings by fighting corruption and idleness in the town hall.[13] Šešelj and his SRS are not to be underestimated. Although the votes cast for his party are not all extremist votes, but also disgruntled previous voters from the SPS or SPO, this party could in given circumstances prove extremely dangerous by picking up the 'Leninist debris' and heading for even more authoritarian populist solutions.[14] From oppositional party the SRS has become ruling party having joined a coalition with Milošević, who, many surmise, has brought Šešelj into the fold so that he could control him and not let him obstruct any major planned future political moves.

Whereas with the ousting/cleansing of the Serbs, Croatia has become a largely mono-ethnic country (now 5 per cent of the population are Serbs),

FR Yugoslavia retains its multi-ethnicity with 60 per cent of the population being Serbs. In the Sandzak region of Serbia where a notable minority of Muslims/Bosniaks live, they are represented by their ethnically based party the SDA (Party of Democratic Action), while in the south of Serbia in the three municipalities of Bujanovac, Preševo and Medvedja the Albanian population is represented by its political party and the Albanian voters partake in the elections (two members in the current Serbian Assembly). Much more importantly, in Kosovo the Albanian electorate has been systematically boycotting the elections and living in a parallel polity with their own clandestine elections for their self-declared Republic of Kosovo. This has meant that the electoral picture of Serbia has been faulty due to the absence of this important electorate. During the winter 1996–7 demonstrations a new note had been struck by Adem Demaci, the President of the Kosovo Committee for Human Rights (and key figure in the Kosovo opposition), when he declared 'I believe we should support the demonstrations in Belgrade and other Serbian cities, because the democratization of Serbia is the precondition which shall lead to a quicker liberation of Kosovo', and opposed any radicalization of the situation in Kosovo.[15]

The Croatian oppositional parties are represented by the Croatian Social Liberal Party (HSLS), the Social-Democratic Party (SDP) and the Croatian Peasant's Party (HSS). Three additional smaller parties and potential coalition partners are the right-wing nationalist Croatian Party of Rights (HSP), the liberal regional Istrian Democratic Assembly (IDS) and the centrist and urban Croatian Party of Rights (HNS).[16] As with the Serbian opposition, the main problem is unity, the need to overcome party rivalry and concentrate on electoral efficiency, especially in a heavily majoritarian electoral system. In the last major elections held in Croatia on 14 April 1997 for the upper house of parliament, the House of Counties (Zupanijski Dom), the ruling HDZ scored an impressive victory over the opposition and also regained votes and seats in Zagreb where there had been a long standoff during the previous year in which Tudjman, in a show of authoritarian strength, did not allow the formation of an oppositional city government simply because he did not want to see an oppositional political figure in the seat of the mayor of the capital city. Nonetheless, much as in Serbia, in practically 'all but one of Croatia's larger cities and towns (accounting for well over half the country's total population), opposition tickets were victorious. The biggest gains were won by the SDP . . . [thus] the opposition has taken over municipal governance throughout the country.'[17]

The opposition parties in both Croatia and Serbia have had to learn the art of politics and electoral competition in highly adverse conditions. There is no 'rational voter' in these territories, nor is there a pool of professional politicians or for that matter individuals of stature ready to engage in the struggle against arbitrariness and for political change; party affiliation or identification is extremely weak. Lack of professional politicians and the need to learn to navigate in high seas has not eased the forging of this main tool of a democratic polity. The political culture of both countries still dictates the behaviour of the electorate as one in which the majority expect that someone else will bring change for them, while bringing support in the minimally necessary number (often with a little help of fraudulent practices) for the perpetuation of the powers that be.

Montenegro

That the situation in FR Yugoslavia is not as simple and one-sidedly authoritarian and sultanistic as it may seem, and that the desire of control over everyone and everything is not always and everywhere the case, is most clearly visible in Montenegro. In the lopsided federation composed of Serbia and Montenegro, a large and a very small unit, the latter's population constitutes only 6 per cent of the population of the whole country. What it lacks in size it compensates for in democratic political will and activity.

One of the most positive recent political developments has been the election of Milo Djukanović to the presidency of Montenegro on 19 October 1997. This has meant the creation of an alternative, pluralist pole of government within the Yugoslav federation of Serbia and Montenegro. Because there is parity of representation in the second chamber of the federal parliament between the two federal units, Montenegro is able to forestall any attempt by the federal President Milošević to usurp the otherwise constitutionally relatively weak position of the federal presidency. Even so, power is where Milošević is situated regardless of constitution and law.

Although far from being a model democrat, Djukanović has persistently and firmly advocated and struggled for democratic reform and market regulation in the Yugoslav political and economic arena. In the Montenegrin presidential he won a hard-fought political battle against his arch rival, former friend and former Montenegran President Momir Bulatović, who was, and still is, being backed in the strongest manner by President Milošević and his political team. This is an extremely dangerous political game because it could lead to open conflict in Montenegro and possible desires for secession, although Djukanović has over and over again restated that he has no intention of changing the status of Montenegro in the federation, but rather of changing the (authoritarian, anti-modern, anti-rational) politics within the federation. With this in mind he has launched a political initiative with the aim of assembling the democratically oriented parties and groups of FR Yugoslavia (and possibly Republika Srpska in Bosnia-Hercegovina) in a joint endeavour for democratic and market reforms.

Kosovo

At present Kosovo is the most burning political issue not only of FR of Yugoslavia, but of the whole Balkan region and of Europe. It threatens to lead to a further breakdown of the country itself and also a general conflagration in the region. It could unfortunately easily leap out of control and develop into a wholesale war, which could at any one moment involve the Republic of Macedonia, Albania, Bulgaria, Greece and Turkey. Milošević's lack of initiative and statesmanship concerning Kosovo, and his preference for the maintenance of the *status quo*, simply reinforced the already notable separation between the Albanian and Serbian populations of the province

The appearance since the autumn of 1997 of the Kosovo Liberation Army (KLA, UCK in Albanian) has been the dual result of Milošević's policy of *status quo* support and of the radicalization of a part of the Kosovo Albanian opposition, impatient with the non-violent policies of Ibrahim Rugova's Democratic League of Kosovo (LDK). This international dimension of the future status of Kosovo as well as the disastrous experience with the break-up of former Yugoslavia and the ensuing wars have led to a flurry of diplomatic activity attempting to foster preventive diplomacy – very simply the prevention of a possible all-out *fin de siècle* Balkan war and the chaotic reconfiguration of borders in a precarious region of Europe.

International and Balkan dimensions

Croatia has been accepted as member of the Council of Europe in 1996 after several unsuccessful attempts. This has been hailed by the political opposition and NGOs as a welcome step which will enable the use of the full scope of European human rights legislation and European institutions to put forward grievances concerning the abuse of power and violation of civic and human rights in Croatia. As for Serbia/Montenegro, the Federal Republic of Yugoslavia still remains unrecognized by the UN, the OSCE, the IMF, the World Trade Organization, the World Bank and the USA although recognized by the countries of the European Union. It is unlikely that it will benefit from any rapid entry into international institutions. Croatia, though, has been recently admonished for its 'extremism' and uncooperativeness exemplified by Tudjman's adamant rejection of the South-East European Co-operation Initiative, advanced by the USA in view of fostering commercial and other links which would enhance confidence-building measures.[18]

International involvement and intervention in the former Yugoslav wars and their resolution has meant that, apart from bringing peace or at least easing of tensions, it has also reinforced the power of those with whom those deals have been brokered. Thus the signatories of Dayton from the three countries emerging from the ruins of former Yugoslavia, Izetbegović,

Tudjman and Milošević, are still strongly positioned and in subterranean ways reinforce each other's power as in a well-orchestrated piece of music. The 'West' is very simply at the level of *realpolitik* reliant on the 'good offices' of these three leaders, it expects them to 'deliver' the goods of peace, and thus is ready to turn a blind eye to the way they conduct their domestic affairs, however harsh, anti-democratic and retrograde these may be. The three leaders have amply used this to their advantage. Vice versa, the fact that all three are in fact under some sort of tutelage and themselves depend on the 'West' to stay in power by continuing to offer their services means that ultimately these three are not allowed an 'anything goes' domestic approach – because the big stick will be upon them sooner or later.

Irrespective of these external constraints the destinies of these three neighbouring countries are very much interdependent. As well as sharing the same language (in spite of all the nationalist rhetoric about the differences between Serbian, Croatian and Bosnian), they share the same type of political regime with strong authoritarian traits, based on personal rule and a small inner circle of confidants. When reform processes, democratization and market reform begin in earnest in one of these countries there will be spill-over effects in the others. Thus, even though one observes these countries separately for analytical purposes, it is important to realize that they nonetheless have many a common feature.

Winners and losers

The ruling parties, their major figures and families and their coalition partners have been the political, economic and social winners, while the societies around them have been, if not scorched to the earth, then at least dramatically set back. The break-up of former Yugoslavia through war and violence has delayed the economic reforms and move toward a market economy in both Serbia and Croatia. Montenegro has interestingly made some steps forward. Also in these states 'a further slowing down of the reform process has been caused by the direct and indirect effects of nationalism [such as] reinforcement of state paternalism, renationalization and creation of a strong state sector, hidden privileges for the non-private/ state firms, confiscation of property of non-nationals, high budget deficits and military expenditure, maintenance of soft-budget constraints, thus to postponement of the transition and privatization'.[19]

These attitudes manifest a desire on the part of the leaderships to remain in near-total control of the economy. And yet the lack of internal financial resources is pushing them ever increasingly to open up their markets and to sell/privatise large state enterprises and infrastructure, which will most certainly occur in the not so distant future as it has in other East-Central European countries. In the meantime the pockets of former or current ruling party politicians have been largely filled by profits from the war economy, and are further being filled by the rapacious activities which are beyond the control of relevant state institutions and public officers.

Hybrid systems

I have argued elsewhere[20] that in the countries of East and Central Europe a *sui generis* model of democracy is emerging. It combines elements of existing models and the strong influence of the legacies of the past. Some countries have already undergone several alternations in power and seem to exhibit tendencies toward stability and consolidation, combined with 'velvet restoration'.

Croatia and Serbia have recently been categorized as 'laggards' (along with Albania, Bulgaria, Romania, Bosnia-Hercegovina, Macedonia, Russia, Ukraine, Moldavia and Belarus) between winners and losers.[21] It is obvious that the behaviour of leaders such as Sali Berisha or Lukashenko resembles that of Tudjman or Milošević. An arrogance and disregard for the rules of the game, and in particular for the opposition (Milošević has barely ever even pronounced the name of an oppositional politician or of an oppositional party, let alone seriously envisaged entering into dialogue with one), a will to dominate completely the most important media (TV and radio) channels, and a tight grip on the military and police are common characteristics. Tudjman's son Miroslav is head of the Croatian secret services; Milošević has created one of the most numerous police forces (per capita) of 80,000 strong for a population of 10.5 million in Serbia/Montenegro. In the autumn of 1998 he dismissed the army and secret service chiefs at a time when he was purging the universities of dissenters and cracking down on the independent media, filling the vacancies with loyalists of his wife. Thus facing increasingly hostility from the West as the economy grows increasingly enfeebled and Kosovo drifts from his control, Milošević is building a private regime composed of loyalists who are completely dependent on the patronage of the duopoly in control of the state. As the Kosovo situation is once more showing, conflict has incited extreme attitudes and turned the energy of citizens not towards democratization but towards the outside. This is one of the main reasons why autocratically bent leaders in power are able to remain in their positions.[22]

In Serbia during the 1996–7 demonstration[23] the regime was described as a dictatorship (mostly by the oppositional leaders in their daily speeches to the demonstrators) and totalitarian as opposed to authoritarian,[24] while others have surmised that it is somewhere between a democracy and a dictatorship.[25] What is clear is that these are regimes with democratic legitimacy (whatever level of fraud exists in elections and it is obvious that there has been fraud to some degree) but without substantive democracy, rule of law, and safeguards for human rights. Kosovo remains a dismal story of repression of the Albanian population. The few Serbs remaining in Croatia and in particular those living in Eastern Slavonia, the last territory to be reintegrated in July 1997 into Croatia, need to be further reassured with concrete gestures about their rights. The media are constantly under threat and in Serbia have been the object of a massive clamp-down since the autumn of 1998 . The main forces hostile to democracy are in power in both Croatia and Serbia.

Conclusion

One of the most difficult legacies of communism is the destruction of civil society. Society has been disabled, atomized and fragmented. People had been brought up in a spirit of (enforced) collectivism in which individualism was a hunted animal. The absence of democracy and freedom of speech and association have left the deepest of scars on the texture of social life.

There are serious fractures and negative traits in all three key levels of state, political society and civil society. The state is still strongly in the hands of a monopolistic apparatus of power. It has not undergone any substantial transformation and an efficient, neutral, civil administration is a distant dream. The separation of powers between the executive, legislative and judiciary is largely illusory, although there have been notable attempts in particular by some representatives of the judiciary to confront these issues and work on them. The institutions of political society, the meso-level between state and civil society, exist only in a fragmentary state. Political parties and intermediary associations are in their initial birth pangs and not sufficiently structured and organized to bear the brunt of seriously engaging in a reform movement. The independent media have played in many cases an immensely important role. Daily newspapers, weeklies and most of all radio stations have been the voice of independent, investigative journalism and have by proxy given the opposition a voice, since the opposition was barred and still is from the state-owned media and in particular from the most influential media of all, the television.

The simultaneity issue of transition from authoritarian/totalitarian rule towards an open society (meaning the parallel radical transformation of politics, economy and society all at once) and its consequent complexities still await these two countries, in which there are in spite of all the authoritarian dynamics thriving small businesses, enterprises, groups, collectives, individuals, artists, scholars, sports people, who live in the 'real' world, not closed in by the regimes' blunders.

Ingenuity and resourcefulness are used to survive and strive while maintaining a sense of ethical responsibility and of public good. In these still illiberal societies it is at the level of local government, in cities where the opposition parties have taken over governance, that a new breed of democratic politician is appearing. Not all of these local oppositional governing coalitions are successful, but some will make their mark and constitute the seeds of the democratic future. It is such largely 'invisible' individuals and their daily appearance and perseverance that give hope. It is they, these individuals and groups, who will constitute the core of future developments in all spheres of society. Relationships with them based on solidarity, mutuality and reciprocity are the way to foster future co-operation and integration into the multiplicity of European networks. This should not be left for ideal times.

Even though written more than a century and a half ago, Tocqueville's *The Old Regime and the Revolution* depicts this kind of regime as one of an oligarchic power structure cloaked in democratic institutions, and names it democratic despotism. The question is whether the current opposition, once it wins power, will turn the tables on this situation and open the road from this form of democratic 'sultanism' toward an earnest endeavour of democratizing these belated nations or or whether it will leave these societies in a 'frozen post-totalitarian'[26] stage, while enjoying the benefits of power as its predecessors did.

Coda

Despotism faces three possibilities: it may cause the people to revolt, and in this case the people will overthrow it; it may exasperate the people and then, if it is attacked by foreigners, it will be overthrown by them; or, if no foreigners attack it, it will decline, more slowly but in a more shameful and no less certain manner.[27]

Notes

1 Charles Tilly, *European Revolutions 1492–1992*, Oxford: Blackwell, 1995, pp. 53, 89, 91, 101.

2 See Zagorka Golubovic, *Kriza identiteta jugoslovenskog drustva*, Beograd: Filip Visnjic, 1987.

3 Ibid., p. 47.

4 See Robert Hayden, 'Constitutional nationalism', *Slavic Review*, 51, 1992, pp. 654–73.

5 See Claude Lefort, 'The logic of totalitarianism', in *The Political Forms of Modern Society: Bureaucracy, Democracy, Totalitarianism*, Cambridge: Polity Press, 1986.

6 *The Economist*, 7 December 1996, pp. 17–18.

7 See Ivan Vejvoda, 'The ancien régime in Serbia', in Elzbieta Matynia, ed., *Grappling with Democracy: Deliberations on Post-Communist Societies (1990–1995)*, Prague: Sociologicke Nakladatelstvi / New York: New School for Social Research, 1996, pp. 40–50.

8 See Vesna Pusic, 'Croatia at a crossroads', *Journal of Democracy*, 9, 1, January 1998.

9 See Attila Hoare, 'The Croatian project to partition Bosnia-Herzegovina, 1990–1994', *East European Quarterly*, XXXI, 1, March 1997, pp. 121–38.

10 Lino Veljak, *Nasa Borba*, November 1996.

11 Claus Offe, 'Ethnic politics in East European transitions', Papers on East European Constitution Building, no. 1 (1993), Zentrum fur Europaische Rechtspolitik an der Universitat Bremen.

12 See Fareed Zakaria, 'Democracies that take liberties', *New York Times*, 2 November 1997.

13 Vojislav Šešelj perfectly matches the agitator-leaders portrayed in Leo Lowenthal and Norbert Guterman, *Prophets of Deceit: A Study of the Technique of the American Agitator*, New York, 1949, and Theodor W. Adorno *et al.*, *The Authoritarian Personality*, Harper & Row, New York, 1950.

14 See Vladimir Tismaneanu, 'The Leninist debris or waiting for Peron', *East European Politics and Societies*, 10, 3, Fall 1996, pp. 504–35, and Daniel Chirot's answer, 'Why East Central Europe is not quite ready for Peron, but may be one day', ibid., pp. 536–40.

15 In *Nasa Borba*, 19 December 1996.

16 Pusic, 'Croatia at a crossroads', p. 119.

17 Ibid., p. 120.

18 See the *New York Times*, 12 April, 20 April, 14 May 1997; also the *Guardian*, 16 May 1997, p. 14.

19 Milica Uvalic, 'Nationalism and economic policy in former Yugoslavia', *Moct-Most*, 5, 3, 1995, pp. 47–8.

20 See Mary Kaldor and Ivan Vejvoda, 'Democratisation in Central and East European countries', *International Affairs*, 73, 1, January 1997, pp. 59–82. Also now as chapter 1 in M. Kaldor and Ivan Vejvoda, eds, *Democratisation in Central and Eastern Europe*, London: Cassell, 1998.

21 Charles Gati, 'The mirage of democracy', *Transition*, 2, 6, 22 March 1996, p. 11.

22 Vladmir Goati, 'Vlast placa danak kratkorocnim ciljevima', *Nasa Borba*, 22 December 1996.

23 See my 'Cogito ergo ambulo: first steps in Belgrade', in Bulletin of the East Central European Program, Graduate Faculty, New School for Social Research, Vol. 7/2, February 1997, pp. 1–2.

24 Zagorka Golubovic and Ivan Siber, 'Gradjanski pokret otpora', *Nasa Borba*, 3 December 1996.

25 Aleksa Djilas, 'Demonstranti na politickom karnevalu', *Duga*, 7 December 1996.

26 Juan J. Linz and Alfred Stepan, *Problems of Democratic Transition and Consolidation*, Baltimore and London: Johns Hopkins University Press, 1996, p. 42.

27 Benjamin Constant, 'The spirit of conquest and usurpation and their relation to European civilization', in *Political Writings*, Cambridge: Cambridge University Press, 1988, p. 133.

11 Albania

The democratic deficit in the post-communist period

James Pettifer

As the poorest of the Balkan countries which had also endured a severe and particularly repressive communist regime, Albania was bound to encounter basic problems in the transition to a post-communist society. Albania has had a difficult history in this century, and did not develop democratic institutions prior to the communist era. This chapter examines the impact of the country's daunting democratic deficit on attempts to build a multi-party democracy that if successful would enable Albania gradually to enjoy closer ties with Western economic and security organizations and move away from a political history shaped by chronic isolation, political in-fighting and desperate poverty.

In general, it will be shown that Albania does approximate in many crucial ways to the worst image of the Balkans as a case of chronic instability and absent socio-economic modernization with poor prospects for democratization. Historical and communist legacies have proved powerful forces, while the political dynamics of transition have not, as a whole, allowed much progress towards democratization. Albania has therefore acquired some characteristics of a formal democracy, having recently acquired a new constitution, but has in practice demonstrated several features of a hybrid regime – suggesting, therefore, an unclear outcome so far to transition.

A legacy of deep insecurity

The small Balkan country only became independent from the Ottoman empire after 1913, and immediately plunged into involvement in the First World War. Foreign troops, principally from Serbia, but also from Austria and Greece, occupied parts of its territory and a period of chronic instability followed in the 1920s. This was only ameliorated by the close relationship which King Zog formed with Italy and by subsequent annexation by Mussolini. The communist state emerged out of the chaos of the struggle against Axis occupation in the Second World War, and in turn the regime of Enver Hoxha and the Party of Labour was threatened by disputes with Tito's Yugoslavia and the West. All Albanian governments since 1913 have thus had to contend with an insecure and fragile state, linked to a variety of real and imagined external and internal threats. Against this background, xenophobia has been a common component of Albanian government policies and attitudes in many periods, and it has underpinned the foreign policies of the Enver Hoxha regime.

Against this difficult historical background, prior to the Second World War there had been little formation of political parties in the conventional sense. The extreme economic backwardness and geographical remoteness of much of the country meant that archaic productive and social relations dominated much of the economy, and there were equally strong tribal and clan relationships. Modern political parties of a nationally organized character did not exist, nor did national political leaders outside the local and regional clan and tribal framework, particularly in northern Albania.[1] The communist party, the Party of Labour (PLA), had a monolithic Leninist structure but it also embodied internal clan relationships, particularly among southern veterans from the partisan leadership from the Second World War period. In the Zogist period, the middle class had been very small indeed, and had little independent political culture. After the Second World War, under communism, the idea or notion of a political party in the 'bourgeois' sense was portrayed as a betrayal of the 'nation', something that would cause division, internal conflict and national weakness. Similarly, the notion of an opposition as having a necessary and valuable role in a democratic system and democratic parliament was totally absent.

It is worth bearing in mind in this context that the Party of Labour was only founded in 1941, on the basis of tiny local communist groupings with Yugoslav help. It totally lacked any experience of working with non-communist forces in a wider framework of anti-fascist struggle, such as that of the popular front stage of Comintern policy had given many other European communist parties in the 1930s.[2] Unlike countries such as the old German Democratic Republic or Poland under communism, there was no vestige of a multi-party system at all in Albania, although of course such systems in many Warsaw Pact countries were in practice a mere façade. Pluralism could only exist, tenuously, in the form of pluralism of ideas within certain limits laid down by the PLA, and within the PLA. Outside the PLA, open political debate of any kind was virtually impossible until the slight liberalization of the late 1980s under Enver Hoxha's successor, Ramiz Alia. The first organized oppositional political movement was not founded until December 1990, much later than in most East European states. This became the Democratic Party (DP) that soon became the government after the spring 1992 elections.

In the later stage of the communist period, especially after the death of Enver Hoxha in 1985, the actual party organization of the PLA became sclerotic. Some observers believe that the moral and political force of Albanian communism was spent by the end of the pro-Chinese period in

1978, when the dictates of pro-Maoist policy had exhausted the commitment of even the most loyal party members.[3] These years were dominated by total international isolation and economic stagnation, with bankruptcy only being avoided by relatively high revenues from the extractive industries. The equally limited development of a national intelligensia also retarded the development of dissident anti-communist groups along the lines that developed in most other East European communist and Warsaw Pact countries. For instance, urban political opposition based upon the universities was slow to emerge. Outside the PLA, there was very little in the way of any independent and functioning civil society, with PLA control of all popular organizations and no non-party clubs, associations or private bodies, while all churches and religous institutions closed after 1968. A large network of informers controlled by the secret police, the Sigurimi, prevented the emergence of any normal civil society and clandestine, oppositional organizations whatsoever until 1989–90.

A problematic transition

There was thus a substantial democratic deficit when communism collapsed in Albania between 1989 and 1992, leading to the National Unity government being replaced by the government of Sali Berisha and his Democratic Party. The notion of political parties was almost wholly absent or undeveloped outside Tirana and the educated Tirana elite. Even those who were never communists often had highly undemocratic attitudes to politics and adhered to a political culture of a very elitist kind. Among the general population, some 65 per cent of which were peasants, there was even less grasp of modern politics in a European sense. Also, the legacy of regional and clan differences was to play an important part in national life in the next few years. The communists had come to power on the back of the anti-fascist war of national liberation, most of whose victories had been won under communist leadership in the south and centre of the country. The north had tended to support royalist and nationalist parties, some of whom had remained close to the German and Italian occupiers for most of the wartime period until their military defeat in 1944.[4]

The overthrow of communism was nevertheless marked by a mass movement of peasants and workers against the one-party state. This often took violent and anarchic forms, with random attacks on all symbols of state property and institutions, not merely those associated with the PLA and the communist system. The urge to leave Albania was paramount with many people, and there were widespread seizures of ships by refugees that led to very adverse publicity for Albania. This was particularly the case in the summer of 1991. It had not, though, been common to have physical attacks on leading communist personalities, and this remained the case in the early Berisha period. The old communist and communist-educated elite remained virtually intact despite the dramatic changes in the country. New leaders had been thrown up by this mass movement, such as the student leader Azim Hajdari, and they quickly became leaders of the Democratic Party. Many of them inevitably had some communist associations, including Sali Berisha himself who had been a PLA member for twelve years. The habits and mentality of this elite were continued in the Berisha government after 1992, although international community backers of this government went to great lengths to try to disguise the fact that this was so, mainly by directing publicity around the energetic personality of the President himself.[5]

In the provinces, the Tirana elite was widely distrusted, and this has remained the case under post-communist society. It is seen as a privileged and exploitative group, particularly in northern Albania. The fact that members of it played a leading part in many aspects of the destruction of the one-party state has been unhelpful to the development of liberal democracy. Sali Berisha was widely seen as a hardline communist when he was a party member. His inherently authoritarian personality combined with this background led directly to many of the difficulties faced beween 1992 and 1997, when he fell from power. Within a few months of his election in spring 1992, he had had major breaches with trusted associates from the founding circle of the Democratic Party, such as the economist Gramoz Pashko, and threats to the judiciary and the rule of law emerged.

The policy of outside backers of Berisha, particularly the United States in this early period, was to build a powerful central presidential government to try to solve the major public order problems of the 1989–91 period, and to act as a restraining influence on Albanian involvement in the growing Yugoslav crisis. In return Albania would receive special treatment from the World Bank and other international financial institutions in its efforts to promote economic development. Although these objectives were very understandable at the time, this foreign backing of President Berisha had the effect of legitimating different elements of the democratic deficit that Albania faced, in particular the lack of a properly functioning parliament, an independent judiciary, and independent civil service. As all important decisions were channelled through the presidency, the potential for a highly authoritarian style of government that eventually threatened dictatorship quickly emerged.

This problem was accentuated by the lack of a democratic constitution. Under democracy after 1992, the President ruled by decrees which were rubberstamped by the DP-dominated parliament. These powers derived from the old communist constitution and had been invoked by Ramiz Alia in 1990 to deal with civil unrest then. Although groups of Tirana legal experts and international advisers had been formed to write a new constitution, progress was slow and power quickly centralized around Berisha in the 1992–3 period. After many disagreements between the parties, a group of American legal experts put forward a constitutional draft that was put to popular vote in a referendum in November 1994. Much to the surprise of international observers and supporters of the Berisha regime, the Albanian people decisively rejected the proposals, which were seen as legitimating the centralist and authoritarian aspects of the Berisha government that were highly unpopular. Particular concern was directed at the provisions for government appointment of judges, the powers that would be given to the President to stop criminal investigations for corruption (a growing problem in Albania), and the lack of any provisions for appeal against presidential actions. The influential Greek minority strongly objected to the provisions concerning Albanian citizenship for religious leaders, as these would have hindered the development of the Orthodox Church. But at least religious conflict was largely conspicuous by its absence in a country where Catholicism, Islam and Orthodoxy each possessed numerous adherents.

Democratic despotism in the making

In retrospect, the real crisis in the Albanian transition from communism began with this referendum result, although that was not immediately apparent at the time. Economic growth rates were still high, and the government was still in good standing with the international financial institutions. Against the background of the war in other parts of ex-Yugoslavia, the international image of Albania was still rather positive. Although concern about human rights was being expressed in some quarters, and political trials of socialist and communist party leaders were beginning, the good international image of the Berisha regime made it difficult for Albanians with genuine human rights problems to attract much attention or support. The relatively unreformed nature of the main opposition party, the Socialists, was a further obstacle to progress. Although the leaders with direct personal links to Enver Hoxha had been shed in 1990 and 1991, there were many senior party members in positions of authority from this period after 1992, and party organization and policy were ossified on many issues. It was difficult for socialist parties in Europe and elsewhere to take up the cause of the anti-Berisha opposition without seeming to support a fairly unreconstructed ex-communist party, as the Socialists were at that time.[6] The Socialists also had many links with Greece, which were unhelpful in terms of internal Albanian politics. And quite a high proportion were from the country's 10 per cent Orthodox minority, whereas the Berisha government was dominated by Muslim and Roman Catholic northern Albanians.

Another important factor was the considerable amount of time and energy spent by better-educated people on constructing organizations of a previously absent civil society, which weakened the forces of direct and organised political opposition. The years 1991–5 saw a genuine flowering of independent cultural, economic and, especially, religious organizations, with the construction of hundreds of new mosques and churches throughout the country. Although many people involved in this work may have been very critical of the democratic deficiencies of the Berisha regime, they were willing to forgive it much in exchange for the limited, largely foreign financed economic progress that seemed to be taking place, and the opportunity to build a civil society without open state repression. The fact that many of the economic achievements were based on sand was not apparent at the time, nor was the lack of real foreign investment seen as a barrier to economic progress and a high GDP growth rate. As a result, the Berisha government was led to believe that it would be immmune from serious international criticism over its authoritarian tendencies.

In 1993–4 the government's impatience towards its critics was high-lighted by regular threats and attacks on the print media, which were free and independent by comparison with most Balkan countries. Albanian television was closely controlled by the government, however, unlike the 1990–2 period of the disintegration of communism when the emergence of the democratic opposition was reasonably fairly reported. A symbol of this was the almost total non-reporting of the activities of the trade unions, although strikes were frequent in the 1992–4 period. The trade unions had played a critical role in the process of democratizing the one-party state, with the General Strike of May 1991 being a decisive nail in its coffin. But popular action of any kind was anathema to the Berisha government, so many of whose members were deeply inbued with the authoritarian mind-set inherited from Leninist conditioning under Hoxha. Trade unionism was seen as having no legitimate role in the fundamentalist free-market ideology espoused by the new government, nor were trade unions seen as having any principled role to play in defending workers rights in a demo-cratic society under the rule of law. The encouragement of civil society by the Berisha government was a highly partial process, with strong state support for business and religious institutions but undermining of basic rights in many fields. Intellectual life suffered deeply from these aspects of the transition, with the main academic institutes in Tirana very adversely affected by the emigration of personnel and the appointment of Berisha placemen. As these bodies had no 'market' function, they were left to wither away.

But a central feature of the crisis that was beginning to develop in 1995 and which would overwhelm Albania in late 1996 and early 1997 was by now apparent. There was a severe and increasing divergence between the real political and cultural and economic world, where Berisha's govern-ment had brought only very limited improvements to the lives of the vast majority, and the imagined world of the international community, where Albania was seen as moving towards stability and prosperity in stable conditions.

Another defining feature of the later years of the Berisha government was the increasing development of a kleptocracy.[7] The unparalled oppor-tunities for economic activities linked to breaking United Nations sanctions imposed on rump Yugoslavia had overtaken the country, and led to a vast and rapid expansion of organized crime. The main focus of this was in northern Albania, where there was a huge demand for diesel fuel from war-torn Serbia and Montenegro. Locally produced Albanian diesel fuel from the oilfields in the south near Fier was brought north by tanker and then smuggled across the Albanian border at Han i Hoti, or by boat across Lake Shkoder. Later on in the war, in the 1994–5 period, there was a use of Durres harbour for this trade, where boats and small tankers transported fuel to the Montenegran port of Bar.

Some members of the Albanian government were involved in sanctions-busting, and a web of massive corruption soon developed, as a new class of people became extremely rich in the process. This kleptocratic group became a decisive factor in the subsequent 'pyramid crisis' and the over-throw of the Berisha government. Native Albanians were joined by experienced Mafia people from Italy and elsewhere, and very soon they came to dominate many areas of economic life. The booming pyramid banks offering high-interest deposits were very closely tied to the klepto-cratic elite, with substantial money-laundering of sanctions-busting and drug-trade generated funds a particular feature of their activities. At the same time, there was large-scale peculation and embezzlement of the large flow of foreign funds from the World Bank and International Monetary Fund into Albania by government officials and civil servants. This money needed to be laundered by the pyramid banks before it could be placed securely abroad. Thus, the democratic deficit existing in Albania was greatly increased by social and economic developments in the years of UN sanctions. The new semi-criminal and criminal kleptocracy was increasingly entrenched. As government became more and more identified with the Democratic Party and President Berisha, a right-wing dictatorship beckoned.

In retrospect, the international community did little that was substantial towards ameliorating this dark progress away from democracy. Only in the United States had there been any significant protests at the human rights violations of the Berisha government before the May 1996 general election. European Union countries led by Germany and Austria, which had traditionally strong links with the Albanian right, soon took the place of the USA as the main international supporters and advocates of the Berisha project.[8] In international relations terms, this 'neo-Hapsburg' bloc saw Albania as a valuable counter to Serbia, traditionally the strongest opponent of the Hapsburg empire, and a country which was increasingly being cast by media-influenced liberal opinion in the West as the root of all evil in the region. On superficial examination, Albania appeared to be everything that Serbia was not, in terms of economic progress, a Western policy orientation, and a pro-NATO stance in the Balkans.

Britain was also an important minor prop of the Berisha government, largely because of the distortion of Foreign Office policy through the influence of a small group of senior Conservatives who had served with anti-communist forces in Albania in the Second World War.[9] Despite the generally pro-Serbian British policy stance in the Balkans, a position also shared by France, for all the traditional historical reasons Albania was seen as a developing and favoured democracy, despite so much independent evidence to the contrary. The virulently anti-Serb propaganda lobby that grew up as a result of alleged Serb war crimes in the Bosnian war inadvertently assisted the Berisha regime in maintaining the image of itself as a democracy, particularly on Capitol Hill in the United States where there was very little knowledge of Balkan realities even among the politial elite. Because it was anti-Serb, Berisha's Albania was seen in a wholly positive light. And some critics of the Berisha regime, even Albanians, were accused of pro-Serb leanings if they supported the Albanian opposition. In the same way, when leading members of that opposition, such as Neritan Ceka, the Albanian Interior Minister from 1997 to May 1998, engaged in peaceful dialogue over the Kosovo problem with members of the Serbian opposition in 1995, they were denounced as traitors to the nation by the Berisha-controlled television and pro-government newpapers.

The unravelling of a state?

The events in the late winter of 1996 and the spring of 1997 leading to the downfall of the Berisha regime are well known. A financial crisis, which had begun by October 1996 with the collapse of one or two small high-interest-rate institutions, had spread to the entire financial system by early January 1997. The pyramid institutions were unable to repay depositors' money, particularly if their deposits were in hard currency. Social unrest accompanied this crisis, which was centred on the southern port of Vlora and the Greek minority areas in the south of the country. A mass popular uprising began, which soon took control of most of the south and centre of the country.

To prevent a complete meltdown of society, the UN mandated an international peacekeeping force led by Italy to be sent to try to restore a semblance of stability. Shortly beforehand, in March 1997, the Organization for Security and Co-operation in Europe (OSCE) successfully mediated an agreement between President Berisha and the opposition. Both sides agreed to early elections and to a government of national reconciliation under the Socialist politician Bashkim Fino. Elections held in two stages on 29 June and 6 July were judged a success, even though the government and the OSCE barely had two months to prepare. There was a clear-cut result with the Socialists winning an overwhelming majority. In August 1997 a Socialist-led coalition government took office under Fatos Nano, the former Socialist leader who had been imprisoned under Berisha. Several important ministries were given to non-Socialist figures. Berisha resigned the presidency, his successor being a second-ranking Socialist, Rexhap Meidani, a physicist, who tried to promote national reconciliation.

Despite winning a two-thirds parliamentary majority, the Nano government proceeded cautiously against Berisha and the Democrats. It did not use its new-found position of strength to seek retribution for the misdeeds of its implacable rivals when they were in office. This would have been a perilous course since the Nano government found it hard to gain physical control of all of the country. Many places in northern Albania remained under the control of militant Berisha supporters.[10]

The challenge facing such a new government will be to try to remedy the democratic deficit in Albania that led to these events – to build liberal political institutions, with genuine multi-party pluralism, and to develop a civil society and genuinely free media to underpin these institutions. Whether a freely elected government can restore its authority will depend on the degree of progress made in restructuring the economy. Inflation is high, over 50 per cent and rising, and there is widespread popular hardship caused by rising food prices in particular, and serious problems with power and water supplies in many towns. The government needs to restore its authority by collecting taxes and customs duties and establishing some degree of control over the black economy, one that is based on smuggling fuel, narcotics, arms and, not least, people (to Italy). If a semblance of economic order is restored, the chances of being able to create new jobs and rebuild the infrastructure will increase; but it is a very demanding task.

Bitter polemics between the Socialists and the Democrats had resumed by the start of 1998. In and around the city of Shkoder in particular this was evident, and troops had to be deployed to secure the city from armed bands supporting ex-President Berisha in February 1998. The Democrats refused to take their seats in parliament and remained active in the extra-parliamentary opposition. They thus refused to participate in the process of instituting and consolidating reforms necessary to overcome the inherited democratic deficit. The new constitution, which parliament began deliberating in late 1997, would not just be the expression of the Socialists, given the presence of other forces in the government. But Albania seemed as far away as ever from renouncing the politics of partisanship and embracing a formula based on bargaining and pacts between the chief political contenders in order to devise a peaceful framework for competitive politics.

Relations with neighbouring Balkan states improved for a time in 1997–8 with the first contact between Yugoslav and Albanian leaders for over fifty years taking place at the South-East Europe conference held in Crete in November 1997. A number of important border and trade agreements were signed with Macedonia; while progress was made in finalizing an agreement with Greece for the legalization of Albanian guest-workers. Although formal relations were cordial, the United States and European Union powers kept some distance from the Nano government, perhaps waiting to see whether it succeeded in its basic objectives, particularly security, before undertaking a deeper commitment to Albania.

In 1998, full-scale violence erupted in Kosovo as the Albanian militants of the Kosovo Liberation Army (KLA) attempted to wrest control of the disputed Yugoslav province from Serbia. This soon succeeded in destabilizing the fragile Nano government. Albania endorsed the view of most Western powers that the best short-term answer for resolving the Kosovo crisis was sweeping autonomy for the Albanian majority within a decentralized Yugoslavia. But, in the summer of 1998, as Yugoslav forces employed scorched earth tactics to defeat the KLA insurgents, destroying dozens of villages and turning hundreds of thousands of Albanian Kosovans into refugees, Nano's policy faced a major challenge at home. Berisha accused the government of pursuing a policy of squalid betrayal towards co-ethnics in Kosovo. The opposition demanded that Tirana recognize Kosovo as an independent Albanian state and that all necessary assistance be provided by the government to the KLA.

As the crisis deepened, the Nano government's hold on power grew increasingly shaky. With the country remaining awash with an estimated 600,000 guns looted from army depots in the 1997 disturbances, the disintegration of its authority seemed a real possibility. Its inability to control arms and smuggling and deal with the political fall-out from the thousands of refugees fleeing into the country from Kosovo exposed its vulnerability.

Fatos Nano resigned on 28 September 1998, citing as his main reason that 'he was not receiving any credible signs of solidarity' either from parts of the Socialist Party or from his coalition partners.[11] His inability to find a new Interior Minister acceptable to all parties hastened his departure. In the preceding days, it looked as if Albania was going to witness a repeat of the anarchy of 1997. Following the murder of Azem Hajdari, a leading Democratic Party official, who was well known for his open support for the KLA, Nano's offices were set on fire and state-run television was briefly seized by gunmen. Berisha, addressing rallies of his supporters, seemed to lend his backing to such extra-parliamentary action. But the opposition failed to acquire sufficient popular backing to topple the government by force, and the armed revolt in Tirana was contained after several days.

A new Prime Minister was appointed whom commentators believed might stand a greater chance than Fatos Nano of establishing a degree of common ground within Albania's fragmented political elite to facilitate the reconstruction of the country. Pandeli Majko had never been a member of the former ruling PLA and had been one of the leaders of the student revolt that helped end communist rule. At 31 he was Europe's youngest Premier, having become a member of the Socialists after the party's internal reform in 1991. Thereafter he came across as a social democratic reformer keen to align the successors of the communists with a Western pluralist outlook.

Majko's government was almost identical in composition to that of Nano's, so a testing time lies ahead to convince critics that the polarization

12 Macedonia

An unlikely road to democracy

Bogdan Szajkowski

The Republic of Macedonia, the small but strategically important buffer state in the southern Balkans, has faced a battle to survive since its declaration of independence in 1991. Discussion of its future is often overshadowed by spectres from the past and the seemingly insuperable internal problems and conflicts in neighbouring countries. The war in Bosnia-Hercegovina, the continuous emergency in Kosovo, the restlessness of its Albanian minority and previous aggressive actions by its larger neighbours, Serbia, Greece and Bulgaria, are all major destabilizing factors. Yet against all the odds Macedonia remains a peaceful, stable and quite confident country.

Democratization in Macedonia has therefore been taking place against the background of regional insecurity, plunging living standards, and corrosive inter-ethnic suspicions. Rivalries between Macedonian and Albanian political contenders as well as within the elites contesting power in both communities have occasionally strained the political system to breaking point. President Kiro Gligorov, who played a very major stabilizing influence in preventing these antagonisms overwhelming what was, until recently, a weakly implanted multi-party system, will relinquish his post before the turn of the century. A new generation of untested politicians will have to steer Macedonia into a new millennium as shockwaves from the violent collapse of federal Yugoslavia after 1991 complicate the process of state- and nation-building for Macedonia.

The question of identity

The geographic name Macedonia is applied to three regions: Vardar Macedonia (former Yugoslavia), Aegean Macedonia (in northern Greece), and the Pirin Macedonia in Bulgaria. Throughout history these Macedonian territories have been highly valued strategic points of transit between West and East and much fought over. The Macedonian territories included in Serbia were brought into the Kingdom of Serbs, Croats and Slovenes in 1919 (renamed Yugoslavia in 1929). Following partition under Axis occupation in 1941, Yugoslav Macedonia was occupied principally by the Bulgarians, with the western part allocated to the Italian client state of Albania. At the end of the Second World War, Bulgaria, Greece and (what came to be) Yugoslavia carved up the region of Macedonia in a tripartite agreement. Yugoslavia took control of 'Vardar' Macedonia.

The Macedonian Republic was proclaimed on 2 August 1944, as a part of the Socialist Federal Republic of Yugoslavia. Thereafter Yugoslavia's leader, Josip Broz Tito, encouraged the reinforcement of a Slavic Macedonian nation through an intensive period of state-building. This in particular included the refinement of the Macedonian language and alphabet (which became the republic's official language), the re-establishment of the autocephalous Macedonian Orthodox Church as one of the fundamental features of national identity, re-examination of Macedonian history, and the introduction of policies designed to instil and strengthen Macedonian identity in the republic and to make the Macedonism of Macedonia clearly recognizable within the federation.

Macedonia was the fourth largest of the six republics within the Yugoslav Federation but the least developed. It was strategically significant in that it provided a corridor through the Balkan mountains from north to south and from east to west. Tito's Yugoslavia has been good to Macedonia, which meant that inside the republic there was a strong level of commitment to the idea of Yugoslavia. In part, at least, this commitment could be explained as a way of overcoming the multitude of issues related to the insecurities of Macedonian identity. At the same time it should be seen as a way of resisting predatory moves and challenges by the Albanians, Greeks, Bulgarians and Serbs.

Macedonia's identification with Yugoslavia could obviously last only as long as Yugoslavia itself. When the disintegration of Yugoslavia became a possibility after 1989, Macedonian opinion was initially strongly in favour of the maintenance of the federation. Leading Macedonian politicians, including Kiro Gligorov and Vasil Tupurkovski, were actively engaged until the last minute in negotiations that might have prevented its disintegration. The collapse of the federation only held out the prospect that this small country of some two million people would be exposed to irredentist claims by its neighbours. In the spring of 1991 President Gligorov of Macedonia produced a compromise plan to transform the Yugoslav Federation into a loose Alliance of Sovereign States.[1] Macedonia pinned its hopes on a reconstituted federation that would operate on loose confederal lines.[2]

Consequently it was not until 8 September 1991 that a referendum was held, seeking popular approval for independence. In the referendum voters were asked: 'Are you for a sovereign and independent state of Macedonia, with the right to enter in a future alliance of sovereign states of Yugoslavia?'. It is worth noting that the terms of the referendum motion mentioned that Macedonia retained 'the right to join an alliance of sovereign states' – implicitly some revived future version of Yugoslavia. In the referendum, in which 75.74 per cent of the registered electorate participated, 95.26 per cent voted in favour. On 18 September 1991 the Macedonian parliament, the Sobranie, declared the independence of the republic from the Federal Socialist Republic of Yugoslavia. For the first time in history Macedonians achieved the goal of having their own sovereign and independent state. Unlike the other republics of the former Yugoslavia, Macedonia achieved its independence in a peaceful way. The Yugoslav National Army left Macedonia as a result of an agreement, without a single shot being fired, in the spring of 1992.

The declaration of independence, however, resurrected some old issues and questions concerning the identity of the Macedonians, their historical claims and what is more important their position within the new state. This complex set of problems will be discussed throughout this chapter. For the moment it is worth noting that whether the Macedonians form a genuine ethnic group in their own right is disputed by virtually all of Macedonia's neighbours. Only Albania has recognized the existence of the Macedonian people. Bulgaria and Serbia view 'Macedonians' as being either Bulgars or Serbs respectively. Greece points to the way in which under Tito a Macedonian identity was deliberately encouraged, and rejects any historical connections of the Macedonians and the new republic to the Royal House of the Makedons.

Whatever is the perception of Macedonia's neighbours, the fact remains that at least two generations have grown up with Macedonian identity. Developments since 1991 have further strengthened the argument in favour of 'the Macedonian nationality'. For the overwhelming majority of the population of the Republic of Macedonia there is little question about their sense of belonging regardless of their national/ethnic association. They consider themselves as citizens of the multi-ethnic republic and wish to live and work in Macedonia, which offers much better opportunities and standard of living than most countries in the area.

Ethnic challenges

Perhaps the most fundamental challenge facing the republic is finding a successful resolution to ethnic tensions given its heterogeneous population. This challenge is particularly formidable with respect to Macedonia's Albanian population.

The constitution adopted on independence designates Macedonia as a 'citizen state'.[3] The aim of such a designation has been to minimize inter-ethnic problems by stressing that the state belongs to individual citizens irrespective of their ethnic origins. This formulation as one of the cornerstones of the ideology of the new republic has been also intended to forestall the emergence and consolidation of ethnocentric political culture as a reaction to the Yugoslav system which officially laid stress on 'brother-hood and unity'. The preamble to the constitution declares that

'Macedonia is established as the national state of the Macedonian people, in which full equality as citizens and permanent co-existence with the Macedonian people is provided for Albanians, Turks, Vlachs, Romanies and other nationalities living in the Republic of Macedonia'. The constitution makes no reference to ethnic minorities in Macedonia[4] in order not to imply 'second' or 'lower' class of citizenship. Instead the term nationality or nationalities is used for all peoples of any ethnic background.[5]

The largest of Macedonia's ethnic minorities are the Albanians. In the former Yugoslavia they were heavily discriminated against. Consequently they reacted to Macedonia's independence with a sense of impatience and opportunity, hoping that an independent Macedonia would redress their grievances.[6] However, the spectre of Greater Albania uniting the Albanians in Macedonia, Kosovo and Albania under one state increased Macedonian anxieties for the security and territorial integrity of the new republic.

The Albanians live in western and north-western Macedonia near the Albanian and Kosovo borders where they form a compact majority. They have always been set apart from Slavs and others. Their language, customs, social organizations, and traditions have very little if anything in common with those of their Slav and Greek neighbours. Organized in tightly-knit clans and following their own centuries-old 'custom' law, the Albanians have had little meaningful social interaction with others. While most speak Macedonian, members of other ethnic groups do not speak Albanian. Albanians, like the Turks in Macedonia, are predominantly Muslim. Unlike the Turks, however, who are largely assimilated into the mainstream of Macedonian society, Albanians have remained fairly isolated socially. Macedonian Albanians have strong ties with Kosovo. They tend to be low-paid manual workers with a significant percentage being unemployed and involved in the 'grey economy'.[7]

The mistrust between the two communities is significant and noticeable, with each suspecting the other's intentions and motives. This is often reinforced by the conspiratorial nature of Balkan political culture. There is a widespread belief among ethnic Macedonians that the Albanians in Macedonia have rights but no obligations and that their real goal is union with Albania. A survey conducted among Muslims and Orthodox concerning 'rights' and 'obligations' (loyalty) produced interesting but predictable results. Some 91 per cent of Muslims said that they do not have enough rights, while 53 per cent of the Orthodox group of respondents thought that 'the others' have enough rights – the remaining 47 per cent thought that they had too many rights.[8] While the survey was conducted amongst the two religious groups it should be remembered that since most of the Muslims are ethnic Albanians and most of the Orthodox Christians are ethnic Macedonians, people seldom make a distinction between their ethnicity and their religion. Most of the Muslims consider themselves to be 'second-class' citizens because of their ethnic and religious identity. This provides fertile ground for political manipulation.

Indeed, the Muslim population has from time to time been targeted by political activists and encouraged to use different forms of political pressure (such as boycotting obligations towards the state). Naturally, the reaction of the majority of the population is to consider such actions 'disloyal', so widening the gulf between the two groups. It is clear, however, that the apparent 'disloyalty' stems more from a sense of inequality – thus indicating that the integration of the Muslim communities has not been as successful as it might have been.[9]

This also provides broad scope for religious feelings to be used for political ends.

Among the Orthodox population, 75 per cent would not marry a person of different confession and almost all of these rejected the idea of a mixed marriage with Muslims (only 8 per cent referred to Catholics as a 'non-desirable combination'). Among the Muslim population, 78 per cent would not choose a non-Muslim partner (57 per cent singled out Orthodox Christians, and a smaller number did so with Catholics).[10]

There is a dispute about the size of the ethnic Albanian population in Macedonia. According to the census conducted in 1991 by the Macedonian Statistical Office, Albanians comprised 21.73 per cent of the population of the republic. The census was, however, boycotted by the Albanians who claimed that the census was unfair because instructions explaining how to fill out forms were in fact written in Macedonian. The 1994 internationally supervised census recorded 442,914 persons (22.87 per cent of the total population) who declared themselves as Albanians. Leaders of the Albanian community who claimed that their people comprise about 40 per cent of Macedonia's population again questioned the census results. Most specialists regard the ethnic Albanian's claims as highly exaggerated.

The question of the size of the ethnic Albanian population is not simply one of numbers as it has a direct bearing on the political and social role of the Albanians in the new Macedonia and naturally also on inter-ethnic relations in the country. Albanians consider it crucial for their status in the new state. They demand equal status for the Albanian language,[11] much wider access to Albanian-language secondary and tertiary education, the right to be named as a co-nation of Macedonia, together with the Macedonians and not as an ethnic minority. The Albanians believe that their status as defined by the constitution is inappropriate. Since the constitution describes the state as 'Macedonian' the Albanians maintain that it accords 'minority status' to other ethnic groups. This formulation, they stress, gives them second-class citizenship. They argue that in Macedonia they have lost even the limited recognition they enjoyed in the former Yugoslavia.[12] They request that they should be accorded equal 'state-building' status.[13] The political implications of this demand are quite considerable, as this would have substantial repercussions, not only on political representation at national and local level but also on bilingualism, education and employment.

The claims of Macedonian Albanians that they enjoy less than equal status with Macedonians are supported by some data. The number of Albanians in tertiary and higher education clearly does not reflect their proportion in the society. During the Yugoslav period, of those who embarked on higher education, most chose to attend Pristina University.[14] After the independence of Macedonia this became extremely difficult if virtually impossible, as it meant crossing the state border with Serbia, long queues and regular harassment. The inability to attend Pristina University resulted in demands for increasing opportunities in higher education in the Albanian language. The Macedonian government was slow to respond to these requests.

Of the 71,505 students attending all institutes of higher learning in Macedonia in 1989–90 academic year, only 2,794 (3.9 per cent) were Albanians. At the university level the attendance figures were even worse: of the 22,994 students registered for 1991–2 academic year, only 386 (1.68 per cent) were ethnic Albanians; 172 (0.75 per cent) were Turks; and fourteen (0.06 per cent) were Roma. At that time courses were taught only in Macedonian.[15] Since 1992 the government had taken steps to improve the situation. In 1995 Albanians constituted 6.5 per cent of all university students. The Albanians consider this increase insufficient. This led in February 1995 to the opening of the private Albanian-language Tetovo University in the Mala Recica suburb of Tetovo.[16] The authorities declared this an unconstitutional act and the police used force to prevent it from opening, one person being killed. The university's rector, Fadil Sulejmani, was sentenced in July 1995 to two and a half years in prison for stirring unrest during the February incidents. He was released in February 1997 on probation.[17]

The Macedonian authorities have defended their position on the grounds that permitting higher education exclusively in Albanian would amount to 'educational ghettoization' of the Albanian minority. Moderate Albanian leaders appear to support this view. 'We don't want to create American-style reservations for Albanians in Macedonia . We would like to live in a multi-ethnic environment.'[18] Many Macedonians fear that such a university would become a stronghold of separatist and nationalist ideology, as in the case of the Albanian Studies Department of Pristina University.

In face of the long-standing demand of the Albanians for university education in the Albanian language, the authorities have granted the Albanians a few concessions, including the use of Albanian language at the Pedagogic Faculty at the Sainst Kiril and Methodij University in Skopje. When the Albanian students complained that their teachers were not qualified to teach them in Albanian, the government produced a regulation stipulating that Albanian students should only attend classes taught by 'qualified teachers'. This decision, however, met with strong opposition by Macedonian students who organized peaceful protests in front of the Rector's office calling for 'a unified university'. Despite opposition the Albanians managed to secure limited gains in their demands for Albanian language education.

Gostivar, a prosperous town in western Macedonia where Albanians form an overwhelming majority, became a scene of major confrontation on 9 July 1997 in which three people died, more than seventy were injured, and some 320 were arrested. The riots began when the Macedonian police took down an Albanian flag hoisted from the municipal building. Following the sentencing of the mayor of Gostivar the Democratic Party of Albanians withdrew its mayors and councillors from local government throughout Macedonia and asked its MPs to stop participating in the parliament. Significantly the Party of Democratic Prosperity continued as a member of the government coalition.

The flag issue was only a catalyst that brought long-simmering tensions to the surface. At the root of the dispute is a strong mutual distrust between ethnic Albanians and Macedonians, who fear the separatist aspirations of Albanians and see Albanian irredentism as an existential danger to their young and volatile state. Most of the young Albanians, especially the large number of young unemployed, feel discriminated against by the Slavic-speaking majority. The Albanians' repeated failure to achieve their most basic aim of political and social equality through Macedonia's political institutions reinforces that frustration and feeds nationalism.

Electoral politics: the construction of a viable party system

The first multi-party elections were conducted in three rounds, on 9 and 25 November and 9 December 1990. Because of massive irregularities in the conduct of the first round of the elections on 9 November 1990, it was necessary to declare the first round void in 176 voting districts. The elections returned the candidate of the former communist Party of Democratic Change, Kiro Gligorov, as the state President, and an Assembly (Sobranie) of 120 seats.

After the December 1990 elections no single party was able to form a majority within the single chamber of the Sobranie. The Internal Macedonian Revolutionary Organization–Democratic Party for Macedonian National Unity (VMRO–DPMNE), the principal exponent of Macedonian nationalism and the largest single party, with 38 of the 120 seats was asked to form a government. Since the largely working-class and populist VMRO–DPMNE was unable to provide persons with sufficient experience and qualification from within its own ranks, many of the ministers were recruited from outside the parties themselves. The government thus came to be known as the 'government of experts'.[19]

In the Sobranie, the opposition to VMRO – DPMNE came from the former communists the Party of Democratic Change,[20] and from parties representing other national interests, especially from the Albanian Party of Democratic Prosperity (PDP). The government of experts collapsed after a vote of no confidence on 16 July 1992. During the period of instability that ensued, the leader of the Social Democratic Alliance of Macedonia (formerly the League of Communists of Yugoslavia), Petar Gosev, was asked to form a government. He declined after an initial round of negotiations. After a month of impasse, on 13 August 1992 a new coalition was put together by Branko Crvenkovski. It was based on the Social Democratic Alliance of Macedonia (SDAM), the PDP, the Liberal Party (LP) and the Socialist Party (SP). The drawing of the PDP firmly into the governmental process was particularly significant as an attempt to undercut the prevalent suspicion and sometimes outright hostility between the Macedonians and Albanians. To some extent the inclusion of an Albanian party in the governmental coalition involved recognition of some of the problems faced by the Albanians and preparedness to put inter-ethnic relations high on the agenda. These included demands for a higher profile and higher recognition in the Republic of Macedonia, equal status for the Albanian language and Albanian-language university-level education. The balancing act involved giving serious consideration to Albanian expectations without at the same time antagonizing Macedonian nationalists, who claimed that national interests are being compromised in order to appease Albanians.

In the October 1994 elections for the Sobranie, the Alliance for Macedonia, a grand coalition, led by the Social Democratic Alliance for Macedonia (SDAM), comprising the Liberal Party (LP) and the Socialist Party of Macedonia (SPM) , won more than a three-quarters majority of the 120 seats. However, this was to a large extent facilitated by the boycott of the second round of elections by the two main opposition parties, the conservative nationalist VMRO–DPMNE and the moderate Democratic Party (DP). They both claimed election fraud after they obtained disappointing results in the first round of voting. Following the election, the largest ethnic Albanian party, the Party for Democratic Prosperity (PDP), joined the Alliance for Macedonia in forming a government which gave it the support of seven-eighths of the Sobranie. In addition to the coalition parties only fourteen members representing smaller parties or independent candidates were elected to parliament.

The lack of an effective opposition allowed the Social Democrats to enjoy an easy ride until February 1996 when the four-party coalition broke up. The 1994 elections highlighted, however, the growing differences between the two traditional coalition partners who also represent two divergent approaches to economic policy. Differences between the Liberals, who were in favour of a quick transition to market economy, and the Social Democrats, who represent Macedonia's old political establishment, deepened after the elections and led in February 1996 to the break-up of the four-party coalition and the collapse of the established coalition patterns that had dominated Macedonian politics since independence. The withdrawal of the Liberal Party from the coalition meant that the majority of ministers (ten) included in the new government came from the Social Democrats, five from the largest political grouping of the Albanians, the PDP, and three from the Socialist Party. The composition of the new government was also clearly aimed at securing the support of the moderate Albanians who aim to win concessions through co-operation with the government, rather than the Albanian radicals who sought increased confrontation with the Social Democrats. Even after the Gostivar riots the PDP continued to support the government coalition. The November 1996 local and mayoral elections offered the first opportunities since 1994 to test the parties' support in the country. Overall the results clearly showed growing support for more radical parties in both ethnic communities, particularly the Albanians.

Electoral politics: towards the consolidation of the party system

The ethnic problem is certainly one of the most difficult and sensitive issues in Macedonia. The demands for recognizing the status of the Albanian minority as a 'constituent people', amendments to the constitution, confederalization of the state (with parallel institutions of power), the demand for education, culture, mass media in Albanian and Albanian envisaged as the second official language in the country, have all turned into a political project. The Albanians have however been divided about how to realize their demands. The dispute came to a head in February 1994 when the PDP, partner in the government coalition, split. The 'moderate' PDP was recognized as successor to the original PDP. The more radical Albanians, led by Arben Xhaferi, formed the Party of Democratic Prosperity of Albanians (PDPA). The growth of the Democratic Party of Albanians (DPA) has posed a direct challenge to the government's policy of gradual integration of Albanians into the post-independence Macedonian society. The three main ethnic parties, VMRO–DPMNE, PDPA and the People's Democratic Party (NDP) thus far tended to encourage ideologization and politicization on an ethnic basis. This process of ethnic identification has gained considerably in value in the political marketplace. It has led to ethnic segregation and some ghettoization, the preference of the collective over the individual and the concept of parallel institutions based in the case of the Albanian minority on ethnic Albanian exclusivity.

The October–November 1998 parliamentary elections offered an opportunity to re-examine the principal foundation of Macedonia's internal and external policies and critical realignments within the structures of the main contenders for power. Such realignments were essential particularly within both Macedonian and Albanian nationalist camps. Without this Macedonia's peace, stability and position in the international community, in short the country's future, hangs in the balance. The elections also offered an end to the four-year-long blockage of the democratic process when after the 1994 elections the ruling coalition enjoyed an abnormal parliamentary majority which enabled it to govern often in high-handed, sometimes 'absolutist manner'.[21]

The two major Albanian minority parties PDP and DPA signed an electoral coalition agreement[22] and competed jointly in the 1998 elections. It allowed for ethnic bloc voting that concentrated virtually all the votes of ethnic Albanians. More importantly, however, it meant no debate concerning ideological and policy issues, despite differences in the programmes of both parties, in order to allow for a period of rationalization of the 'Albanian political space'. The agreement committed the parties to co-operate to achieve the following joint political goals:

1   A guarantee for the equal status of the Albanians in the Republic of Macedonia;
2   Albanian-language education at all levels, and especially a solution to the issue of higher education in Albanian and the status of Tetove (Tetovo) University;
3   The extension of the scope for the official use of the Albanian language centrally and locally;
4   The proportional inclusion (according to their proportion of the population) of the Albanians in political and state institutions, public administration centrally and locally, public enterprises centrally and locally, and centres of economic and financial decision making centrally and locally;
5   The real decentralization of government and a stronger position for local government;
6   The commitment of both parties to the release of political prisoners.[23]

Both parties undertook 'to embark on joint action, especially in their future parliamentary work, while respecting each other's identity and political individuality, while not restricting their autonomous activities, respecting their equality, and defending their common interests as defined in this agreement'.[24]

VMRO–DPMNE, promoting the image of a modern, pragmatic and moderate nationalist party, formed an election coalition with the Democratic Alternative (DA), a new centre party headed by Vasil Tupurkovski, Professor of International Law at the Sts. Cyril and Methodij University in Skopje. Tupurkovski was the last member of the Presidency of Socialist Federal Republic of Yugoslavia from Macedonia and apart from a brief involvement in politics in 1992 had been absent from political life in the country. Despite that, he remained the most popular politician in the country.[25] In March 1998 he formed the multi-ethnic Democratic Alternative which in a space of eight months became the third political force in Macedonia.

The ruling Social Democratic Union of Macedonia (SDSM) formed a complex set of election agreements with the Socialist Party of Macedonia (SPM) and a number of smaller parties, bringing only slight modification to the government's policies. The party has been losing its ideological coherence since May 1997 when Prime Minister Branko Crvenkovski removed all the reformers from his cabinet and surrounded himself with his own personal supporters. Increasingly the party deserted its left-wing vocation. Over the past two years in particular it became evident that it was merely interested in occupying power. The leadership of SDSM became increasingly arrogant. What became quite obvious is that the party failed to deliver on reforms which were implemented exceedingly slowly, not to mention its approach to the Albanians which became increasingly inflexible. Quite clearly a very large section of the electorate expected that the SDSM would address during the election campaign how to overcome the main defects of its seven years' rule – fallen living standards, rising unemployment,[26] crime and corruption. The SDSM did not offer new solutions and instead put an emphasis on the continuity of existing policies. The result was the collapse of the SDSM vote. The overwhelming majority voted for change and largely in protest against the failed policies of the SDSM.

The results of the elections gave 62 seats to the VMRO–DPMNE/DA coalition – an absolute majority which would have allowed the parties to form a government. The Albanian bloc parties secured 25 seats (PDP 14 and DPA 11), the highest ever,[27] while SDAM managed only 27 MPs. The critical issue in the ensuing negotiations became the participation of the Albanian parties in the next government. The winning alliance found itself under strong pressure from the international community to offer open co-operation with Albanian parties.[28] There was a clear danger that a government without representatives of at least one of the major Albanian parties could soon be presiding over an ethnic crisis.

There was an expectation that both Albanian parties would enter the VMRO–DPMNE/DA coalition. However, the DPA publicly asked the PDP to conduct a reshuffle of its leadership and to suggest new people for ministerial offices – persons who held no positions in the old government. The DPA argued that the participation of PDP in the structures of power under the Social Democrats, as transparent as it was, did not bring the Macedonian Albanians any significant gains by which they could now justify before the electorate their presence in the new executive. PDP's refusal to purge its leadership brought about a historical agreement between two nationalist and radical parties VMRO–DPMNE and DPA. Consequently the DPA joined the new government and received five ministerial posts with VMRO–DPMNE having fourteen and DA eight portfolios. The PDP and its old allies the Social Democrats moved into opposition. While accepting participation in the government, the DPA issued a public warning to its coalition partners.

The DPA has acquired its reputation among Albanians with the fight for realization of the basic social, educational and cultural rights and de-blocking of some relations which cause irregularities in the education process. If it turns out that our hopes for resolving these key problems were in vain, we will step out of the government. If it turns out to be that way, this will in fact prove that Macedonia has not altered the Yugoslav syndrome.[29]

Having accepted posts in the government the DPA also announced that its mayors and councillors 'should withdraw their resignations and return to the municipalities they abandoned as an expression of discontent about the imprisonment of the mayors of Tetovo and Gostivar'.[30]

The results of the October 1998 parliamentary elections allowed for the first time in the history of the Republic of Macedonia a change in leadership through the democratic process. More importantly they show the effectiveness and robustness of democratic institutions under conditions of considerable internal conflict, not to mention the war in neighbouring Kosovo. Both parties would be expected to make further compromises in their position and adopt conciliatory policies. Provided that there is an improvement in the economy of the country that would bring direct benefits to all citizens of Macedonia, there is good reason to hope that the agreement between two principal nationalist parties will have an enduring effect on the country as a whole.

The economy

During 1994–5, the transition to a market economy and indeed Macedonia's economic survival were jeopardized by regional developments. First, the country was badly affected by the UN sanctions on Serbia which isolated Macedonia from its traditional Yugoslav markets. Second, the Greek embargo of Macedonia was a near-disastrous blow for a country so dependent on foreign trade, both for markets for its agricultural produce and for supplies for its industries.[31] The rate of registered unemployment increased from 17 per cent in 1990 to 24 per cent in 1995 and a large section of the working population dropped out of the labour force. By 1997 GDP per head averaged just 1,659 US dollars.[32] But Macedonia managed to maintain a budgetary balance and preserve stability of prices in the fraught mid-1900s. In terms of macro-economic stability, Macedonia ranks surprisingly high, scoring a mark of 3.76 on a scale of one to five, putting the country on the level of high performing transitional countries.[33]

Foreign assistance, both from multilateral organizations and citizens working abroad (particularly Albanians), has been crucial for economic survival. In 1998 the World Bank agreed to provide Macedonia with a 200 million US dollar loan over three years to assist economic reforms; and important negotiations between Western creditors and the new government are due in 1999.[34] 'The good economic situation is improving inter-ethnic relations', according to Gazmend Ajdaraga, an Albanian MP in the PDP from 1994 to 1998.[35] But because Albanians were under-represented in the public sector many feel that they have been left out of the privatization process. In Macedonia privatization has involved management buy-outs with employees also obtaining compensation. Capital in the former state sector as well as access to jobs is mainly controlled by Macedonians, but Albanians prominent in the service sectors (which accounted for 58.7 per cent of GDP in 1997) have prevented this imbalance enflaming politics, though that might yet happen.[36]

Finally, there is the role of the black economy. During the years of the economic embargo, it was illicit economic activity that helped Macedonia to survive. But the state's ability to create an economy based on rational criteria that serve the public good is jeopardized as long as much of the economy is untaxed and based on drugs and arms-trafficking. President Gligorov's willingness to bring the black economy to heel is reliably thought to have inspired the attempt on his life in November 1995 which left him badly injured but able to return to office.

The international dimension

Apart from the resolution of the ethnic problem central to Macedonia's peace and prosperity, there are also problematic relations with her four neighbours, Albania, Bulgaria and especially Greece and Serbia. International factors have played a very important role in threatening to undermine as well as promote Macedonia's stability. In particular, the prolonged instability in neighbouring Kosovo has had a profound impact on Macedonia in terms of politicizing the ethnic Albanian minority in Macedonia. As the prospects for a peaceful settlement in Kosovo declined and many saw no alternative to violent resistance, there was an ever-increasing threat that Albanians in Macedonia could rise up or try to help their Albanian brothers in Kosovo. At the same time, other developments have tended on balance to support the democratization process. These include the eventual resolution of tensions with Greece, restraint in relations with Albania, surprising progress in links with the Federal Republic of Yugoslavia and the UN presence in Macedonia.

Dispute with Greece

The dispute with Greece which began in earnest in 1991 centred over the Republic's use of the name Macedonia, the inclusion of Star of Vergina[37] as a symbol on its new flag, and articles of the Macedonian constitution. Greece claimed that Macedonia was a Greek name and that formulations in the Republic's constitution implied territorial claims to the adjacent Greek province of Macedonia. In particular it objected to formulations in the preamble to the Macedonian constitution which stated that the document takes as a point of departure 'the historical, cultural, spiritual and statehood heritage of the Macedonian people and their struggle over centuries for national and social freedom as well as the creation of their own state, and particularly the traditions of statehood and legality of the Krushevo Republic *(1903)* and the historic decisions of the Anti-Fascist Assembly of the People's Liberation of Macedonia' *(ASNOM, 1944)*. What antagonized Greece was that apparently both texts refer to Macedonian independence. Greek interpretations stressed that the one relating to the Krushevo Republic refers to the declaration of an autonomous Macedonia in the whole of the Macedonian territory of the Ottoman empire. The second gathering of (ASNOM) launched an appeal to the Greek and Bulgarian 'Macedonians' to incite a rebellion against the 'conqueror', in order to achieve their union with their brothers in the Yugoslav Macedonia and all together, as a single federal republic, to integrate in the Yugoslav Federal Republic.

Greece also objected to the formulations of Article 3 on the grounds that it stated that the territory and the borders of the Republic of Macedonia are 'indivisible and inalienable'. Despite the fact that the same article also declares that Macedonia has no territorial claims against neighbouring states, according to Greek interpretations the fact that it refers to the possibility of changing the borders 'in accordance with the Constitution' connotes territorial expansion. The Greek view has been that the formulation of Article 3 insinuates that the only territorial changes that could take place in the Republic of Macedonia are those of annexing new territories. Greeks charged Macedonia that taking together Article 3 and the Preamble they provide a legal base for accomplishing, in the future, territorial annexation from neighbouring states.

Another Greek objection referred to Article 49, which deals with the right of the Republic of Macedonia to care 'for the status and rights of those persons belonging to the Macedonian people in neighbouring countries, as well as Macedonian ex-patriates, assists their cultural development and promotes links with them'. Greece maintained that this provision creates a constitutional obligation for the Macedonian government to interfere in the internal affairs of neighbouring states with the pretext of concern for the existing minorities. The (at least publicly) unspoken fear for some groups in Greece related to the experience of the Greek civil war between 1946 and 1949. Many Slav Macedonians fought for a separate Macedonia during that conflict and several thousands were expelled after the war ended. Many who fled north to Varda Macedonia still lay claims to property in northern Greece around Florina and Kastori.

Macedonia and Greece began to make considerable progress towards the normalization of relations when, after more than two years of negotiations, brokered by UN mediator Cyrus Vance, they signed an Interim Accord on 13 September 1995. Under the Agreement[38] the two parties confirmed their existing borders and established diplomatic relations. Greece recognized the country as the Former Yugoslav Republic of Macedonia and agreed to lift its embargo on Macedonia within thirty days.[39] Macedonia agreed to remove the controversial Star of Vergina from its flag and to make a solemn declaration concerning some articles of the constitution that Greece found objectionable. Negotiations were to continue regarding the issue of the Republic's name. Resolving some of the most important aspects of the dispute has allowed Macedonia to join international organizations where Greece previously obstructed this. Clearly good relations with Athens are essential for Macedonia's progress in joining Euro-Atlantic structures. It would be extremely difficult, if not impossible, for Macedonia to negotiate close co-operation with the EU without the support of Greece. Just as Estonia, in its negotiations for EU membership, benefited directly from the support from Finland, Macedonia could clearly benefit from a similar arrangement with the Hellenic Republic.

Since the heyday of the dispute, when in 1992 the Greek authorities were able to organise over one million people in a protest march again Macedonia in Athens, the sense of insecurity in Greece has declined. At the governmental level, a pragmatic approach to Macedonia increasingly prevails. What is of utmost importance is that the border between Greece and Macedonia is open to private and commercial traffic.[40] The dispute has faded into the background amid increasing investment by Greek companies and a recovery of tourism, which brought more than 400,000 Macedonians to Greece in 1996.[41] In sharp contrast with past policy Greece now enthusiastically promotes economic ties with Macedonia. Macedonian companies have regained access to the port of Thessaloniki – the country's nearest gate to the sea, just three hours drive from Skopje.

This approach has allowed both sides to restore relations to a normal level and to leave the delicate and legal issues in abeyance for future consideration. In a 1998 interview, the Greek Foreign Minister Theodoros Pangalos declared:

> I believe that both sides badly managed the approach towards this issue. Exaggerations, mobilizations, politicians who used the problems instead of attempting to handle them – all of this appeared on both sides. However, this is over and it is a fact it was not a real question in its essence, but rather a question of semantics, since we have nothing to share, we do not have territorial pretensions one towards the other. Our interest is joint. Our reality in the relations between the two nations and countries and the promises and prospects for the future are so strong that it would be neither wise nor flattering for both sides if they remain in the world of semantics, instead of endeavouring to live in the world of reality.[42]

There is a silent agreement on all the major issues, including the name.[43] After the October 1998 parliamentary elections the new Prime

Minister Ljubco Georgievski pledged that his government would create a positive political and economic atmosphere towards Greece and maximum openness for Greek investors.[44] Diplomatic contacts have led to a tacit agreement on the resolution of the name problem with Greece suggesting the name of Republic of Macedonia–Skopje for the use between the two countries. This would allow for the Republic to retain its constitutional name of the Republic of Macedonia in its contact with the outside world and be acknowledged appropriately at the United Nations.

Relations with Albania

Albania and Macedonia have both shown considerable restraint in their inter-state relations; and Tirana has not usually exploited the difficulties of the Albanian community in Macedonia. Albanian–Macedonian relations improved quite considerably after the enforced resignation of Sali Berisha and the election of the Socialist government in Tirana in May 1997. In October 1997 the two countries signed an agreement in Skopje to improve security on their common border. Armed gangs and smugglers have often crossed the frontier since law and order broke down in Albania early in 1997. In December 1997 talks at foreign minister level between the two states led to the signing of six agreements aimed at strengthening security along the common border. In an interview for the Macedonian daily *Nova Makedonija* Paskal Milo, the Albanian Foreign Minister, emphasized that Macedonia's ethnic Albanians should be allowed to 'manifest their national identity and participate in the leadership and administration of the Macedonia state'. He added, however, that Albania does not encourage separatism and has no territorial ambitions in Macedonia.[45]

On 15 January 1998 Fatos Nano and Branko Crvenkovski, the Albanian and Macedonian Prime Ministers, signed co-operation agreements in economic and transportation matters. Speaking in the largely ethnic Albanian city of Tetovo, Nano attempted to discourage separatism by telling local people that the 'only future of all citizens in the Balkans, wherever they live . . . is their integration into a new Europe'.[46] He also told the Albanians of Macedonia that they should be satisfied with their position and should seek their rights only within the system. The two Prime Ministers met again on 22 August 1998 in Ohrid. It was their fourth meeting to date (three previous meetings took place in Macedonia and one in Albania). On that occasion Fatos Nano said that the Albanians and Macedonians 'are the best example of how Albanians can live together and govern together with Slavs. . . . This must be the future for all the peoples in the Balkans.'[47] His statement caused considerable indignation among sections of the Albanian population who claimed that the statement was very damaging and that it does not reflect reality.

Relations with the Federal Republic of Yugoslavia

Macedonian and Yugoslav relations have been improving steadily despite a number of unresolved problems, including the final demarcation of several stretches of the border between the two countries, and the formal position of Serbs in Macedonia.[48] The Federal Republic of Yugoslavia was the last of the Yugoslav successor states, and the last of Macedonia's neighbours to recognize the Republic of Macedonia. An Agreement on Mutual Recognition signed on 8 April 1996 allowed for the establishment of diplomatic relations and represented a significant progress towards confidence-building in the entire region and the consolidation of the regional peace process. At the same time Serbia regained a valuable trade corridor through Macedonia into the Aegean. For Macedonia the obvious benefit was the restoration of its customary markets to the north.[49] In the first quarter of 1998, 98.25 per cent of Macedonia's exports went to the former Yugoslav republics of which some 60 per cent to the rump Yugoslavia.[50]

The Bulgarian dimension

Bulgaria was the first country to grant Macedonia full diplomatic recognition. However, Sofia has consistently refused to recognize the Macedonian nation and the Macedonian language. It considers Macedonians merely as Bulgarians and the Macedonian language as a dialect of Bulgarian. This Bulgarian manifestation of nationalism should also been seen as a measure against the assertion of Macedonian national consciousness in Bulgaria's Pirim region. The dispute has held up the signing of over twenty bilateral agreements drawn up in Macedonian. Macedonia has successfully averted Bulgarian attempts to exacerbate the language issue and to give up its right to call the language as it wishes.

The United States

The United States has played a vital role in the preservation of Macedonia's sovereignty. The American moral and on-the-spot political, diplomatic and military presence has been consistent and quite considerable. The United States sees Macedonia as a buffer against a regional war that can involve two members of NATO – Greece and Turkey. The Americans have consistently supported President Gligorov and his policies and have bank-rolled Macedonia's trade deficit of some 7.4 per cent of GDP in 1997.[51]

However, the United States extended uncritical support to the SDAM and Branko Crvenkovski and has clearly neglected ties with VMRO–DPMNE and the Democratic Alternative, viewing the former in stereotypical terms. 'Unqualified backing for the SDAM, especially from Washington, sent the message that human rights abuses, the lack of democracy, and even corruption would be tolerated in the name of short-term stability.'[52] The Ambassador of the United States, Christopher Hill, appears to have chosen an ill-advised American tactic in the post-communist world: choose a local partner (Branko Crvenkovski) and back him to the hilt over the development of democratic institutions.[53] In spite of the noticeable American political, diplomatic and other presence in Macedonia, the US appeared somewhat surprised and certainly uncomfortable with the results of the October 1998 elections. One Macedonian newspaper captured this when it published a list of top-ten election losers – it included Ambassador Hill.

UN role

The presence of the United Nations Protection Forces (UNPROFOR) in Macedonia was established under the UN Security Council resolution 795 (1992) of 11 December 1992 when the first troops were sent. The mandate was subsequently re-defined under the Security Council resolution 983 (1995) of 31 March 1995 when the United Nations Preventive Deployment Force (UNPREDEP) was established. The force is drawn mainly from the USA and Nordic countries and there are 168 civilians, mainly police monitors, drawn from 23 countries. In addition the UNPREDEP political affairs component also plays a major role in promoting reconciliation among various political and ethnic groups. The presence of civilian police monitors has considerably strengthened the mission's outreach to local civil authorities and institutions, in particular the police. Civilian police have also played an indispensable role in regular monitoring of areas populated by ethnic minorities.

The deployment of UNPREDEP in Macedonia has been an important factor in the maintenance of a degree of peace and stability in the region. It has played a significant role in preventing the conflict in the former Yugoslavia from spreading to that Republic. It has contributed to alleviating that country's serious concerns about external security threats and has served in part as a substitute for its minimal self-defence capacity.

Conclusions

Since the declaration of independence Macedonia has faced considerable internal challenges and enormous external risks. It has had to cope with substantial hardships of transition, compounded by difficulties in inter-ethnic relations, and external embargoes and blockades. The costs of fundamental economic and social reforms led to a drop in living standards, and an increase in unemployment, crime and corruption. Despite all this it has managed to preserve peace and stability and create a functioning party system, confounding the widely held stereotype about the Balkans that in fragile and divided states it is the worst-case scenario that often prevails.

In terms of inter-ethnic relations a silent consensus has emerged on issues that both divide and united the national communities. However, the concept of the citizen state has not really worked in Macedonia. The society remains deeply divided. The ordinary Macedonian knows little about the ordinary Albanian and vice versa. They never really socialize except when they are involved in work arrangements and business deals. To a certain extent the two communities live in different worlds; however, these worlds are not so distant. People who are involved in negotiations think in different terms from people who operate separately, and some common ground is possible. There are layers of consensus between these two national groups. As far as the majority of Macedonian Albanians are concerned, the Republic of Macedonia offers them the best material and political environment in the region – living standards reasonable for the region, freedom to engage in economic activity, good education, and their own social and political institutions which have international backing. The overriding aspect of the consensus between Macedonian and Albanian political elites is to share power in order to promote and safeguard the interests of each national group. The difficulties are primarily in terms of bridging the different layers of the power-sharing consensus. While it has acquired the status of a common currency at the elite level, the degree of its acceptance amongst the ordinary public remains low primarily because the returns (benefits) of such arrangements are hardly noticeable by the man and woman on the street.

Both of the main communities have been talking a different discourse. The Albanians do not want to accept any kind of minority status. It is clear that they will never accept anything less than equal rights. The Macedonians on the other hand maintain the position – you are a minority and we can discuss your rights.What has prevented an explosion is the creation and use of robust democratic institutions. The central aspect of the power-sharing consensus has been talking through the democratic institutions. This is probably one of the most fundamental achievements of democratic transformation in Macedonia. However, while this might have been sufficient during the post-independence period during which the construction of democratic structures and intense economic and social transformation took place, it is unlikely to suffice now when the country has entered a new phase of consolidation of the earlier democratic gains. The relations between the two principal national groups cannot be resolved without a new historical agreement between the Macedonians and the Albanians to confirm what kind of state they want to share. Approval and active support of the Macedonian–Albanian consensus by the international community has been and will continue to be an essential part of process of democratization in Macedonia and the consolidation of democratic institutions. Indeed, it can be argued that to a large extent it has been the pressure from the international community that has kept Macedonia together.

The participation of the Albanian party in the government not only holds together the institutions of the state against large and often articulate opposition from dissatisfied Macedonian and Albanian groups, but more importantly it provides a very important channel for back-room dialogue between the officers of state and the Albanian leaders. Albanians want concrete results from the presence of Albanian ministers in the government and don't want them to be seen as decorative elements underpinning political arrangements that primarily suit the Slav Macedonians. Albanians, in turn, will need to show restraint in the face of the intense fighting in Kosovo, a conflict in which the casualties have been predominantly from the territory's Albanian majority. If the Kosovo Liberation Army insurgents try to establish a presence in Macedonia or encourage bold solidarity actions from their co-ethnics there, Macedonia could be directly sucked into the conflict. As for the ruling VMRO, it will have to avoid any return to the nationalist rhetoric which marked its debut in politics. If the VMRO-led government suffers economic reverses that prove damagining for ordinary citizens, there may well be a temptation to strike nationalist poses, which will need to be resisted to preserve the peaceful fabric of inter-ethnic relations.

Much of the democratic success of Macedonia is due to the country's first President, Kiro Gligorov. He played a crucial role in guiding the republic to its independence in November 1991 and presiding over the transformation of Macedonia into a modern Balkan state with a market economy, parliamentary democracy and respect for fundamental human rights. He was instrumental in getting political institutions off the ground and popularizing the politics of consensus and compromise. The distinctiveness of Gligorov's visions for Macedonia lies in the philosophy and politics of Europeanization of the Balkans. Its roots are in a formulation that for too long the people of the region have avoided planning for the future while fixed on the myths of the past. What is needed is to turn for once to the future and in the name of that future embark on the building of a new Balkan architecture through its Europeanization. President Kiro Gligorov has announced that he will not stand for re-election in 1999. His departure from office will produce an inevitable gap in the skills, expertise and sophisticated statesmanship that he demonstrated over the years. At the same time it will hopefully allow his successor to refine the pragmatic approach to the settling of disputes that the post-Gligorov era will certainly demand.

Altogether, it is evident that in several important ways Macedonia's new democracy is not yet consolidated. There remains a distinctly fragile edge to the inter-ethnic consensus, which needs stabilizing especially at the societal level; and, to this degree, there must be some doubts about the future. However, the story of Macedonia in the 1990s is one of unlikely success in democratic transition, due to a combination of above all skilful and restrained political leadership but also economic progress and the resolution of a whole range of difficult issues that appeared for a time to conspire against this outcome. Macedonia tends to support the assumption in political choice theories of regime change that elite decisions count for much in situations of systemic uncertainty. Thus, a picture emerges which is mildly optimistic but it remains subject to further developments that may or may not reinforce the path to democracy.

Notes

1 This proposal, which closely reflected the Slovene and Croatian position, was put forward jointly with President Alija Izetbegovic of Bosnia-Hercegovina.

2 In his address to the Assembly of the Western European Union in Paris in June 1995, President Kiro Gligorov acknowledged that the 'former Yugoslavia has fallen apart because it was an artificial creation . . . All former six members of the Federation are equal successors of former Yugoslavia. Another experiment of an imposed or violently created new state community on this territory is impossible' (MIC news bulletin, 26 June 1995).

3 The EU Badinter Commission which assessed the constitution concluded in 1991 that it is a modern European constitution, the only one developed by states of the former Yugoslavia that satisfies standards for democratic, independent statehood.

4 The word minority or minorities is not used even once in the constitution.

5 The Macedonian constitution was approved by the Sobranie in November 1992. The Albanian members of the parliament refused to vote for the constitution.

6 Robert W. Mickey, 'Citizenship, status and minority political participation: the evidence from the Republic of Macedonia', in Gerd Nonneman, Tim Niblock and Bogdan Szajkowski, eds, *Muslim Communities in the New Europe*, Reading: Ithaca Press, 1996, p. 55.

7 Robert W. Mickey and Adam Smith Albion, 'Success in the Balkans: a case study of ethnic relations in the Republic of Macedonia' (unpublished paper).

8 Mirjana Najcevska, Emilija Simoska and Natasha Gaber, 'Muslims, state and society in the Republic of Macedonia: the view from within' in Nonneman, Niblock and Szajkowski, eds, *Muslim Communities in the New Europe*, p. 81.

9 Ibid.

10 Ibid., p. 91.

11 At present the Albanian language can officially be used only at local government level in districts and municipalities where the Albanians constitute a majority of the population. It cannot be used in parliamentary debates even by Albanian-speaking members of the Sobranie.

12 The constitution of the Socialist Federal Republic of Yugoslavia described the Socialist Republic of Macedonia as a 'state of the Macedonian people and the social union of the Albanian and Turkish nationalities'. This formulation, according to the Albanians, gave them a direct constitutional recognition which they do not have currently in the Republic of Macedonia.

13 Hugh Poulton, 'The Republic of Macedonia after UN recognition', *RFE/RL Report*, 2, 23, 4 June 1993, p. 24.

14 Pristina University was closed down by the Serbian authorities in 1989.

15 Aleksander Soljakovski, 'An education in ethnic complexity', *Balkan War Report*, 15, October 1992, quoted by Hugh Poulton, 'The Republic of Macedonia'.

16 The Tetovo University was set up in 1998 by the local community with support from the Kosovo Albanians. Some 400 students attend the university. It is financed by contributions from ethnic Albanians in Macedonia and the Albanian diaspora. Lectures are held in private houses. The establishment of the university was clearly a political act

of protest and an attempt to force the Macedonian government to rectify the grievances of the Albanian community. It can be argued that an ethnically clean university in the long run has little value. The graduates will probably find themselves in the same situation as their colleagues from Pristina who with their unrecognized diplomas are fighting to transfer to a recognized university but find that none except the University of Tirana are prepared to have them.

17 1997 Annual Report Compiled by the International Helsinki Federation For Human Rights, MAK News, 5 July 1997.
18 Dzemail Hajdari, Minister without portfolio, quoted by Kerin Hope in 'Image shattered by clashes', *Financial Times*. Survey of the Republic of Macedonia. 17 December 1997.
19 John B. Allcock, 'Macedonia', in Bogdan Szajkowski, ed., *Political Parties of Eastern Europe, Russia and the Successor States*, Harlow: Longman, 1994, p. 281.
20 The Party of Democratic Change, formerly the League of Communists of Macedonia–Party of Democratic Change (LCM–PDC), in April 1991 became Social Democratic Alliance of Macedonia (SDAM).
21 *Dnevnik*, 'Democracy and will for change have won', quoted by MIC news bulletin, 3 November 1998.
22 For text see *Koha Ditore* (Albanian-language newspaper published in Pristina), 10 September 1998. The text has been re-published by BBC Summary of World Broadcast, EE/3332 A/9, 15 September 1998.
23 Ibid.
24 Ibid.
25 In 1992 President Kiro Gligorov sent Tupurkovski on a diplomatic mission to Washington DC which lasted very briefly, because of the disagreements between Tupurkovski and Gligorov concerning the international recognition of Macedonia.
26 Data produced by the Bureau of Statistics in November 1998 gives the unemployment rate as 34.5 per cent of the total workforce. The largest section, 70.9 per cent, are persons between 15 and 24 years of age, while those between 25 and 49 constitute 15.2 per cent. The unofficial estimates of unemployment vary from 40 to 60 per cent.
27 There is a widely held assumption that the Albanian parties have secured 100 per cent of the vote of the Albanian electorate. Although it is difficult to authenticate this, my own inspections of the electoral count as an Election Observer would support this assumption.
28 The pressure appears to be quite overt. For example the US Secretary of State Madeleine Albright, in her message of congratulations to the new Prime Minister Ljubco Georgievski, stressed 'Now as you seek to form a government I ... encourage you to consider carefully to offer governmental representation to Macedonia's significant Albanian minority' (MIC new bulletin, 6 November 1998).
29 MIC news bulletin, 1 December 1998.
30 BBC Summary of World Broadcast, EE/3406 A/8, 10 December 1998.
31 David A. Dyker, 'The economy', in *Eastern Europe and the Commonwealth of Independent States, A Political & Economic Survey*, London: Europa Publications, 1999, p. 526.
32 Hellenic Foundation for European and Foreign Policy – ELIAMEP, *South-East Europe Factbook & Survey: 1996–1997*, Athens, 1996, p. 160.
33 Lujiza Ismasili and Mirce Jovanoski, 'Economy: putting profits over politics', in *Reporting Macedonia: The New Accommodation*. London: Institute for War & Peace Reporting and Search for Common Ground Macedonia, 1998, p. 59.
34 Ibid.
35 Ibid., p. 60.
36 Dyker, 'The economy', pp. 526, 528, 111.
37 The Star of Vergina adorns the cover of the golden larnax (dated 335 BC) in which bones were found believed to be those of Philip II, King of Macedonians and father of Alexander the Great. The larnax was discovered in 1977 in the unplundered tomb

which is assumed to be that of Philip II. Since the declaration of independence of the Republic of Macedonia the Greek government has asserted that it has exclusive copyright to the use of the Star of Vergina. But it has been argued that since modern-day Greeks are not descended from ancient Greeks: 'The Star of Vergina is not a Greek symbol, except in the sense that it happens to have been found on the territory of the present-day Greek state. The modern day Greeks appropriated ancient Greek cultural symbols because they happen to live in more or less the same part of the world as the ancient Greek did' (Peter Hill, 'Levelling the Levendis', *The Age*, Melbourne, 20 April 1994, quoted by John Shea, *Macedonia and Greece: The Struggle to Define a Balkan Nation*, North Carolina: Jefferson & Co., 1997, p. 190). It is widely recognized that 'national symbols are often modern creations which do not reflect the reality of the circumstances they purport to represent. Tradition can be invented. Modern Greece, for example, is a relatively new creation and bears little resemblance to the ancient Greece which is the source of much of its symbolism' (Jeremy Moon, *Making Macedonia*, Department of Political Science, University of Western Australia, March 1994, quoted by Shea, *Macedonia and Greece*, p. 190).

   In the case of the flag of the Republic of Macedonia which included a version of the Star of Vergina the difficulties had arisen because the Macedonians and the Greeks wanted to appeal to same history and make a similar statement about themselves to the outside world. It is worth recalling that the new flag of the Republic of Macedonia, to which there has been no objections, portrays an eight-rayed sun. Perhaps historical validation of the eight-rayed sun as the symbol of the royal house of the Makedon made it easy for the new republic to change its original flag.

38 The Interim Agreement expires after seven years.
39 The Greek embargo on Macedonia started on 16 February 1994. It was lifted on 20 September 1995, one week after the signing of the Interim Agreement. It lasted nineteen months. According to the UN methodology for calculations of the cost of embargo, the total cost amounts to $US 1.9 billion. An average cost is $US 1 million per month.
40 A high-speed train link between Skopje and Thessaloniki was opened in April 1998.
41 Kevin Done and Kerin Hope, 'Brighter prospect for buffer state', *Financial Times*. Survey of the Republic of Macedonia, 17 December 1997.
42 Interview with the Greek Foreign Minister, Theodoros Pangalos, *Dnevnik*, 11 April 1998.
43 In the latest of complex suggestions concerning the name, Cyrus Vance, the UN negotiators proposed in 1998 the name of the Republic of Macedonia–Skopje. Similar was a proposal made by President Kiro Gligorov some six years earlier. He informed the Macedonian Assembly on 9 December 1992 that if the EU recognized Macedonia as the Republic of Macedonia (Skopje), Macedonia would formally accept that name.
44 BBC Summary of World Broadcast, EEW/0567 WA/6, 10 December 1998.
45 RFE/RL Newsline, 4 December 1997.
46 RFE/RL Newsline, 16 January 1998.
47 BBC Summary of World Broadcast, EE/3318 A/12, 29 August 1998.
48 While the Preamble to the Macedonian constitution states that 'full equality as citizens and permanent co-existence with the Macedonian people is provided for Albanians, Turks, Vlachs, Romanies and other nationalities living in the Republic of Macedonia', it fails to mention the Serbs. The Serbian minority has been demanding changes to the document and the inclusion of Serbs among the list of ethnic minorities in Macedonia. The omission of Serbs is explained by the fact that at the time of the writing of the Macedonian constitution Serbia insisted on acknowledging Serbs in all the former Yugoslav republics as a constitutive nation and not a minority. The legitimacy of Serbs living in Macedonia is not disputed now and they have been promised inclusion in the constitution when it is next revised. The process of revising the constitution is expected to begin in January 1999.

49 There have been speculations that the 'Albanian factor' played a major role in reaching the agreement. The speculations are apparently linked to several well-known factors. The first is the explosive birth rate of the Albanian minorities in both countries. The second is that the land border with Albania is rather leaky with insufficient police controls to stop thousands of hungry Albanians pouring across for casual jobs or selling arms captured from the Albanian army. The centrepiece of this speculative scenario is that President Slobodan Milosevic plans some form of tightly controlled local autonomy for Kosovo and that this would need support from both Macedonia and Albania.

50 Katerina Blazevska and Kim Mehmeti, 'Steering through the regional troubles', in *Reporting Macedonia*, p. 27.

51 'Macedonia. Next domino?', *The Economist*, 7 March 1998, p. 54.

52 Fred Abrahams, 'The new accommodation', in *Reporting Macedonia*, p. 8.

53 Similar unqualified US backing for Boris Yeltsin and Sali Berisha are other examples of somewhat strange choices made by the United States.

Index